v'

D1566808

WITHDRAWN

THE RENAISSANCE CHAUCER

THE RENAISSANCE CHAUCER

Alice S. Miskimin

New Haven and London, Yale University Press

1975

Designed by John O. C. McCrillis
and set in Baskerville type.
Printed in the United States of America by
The Murray Printing Co., Forge Village, Mass.

Published in Great Britain, Europe, and Africa by
Yale University Press, Ltd., London.
Distributed in Latin America by Kaiman & Polon,
Inc., New York City; in Australasia and Southeast
Asia by John Wiley & Sons Australasia Pty. Ltd.,
Sydney; in India by UBS Publishers' Distributors Pvt.,
Ltd., Delhi; in Japan by John Weatherhill, Inc., Tokyo.

For

E. T. D.

docere et delectare

Consideryng that wordes ben perisshyng / vayne & forgeteful /
And writynges duelle & abide permanent / as I rede Vox audita
perit / littera scripta manet
William Caxton, *The Mirrour of the World*

Omnis mundi creatura
Quasi liber et pictura
Nobis est et speculum
Alan de Lille

Contents

Acknowledgments

It is a pleasure to acknowledge and to thank friends and colleagues to whom I am indebted for their advice, kindness, and encouragement: Whitney Blake, Harold Bloom, Marie Boroff, Loretta Bulow, Thomas Clauss, Thomas Greene, Eugenia Herbert, Alvin Kernan, Elizabeth Kirk, Lowry Nelson Jr., and Richard Sylvester. I am especially grateful to James Heaney and to Doris P. Nelson for their unfailing patience and accuracy in preparing this manuscript, and to James P. Reilly Jr., director of the Leonine Commission at Yale University for checking my translations of Gower and Bernard Silvestris. I would also like to thank the librarians and staff of the Sterling and Beinecke libraries of Yale University for their assistance, and for allowing me to use their Chaucer incunabula. All quotations from early printed texts of Chaucer are from editions of Caxton, Pynson, Thynne, Stowe, and Speght in the Beinecke Library unless otherwise noted.

My gratitude to Sidonie, Matthew, and Harry Miskimin is immeasurable in words.

Introduction

It might be said that the defense of poetry has become in modern times a defense of criticism. René Wellek and Austin Warren, however, begin and end their *Theory of Literature* with a plea for a higher literary history to which both theory and criticism are indispensable:

> We must conceive of literature as a whole system of works which is, with the accretion of new ones, constantly changing its relationships, growing as a changing whole. But the mere fact that the literary situation of a time has changed compared . . . to a century before is still insufficient to establish a process of actual historical evolution.

> The total meaning of a work of art cannot be defined merely in terms of its meaning for the author and his contemporaries. It is rather the result of a process of accretion, i.e. the history of its criticism by its many readers in many ages.

> The real critical problems arise when we reach the stage of weighing and comparing, of showing how one artist utilizes the achievements of another artist, when we watch the transforming power. The establishment of the exact position of each work in a tradition is the first task of literary history.[1]

This book is concerned with "the real critical problems" involved in the inheritance of the Renaissance Chaucer. Let us assume that an ideal literary history of "England's Homer" should attempt to interpret the reflections of medieval Chaucer in the works of Elizabethans—the after-images left on the surface and still perceptible echoes that transmit "influence" in poetry. The modern historian may also seek to see more, in the transmission of "England's Homer" as Chaucer's book: the gradual and continuous "process of accretion" which clouds over the text, apocryphal poems, scribal and linguistic change. He should try to assess the parallel growth of Renaissance criticism, as new theories of poetry emerged for reinterpreting the medieval past. The horizon for

1. René Wellek and Austin Warren, *Theory of Literature*, rev. ed. (New York, 1956), pp. 255, 42, 259.

criticism includes as well the surviving monuments of the Gothic world that surrounded Elizabethans in architecture, in design, in obscure and commonplace artifacts taken for granted and ignored, as well as the spectacular rejections: statues defaced, frescoes painted over.

In every age, the critic tries to establish "the exact position" of the great originals and to trace the sources and significance of such reflected images as can still be seen. In the following chapters my intention has been to explore how the 200-year growth of the Renaissance Chaucer retrospectively casts light both on medieval Chaucer and on his Elizabethan heirs. When the modern critic compares his readings with those of his Elizabethan forebears and observes discrepancies in the diverging perspectives of three eras at once, he may expect to see more, in spite of the distance in time and the ultimately mysterious concealments of art "when we watch the transforming power." But if history is a form of criticism, such reciprocal interpretation opens the way to further questions.

In the following chapters, I have sought to reexamine the well-known evidence of the metamorphosis of medieval Chaucer into the Elizabethans' "English Homer"; not, however, by retracing the long, widening spread of his famous influence on younger contemporaries and later disciples. The line traditionally begins with Hoccleve, Clanvowe, and Lydgate, develops new growth in Dunbar and the Scots Chaucerians, and evolves further in the sixteenth-century English poems of Skelton, Hawes, Wyatt, and Gascoigne. A broad historical survey of Renaissance readings of Chaucer should of course include studies of all these poets and of other minor figures, many nameless. It might also reassess in depth (far more precisely than I have done) the anonymous apocryphal additions to the Chaucer canon which were taken to be authentic and "medieval" by Elizabethans, although it is now apparent they are derivative and for the most part weak poems, inferior imitations.

My intention, however, has been not to examine the broad impact of Chaucer's influence on the lesser poets who came after him but rather to reconsider the changing shape and meaning of the original source itself. A number of metamorphoses occur—in the language, in the texts, and in the very image of the poet—the primary evidence for the historical rise of Chaucer's fame as Father of English poetry, from his death in 1400 to his apotheosis in Spenser. In choosing this perspective, I have reduced and foreshortened the panoramic backdrop of two centuries of literary history, from the interchange between Chaucer and Gower to that between Chaucer and Spenser and attempted to maintain focus on the figure of the poet: Chaucer the dreamer, Chaucer the pilgrim, Chaucer the maker of *Troilus and Criseyde*. It is appropriate to state here some of the reasons for eschewing the more obvious approach.

While there are several relevant modern studies, such as Derek Pearsall's excellent book on Lydgate and Stanley Fish's on Skelton, the fifteenth- and sixteenth-century Chaucerians deserve a whole volume unto themselves. The tradition is perhaps broader and more interesting than has hitherto been thought. I hope to pursue these themes in a later study, which will explore the full-fledged revival of Gothic enthusiasm beginning with Dryden and growing in the eighteenth century, which received fresh impetus in the Romantic "medievalism" renewed from Blake to Keats. The present work, it should also be stated, considers only some of the difficult problems of reinterpretation surrounding the Renaissance Chaucer and touches many topics briefly, if only to invite speculation. In effect, my purpose has been to reopen the larger, more philosophical questions of the status of the poet and of his fiction which I think Chaucer himself was the first English poet to raise. His enigmatic and ironic attitudes toward his art are my starting point, and they lead the way, not to minor imitators, but to the major Elizabethans, Sidney, Spenser, and Shakspere, who reformulate the terms in which the poet may be said to be a maker of art.

In order to establish perspective for criticism, in the first six chapters of this book I have attempted to read Chaucer's poems as works of self-conscious fiction—"fables freely being formed in the mind of the author," in Spitzer's fine phrase—created behind a screen of deference to his *auctors* and *olde bookes*.[2] These conventions conceal subtle relations among the speaker, the poet, the audience, and the reader and suggest problematic meanings in the poems we read. At the same time, I have reexamined the implications of *allegoria* and *ironia* as distinctive modes of Chaucerian rhetoric, in order to approach the poems as works of philosophical intelligence, concerned with the question of the autonomy of the imagination, which becomes Sidney's, Spenser's, and Shakspere's question as well. It is a famous paradox in all the arts that the splendor

---

2. Leo Spitzer, "A Note on the Poetic and Empirical 'I' in Medieval Fiction," *Traditio* 4(1946): 414–22. H.L. Levy, " 'As myn auctor seyth,' " *Medium Aevum* 12(1943): 25–39, traces vernacular formulae for affirming truth and referring to sources of authority to early English hagiography, wherein distinctions between history and fiction have to be overcome. The "credibility topos" descends from pagan antiquity; see below, ch. 5, 6, and 7.

of the Renaissance casts a long backward shadow which obscures medieval elements in the process of mutation. In poetry, one way to see this more clearly is to test the premisses of Renaissance poets against their own evidence, just as one tests the claims of Chaucer: one regards what he says he is doing against what he in fact achieves. There being few precedents for such inquiries, the methods of analysis I have used are necessarily, perhaps, both eclectic and subjective; in the main I have relied on juxtapositions, both direct and oblique.

It has been taken for granted since the turn of the seventeenth century that Chaucer's primary heir in the Renaissance of English poetry was Spenser, who sought his native *matere* in the *Knight's* and *Squire's Tales*, *Sir Thopas*, and the *Book of the Duchess*, as well as in Ariosto and Tasso, and who first practiced his art in the *Shepherd's Calendar* by claiming to imitate Chaucer's voice. There remains much to be said concerning Spenser's relation to Chaucer and his special sense of the medieval English past; within the scope of the present study, I have called attention to certain of the issues in chapters 2 and 9. But I wonder whether there are not perhaps deeper differences between the style of Spenser's mind, what he claims he wanted to achieve as a poet, and his declared homage to "Tityrus," "Dan Geffrey," than exist between Chaucer and Shakspere, who never names him. Juxtapositions of this kind, it is true, are speculative and old-fashioned and add little to our knowledge of either poet or to literary history per se. But in the limbo of the *olde bookes*, where all poetry is simultaneously present as "the tradition," it seems to me that Chaucer's *matere*, his dramatis personae, his tolerance of human limitation, and his allegorical ironies are nearer to Shakspere's than to Spenser's.[3]

Both Chaucer and Shakspere are, in this sense, anomalous—beyond all dogmas, beyond philosophies, and unclassifiable—except, perhaps, for the few common terms that link them, closer than any other great English poets, to classical antiquity: their compassion and their detachment. Neither belongs with the majority of his contemporaries, the Ricardian "medievals" or the Elizabethan humanists. Shakspere's poetic imagination need not be compared with Plato's, as I have tried to highlight Chaucerian irony by Socratic parallels, but both Shak-

---

3. This view contrasts with the assumptions of Abbie F. Potts, *Shakespere and the Faery Queene* (Ithaca, 1958), and W. B. C. Watkins, *Shakespere and Spenser* (Princeton, 1950), for example, as well as with many who glance at, but rarely analyze, "Spenser's debt to Chaucer." Studies of Spenser's poetic language and "archaism" are noted in chapter 9 below.

spere's and Chaucer's art reciprocally illuminate each other. I would suggest here no more than one other likeness between them: the rare, shared transcendence of everything that could be predicted of a poet in the Middle Ages and the Renaissance, which each in turn achieved by self-abnegation; their withdrawal from the invented mirage, thus making their fictions self-sustained. In these terms, it becomes irrelevant whether we ever know more than we do now about the London civil servant who served three fourteenth-century kings—Edward III, Richard II, and John of Gaunt's son, Henry IV (however briefly)— and the Warwickshire actor who served Elizabeth and James I. Their biographies have little in common, and probably less is known of these two than of any other great English poets, but their works significantly intersect. I think we may see more of both, and further toward the limits of art—toward what poetry defends as fiction making—by setting Chaucer and Shakspere together than by any other such juxtaposition. Of course, to make such parallels is no more than a game, but fiction itself is a paradoxical game, playing with illusion to see if it can be made to last—unless it be taken for truth. Neither Chaucer nor Shakspere claims certainty for himself, nor makes, for poetry, Sidney's commitment to truth: 'Nature can make only a brazen world, poets deliver a golden.' Spenser belongs with Sidney and with passionate desire for poetic truth. Chaucer's and Shakspere's ironists leave truth to others.

In turning from Chaucer's poetry in the Middle Ages to his new role among old *auctors* in the Renaissance, I turn in chapter 7 to his most famous poem from the fourteenth century to the seventeenth, *Troilus and Criseyde*, to examine the evolution by mutagenesis of new form through which it became Shakspere's and Dryden's plays. In the following chapter, I look back to Chaucer and medieval poetry from the point of view of the Renaissance editor, reader, and critic, through the series of folio editions of the *olde bookes* published in the sixteenth century. Finally, returning to Spenser's Chaucer in chapter 9, I have sought to observe some phenomena of mutation in the theory of poetry proclaimed in the *Shepherd's Calendar*. From this perspective, the Socratic Chaucer of the Middle Ages is no longer strongly apparent. We see instead Boccaccio's magnified figure of the Poet whose visions come from the bosom of God—in Sidney, in Spenser, and parenthetically, in Dryden, all of whom acknowledge Aristotle as well as the Renaissance Plato.[4] The Chaucerian metamorphosis has occurred.

4. Spenser's Platonism and Neoplatonism, widely cited in the *Variorum* and in many early

The evolution of philosophy in the Renaissance is beyond the scope of this book, as is the contiguous revolution in religious thought, from its precarious medieval synthesis to the breakthrough forced on the Church by Luther and Calvin. The crisis had begun before the Great Schism in 1378 and still seethed in the issue of the Elizabethan succession. But these outermost dimensions of the history of English poetry are paradoxically also at its inmost point of growth: the conception of the individual and the autonomy of the individual mind. The study of the self is the subject of an increasing portion of Renaissance poetry after the public poems of the fifteenth century,[5] but "individuality" was not conceived as the Renaissance inheritance from the Middle Ages, by men who then looked back—nor now, by many moderns. From the vantage point of two centuries later, however, it seems to me that indeed the study of the self, externalized in poetry, was one of the great legacies medieval poets left, and that in Chaucer self-doubt becomes creative of a sense of self uniquely enigmatic and enduring. Twentieth-century fascination with psychic experience has stimulated reappraisals of poetry which find relevance in Chaucer no earlier age discerned, and we read him as we read Shakspere and Spenser, convinced that we have fewer misconceptions than our ancestors. That, of course, remains to be seen, and is probably irrelevant. What we can observe are analogies important to ourselves, and something of our ancestors' more interesting errors.

Many sophisticated and complex comparisons remain still to be made. Given the scope of this study, burdened with countless unknowns and masses of evidence, I have found that even the simplest analogy begins to proliferate beyond its immediate context and the limits of one book. One reason is clear from the start: in the flowering of English poetry at the end of the sixteenth century, we find both the greatest

twentieth-century interpretations, are critically reassessed in the more recent studies of Robert Ellrodt, *Neoplatonism in the Poetry of Spenser* (Geneva, 1960); Alfred W. Satterthwaite, *Spenser, Ronsard and Du Bellay* (Princeton, 1960): Rosamund Tuve, *Allegorical Imagery* (Princeton, 1966); and John E. Hankins, *Source and Meaning of Spenser's Allegory* (Oxford, 1972). The philosophical aspects of Spenser are debated in all but the most narrowly philological studies of his work: the reader is referred to the bibliographies of Paul Alpers, in his *Elizabethan Poetry: Modern Essays in Criticism* (Oxford, 1967): idem, *Edmund Spenser* (Baltimore, 1969); and William E. Nelson, *The Poetry of Edmund Spenser* (New York, 1963).

5. See the fine study of Lydgate by Derek Pearsall, *John Lydgate* (London, 1970), passim; and two recent studies by N. F. Blake, *Caxton and His World* (London, 1969), and "The Fifteenth Century Reconsidered," *Neuphilologische Mitteilungen* 71 (1970): 146–57. V. J. Scattergood's *Politics and Poetry in the Fifteenth Century, 1399–1485* (London, 1971), is the most recent broad survey.

change and the highest elevation of Chaucer's fame. To discover how and why it occurred, and what it meant to the Renaissance self–image of the English poet, requires a synthetic approach, at once critical and historical, which runs the risks of subjectivity in pursuit of what seem to me to be real issues. What does it mean to demur, *myn auctor seyth, the boke seyth*, and what are the effects of the disappearance of such cues? What is the role of the poet vis à vis his power to make fiction and to move us to see, and to believe? At the beginning of the modern English literary tradition, Chaucer raised these open questions, to which each in turn his greater successors tacitly respond. The best answer to a poem is, of course, another poem: the Chaucerian legacy we still possess.

I

From Medieval to Renaissance: Some Problems in Historical Criticism

> History . . . cannot say, and indeed hardly ever knows, what it is
> omitting, nor can it ever know how this comes about.
>
> Paul Valery

The Rise of Chaucer's Fame

Study of the influence of a masterpiece in any art reveals that from the
very first, in the accumulating frames of its early reputation and
imitation, its fame becomes a part of the artifact itself. As for poetry, as
Wellek put it, "Every reading of a poem is more than the genuine
poem."[1] It is virtually impossible now to read the Great Books—the
Odyssey, the *Aeneid*, the *Commedia*—without knowing that they are
Great Books; they have been read for us.

"So it is, that here as elsewhere, what men seek for, that generally
do they find. . . ." Thus Caroline Spurgeon somewhat wearily concluded the introduction to her monumental history of Chaucer's fame,
Five Hundred Years of Chaucer Criticism and Allusion, 1357–1900. Ideally,
criticism should attempt to refer a work of art, or a poem, both to the
values of its own time and to all periods subsequent to its own, for
"a work of art is both 'eternal' (it preserves a certain identity), and
'historical' (it passes through a process of traceable development)."[2]
Such a historical critique of Chaucer is worthy of aspiration, but it
has yet to be achieved. Modern medievalists are still embroiled in
questions of methodology, following the precedents set for the classics.
Confronted with a judgment with which he cannot agree, Peter Dronke
asks, "Is not *this* the anachronism, reading into the text what the
writer has not intended, in order to comply with modern notions of the

---

1. Wellek and Warren, *Theory of Literature*, p. 145.
2. Ibid., p. 43.

medieval?"[3] From the other side of the historians' circle, perhaps we hear Curtius's reply: "It is immaterial whether the catalogue of ships is [interpolated] by a Homerid or not: we should read Homer as he was read for two thousand years."[4] For Chaucer, five hundred years have certainly not been long enough.

Almost three-quarters of another century have been added to Spurgeon's *Five Hundred Years*; the "Chaucerians" have been disposed of, sooner and more easily than the Homerids. The manuscripts, all posthumous, are being reedited, for the second time in this century, and the *Chaucer Life Records*, edited by M. M. Crow and Clair Olson, finally published in 1966, seem to have established the biographical facts for the first time since the fifteenth century. Hammond's *Bibliographical Manual* of 1908 has been brought up to date by D. D. Griffith's volume for 1908–53 and William Crawford's for 1954–63; student guides to the literature, such as that of Albert Baugh, provide virtually annual supplements. It has become clear that Chaucer the poet is no longer in danger of being buried under the weight of his reputation, but he is still imprisoned in it. The purpose of this book is to look back to the beginnings of his poetic influence, to the earlier periods of Chaucer's fame, when the medieval Chaucer gradually evolved into the forefather figure of Renaissance English literary history.

As with Homer, so with "English Homer," as Chaucer was named by Renaissance historians. It is unlikely that a modern critic can find a single line left in the canon that has not been glossed, a date or occasion yet to propose. But of course the work still flourishes, and old certainties are open to challenge. The only presumably fixed date in the chronology of Chaucer's poems, that of the elegy for Blanche of Lancaster, *The Book of the Duchess*, has recently been questioned,[5] and the vexed issue of final-*e*—Chaucer's rhythms–submitted to a new scrutiny.[6] In any review of the conflicting testimony to the vigor of medieval poetry, in the past half-century's yield of brilliant scholarly and critical readings of Chaucer and his contemporaries, it soon becomes clear that new orthodoxies and true believers, as convinced as those of the nominalist and realist parties of late medieval theology,

3. *Poetic Individuality in the Middle Ages* (Oxford, 1970), p. 196.

4. Ernst Curtius, *European Literature and the Latin Middle Ages,* trans. Willard R. Trask (New York, 1953), p. 229.

5. See Edward I. Coudren, "The Historical Context of the *Book of the Duchess,*" *Chaucer Review* 5 (1971): 195–212.

6. See Ian Robinson, *Chaucer's Prosody* (Cambridge, 1971), passim.

still are at odds in the field, occupying positions as diametrically opposed as the schoolmen. "If Chaucer means what Professor X says he does, he cannot possibly be saying what Professor Y explains he means." Provided with facing pages of gloss, interlinear translations, prose paraphrase, and heavy annotation, readers are reminded of their own ignorance and become humbly confused, diverted from the poems to the marginalia, the spectacular display of critical scholarship that would seem to illuminate every detail. All too often contentious, however, and incongruous to Chaucer's wit and humility, the debates of modern expositors are in effect un-Chaucerian in tone and conviction, but to readers of Spurgeon's anthology, classically familiar.

In criticism as in logic, it should be never forgotten that *negativa non sunt probanda*: absence of particular meanings can never be proved. An interpretation can be said to be corroborated only if we are unable to find refuting evidence, rather than if we are able to find supporting evidence; it is a historical commonplace that "of nearly every theory it may be said that it agrees with many facts," which are a dime-a-dozen, empirically, and easily chosen a priori to confirm hypotheses.[7] Circular reasoning and the selection of evidence in the light of the very theory the evidence is supposed to test flourish in all our criticism and are rooted deep in the past. In the readings of the medieval and Renaissance Chaucer which follow, I shall question and try to test some of the assumptions of contemporary criticism as to the varieties of meaning in allegory and the uses of analogy, against historical evidence. The metamorphosis of one poet's book, from manuscript to print, provides a paradigm of literary evolution. As a case history, we can inquire how the medieval Chaucer's book became an antiquity within two hundred years by processes of which contemporaries were becoming acutely aware.

This study, based on facts long known and commonplace formulae, is presented, then, not as a new approach or prologue to Chaucer, but as a supplement or epilogue, an ex post facto inquiry into early "readings" of Chaucer which in striking ways both resemble and parody his own readings of his *auctors*. The familiar tag, *as the book seyth*, however, implies questions of poetic originality and elements of imitation which in late medieval and early Renaissance poems are concealed, controversial, and perhaps insolubly conjectural. The disap-

7. See Karl Popper, *The Poverty of Historicism* (Boston, 1957).

pearance of such phrases in the early sixteenth century is itself revealing and raises the question of what takes their place. As has long been known, the first translation of a Petrarchan sonnet into English–more than a century before Wyatt–is Chaucer's borrowed, and unacknowledged, version of "S'amor non e," which Troilus sings in *Troilus and Criseyde*.[8] Chaucer has altered the Italian in significant details which affect interpretation, but, given the variables, what conclusions can be drawn? Was it a bad manuscript, or scribal error, or inadequate knowledge of Italian, or conscious revision, intended for characterization of the speaker? How can ironies be certified? The questions of Chaucerian irony, latent in the text, unlike those of his "sources," remain open for speculation, for they underlie the "medieval" reading of the poems, and their rereading in the Renaissance.

Given the richness and variety of the historical evidence we have inherited, it is possible to reexamine and reassess the literary implications of *myn auctor* and the *olde bokes* in Chaucer's poems, and observe their afterlife in literary history, as topoi—means by which *auctoritee* and postmedieval poetic influence descend during the two-hundred-year evolution of the English humanists. Within five years of Petrarch's coronation in Rome as poet laureate, Richard de Bury, the former tutor of Edward III and later bishop of Durham and lord chancellor of England, described the peregrinations of the Muses to the North—the arrival of the first seeds of the Renaissance, in his *Philobiblon* (1345). The *translatio studii* topos is proudly applied to England:[9]

> The admirable Minerva seems to have made the tour of the nations of mankind, and casually come in contact with them all, from one end of the world to the other, that she might communicate herself to each. We perceive her to have passed through the Indians, Babylonians, Egyptians, Greeks, Arabians, and Latins. She next deserted Athenas, and then retired from Rome; and having already given the slip to the Parisians, she has at last happily reached Britain, that most renowned of islands . . . the Microcosm.

8. The stanza is discussed by Theodore Maynard, *The Connection between the Ballade, Chaucer's Modification of it, Rime Royal and the Spenserian Stanza* (Washington, 1934), p. 73; and by Patricia Thomson, "The Canticus Troili: Chaucer and Petrarch," *Comp. Lit.* 11 (1959): 313–28. Chaucer's source was first noted by Thomas Watson in 1582.

9. *Philobiblon*, in *A Miscellany*, ed. Henry Morley (London, 1888), ch. 9, p. 52; the Latin text, with English translation of E. C. Thomas (1888) was edited by Michael Maclagen (Oxford, 1959, repr. New York, 1970). My quotations are from Morley's edition.

One of the most learned men in England, de Bury was one of the first to read Greek, and he quotes, with approval, Plato's *Phaedo*. The library he founded at Durham College, Oxford, was scattered when the college was dissolved by Henry VIII, but his passionate little treatise in defense of learning and vindication of poetry was printed in 1473; it prophesies Sidney's *Apology*. The literary history of the English Renaissance began in the fourteenth century, as the Renaissance historians themselves saw.

But after 1400, Chaucer's late fourteenth-century world became immediately, then ever more distantly, a shadowed past. The deposition of Richard II, virtually coincident with Chaucer's death, was to contemporaries truly an end, and the Lancastrian accession a new order. The new century began with a turbulent sense of transition and sharp memories of the ending century's turmoil, in both politics and religion. Paradoxically, it is often the case that the immediate successors of those familiar with a historical episode are the ones who have the greatest difficulty remembering what it was really like. The blur of change—in language as in the image of events—occurs in a single generation. Imagination, memory, and the invoking of authorities begin to conflict. Then revision is under way. Vico found his historical theory, the *universali fantastici*, in this very conflict: those universal ideas return, originating in fantasy, by means of which the imagination seeks to ward off chaos. He saw them as formulae which become institutionalized, stereotyped—as magic, ritual, social orders—ultimately reducible to rhetoric. For Vico, anticipating Freud, poetry is an autonomous mode of perception, of self-orientation, a defense against the flux. For poets within the flux, from Chaucer to Spenser and Shakspere, the issue of time's disintegration is not so simply stated. Mutability, as a reflex of the invocation of authority, becomes a constant theme in evocations of the medieval past. The mutability of language, and of the meaning of poetry itself, confront every reader of Chaucers's book.

The Middle Ages slowly became "medieval" as the paradox of receding time seemed gradually to reveal the periodization of events, of ideas, of culture itself—as in de Bury's welcome to the Muses. The German Protestant annalist Cellarius appears to have been one of the first to use *medii aevi* in its present sense, in the seventeenth century. He saw the period as extending from the fall of Constantine to the fall of Constantinople, from 340 to 1453 A.D. As Curtius drily comments, "Middle Ages is (as a concept) . . . scientifically preposterous, but indispensable for mutual comprehension; whether one is to distinguish 'renaissances' is a question of expedience."[10] The present, still indefinite, meaning of Middle Age, the period between "ancient" and "modern" times, seems to have become common shortly after 1700, competing with "Gothic." The earliest citation in the Oxford English Dictionary, for 1722, indicates prevalent common usage of the term. *Medieval* (translating the scholarly *medium aevum*) is quoted from the *Gentleman's Magazine* in 1827, twenty-five years before Ruskin's lectures refined and popularized it.[11] Nevertheless, it would seem that soon after 1400, men were already conscious of the end of an era, and looked back to it, ambivalently, as inheritors. In the historical framework of this book, the relationships between medieval Chaucer and his *auctors*, and those of his Renaissance successors who then looked back to him as their progenitor, are separated as two contingent problems. The time span is roughly two hundred years, from the reading of Chaucer's poems by his audience of contemporaries to the readings of Elizabethans, as witnessed in Shakspere and Spenser. It goes without saying that modern interpretation of the Renaissance Chaucer is probably no less biased and arbitrary than theirs was of their medieval forebears. Our chief advantage is the purity of our texts.

Chaucer's Renaissance reputation and his poetic influence, as himself an *auctor*, among literary historians and poets, are distinct phenomena which are in turn distinct from a third, the poems on which the fame and *auctoritee* depend: manuscripts, printed texts, editions. The original manuscripts have long been gone, but early copies and the Renaissance editions remain to be read for what they can tell us of their readers. Among readers in the Middle Ages and in the Renaissance we need to distinguish between poets, who read one another with special privileges, critics, whose interpretations may be disinterested or not, and finally, the silent audience addressed within the poem: *thou, redere,* the hypothetical ideal solitary for whom poems are written. The last is the most important of all and, for the reading of Chaucer, indispensable. Anticipating the structuralists, T. S. Eliot in 1919 restated more elegantly what scholiasts and pedants from the Alexandrian librarians to Isidore of Seville had always assumed: poetry exists in

10. Curtius, *European Literature*, p. 20.
11. See the summary in J. R. Hale, *England and the Italian Renaissance* (London, 1954), ch. 6; and Roberto Weiss, *Humanism in England During the XV Century*, 2nd ed. (Oxford, 1957); and idem, *The Spread of Italian Humanism* (London, 1964), passim.

horizontal time, in the synchronous limbo of the *olde bokes*. There, medieval poems live with all poems, their literary ancestors, contemporaries, and successors. We read Chaucer as we read his Virgil, Ovid, Boethius, and Dante, as did Shakspere, Dryden, Spenser, and Keats. In Eliot's sense, we might disregard the medieval and Renaissance audience, *ars poetica, movere et docere,* as irrelevant to us. Thus we may immediately avoid the infinite regress of revisionary history in which every age redefines and reinvents its past. To do so seems to escape the traps—the questions of Langland's audience and Chaucer's contemporaries, the early marginalia and annotations in the manuscripts, the accretions of Chauceriana in the new editions of the poems after 1500—the only evidence that survives to witness medieval and early Renaissance readings of the poems. The difficulties and risks of error in historical interpretation are admittedly real and not irrelevant, but excessive caution is as misleading as excessive boldness, and a half-truth is a half-truth in any period. For both the medieval Chaucer and the Renaissance Chaucer, the contemporary world has to be taken into account as an imperfect historical given, by inference and implication, insofar as the limitations of our knowledge and subjectivity permit. Few have entered the labyrinth of literary history between 1400 and 1600, and fewer still have emerged able to say what they saw. The phenomenon of metamorphosis takes place, but no one has yet fully understood and described how. C. S. Lewis has surely gone further than any other modern reader, and all who come after pay him homage. I have found, however, that his account of the Renaissance Chaucer raises almost as many questions as those he answered, and instead of certainty, left much in doubt. My debt to him, and to other great modern Chaucerians, will be apparent in these studies, as will my divergence from prevailing views.

Anonymity and Acknowledgment: The Medieval Author, *Auctoritee,* and Time

It has often been suggested that Chaucer momentarily drops his mask as narrator and becomes himself, in replying to the nameless Friend who stops him on the way out of his House of Fame:[12]

12. For example, Ann C. Watts, "Chaucer's Two Selves," *Chaucer Review* 4 (1971): 229–41; Chaucer, *The House of Fame,* in *The Works of Geoffrey Chaucer,* ed. F. N. Robinson, 2nd ed. (Boston, 1957), ll. 1871–82, pp. 299–300. Unless otherwise noted, all quotations from Chaucer are from Robinson's text.

> Frend, what is thy name?
> Artow come hider to han fame?
> Nay, for sothe, frend, quod y;
> I cam noght hyder, graunt mercy,
> For no such cause, by my hed!
> Sufficeth me, as I were ded,
> That no wight have my name in honde.
> I wot myself best how y stonde;
> For what I drye, or what I thynke,
> I wil myselven al hyt drynke,
> Certeyn, for the more part,
> As fer forth as I kan myn art.

But Chaucer has of course already begged the question, having named his narrator "Geffrey" in the self-ridiculing comedy of the second part of the poem. Chaucer's thirst for fame is a curious corollary issue in this poem, and it is worth comparing it to Petrarch's imagined confession of his egotism to "Augustine" in the *Secretum*. In this dialogue, Petrarch tries to defend his insatiable desire for earthly glory as the first natural step toward "that which awaits us in heaven." More Boethian than the *Trionfi*, the *Secretum* expresses the anxiety of the Christian humanist poet confronting his ignorance and mortality and the ambiguity of Fame. Petrarch imagines Augustine's rebuke:[13]

> Augustine: You trust to your intellectual powers and your reading of many books; you glory in the beauty of your language and take delight in the comeliness of your mortal frame. But do you now perceive in how many respects your skill does not equal that of the obscurest of mankind, not to speak of weak and lowly animals,

13. "Est autem aliqua propositii mei ratio. Eam enim quam hic sperare licet gloriam, his quoque manenti quaerendam esse persuadeo ipse mihi. Illa maiore in coelo fruendum erit, quo qui pervenerit hanc terrenam ne cogitare quidem velit. Itaque istum esse ordinem ut mortalium rerum inter mortales prima sit cura: transitoriis aeterna succedant: quod ex his ad illa sit ordinatissimus progressus." *Secretum*, in *Coloquium tertii diei* (1496). The dialogue is undated, but J. R. Robinson and H. W. Rolfe, editors of Petrarch's correspondence, suggest it was finished between 1342 and 1353. They translate as follows: "There is a certain justification for my plan of life. It may be only glory that we seek here, but I persuade myself that, so long as we remain here, that is right. Another glory awaits us in heaven, and he who reaches there will not wish even to think of earthly fame. So this is the natural order, that among mortals the care of things mortal should come first; to the transitory will then succeed the eternal; from the first to the second is the natural progression." See Robinson and Rolfe, eds, *Petrarch,* 2nd ed. rev. (New York, 1914; reprinted 1969), pp. 412–426. Cf. Ernest Wilkins, "On Petrarch's Accidia and His Adamantine Chains," *Speculum* 37 (1962): 589–94.

whose works no effort on your part could possibly imitate? Exult
then if you can in your abilities! And your reading, what does it
profit you? From the mass that you have read, how much sticks
in your mind, how much takes root and brings forth fruit in its
season? Examine your mind and you will find that all you know,
if compared with your own ignorance, would bear to it the same
relation as that borne to the ocean by a tiny book, shrunk by the
summer heats.

Both Petrarch and Chaucer (unlike Gower in his *Confessio*) defied their
imagined confessors; the unfinished *Trionfi* and the broken-off *Book of
Fame* were set aside, but not to spurn poetry, and both finished other
poems more immediately apprehensible. Difference, however, tells more
than likeness: Petrarch's fear that Laura's name might be misconstrued
forever with his own laurel, his anxiety that men might think he envied
Dante, could never disturb his English reader Chaucer, who hardly
presumed so much, never named a Lady of his own (although he suffered for Criseyde and for Alison of Bath), and borrowed Dante's golden
eagle to satirize his own narrator's unsurpassed *lewedness*. Perhaps he
did not invent the Temple or the *Book* "to han fame," but Chaucer did
leave his name, as Bennett points out, for the first time in an English
poem in which the narrator names himself. He set a precedent and left
the enigmatic identity of "Geffrey the poet" as a conundrum for
criticism. In spite of the modest disclaimer, "Sufficeth me, as I were ded
That no wight have my name in honde," Chaucer knew how he stood,
and he went on, "as fer forth as I kan myn art."

The *Book of Fame* explores the limits of poetic ambiguity, and Bennett
is surely right to emphasize Chaucer's ambivalence everywhere in it, as
he hovers "between two worlds, celestial and terrestrial . . . between
jest and earnest, faith in dreams and scepticism." Perhaps he is also
right that the chief difference between Boethian resignation to the
mutability of time's curse on poets, "the whiche writynges long and dirk
eelde / doth awey, bothe hem and ek hir auctours" (*Boece*, 2.7.88–90),
and the attitude of Petrarch and Chaucer lies in Boethius's despair of
the "trustworthiness of writers and the permanence of their works,"[14]
which Renaissance poetics affirm, and medieval poetics doubt. The
questions raised in the *Book of Fame*, and therein left unanswered,
epitomize Chaucer's allegorical irony, "that which affirms and denies
at the same time," as I shall subsequently attempt to describe it.

14. J. A. W. Bennett, *Chaucer's Book of Fame* (Oxford, 1968), pp. 82, 112.

As everyone knows, Chaucer invented very little of his own; like Shakspere, he found what he needed at hand. The brilliant source studies of modern scholars—Bennett, Bloomfield, Payne, Pratt, Muscatine—have revealed the dovetailing procedures under the surface of Chaucer's synthetic dream visions, as well as in *Troilus* and the *Canterbury Tales*. The Temples of Venus and Fame are variously modeled on Claudian, Guido de Columnis, and the Temple of Juno in the *Aeneid*. The earthly paradises variously come from Jean de Meung, Dante, and Alan de Lille; the lists of trees from Guillaume de Lorris and Statius, and the catalogue of trees burned at Arcita's funeral in Boccaccio's *Teseide*. Translated elements are always fused by the devices of the Chaucerian dreamer, but, named and unnamed, the *auctoritees* lie under the patterns of allusion and figurative imagery like a mosaic floor seen through water. It is still difficult to tell whose dreams these are, but to the reader of the Renaissance Chaucer, as we shall see, it was virtually impossible to distinguish Chaucer's from these of his imitators. The dream visions are, we now know, more authentic than the "Chaucers Dreme" Speght unveiled in his folio of 1598, but authentic in a highly sophisticated sense. The modern recovery of so many of Chaucer's *auctoritees* in effect heightens the sense of the dubious meanings of *auctor* associated with Rumor, Alison, the Pardoner, and Pandarus—masters of quotation—and intensifies the incongruity between the naive Dreamer and his very subtle dreams. It is more apparent to us than it could have been to the Elizabethan reader that the autonomy of the poet as a "maker" of fictions was already a problem, concealed in the circumlocutions of medieval poetics, and that new meanings of the word "invention" were coming to the surface, soon made explicit in Henryson's most Chaucerian poem. No less self-conscious than Petrarch in feigning simplicity, Chaucer was as aware as the Italians he admired of the unpredictable secret arts of writing, not merely for a present audience but for unseen readers and for the future. The "new" poet is not just a compiler of stories or transmitter of authorities, but the originator of a complex, silent, and irreversible creative process. Acute awareness is also the indispensable element in Chaucer's irony—his detachment—and, for whatever other virtues they may share, Petrarch's fame was not for wit, the special wittiness that transcends the comic and becomes philosophical. Chaucer's irony is closer to Boethius's, in his cross-examination of Philosophy, than to Petrarch's in his homage to Fame; he is always nearer to self-doubt than to pride. But the medieval Chaucer has more in common with the

irony of Socrates, it seems to me, than with any of his contemporaries
or successors. The Renaissance Plato and the Renaissance Chaucer
were venerated for myths that confirmed the sixteenth-century image;
hence Chaucer's scepticism, and Plato's attacks on poetry, had to be
explained away, rationalized, or forgotten. So Chaucer was taken for a
Wycliffite and a precursor of the Reformation; his more profound
doubts as to the efficacy of any *auctoritees* at all were no longer apparent.

Beginning with Caxton, who in the 1480's first supplied an "ending"
for the unfinished *Book of Fame*, through the early sixteenth-century
editions of Pynson, Thynne, and their successors later in the century,
the emergent Tudor revisions of the historical, public aspects cf
Chaucer's world were revising at the same time the conceptions of
"medieval" art, always excepting Chaucer and Gower from censure.
The interdiction of the old Catholic hegemony was finally proclaimed
in England by statute and made official in the Act of 1542, "For the
Advancement of true Religion and thabolissment of the contrarie. . . ."[15] The act provides for utter abolishment of forbidden
books, but "Chaucers bokes, Caunterburye Tales, and Gowers books
[are exempt] and shall not be comprehended in the prohibicions of this
acte." The intervening historical events, before and after 1542–43,
permitted and indeed stimulated increasing self-consciousness among
later Tudor humanists and earlier Elizabethan poets and their audiences, who now looked back to Chaucer's and Gower's proscribed
medieval world through the Renaissance new vision of society, a world
to be enriched by the making of new art. One honors one's ancestors,
but were they indeed greater or lesser than ourselves? Who can see
more? Lucan's aphorism, "We are but pygmies, standing on the
shoulders of giants" (*nani gigantum humeris insidentes* in Bernard of
Chartres), is the theme of homage in Petrarch's letters to Cicero and
Homer. It is heard again and again, and interpreted both ways: to
repudiate, and to revere, the past.

The proud Elizabethan sense of advance beyond the predecessors is
stated clearly in Puttenham's praise of Wyatt and Surrey in 1589, as
the first reformers of English meter and style,

> hauing trauailed into Italie, and there tasted the sweete and
> stately measures and stile of the Italian Poesie as nouices newly

15. Statutes 34 and 35, Henry VIII, ch. I, sec. v, *Statutes of the Realm* 3 (1817): 895. See
below, ch. 8, n. 1.

crept out of the schooles of Dante Arioste and Petrarch, they greatly pollished our rude and homely maner of vulgar Poesie, from that it had bene before.[16]

Webbe speaks with similar contempt of the "brutish poetry of rhyme" in 1586, exempting Chaucer, and oddly, Langland, for his anticipation of the blank verse line. But it is not until Francis Bacon, after 1600, that the new conception of time's maturing is stated with full confidence and without equivocation: "The old times are in reality the youth of the world, and the present is therefore more mature and wiser."[17] Bacon's fuller statement of the theme comes in the *Novum Organum* of 1620, in the eighty-fourth aphorism of the first book:

Men have been kept back as by a kind of enchantment by reverence for antiquity, by the authority of men accounted great in philosophy, and then by general consent. As for antiquity, . . . the old age of the world is to be accounted the true antiquity, and this is the attribute of our own time, not that in which the ancients lived . . . which, though in respect of us it was the elder, yet in respect of the world it was the younger. . . . Surely it would be disgraceful if, while the regions of the material globe of the earth, of the sea, and of the stars, have been in our time laid widely opened and revealed, and the intellectual globe should remain shut up within the narrow limits of the old discoveries. . . .

And with regard to authority, it shows a feeble mind to grant so much to authors, and yet to deny time his rights, who is the author of authors, nay, rather of all authority. For rightly is truth called the daughter of time, not of authority. It is no wonder if those enchantments of antiquity and authority and consent have so bound up men's powers that they have been made impotent, like persons bewitched, to accompany with the nature of things.[18]

Carlo Cipolla, commenting on the coincidence of the emergence of

16. George Puttenham, *The Arte of English Poesie* (facsimile ed., Kent, Ohio, 1970), 1. 31, p. 74.

17. *The Advancement of Learning* (1605), 1.5.1: "*Antiquitas saeculi juventus mundi.* These times are the ancient times, when the world is ancient, and not those which we account ancient *ordine retrogrado*, by a computation backward from ourselves" (William Aldis Wright, ed., [*Francis*] *Bacon, The Advancement of Learning*, 4th ed. [Oxford, 1891], p. 38).

18. Edwin A. Burtt, ed., *The English Philosophers from Bacon to Mill* (New York, 1939), p. 58. Burtt reprints the standard text edited by J. Spedding, R. L. Ellis and D. D. Heath London, 1858–74).

printed books, the Reformation, and the Counter-Reformation, noted
that as more men learned to read, supply was stimulated to keep pace
with demand: books become increasingly cheaper and their use more
widespread. But both the growth of pedagogy and the rise of vernacular
literatures in Europe are "the unfortunate byproducts of the religious
feud . . . of book-burning, bigotry, control over schools, and censorship of publication."[19] Printing, after 1500, speeded up the growth of
literacy and spread of reading, and it also heightened scholarly consciousness of linguistic evolution. In England, new editions of old books
aroused interest in Anglo-Saxon studies and called attention to the
primitive state of medieval literature; antiquarian research began to
bring back to life archaisms frozen in the texts of Caxton, Pynson, and
William Thynne.[20] Francis Thynne, in his *Animadversions* on Speght
(1599), speaks for the first time in English since Caxton as a textual
critic of Chaucer's language:[21]

> so that, of necessyte, both in matter, myter, and meaning, yt must
> needs gather corruptione, passyng through so manye handes, as
> the water dothe, the further it runneth from the pure founteyne.

Thynne is well aware of his "source"—Spenser's Chaucerian "pure
well of English undefil'd"—and he is using the water imagery ironically. Speght's 1598 edition of Chaucer's *Works* is the first to contain
a separate glossary of obsolete and difficult words, consciously anticipating the reader's needs; the list is nearly doubled in size in Speght's
"revised" edition of 1602. Writing in the same year, Samuel Daniel
concluded his *Defence of Rime* with a troubled awareness of uncertain
judgment, not of the present, but of the future—without Bacon's opti-

19. *Literacy and Development in the West* (Baltimore, 1969), p. 51.

20. René Wellek's *Rise of English Literary History* (Chapel Hill, 1941), and May Mckisack, *Medieval History in the Tudor Age* (Oxford, 1971), copiously document the consequences of the efforts of Leland and Bale to save the manuscripts dispersed from monastic libraries: Aelfric's Easter sermon, published in *A Testimonie of Antiquitie* (1567); the Anglo-Saxon Laws, in William Lambarde's *Archaeonomia* (1568); Asser's *Life of Alfred* (1574); the Anglo-Saxon Gospels, published by Archbishop Parker's assistant John Joscelyn (1577). Hakluyt's *Voyages* (1589) included a translation of Alfred's *Orosius* ("Othere's Voyage"), and Camden's *Remains* (1589) included the Lord's Prayer in two Anglo-Saxon versions, with three other versions (twelfth-, thirteenth-, and fourteenth-century Middle English) given to demonstrate the "antiquity" of the English church. Inadvertently, Camden illustrated the stages of develop-ment through which the language had passed; Old English studies may be said to have be-gun, and continued virtually uninterrupted, from this point to the present.

21. *Animadversions . . . by Francis Thynne*, ed. G.H. Kingsley, rev. F.J. Furnivall, *EETS* 9 (1865): 6. Thynne's *Animadversions* will be discussed below in chapter 8.

mism—as it seemed to a poet defending both the *olde bookes* and his own. His *Defence* of native English style is on historical grounds, in answer to Campion's humanist contempt for the barbarous vernacular:

> [Literary standards are] things that are continually in a wandring motion, carried with the violence of our uncertaine likings, being but onely the time that gives them their power. . . . [This inordinate desire of innovation] is but a Character of that perpetuall revolution which wee see to be in all things that never remaine the same, and we must heerein be content to submit ourselves to the law of time, which in a few yeeres will make al that, for which we now contend, Nothing.[22]

But what is more significant is what is omitted in Daniel's *Defence* of the English past. In reply to the charge that "all lay pittifully deformed in those lacke-learning times, from the declining of the Romane Empire, till the light of the Latine tongue was revived [by the Renaissance humanists Erasmus, Reuchlin, and More]" Daniel chooses to cite the eloquence and learning of the Venerable Bede, Joseph of Exeter, Roger Bacon, and Occam, but not one English poet of the later Middle Ages. He does not name Chaucer or Gower in his list of precedents for the poetry of his own time, but be eulogizes instead Petrarch and Boccaccio, whose excellence in Italian surpassed anything written "in any other form." It was Italy, "the miracle and phoenix of the world, which wakened up other Nations likewise with this desire of glory," long before time brought forth Reuchlin, Erasmus, and More. Of Chaucer's "ancient" English rhyme, Daniel has nothing to say.

Although it is taken for granted that we know what "medieval" and "Renaissance" mean, it is very difficult to persuade historians to define them. In effect, since Ruskin's popular triumphs finally established the French term *renaissance* in English in the 1850's the old idea, once clear in Italy, has become an elastic historical illusion. In literary history, "Renaissance" encompasses the diverse succession of period styles from Chaucer's descendants Skelton, Wyatt, Surrey, and Spenser ("Tudor," "Humanist," "Elizabethan") through the early years of Milton's poetic apprenticeship ("Metaphysical," "Jacobean," "Caroline," "Baroque"). Our anachronisms and overlapping terms are the obvious result of nineteenth-century pattern making, as interesting phenomena

---

22. In *Literary Criticism of Seventeenth-Century England*, ed. Edward W. Taylor (New York, 1967), pp. 58, 71, 73. Taylor gives the complete text of the *Defence*, pp. 48–73.

in themselves as Vico's spirals. The term "Renaissance" was, however, in origin continental, and it seems, in English, to obscure rather than to make things clear. Cultural phenomena occurring in the north of Europe after ca. 1500 are seemingly made analogous to the Italian humanists' enunciation of recovery of the ancient world, which began before Chaucer was born. English literary theory in ·the sixteenth century rests in part on the premises of Italian poets and critics of the fourteenth. Thus Boccaccio and Petrarch, first translated by Chaucer before 1400, returned to England in the second, greater wave of Italian translations from 1550–1600. But Italian as a foreign language did not seem to have so profoundly changed, as the Middle English of Chaucer had become decayed: to Elizabethans, fourteenth-century English poetry looked far more "antique" than fourteenth-century Italian.

Of course, both "medieval" and "Renaissance" are opinions, anachronistic, and no more than convenient abstractions, to be redefined each time a new historian announces he has found proof they ever—or never—existed, in the twelfth, fourteenth, or sixteenth century. As classifications for art and ideas, they are at once usefully vague and irritatingly specific. They frequently obfuscate the mind, rather than free it to see more in the light of general meaning. It is paradoxical to alternate comparisons by epithet of this kind, "medieval Chaucer," "Renaissance Chaucer," for they coexist in the same body, the same mind, the same poems. As Donaldson remarks of the Wife of Bath, "if [her] Prologue were the only literature to survive between 1200 and 1600, one might say that in her character the Renaissance sprang from the Middle Ages."[23] Reading the same Chaucerian text, Auerbach comments:

> There is hardly a sign of humanism. Chaucer still makes a considerable display of semi-erudite exempla, taken over from the earlier Middle Ages; the effect is often rather grotesque, as in the case of the misogynous tales which the Wife of Bath represents as the learned literary gleanings of her late fifth husband.[24]

How shall we read Jankyn's Book? Our first tasks, then, in the following chapters, are to reexamine the medieval Chaucer, and then to see what was claimed by his heirs.

23. E. T. Donaldson, *Chaucer's Poetry* (New York, 1958), p. 915.

24. Erich Auerbach, *Literary Language and Its Public in Late Latin Antiquity and in the Middle Ages*, trans. Ralph Mannheim (New York, 1965), p. 326.

"Sources": Translation, Parody, and Concealment

Claiming and naming of ancestors evidently depend upon what is wanted by the inheritor, who discovers meanings in a given tradition for his own acknowledged or unconscious purpose. In 1555, Michelangelo carved the Pietá he intended for his own tomb out of a fragment of a fallen pediment from the Temple of Victory, as a last measure of his own achievement. In the marble lies a symbolic metamorphosis, from Greek original to pagan Roman copy to Florentine Christian triumph. Ideally, literary history should study the reflexive relations in which the present openly or subtly alters the past, in newly perceived hierarchies, readjusted values, as the modern is simultaneously transformed by the past in the process of confrontation: Virgil in Dante, Dante and Virgil in Chaucer, all three simultaneously in Spenser. In such dialogue, whether or not names are used or allusions suppressed, there is adversary relationship. The colloquies of poets perhaps rarely come close enough to the surface of consciousness to be recognized, and the recognition of sources opens new horizons for misinterpretation, as hazardous as the indefinable limits of historical ignorance. For literature, as Wellek reminds us, has a temporal reality; it is a public artifact, and the poet has first a role, an audience, and social status in the real world. Attempts to describe his role and his audience soon reveal the poverty of criticism without history; but to describe the influence of the contemporary audience or the social milieu upon the poet is a task for the biographer. The roles of poet and audience and the history of ideas within the poem are not, in this sense, "historical," they are self-reflexive perspectives of the poem itself.

Like all works of art, ancient and modern, fictions have antecedent sources and histories, but only copyists—plagiarists and verbatim translators—can, with luck, be traced to their true originals in place and time. In 1345, Richard de Bury commented ironically on the fakery and deception practiced by his contemporaries, speaking as the voice of his "counterfeit" books, in the imagery of Renaissance "rebirth":

> What wonder is it then, if clerical apes magnify their margins from the works of authors who are dead, as while they are yet living they endeavor to seize upon their recent editions? Ah, how often do you pretend that we who are old are but just born, and attempt to call

us sons, who are fathers? and to call that which brought you into
clerical existence, the fabric of your own studies? In truth, we who
now pretend to be Romans are evidently sprung from the Athenians . . . and we who are just born in England shall be born again
tomorrow in Paris, and being thence carried on to Bologna, shall
be allotted an Italian origin, unsupported by any consanguinity.[25]

While the Southwark tavern in Chaucer's *Prologue* bears a strong
and suggestive resemblance to an actual tavern known to the fourteenth-century London world of Chaucer's audience, the Tabard—like
the Mermaid, and the Spouter Inn in New Bedford—requires no
corroboration beyond what takes place in it. John Fisher speculates
that Chaucer chose

> to assemble his pilgrims at the Tabard Inn, across from St. Mary
> Overys Priory in Southwark . . . as an acknowledgement that he
> was finally taking his departure from Gower's own metier, the
> vices and virtues and criticism of the estates.[26]

But as the starting point for the fictional journey to Canterbury—to
Becket's shrine, which the pilgrims never reach—the Tabard is a point
of no return, like the Malvern Hills and Santa Maria Novella in
Florence, although Boccaccio's three young men do, in fact, return the
seven young ladies to the church where they had met, "and after taking
leave of them went about their business." The *Decameron* aristocrats,
Langland's Long Will, and Chaucer's thirty pilgrims belong to the same
realm of symbolic reality, of the universal "I" and "you," as the eagles
in the *Parliament of Fowls* and the *Book of Fame*. The true sources and
"historicity" of a fiction can neither be verified nor proved false. Thus
Macpherson's pseudomedieval "Ossian" (1760–63) and Chatterton's
"gothick" "Elinoure and Juga" (1769) are authentic fictions, and the
"Rowley" poems of 1777 truly reflect the Gothic enthusiasm of the
eighteenth century—a literary society apparently outraged by the
printing of Urry's *Chaucer* (1721) in Roman type rather than black
letter, but delighted to be deceived by "Gamelyn," *Shamela*, Pope, and
Gay. Cultural history and the recovery of probable sources enlarge
our conception of meaning and reduce the margin of error in interpretation, but they are rarely more than probable, nor are the most

25. *Philobiblon*, in Morley, *A Miscellany*, ch. 4, pp. 52–53.
26. *John Gower, Moral Philosopher and Friend of Chaucer* (New York, 1964), p. 208.

striking analogues ever a perfect match. Chance parallels are rarer than imitations, but even red herrings are valuable in the study of sources, influence, "evolution."

Homage that is truly disinterested is even more rare. No poet ever alludes to another great name, or names himself, inadvertently. Chaucer's naming of himself and his *auctors* provides a paradigm for "authority" at the beginning of the new tradition in English poetry to which all succeeding generations looked back. The later naming of Chaucer with epithets, as "English Homer," "Dan Geffrey," "Tityrus," like the silent imitations he practiced himself, became a means for an English poet to define himself against what had been done before. Naming him is sometimes merely formulaic apostrophe, but occasionally, as in Milton, significant invocation. Even the humble younger Lydgate, adding his *Siege of Thebes* to the *Canterbury Tales*, attempts to maintain his independence in the immediate context of his powerful master. One of Lydgate's modern defenders, Alan Renoir, declares that even though the tale pays homage to Lydgate's *maister* Chaucer, as in a scholar's Festschrift,

> it allowed him to put a new twist on his favorite topos [affected modesty], . . . [yet] his borrowing was free from the tyranny of a specific model whose example must be constantly followed.[27]

Imitative adaptation and transformation of traditional styles and forms occur commonly in all the arts, beginning with elementary exercises in copying, ending in mastery; out of imitation comes the mutagenesis of new form. Picasso made dozens of studies of Velasquez's "Las Meninas," modifying and playing with the planes of its imagery more than fifty times. Prokofiev's and Stravinsky's uses of Bach and Handel repeat the theme. As in the greatest poems of Pope, imitation is not merely parody or derivative burlesque, but art made new; the *Dunciad* is an appropriation of the epic, which tests the unique strengths of both model and imitator. In major artists, imitation is extension, recognized conquest; in lesser, we find minor exploits and fugitive explorations on a miniature scale. Chaucer, as a translator and borrower from first to last, wrote the first great "imitations" in English poetry; he then in turn became the subject of imitation, conscious and unconscious, by his immediate heirs and their later successors. The study of *Troilus and Criseyde* reveals both dimensions of Chaucerian

27. *The Poetry of John Lydgate* (London, 1967), pp. 111, 114.

imitation: it is the epitome of his own synthetic fiction making, and it became a model, in the Renaissance evolution of the poem, marvellously transformed.

Renaissance Perspective: Chaucer and the *olde bookes*

From Lydgate to Spenser, English poetry acquires a new sense of its own historicity. The word *modern*, apparently first used by Dunbar circa 1520, comes into common use, as distinct from "ancient," in the 1580's. Of course, the concept (*moderna*, from *modo*) belongs to every age, as the sense of *now*. Increasingly remote and finally, as England's historic national literature, distinct from the older antiquities (Roman, then Greek), the poetry of the Christian Middle Ages grew to be an increasingly problematic legacy for the later English poets who inherited all traditions and compared their state with their continental rivals' in the last permutations of the Renaissance. Chaucer, Langland, and Gower, then finally Chaucer alone, became, posthumously, progenitors. As Shakspere's "Gower" says,

> The purchase is to make men glorious;
> Et bonum quo antiquius, eo melius.[28]

Pericles (1607–08) is probably the first of Shakspere's Jacobean romances, and in its choral Prologue, "Gower" renews the medieval devices that conventionally mark departure into fantasy: "I tell you what mine authors say" (1. 1. 20) (*myn auctor seyth . . .*):

> To sing a song that old was sung,
> From ashes ancient Gower is come;
> Assuming man's infirmities,
> To glad your ear, and please your eyes.
> It hath been sung at festivals,
> On ember-eves and holy-ales
> And lords and ladies in their lives
> Have read it for restoratives.
>
> [1. 1. 1–8]

After Speght's two editions of Chaucer's *Works* in 1598 and 1602, no new edition was called for for eighty-five years. The poems of Gower,

28. *Pericles*, 1.1. 9–10. *The Complete Works of William Shakespeare*, ed. Hardin Craig (Chicago, 1961).

printed by Berthelette in 1533 and reprinted in 1554, were not edited again until 1857. The great medievals, as Lounsbury remarked, had become ancestral poets, whom it was respectable to name but no longer essential to read.

Reflecting on his own consciousness of time in his *Account of the Greatest English Poets* (1694), Addison uses a typical Augustan metaphor of "rust" for the medieval past, echoing Shakspere's "ashes":

> Long had our dull Forefathers slept supine
> Nor felt the Raptures of the Tunefull Nine
> Till Chaucer first, a merry Bard, arose;
> And many a story told in Rhime and Prose.
> But Age has rusted what the Poet writ,
> Worn out his language and obscur'd his Wit.
> In Vain he jests in his unpolish'd strain
> And tries to make his Readers laugh in vain.[29]
>
> [9–16]

Six years later, Dryden published his great "Preface to the Fables" and translations, thus setting Chaucer, newly "restored," back again next to Virgil and Ovid. Rust, of course, means the metamorphosis of matter by the transformation of energy in slow fire. What Addison wanted in his commonplace is the negative effect of this process, solidity and clear form turning to shapeless dust, the illegible epitaph. The universality of such clichés for medieval antiquity—but not the "classic" past—"wasted," "crumbling," "decayed," "barbarous"—reveals the poetic imagination recoiling in fear of its own disintegration. What is the power of the word, which cannot be saved, nor save itself? The terrible gothic darkness of the age that ends Pope's *Dunciad*,

> Lo! thy dread Empire, Chaos, is restor'd;
> Light dies before thy uncreating Word:
> Thy hand, great Anarch! lets the curtain fall;
> And Universal Darkness buries all,[30]

is no bleaker than that in Chaucer's satire on the confusion of tongues in his own, in *The Former Age*:

29. Addison's poem is dated April 3, 1694; text in *The Poetical Works of Joseph Addison, Gay's Fables, and Somerville's Chase*, ed. Rev. George Gilfillan (Edinburgh, 1859), pp. 27–28.

30. *Dunciad*, 4. 653–56. *The Poems of Alexander Pope*, ed. John Butt, reprinted in one volume, (New Haven, 1963).

> Yit was not Jupiter the likerous,
> That first was fader of delicacye
> Come in this world; ne Nembrot, desirous
> To regne, had nat maad his toures hye,
> Allas, allas! now may men wepe and crye!
> For in oure dayes nis but covetyse,
> Doublenesse and tresoun, and envye,
> Poyson, manslauhtre, and mordre in sondry wyse.
>
> [56–63]

The mutability of language is a latent element in all interpretations of medieval poems, where the theme of anxiety is consciously struck again and again in the *translatio regni, memento mori,* and *ubi sunt* formulae, lamenting the past and the dead, even in seriocomic execrations of careless scribes. The reader of the Renaissance Chaucer confronts the formulae in the context of increasing linguistic obsolescence and textual obscurity in the early editions of Chaucer's poems. Chaucer's book, now an *olde boke,* is the source of both Elizabethan reverence and condescension toward the past, the theme of Chaucerian irony in the *Book of Fame,* where we first begin to see his own ambivalence toward *auctors.* It became a constant element in everything he wrote.

In the freedom of the Elizabethan stage, where the invisible *auctor* has vanished entirely, replaced by dramatis personae who act out the fiction, one of the problems of authority most relevant to Chaucer and Gower was solved:

> We commit no crime
> To use one language in each several clime
> Where our scenes seem to live. I do beseech you
> To learn of me, who stand in the gap to teach you.
>
> [*Pericles,* 4. 4. 6–10]

Here Shakspere has "Gower, as Chorus" to stand in the gap, as well as the goddess Diana and pantomime: "What's dumb in show, I'll plain with speech." The task of narration, in the staging of Shakspere's *Troilus and Cressida,* is reduced to the brief speech of the Prologue, whose exit symbolizes the disappearance of the omniscient Chaucerian narrator as the maker of the fiction. But for medieval poets, and for Spenser, the problems of *myn auctor,* the audience, and the fictitiousness of speech are entangled with the task of self-impersonation and the presentation of dramatis personae in actions which take place in the mind—in allegory, fable, romance. The study of the poetic influence of Chaucer in the Renaissance must first go back to the open questions of medieval poetry as a written, not oral, art, to the poem conceived to be read. *Allegoria* and *ironia* "intend" multiple meanings, but the interpretation of intention need not be arbitrary. In the metamorphosis of Chaucer from medieval to Renaissance lies the evolution of allegory itself, which became for Puttenham, in 1589, "dissimulacion," *False Semblant*. Chaucerian irony and his allegory demand close reading.

Many of the old ambiguities of the verb *to read*, Middle English *reden*, still remain alive. It means, in its oldest sense (OE *rǣdan, rēden*) 'the giving or taking of counsel,' 'to have or exercise control,' with the sense of considering or explaining something mysterious such as a dream or riddle. It can be used for *think, conjecture,* or *guess*. Spenser was the first to use it to mean 'foresee, foretell,'[31] in 'to read one's fortune,' and he alone used it to mean, 'see, discern, distinguish.' He also used it as a substantive, meaning 'speech.'[32] In Middle English, "to read" may mean to interpret, to peruse without uttering in speech (to scan or interpret in thought); to learn, by perusal of a book; to utter aloud and render in speech something written; to instruct, advise, or to teach. *Rede* is frequently a colorless variant for *say, tell*; it can mean 'to find mention or record of something,' or simply 'to rehearse,' 'speak,' or 'tell of a subject.'[33] The *Lenvoy of Chaucer a Bukton* exploits a range of the ambiguities of *rede* and a written text which suggests almost everything there is to be said about "reading a fiction" and the meaning of *auctoritee*, yet the poem leaves all, characteristically, in doubt. Shall Bukton risk marriage, or not? Chaucer is asked to "advise:"

> This lytel writ, proverbes, or figure
> I sende yow, take kepe of yt, I rede;
> Unwyse is he that kan no wele endure.
> If thow be siker, put the nat in drede.
> The Wyf of Bathe I pray yow that ye rede
> Of this matere that we have on honde.
> God graunt yow your lyf frely to lede
> In fredam; for ful hard is to be bonde.
>
> [25–32]

31. "Mother Hubberd's Tale," 1. 698, cited in *OED*; see below, n. 33.
32. *FQ* IV, x, 34, "Concord she cleeped was in common reed."
33. See *OED*, s.v. "Read," *v.*; "Rede," *sb.*[1], and "Rede," *v.*[1].

"If you are secure, don't put yourself in doubt: 'read' the Wife of Bath. *Yf that hooly writ may nat suffyse, | Experience shal the teche*; as for myself, I say nothing at all." It is this Socratic Chaucer and his subtlety and autonomy—a master, posing as a servant of rhetorical conventions— which are most vulnerable to the mutability and disintegration of language, in his evolution to "antiquity" in the Renaissance.

The Apology for Ficton: Chaucerian and Socratic Irony

Why, one asks, was Chaucer the only medieval English poet still thought worth reading, and why was only he revived, imitated, and revered in the Renaissance? Because of his wit, his love poetry, his vividness as a social historian? In the short run, there are possible answers to such questions, but in the longer run they will not do. The premises are false, and the isolation of Chaucer is misleading. His prolific successor Lydgate, as we shall see, was widely read and admired, and his contemporaries Gower and Langland had, at least in the earlier period, as large an audience. Of the great medieval poets, however, only Langland is truly an Anglo-Saxon original; Chaucer and Gower are chiefly poetic translators. Gower's major works are in three lan-guages: Latin, French, and English, while Chaucer worked from Latin, French, and Italian into English. Chaucer's distinctive achievements as a poet are to be found in his discoveries of means of concealment of himself, of art that seems to be artless. These are certainly not the quali-ties he was praised for by contemporaries, nor did the Elizabethan writers who looked back to him consider him a master of simplicity. To his fifteenth-century heirs, he was the epitome of elegance, Dunbar's "rose of rhetoricians." Spenser, Sidney, and Shakspere saw him as a primitive genius, admirably learned for a barbarous time, handicapped by the very crudeness of his medium in an age ignorant of great art.

All three of the great Middle English poets, Chaucer, Gower, and Langland, were regarded by their contemporaries and descendants as moralists who wrote according to the universal sanction for poetry, sacred and profane: *movere et docere; docere et delectare.* Yet it seems to me that, unlike Gower and Langland, Chaucer alone used poetry as a mode of inquiry as well as of instruction and delight. Unlike his con-temporaries', his poems are difficult to reduce to moral statements, although he begins with the same moral premises and assumes a similar religious context. Chaucerian allegory and Chaucerian irony and ambiguity are unique and distinct from Gower's and Langland's kinds of allegory and irony. At a distance, the frameworks in which all three begin are common and "typically medieval": we find the familiar dream and the dream landscape opening up to be ready symbolically according to cues placed by the narrator, which follow conventional codes external to the poem and may be taken for granted by the audience. The interpretation of the poem is set in motion and conducted by the narrator, who leads the audience toward their goal. It is here, however, that questions arise, far more frequently in Chaucer than in any other medieval poet. In virtually every other poet, answers can be found for difficult questions of intention; in Chaucer's poems, nothing can be taken at face value, and certainty is rarely possible. The uniquely Chaucerian quality, in the dream visions, the *Canterbury Tales*, and most profoundly in *Troilus and Criseyde*, is the uncertainty of the narrator as to what his poem means. He is led, rather than leader; he follows, and he is almost always in doubt.

Chaucer's discoveries as a poet, and his originality, lie not in narrative—plots, myth making, invention—but in voices, and in the controlling of language so that voices other than his own are made to speak. In the chapters that follow, I propose to study some facets of his poetry which seem to me to be unique to him, and which are therefore inimitable. As a translator of extraordinary range, he brought a wealth of new kinds of poetry into English; but so, of course, did Gower. As a moralist and ironist, he explored the world he lived in and exposed its hypocrisy and vice; but so, too, did Langland. More than either of them, or any other medieval poet, however, he questioned the worth of his own art, the ambiguity of language, and the pretensions of poets to know or say more than other men. It is a very ancient ploy to remain ambivalent as to one's capacity to speak, and Chaucer alone among his medieval contemporaries mastered the rhetoric of ambiguity.

I shall frequently find reason, in reading Chaucer in the Middle Ages and in the Renaissance, to turn to Plato. The Platonism that grew and flourished in twelfth-century France provided medieval poetry with a new world of allegorical imagery and cast the poet in a new philosophical role. The higher Platonism of the Renaissance immensely magnified that role, with the adding of the *Symposium*, the *Phaedrus*, and the *Ion* to the medieval *Timaeus* as texts to justify the visionary imagination. The question of poetry in Plato, in the earlier Middle Ages, arises in a dialogue perhaps as well known in medieval

Europe as it was in the sixteenth century, and as indispensable to
both: the *Phaedo*, Socrates' argument for the immortality of the soul.
The *Phaedo* also recounts the last days in prison of Socrates, while he
awaited the end of Apollo's festival, for which his execution had been
postponed.

The relevance of the *Phaedo* for medieval poetry is, I think, very clear
from the opening episode on; the subject there raised is whether or not
death is to be feared. Plato begins obliquely, with Socrates' release
from the chains on his legs, and leads from the subject of pleasure and
pain into the myth of the afterlife, the soul's escape, and its following
of its guide or *daimon* beyond Hades into the other world. The dialogue
concludes with Socrates drinking the hemlock. The portion of the
dialectic that is most interesting for the present study is its introduction,
the means Plato uses to shift the focus from the immediate state of the
body to the survival of the mind, and Socrates' conception of eternity.

Cebes interrupts a remark of Socrates on the double nature of pleasure and pain to ask him if the rumor is true that he has been writing
poems, "putting into verse stories of Aesop and composing a hymn
to Apollo." No one has ever heard of him doing such a thing before,
and his mocking opinion of the rhapsodes is well known. Socrates'
reply amplifies what he said at his trial, about the voice of his *daimon*:

> I was trying to discover the meaning of some dreams, and I wrote
> the poems to clear my conscience, in case this was the sort of art
> that I was told to pursue. It happened something like this: the
> same dream had kept on coming to me from time to time through-
> out my life, taking different forms at different times, but always
> saying the same thing: "Socrates, pursue the arts, and work hard
> at them." I formerly used to suppose that it was urging me to do
> what I was in fact doing, and trying to encourage me in the per-
> formance of that: that like those who shout encouragement to
> runners in a race, so the dream, when it urged me to (*mousiké*)
> pursue the arts, was encouraging me in what I was doing; for
> philosophy is the greatest of all arts, and that was my pursuit. But
> then when the trial took place, and the god's festival prevented
> my execution, I thought that just in case the dream meant, after
> all, that I should follow this popular kind of art, I ought to follow
> it and not disobey. It seemed safer not to depart before salving my
> conscience, by the composition of poems in obedience to the dream.

So I first wrote in honor of the god for whom the ceremonies were being held, and then, after the hymn, realizing that the "poet," if he was going to be a poet or composer at all, must compose not fact but fiction, and that I myself was not a story teller, I used fables that were ready at hand—the fables of Aesop, which I knew —the first of them I came across.

The speech ends with Socrates' farewell message to Evenus, the poet: "Tell him, if he has any sense, to follow me as quickly as he can."[34]

While Boethius and Prudentius are the primary medieval sources for the sacred dream and its allegory, the older pagan forms also survive, and invite speculation. What this Socratic defense provides, then, is Plato's testimony as to the visionary voice in dreams and the two fundamental modes of poetry, the sacred hymn and the "fiction"— the fable that does not have to be true in order to be delightful, that can be invented on the spot, translated, or made to mean anything at all, since it is "composed," a fable. Socrates makes a clear distinction between storytelling as an art and the voice of the *daimon* in his dream, just as he distinguishes between sacred and secular poetry. When he needs myth—or Homer—in order to describe "the shape of the earth as I believe it to be," it is a story. "As Homer describes it," we see the underworld of Hades and its four rivers, and the "pure dwelling place up above" for those who are released "from these regions and depart from them as from a prison"; the cosmic image is made visible by Socrates' imagination. He has the power to envisage and describe it, but as to its truth, he cannot go beyond hope and the risk a rational mind is willing to take:

No man of sense should affirm decisively that all this is exactly as I have described it. But that the nature of the souls and their habitations is either as I have described, or very similar, . . . that, I think, is a very proper belief to hold, and such as a man should risk, for the risk is well worth while. And one should repeat these things over and over again to oneself, like a charm, which is precisely why I have spent so long explaining the story now.[35]

Interpretation of Chaucers' dream–vision poetry properly begins

---

34. *Plato's Phaedo*, trans. and ed. R. S. Bluck (London, 1955), 60D; 59C–61B; 61C. All quotations from the *Phaedo* are from Bluck's edition.
35. Ibid., 114C.

with Boethius. However, the survival of Socrates' *daimon*, his irony, and his ambivalence toward fiction making, in the dialogues of the medieval Platonic tradition, the *Timaeus, Meno, Phaedo*, and the *Apology*,[36] provide a deeper perspective for criticism than the Christian exegetes, rhetoricians, and the literary sources, named and unnamed, we now know he knew. We shall approach the medieval Chaucer indirectly, through Spenser and the Elizabethan defense of allegory, and then through the ending of the *Book of Fame*, the most enigmatic of his visionary poems, because it focusses on the art of poetry, and on the poet. It would seem to me to yield something more of its eccentricity to an oblique approach, through the ambiguous Neoplatonic figure of Genius the poet, than through the traditional study of its *auctors*, the heterogeneous mélange of Virgil and Dante, Alan de Lille and Jean de Meung, medieval science and the texts of *artes poeticae*. All of these are present (as elsewhere in his poems), and all too visible. But the issues the poem confronts are those which its narrator evades, and they suggest risks he was not willing to take. The *Book of Fame* is, I think, Chaucer's most Socratic poem, and its treatment of *auctoritees* suggests the central problems we face in interpreting Chaucerian irony, which grow deeper in the other stories he found, "fables ready at hand," for the poet, "if he is to be a poet at all, must compose not fact but fiction."

36. See Raymond Klibansky, *The Continuity of the Platonic Tradition* (London, 1939), p. 51. See also R. R. Bolgar, *The Classical Heritage and its beneficiaries from the carolingian age to the end of the renaissance* (London, 1954; repr. 1964), ch. 5–8, passim; and Ernst H. Kantorowicz, "Plato in the Middle Ages," *The Philosophical Review 51* (1942): 312–23, reprinted in his *Selected Studies* (Locust Valley, N. Y., 1965), pp. 184–93.

II

Imitation, Allusion, and Originality: Some Renaissance Experiments and Medieval Models

... craft countrefeteth kynde

The Book of Fame

When divine power and wisdom and goodness are beheld in the creation of things, we fear One so powerful, worship One so wise, and love One so benevolent.

Guillaume de Conches, *Glose super Platonem*

"A man carried the inkhorn of a writer at his loins, who set a mark T upon the foreheads of those who sighed," [Ezek. 9] figuratively insinuating that if any man is deficient in the skill of writing he must not take upon himself the office of preaching penitence.

Richard de Bury, *Philobiblon*

Spenser's Chaucer: Mutability and Natura's Gown

By common consent, the following stanza from Spenser's *Mutability Cantos* is primary evidence of the continuity of Chaucer's fame from the Middle Ages to the Renaissance, and of Spenser's debt to his acknowledged English master. Approaching the description of the goddess Nature, Spenser hesitates over the difficulty of his task:

> So hard it is for any liuing wight
> All her array and vestiments to tell,
> That old *Dan Geffrey* (in whose gentle spright,
> The pure well head of Poesie did dwell)
> In his *Foules parley* durst not with it mel,
> But it transferd to *Alane*, who he thought
> Had in his *Plaint of Kind* describ'd it well:
> Which who will read set forth so as it ought,
> Go seek he out that *Alane* where he may be sought.
>
> [*FQ* VII, vii, 9][1]

1. *Spenser's Faerie Queene*, ed. J.C. Smith (Oxford, 1909), 2: 470.

35

The turn of Spenser's phrases, "old *Dan Geffrey* (in whose gentle spright / The pure well head of Poesie did dwell)" suggests not continuity, however, but metamorphosis, traceable in part to the inevitable aging process of literary evolution, and in part to Spenser's conception of himself, projected backward to his chosen literary forefather, whose "owne spirit (through infusion sweete), doth in me survive" (*FQ* IV, ii, 34). An inquiry into the aging and survival of Chaucer's poetry may appropriately begin in the context of Spenser's unfinished meditation on flux and impermanence, which, characteristically, he saw in terms of myth growing into new forms out of deeply rooted traditional sources. Spenser opens canto vi with the cliché of medieval Fortuna:

> What man that sees the euer-whirling wheele
> Of Change, the which all mortall things doth sway,
> But that therby doth find, and plainly feele,
> How Mutability in them doth play
> Her cruell sports, to many mens decay?
> Which that to all may better yet appear,
> *I will rehearse that whylome I heard say,*
> How she at first her selfe began to reare
> Gainst all the gods, and th' empire sought from them to beare.

> But first, here falleth fittest to vnfold
> Her antique race and linage ancient,
> *As I have found it registred of old,*
> *In Faery Land mongst records permanent.*
>
> [*FQ* VII, vi, 1–2, (*italics mine*)]

Chaucer first used the word *mutabilitie* in English in his translation of Boethius's *Consolation of Philosophy*, but Spenser more likely found it in *Troilus and Criseyde*, in Pandar's defense of Fortune's "whirlynge wheel with the turnynge sercle" (*Boece*, II, pr. 2; cf. *Tr I*, 851, quoted below, p. 175). The image that was strongest, I think, for Chaucer's poetry is from *Boece*, III, prosa 8:

> Axestow glorye? Thow shalt so bien distract by aspere thynges that thow schalt forgon sykernesse. And yif thow wolt leden thi lif in delyces, every wyght schal despysen the and forleeten the, as thow that art thral to thyng that is right foul and brutyl (*that is to seyn, servaunt to thi body*). . . . But the schynynge of thi forme (*that is to seyn, the beute of thi body*), how swyftly passynge is it, and how transitorie!

Certes it es more flyttynge than the mutabilite of floures of
the somer sesoun.

But the primary source of Spenser's narrator's knowledge of Mutability, we see, is himself: what he remembers to have heard, and to have
seen, recorded "permanent" in the world of his imagination. In his
Faery Land (the poem itself), the abstraction "Change" becomes
concrete, transformed into "she" who climbs up into the night sky to
push the Moon from her chair,

> And there-with lifting up her golden wand,
> Threatened to strike her if she did withstand.
> Whereat the starres, which round about her blazed,
> And eke the Moones bright wagon, still did stand.
> All being with so bold attempt amazed,
> And on her uncouth habit and sterne looke still gazed.
>
> [*FQ* VII, vi, 13]

Spenser achieves his transitions from abstract to allegorically visualized
concrete so effortlessly that his brief notes (in stanzas 1 and 2) to authenticate his fictional "sources" seem almost gratuitous: who would
doubt that he heard what was said, and saw what only he can describe?
It comes as something oddly stressed, then, that the narrator emphasizes for a full stanza the difficulty of his task—the attempt to describe
the gown of Nature—by alluding to Chaucer's inability to do it, and his
passing it on, in turn, to Alan de Lille. Now the real world of writers
long dead, and of extant poems in old languages, merges into the making of the fictional scene of Mutability's trial, which the narrator says
is beyond his power to tell, were he not under a greater compulsion:

> Ah! whither doost thou now, thou greater Muse,
> Me from these woods and pleasing forrests bring?
> And my frail spirit (that dooth oft refuse
> This too high flight, unfit for her weake wing)
> Lift up aloft. . . .
>
> Yet sith I needs must follow thy behest,
> Doe thou my weaker wit with skill inspire,
> Fit for this turn; and in my feeble brest
> Kindle fresh sparks of that immortal fire
> Which learned minds inflameth with desire
> Of heavenly things: for who but thou alone,

That art yborne of heaven and heavenly sire,
Can tell things doen in heaven so long ygone,
So farre past memory of many that may be knowne?

[*FQ* VII, vii, 1–2]

There would seem at first to be little difficulty in understanding what Spenser means by "my frail spirit," "gentle spright," and "spirit (through infusion sweete)," in his allusions to what will later be called Chaucer's "genius." But to pause over these terms leads to awareness of their entanglement in ancient ambiguities. Spenser's *spright* and *spirit* reflect postclassical developments into new metaphors of the concept most familiar to us in Socrates' *daimon*, from which Middle and modern English *demon* evolved. C. S. Lewis has described the medieval inheritance from pagan mythology of *daemon*, "the tutelary spirit. . . . intermediary between divine and human, which accompanies men from birth to death."[2] In the *OED*, the second sense, "a genius," is compared with Latin *genius* (from *gignare* 'to be born' or 'come into being'), and the early definitions run closely parallel. *Genius* is 'a demon, or spiritual being in general' in the citations up to the sixteenth century. Spenser exploits the fusion of Christianized meanings of *daemon* and *genius* for the third term *spright*, or *spirit*, which is apparently indispensable for the definitions of the two former terms in their common senses of 'a benign attendant,' 'ministering or indwelling spirit.' Thus these words, *spirit*, *genius*, *daemon*, all share and convey the fluctuating cloudiness and transparency characteristic of men's uncertainty over the origin of voices said to be "heard in the mind." They may be of good or evil spirits, a good or evil genius, a benign *daemon* or an unclean devil. Spenser's contemporary James Sanford commented in 1569 on his difficulty as a translator in dealing with these words and their problematic implications: "Grammarians doo expounde this word Daemon that is, a Spirite, as if it were *Sapiens*, that is, wise,"[3] A little over a decade later, Sir Phillip Sidney used a positive sense, in the *Apology*, for

2. See *The Discarded Image* (Cambridge, 1970), pp. 40–44, on Apuleius's *de Deo Socratis*. See also notes 19 and 23 below, and Brian Stock, *Myth and Science in the Twelfth Century* (Princeton, 1973), ch. 4, passim.

3. In his translation of the Renaissance sceptic Henricus Cornelius Agrippa von Nettesheim, *Of the Vanitie and Uncertaintie of Artes and Sciences*, Englished by James Sanford (London, 1569), p. 2. Agrippa's strange diatribe against all intellectual activity was written in 1526; it was translated into Italian and French, and widely published in the early sixteenth century in the original Latin edition. Agrippa is discussed by Richard H. Popkin, *The History of Scepticism from Erasmus to Descartes* (New York, 1969), ch. 2.

the exalted power of the poetic imagination: "A Poet, no industrie can make, if his own Genius bee not carried vnto it."[4] We will not here digress further on the rich phenomena and language of demonology in the Renaissance, which was rising to new heights in the late sixteenth century in England. But it will be useful to look briefly, later in this chapter, at one source relevant to the present context, the fully formed allegorical figure of Alan de Lille's Genius, in the *Plaint of Kind*, and more briefly note its medieval antecedents and later analogues. Although overshadowed in allegorical exegesis by the famous Natura, Genius is an active symbol of the ambiguity latent in all these words for the inner voice that poets "hear," which Socrates trusted but Plato did not. As Chaucer's contemporary John Trevisa put it, in his version of Higden's *Polychronicon* (1385), "We haueþ i-lerned of Socrates, þat was alway tendaunt to a spirit that was i-cleped demon."[5]

The confusions of meaning and the ambivalent associations that cluster around the words *genius, demon,* and *spirit,* from the twelfth-century allegorical image of Alan's Genius to the paradoxes of the Shaksperean supernatural (Prospero's role as "genius," for example), were freely exploited and enlarged by poets for four hundred years. In the *Faerie Queene,* Spenser needs both a good and an evil Genius (for Acrasia's Bower and the Gardens of Adonis), needs Chaucer's *spright,* as well as Archimago's power over the demonic *sprites* of the underworld, and his own spirit's access to the Muses—to name but a handful. Spenser's metamorphic definitions of allegory are expressed everywhere in the landscape of Faerie Land, in its *genii loci.*

The ambiguity of these potent terms, *spirit, genius, daemon,* and their "powers" seem to involve the poet who uses them in risks. The other side of the supernatural comes alive brilliantly, for example, in Chaucer's *Friar's Tale,* where the Devil in Green wins the Summoner; the negative meanings of "demonic" are extended even further in the tale of the friar in the Summoner's reply. The earliest use of the word "demonic" in English occurs in the mordantly anti-intellectual satire at the ending

4. Sir Philip Sidney, *An Apologie for Poetrie,* in *Elizabethan Critical Essays,* ed. G. Gregory Smith (Oxford, 1904), 1: 195 (hereafter cited as Smith, *Sidney*).

5. *Polychronicon Ranulphi Higden monachi Cestrensis; together with the English translations of John Trevisa,* ed. Churchill Babington and J.R. Lumby (London, 1865–86), 3: 279. Higden's chapter on Socrates was rewritten in later versions of the *Polychronicon,* with additional material from the thirteenth-century Franciscan John of Wales's *Compendiloquium.* See the study of Higden's sources and the texts of his chronicle by John Taylor, *The Universal Chronicle of Ranulph Higden* (Oxford, 1966), ch. 5 and passim.

of this tale, certainly one of the most obscene contexts in the *Canterbury Tales* (" . . . Jankyn spak, in this matere / As wel as Euclide dide or Ptholomee," in answering the problem in *ars-metrike*). When the furious friar comes to complain of the *odious mescheif* perpetrated on him, the lord and his lady dismiss it, as the foul deed of a *cherl* "possessed", "whose sike heed is ful of vanytee; / I holde hym in a manere frenesye" (D 2208–09). When the friar persists, the lord laughs away the reverberations in the air and taunts the incensed friar ironically,

> What, lo, my cherl, lo, yet how shrewedly
> Unto my confessour to-day he spak!
> I holde hym certeyn a demonyak!
>
> [D 2238–40]

The final echo of the "demonic" in the tale turns it into a witty negation:

> they seyde, subtiltee
> And heigh wit made hym speken as he spak;
> He nys no fool, ne no demonyak.
>
> [D 2290–93]

The Chaucerian ambiguity of the demonic inner voice and of *wit* and *subtiltee* in the *Summoner's Tale* are, in almost every conceivable sense, the antitheses of Spenser's serious subtlety and the "sweete infusion" of Chaucer's voice in his own. That it is absurd to connect them is self-evident, but the absurdity should not obscure the point, which is the antinomian conception of the demonic voice, deeply implicated in medieval and Renaissance concepts of genius and creativity. The clearest literary source of this ambiguity, common to both Chaucer and Spenser is not, I think, Plato, but the Neoplatonic figure of Genius in Alan's *Plaint of Kind* and the *Roman de la Rose*: the prolific maker of images who is the goddess Nature's scribe, lover, and priest. We shall come back to him, then, after we have looked further at Spenser's *Mutability* stanza, where Chaucer and Alan are linked by name.

In both the *Mutability Cantos* and the *Parliament of Fowls*, the goddess Nature is unambiguous, beneficent, and strong; she is not weeping and distraught, as the Dreamer sees her in Alan de Lille, but in benign control of her domain. She is the natural law that expresses divine law, personified. Both Chaucer and Spenser have separated her from her priest, Genius; Spenser makes use of him elsewhere in the *Faerie Queene*, but, although Chaucer fills several stanzas of the first part of the *Parliament* with allegorical personifications, he seems to have ignored Nature's priest. He does not describe her, but as Spenser says, defers: She is "right as Aleyn, in the *Pleynt of Kynde* / Devyseth . . . of aray and face" (*PF* 316–17), without further detail.[6] The perspectives that open out from Spenser's stanza stretch even further back than we can pursue them here, for what is sought is not evidence of dependence or influence, but of recurring and changing common problems inherent in imitation—both Chaucer's and Spenser's—which entail the double image of the poet and the fading and remaking of his art. The linking together of Chaucer and one of his *olde bokes* exemplifies not only Spenser's and Chaucer's naming of sources, but also the self-projection of the poet in the poem, which becomes measurably stronger in Spenser in the *Mutability Cantos*. Here, it is the narrator himself, not one of his knights, who is directly involved with Mutability and her trial, and here, on his own home ground:

> Whylome, when Ireland florished in fame
> Of welths and goodnesses, far above the rest
> Of all that beare the British Islands name.
>
> [*FQ* VII, vi, 38]

His need to turn to "Dan Geffrey" provides a starting point for this inquiry into Renaissance readings of Chaucer, which examines first some problems in allegory and imitation in the Renaissance, and then some medieval experiments in personification.

Renaissance "Imitation" and the Defense of Art in Ascham, Sidney, and Spenser

Spenser's naming of Chaucer and Alan constitutes a rare double occurrence in the *Faerie Queene* of two medieval poetic conventions which are favorite ploys of Chaucer: the acknowledgment of authority or naming of a source (*myn auctor seyth, as the book seyth*), and (transferred to Chaucer) a rhetorical device far more frequently found in medieval poetry than in the Renaissance, the *occupatio*, or feigned refusal to

---

6. J.A.W. Bennett's *The Parlement of Foules* (Oxford, 1957; repr. 1965) is the fullest study of Chaucer's sources; his appendix on Natura, Nature, and Kind (pp. 194–212) is a more useful survey than the earlier commentaries of Lewis, Curtius, and E.C. Knowlton (see below, note 23).

describe.[7] It is familiar to us, for example, in the brilliant fifty-odd line description in the *Knight's Tale* of the funeral of Arcite, which the Knight ironically professes his inability to describe while he recalls in detail its visible splendor. Spenser's prayer to Clio to "kindle fresh sparks" and inspire his "weaker wit" vary this theme, which is an aspect of the larger group of various devices used for the modesty topos, the strategy by means of which the humble poet apologizes in advance and thus forestalls criticism of his inadequacy.

   In Spenser, the new goddess Nature slowly emerges, brought in to mediate a dispute more profound than the one in Chaucer's *Parliament*, perhaps closer to the bitter grief in the *Plaint of Kind*, where she bewails her ruin after Adam's fall. Spenser develops her against a backdrop of allusions that suggest a genealogy by association with two vaguely familiar, loosely connected mythological characters, Chaucer's Kind and Alan's Natura, who are just enough alike to be understood as a commonplace against which the new image should be viewed. Without the use of the traditional formula, *as the book seyth*, Chaucer and Alan are made to seem Spenser's *auctors*. Nor does he affect the humble occupatio, which he attributes instead to Chaucer ("who durst not . . . tell her vestments and array"). So his own forty-five-line description of the goddess (stanzas 5–13) unobtrusively conceals the originality of its richness, far more ornate and complex than its predecessors. Only at the very end of his long presentation of her, "That richer seem'd than any tapestry / That princes bowers adorne with painted imagery," does the narrator pause to glance aside, as it were, at his own signature:

---

7. Occupatio (or praeteritio) is closely related to two other figures, occultatio ("suggestion, insinuation") and praecisio (or aposeiopesis), the "impossibility" figure, in which the speaker stops, as if unable to continue describing something beyond words; all the modesty conventions may be used in either witty or serious senses, as forms of *ironia*.

   Occupatio ("anticipation") and praeteritio ("omission, something by-passed") like the various rhetorical uses of occultatio ("hidden, concealed, secret") ultimately derive from Cicero (*De Inventione*) and the anonymous treatise *Rhetorica ad Herrenium*; the terms descend as vaguely defined and confusingly interchanged concepts in later medieval grammarians and commentators on proper Latin style.

   The problems of vernacular style and poetic form in the modern languages are first taken up in the fourteenth century, for Italian by Dante in *De Vulgari Eloquentia* (circa 1305) and for French by Eustache Deschamps in *L'Art de dictier et de fere chançons* (1392). For medieval rhetoric in England, the survey of J. W. H. Atkins, *English Literary Criticism: The Medieval Phase* (Cambridge, Eng., 1934) is still useful on John of Salisbury: see also his summary of Geoffrey of Vinsauf, appendix A; on Chaucer, see the discussion in Robert Payne's *The Key of Remembrance* (New Haven, 1963), ch. 1 and 2, passim.

> This great grandmother of all creatures bred,
> Great Nature, ever young yet full of eld,
> Still mooving, yet unmoved from her sted,
> Unseene of any, yet of all beheld,
> Thus sitting in her throne, as I have teld,
> Before her came Dame Mutabilitie.
>
> [*FQ* VII, vii, 13]

All three of these Natures present the concept of the law of fertility and orderly plenitude, which, as Bennett and Lewis have shown, is traditionally personified as a veiled woman in an elaborate gown, mysteriously beautiful and of immense power. Reduced to simple terms, the abstract attributes of the image are important only as they outline the composite stereotype frame, "Nature," a generalization against which each new Natura is to be visualized and understood, in the twelfth-, fourteenth-, and finally sixteenth-century versions of the classic Latin commonplace, derived from the feminine singular noun. But the omission or alteration of her attributes may be significant, as I think will be clear in the case of Natura's gown. Obviously, each new version of the image stands out in turn against its own immediate foreground: the Arlo hill of Mutability's trial, the dream landscape of Chaucer's earthly paradise in the *Parliament*, the flat, indeterminate, flowery plain in the mind of the Dreamer in Alan de Lille. As background and in succession (as in Spenser's stanza), the goddesses Natura cumulatively begin to coalesce with one another, mutations of a basic form; each is unique, none are identical, but all are Natura. She, however, is less important for the present purpose than the process of transference of authority which Spenser uses to stress the difficulty of his attempt to describe her. All men know who she is, but very few have ever been able adequately to envision her, "thus sitting on her throne, as I have teld." By almost imperceptible sleight of hand, Spenser has turned the old modesty formulae and the occupatio into the Renaissance poet's affirmation of art.

Spenser is struggling to reconcile great commonplaces—the many and the one, the bound and the free, time and eternity—in the *Mutability Cantos*, as he had been concerned with themes of illusion, constancy, and change from the beginning of his career as a poet, in his first youthful exercises in translation, the blank verse versions of du Bellay's sonnets on the decay of nature and art in *The Theatre for*

Voluptuous Worldlings. It is hardly surprising that he turns again to acknowledge Chaucer, his "Tityrus," in what may be the last poetry he wrote. In *The Shepherd's Calendar*, Spenser claimed a relationship to Chaucer comparable with Dante's to Virgil—disciple to master, modern to ancient—which is distinctively retrospective, and, with his equally distinctive vocabulary, it gave him a kind of somber eminence among forward facing "modern" Elizabethans. When such a poet calls strong attention to his historical perspective and asserts relationship, it is worthwhile to try to be aware both of what he wants to acknowledge, and of what he may omit, whether the omission be deliberate, unconscious, or something regarded as unimportant. As will be seen, Chaucer's deliberate omissions and allusions to his *auctors*, both real and imaginary, create a significant dimension of his *Troilus and Criseyde*, as well as of other poems, for he explored the potentialities of the authority formulae from the beginning, in his earliest work. Spenser's allusions to Chaucer are, I think, fascinating because they pay homage and seem to define relatedness which reading of the poems does not confirm. Hence, one of the purposes of the following chapters is to examine the grounds for support, or doubt, of Spenser's claims of direct descent and special shared affinity. Obviously Spenser used medieval poetry, Chaucerian and Malorian romance, but how shall we interpret the more elusive implication, made by Colin Clout in the *Shepherd's Calendar*, that, in the self-conscious image of Orpheus, he learned to play his pipe as a poet from listening to Chaucer, his "old Tityrus"? The claim is a clue to its medieval precedents and suggests study of Chaucer's own disavowals of any art, his pose as a bungling amateur. And it is also proper to raise the question of why such devices —*myn auctor seyth, the book seyth*—are used formulaically in medieval poetry, but rarely by Elizabethans. Spenser's homage raises the issues of imitation and authority. Why, and to what effect, does it seem necessary for other witnesses to be called, almost as character witnesses are called in court? The offering of the names of one's poetic ancestors, real or imaginary, is part of the apology for secular poetry, and it implies a need to defend the poet's art (since it is more than a skill) against accusers.

Both the authority formulae and the occupatio, or pretended refusal to describe, as we shall see, are very frequent in Chaucer and relatively rare, or else heavily disguised, in Spenser.[8] The enigmatically deferential

8. I have found only three instances of formulaic use of "as the book seyth" in the *Faerie*

stance characteristic of the medieval master seems to be transformed in the Renaissance disciple into confident gestures, no matter how modest the tone, which call attention to the poet and convey certainty as to the value of his art. If there has been a change, although many of the terms seem to be superficially the same and continuity is asserted, where do the proportions shift? One interesting method of approach might be to examine Spenser's practice in the light of the Renaissance theory of Imitation, as expounded, for example, by Roger Ascham in *The Scolemaster* (1570). Ascham taught his students the six rules for "reading" classical models, which he had learned from Sir John Cheke. In his essay "Of Imitation," Ascham thus describes the process of reinterpretation of models; one must, he says, compare:

i. [The author] reteyneth thus mooche of the matter, thies sentences, thies wordes.
ii. This and that he leaueth out, which he doth wittelie to this end and purpose.
iii. This he addeth here.
iv. This he diminisheth there.
v. This he ordereth thus, with placing that here, not there.
vi. This he altereth and changeth, either in propertie of wordes, in form of sentence, in substance of the matter, or in one or another conuenient circumstances of the authors present purpose.

In thise fewe rude English wordes are wrapt up all the necessarie tooles and instrumentes, where with trew Imitation is rightlie wrought withall in any tonge.[9]

Ascham's rules, intended for comparison of Virgil and Homer or Cicero and Demosthenes, taught his students reverence for the text and also the circuitous means by which "to assimilate" becomes "to transform." I think they may not be enough, however, fully to account for the differences between Spenser's Nature and Chaucer's, nor those between both and their apparent source, Alan de Lille's *De Planctu Naturae.*

From Ascham one can learn how to compare, but not how to

Queene: "As it in bookes hath written been of old" (III, ii, 18.3); "As it in antique books is mentioned" (III, vi, 32.2); "as in bookes is taught" (VI, vi, 9.9). Other references to "old books" apply to particulars in the narrative, e.g., Archimago's book of spells, Guyon's history of Faery Land, Arthur's "Briton Moniments," etc.

9. Roger Ascham, *The Scolemaster,* in *Elizabethan Critical Essays,* ed. G. Gregory Smith (Oxford, 1904), 1:9.

interpret the results of self-conscious Renaissance "imitation." Two other factors limit the usefulness of Ascham's rules for the study of Spenser and Chaucer. One is the ambiguity latent in the word "imitation" itself, and the other is Ascham's prejudice as to proper models. In his opening statement, Ascham seems to define "imitation" inclusively, meaning by it both "copy" (in a vaguely Platonic sense, i.e. that all art copies other art, and writers copy other writers, as Virgil "copies" Homer) and *mimesis* (in a vaguely Aristotelean sense, i.e. that the artist follows nature, and imitates "life"). It is at once freely creative, and yet bound to a model:

> Imitation is a facultie to expresse liuelie and perfitelie that example which ye go about to folow. And of itself it is large and wide: for all the workes of nature in a maner be examples for arte to folow.
>
> But to our purpose: all languages, both learned and mother tongues, be gotten, and gotten onelie by Imitation.

In the entire discussion of *imitatio*, however, Ascham deals only with literary imitations—with who the best classical models are and how they are to be followed. He is a severe humanist, and he scorns those who would ignore the ancients, and prefer more modern models:

> Some that make Chaucer in English and Petrarch in Italian their Gods in verses, and yet be not able to make trew difference, what is a fault and what is a iust prayse in those two worthies wittes, will moch mislike this my writyng. . . .
>
> And you that be able to vnderstand no more than ye find in the Italian tonge, and neuer went farder than the scole of Petrarke and Ariostus abroad, or else of Chaucer at home, though you haue pleasure to wander blindlie still in your foule wrong way, enuie not others that seeke, as wise men haue done before them, the fairest and rightest way.

In spite of his censure of Chaucer in this context, Chaucer's editor Speght found other passages in Ascham's Chaucer criticism useful to quote in his Preface of 1598. But in *The Scolemaster* (twenty years before the publication of the first part of the *Faerie Queene*, and only a decade before the *Shepherd's Calendar*), Ascham will have none of the Italians, nor of the English Middle Ages, which both corrupt and contaminate men's minds:

> There be in man two speciall thinges: Mans will, mans mynde. Where will inclineth to goodnes, the mynde is bent to troth: Where will is caried from goodnes to vanities, the mynde is sone drawne from troth to false opinion. And so the readiest way to entangle the mynde with false doctrine is first to intice the will to wanton liuyng. . . .

> These be the inchantements of Circes, brought out of Italie, to marre mens maners in England; much by example of ill life, but more by preceptes of fonde bookes, of late translated out of Italian into English.

As for medieval English literature, to Ascham it is if anything fouler still, but less dangerous, because *Morte Arthure* is less read now in England than Ariosto and other Italian "subtle, cunnyng, new and diverse" books. Looking back to the darkness of even the recent English past, he sees

> in our forefathers tyme, whan Papistrie, as a standyng poole, couered and ouerflowed all England, fewe bookes were read in our tong, sauyng certain bookes of Cheualrie, as they sayd, for pastime and pleasure, which, as some say, were made in Monasteries by idle Monkes or wanton Chanons.[10]

Ascham goes on in a swinging attack on Malorian romance and its lesser like, having brushed aside Hawes and Lydgate, the most famous poets of the fifteenth century (and devoted "Chaucerians"), without even naming them. In the light of Spenser's avowed predilection for just those models Ascham fears most and virtually repudiates—the seductive Italians and the barbarous medievals—we must look more deeply, beyond Ascham, into the issues at stake in "imitation" and at the underlying theme of "authority." As in medieval rhetoric, the new humanists' terms are curiously elastic. H. O. White observes, in his study of plagiarism in the Renaissance, that

> Elizabethan literary theorists, like their Continental teachers, continually employ the word "imitation" without distinction, for following nature (*mimesis*), and for following other writers.[11]

10. Ibid., pp. 5; 31, 33; 3–4.

11. H.O. White, *Plagiarism and Imitation During the English Renaissance*, Harvard Studies in English 12 (Cambridge, Mass., 1935), p. 61, n. 1. Cf. W.L. Bullock's "The Precept of Plagiarism in the Cinquecento," *Modern Philology* 25 (1927): 293–312.

Similarly, "authority" can be used to refer to the precedents a poet
cites ("old Dan Geffrey," "Alane") and to his own imagination's
autonomy in the domain of his own poem ("As I have found it regis-
tered of old / In Faery Land mongst records permanent").

Because of the wonderful energy and passionate conviction of Sidney's *Apologie for Poetrie*, not written until after 1580, and not officially
published until 1595, the contentious confusion that preceded it in
medieval poetics, which had been growing in the hundred years since
the introduction of printing in England, tends to be underplayed or
relegated to textbook arguments in philology and the history of the
language. The grounds for dispute over the role of the poet and the
language of poetry are, however, not merely matters of style and surface, but, as Ascham takes for granted, moral and psychological as well:
they concern, as he says, "man's will, and man's mynde." I shall not
attempt to deal here with subtler issues involving discrepancies among
the texts of the theorists, and Ascham's and Sidney's predecessors;
merely to describe "imitation" and "authority" invites oversimplifica-
tion of the issues at stake, and the treatment of difficult concepts in
broad and general terms. It is all too easy to become fascinated—
indeed, hypnotized—by the intricacies of detail at both ends of the
poetic spectrum I am tracing, from medieval to Renaissance, in which
theory and practice are just as often at odds as they are sometimes
mutually illuminating. Obviously, in a general sense, and at a distance,
Spenser is in phase with his age; the closer we come, and the more
particular the terms, the less he is like any other Elizabethan. The same
is true for Chaucer and the Middle Ages. In order to deal with both
and to see what continuities may remain after we have sought the
boundaries where one leaves off and the other begins—even in such a
relatively clear case as Chaucer's Kind and Spenser's Nature—it is
necessary to begin with some familiar and fundamental assumptions.

It is a given in poetic theory in the Middle Ages and in the Renaissance that the writing of poetry is the attempt not only to make an idea
intelligible but also to make it powerful: the language beautifies, or
strengthens, the thought. The art is also an attempt to arrest change,
to gain control of the process of mutation by saying something that will
last, and prove to be permanently true. Here, in the mutability of
language itself, lies the disputed territory in which secular poetry has
always been open to attack. For whether or not a poet claims to be
affirming a truth or merely "making a fiction," his art gives him access

to power over other men's minds and the power of the imagination to perceive a plurality of worlds.

The other world is the domain of the gods, and in the early Middle Ages in Christian Europe the poetry that celebrated the one true God and his cosmology survived and flourished in spite of iconoclastic attacks on the other arts and intermittent attempts to control image making. The suppression of art and the control of fiction are still constant elements in the shift from medieval to Reformation Europe, from Chaucer's England to Sidney and Spenser's, and the interpretation of the evidence remains very much in dispute in modern readings of allegorical imagery and symbols which suggest ambiguity, irony, and paradox in both sacred and secular contexts.

Just as devils, apes, rabbits, and peasants at play are found in the foliage in the margins of many manuscripts, so also at the bottom of a Gothic pillar holding up a vault one may find a ring of small, sculptured animals in hot pursuit of one another—commonplace, but fantastic and incongruously amusing shapes made *in playe* by the masons who carved at the top of the column the faces of Matthew, Mark, Luke, and John, with the Lion, the Eagle, the Ox, and the Book, their sacred metaphors. There is a further dimension in poetry: because it is not concrete, at the level of precision in which painting and sculpture are "fixed," its images are, like its linguistic texture, mutable, ambiguous, and capable of misinterpretation, even of opaque obscurity.

As in the stanza of allusion to authority (Chaucer and Alan) where we began, Spenser tries carefully to direct his reader as to how to "read" his images and suggests some of their sources. The narrator is always willing to differentiate between false and true, good and evil, in Faerie Land, and he volunteers interpretations of the action at every turn. Yet, as the history of reinterpretations of the *Faerie Queene* all too well reveals, he could not prevent confusion, contradiction, and "misreading," even by contemporaries. It is a commonplace in poetics, which was old long before Horace, that images conceived and transmitted in the medium of language, and translated from one language to another, can never be fixed, made stable and permanent, in the irreversible flow of time, nor guaranteed of their original significance. This is an undertheme of the *Mutability Cantos*. The Horatian echoes are strong:

As the forest changes its leaves at the decline of the year, so, among words, the oldest die; and like all things young, the new ones grow and flourish. We and all that belongs to us are destined for death. . . . All mortal things shall perish; still less shall the currency and charm of words always endure.[12]

Horace is speaking in this passage about archaism, coinage, and borrowing in the language of poetry, but he ironically admits that poets will go on writing in the teeth of the evidence of futility; a poem has no better chance to last than a harbor built to channel the sea, or a river rechanneled to save the land. The very images of the *Ars Poetica* anticipate the woodcut emblems of Spenser's minor poems, the *Ruines of Time* and the *Teares of the Muses*, which reiterate and rather feebly defy the Horatian theme.

On the other hand, it is of course not always true that the greater the poem the wider its range of potential interpretations; the greater the poem, the more likely it will outlast fashions in criticism and cycles in taste, as the Homeric epics and Virgil survived medieval allegorization, and Dante's *Comedy* its period of neglect. Spenser could neither foresee nor control the reading of his "continued allegory, or dark conceit," nor could he rely on the stability of his medium, the vernacular, highly wrought into new poetic language, beyond the power that the poem itself projects of its own self-referring meaning. That he thought he could and attempted to do so is perhaps one of the definitive differences between Spenser's allegory and Chaucer's allegorical irony. Horace had invented for himself a rhetorical question to which the whole of the *Ars Poetica* serves as a cautionary reply: the Pisos are reported to have said, "Painters and Poets have always had an equal privilege of daring to do anything they wish." The problem for poetics in the Middle Ages and the Renaissance, as in antiquity, is how to set limits on that claim of autonomy, and for poets, how to maintain it intact. Horace began his answer by concession:

> This is true; as poets, we claim this license for ourselves, and grant it to others. But we do not carry it so far as to allow that savage animals should be united with tame, serpents with birds, or lambs with tigers.[13]

But, in the allegory of the *Faerie Queene*, it is taken as a given that Una,

12. Horace, *Ars Poetica*, in *Horace, Satires, Epistles, and Ars Poetica*, ed. H.R. Fairclough (Cambridge, Mass., 1926), ll. 61 ff. I have preferred the English translation in *Criticism: the Major Texts*, ed. Walter J. Bate (New York, 1952), p. 52.
13. Ibid., p. 51.

her lion, and her lamb have their own symbolic unity, which transcends Horatian decorum. Spenser's freedom to invent the monster Error, Red Cross's Dragon, and the Blatant Beast rests on the same premise that Horace concedes to the Pisos: "All poets and painters . . . claim this license, and grant it to others, . . ." but, at the risk of not being taken seriously, or worse, of the charge of immorality. The defense of Spenser's medieval monsters and his dream world of Ariostan romance must also transcend the classical theory of rhetoric and the humanists' elevation of antiquity, without losing the battle for the prestige of poetry fought out in the later Middle Ages. Sidney began, at just this point, to defend the aim and function of "poore Poetry, which from almost the highest estimation of learning is fallen to be the laughing-stocke of children."[14]

Sidney's *Apologie* or *Defence for Poetrie* is, in effect, the Renaissance vindication of allegory, as Spenser too understood it, and an affirmation of art that encompasses not only medieval Chaucer but the modern Italians and their pagan antique ancestors, in myth, legendary epic, and romance. Sidney defends all figurative writing, verse and prose, against not only laughing mockery but the legacy of medieval contempt for counterfeit art—what Abelard called "poetic figments . . . inane fables," epitomized in his citation from the book of Wisdom, "A mouth that lieth destroyeth the soul" (1:1).[15] Sidney lists the charges, without citing their sources in the debates among the Fathers, against poetry: it is "lesser knowledge, . . . the mother of lyes, . . . the Nurse of abuse, . . . and *Plato* banished [poets] out of hys Common-wealth."

I answere paradoxically, but truely, I thinke truely, that of all Writers vnder the sunne, the Poet is the least lier. . . .

Onely the Poet, disdayning to be tied to any . . . subiection, lifted vp with the vigor of his owne inuention, dooth growe in effect another nature, in making things either better then Nature, . . . or quite a new, formes such as neuer were in Nature. . . .

Neither let this be iestingly conceiued, because the works of [Nature] be essentiall, [the poet's] in imitation or fiction; for . . . the skil of the Artificer standeth in that Idea or foreconceite of the work, and not in the work it selfe.[16]

14. Smith, *Sidney*, p. 151.
15. Quoted in Richard McKeon, "Poetry and Philosophy in the Twelfth Century," *Modern Philology* 43 (1946): 217–34.
16. Smith, *Sidney*, pp. 183–84; 184; 156–57.

The strength of Sidney's defense of "imitation or fiction" rests in the
ringing claim that the poet "nothing affirms, and therefore never lieth."
His argument also exhibits the curious Elizabethan ambiguities, pre-
viously noted in Ascham, in the terms for "imitation or fiction": the
words *mimesis* (Aristotle's "imitation") and *poeien* (the Greek "to
make"). Of the latter, Curtius contrasts the classical and Renaissance
senses in the strangely hybrid result:

> To translate *poeisis* as "creation" is to inject into the Greek view
> of things . . . the Hebrao-Christian cosmogony; [to] call a poet
> a creator is [to use] a theological metaphor. The Greek words for
> poetry and poet have a technological, not a metaphysical, still less
> a religious significance. [However], no people has had a stronger
> sense of the divine in poetry than the Greeks. But this divine
> element—precisely because it is divine—is something that exists
> without and above man, which as a Muse, as a god, as a divine
> frenzy, bursts upon him and fills him.[17]

Sidney's noble image of the true poet elevates him above the philosopher in wisdom,

> for hee yeeldeth to the powers of the minde an image of that
> whereof the Philosopher bestoweth but a woordish description:
> which dooth neyther strike, pierce, nor possesse the sight of the
> soul,

and the historian in knowledge,

> for whatsouer . . . the Historian is bound to recite, that may the
> Poet (if he list), with his imitation make his own; beautifying it
> both with further teaching, and more delighting, as it pleaseth
> him: hauing all, from *Dante* his heauen to hys hell, under the
> authoritie of his penne,

because of the scope of the art:

> The Greekes called him a Poet, which name hath, as the most
> excellent, gone thorough other languages. It commeth of this word
> *Poeien*, which is to make: wherein I know not whether by lucke
> or wisdom, wee Englishmen haue mette with the Greekes in

---

17. *European Literature*, p. 146. The transformation of the terms *maker* and *poet* in Chaucer
and Spenser is discussed below in ch. 9, passim.

calling him a maker: which name, how high and incomparable a title it is . . .

Poesie . . . is an arte of imitation, for so *Aristotle* termeth it in his word *Mimesis*, that is to say, a representing, counterfetting, or figuring foorth: to speake metaphorically, a speaking picture: with this end, to teach and delight.

By means of his double etymologies, Sidney engrafts the Christian positive meanings of "spirit," "genius," and *daimon* onto their pagan and classical root senses, producing the eloquent refutation of all from Abelard and Hugh of St. Victor to Ascham and the Protestant zealots who would call the poet a liar and seek to censor epic and romance. "Heroes, Demigods, Cyclopes, Chimaeras and Furies" are defended in the name of "holy Davids Psalms," Moses, Deborah, Job, and the Song of Solomon; virtually the same parade of witnesses, in fact, brought forward by Boccaccio in the same cause more than two hundred years earlier, as we will see further in chapter 6. Sidney includes all fiction making, sacred and secular, poetry and prose, in a single all-encompassing analogy; the human imagination corresponds to the mind of its creator:

> Neyther let it be deemed to sawcie a comparison to ballance the highest poynt of mans wit with the efficacie of Nature: but rather giue right honor to the heauenly Maker of that maker, who, hauing made man to his owne likenes, set him beyond and ouer all the workes of that second nature, which in nothing hee sheweth so much as in Poetrie, when with the force of a diuine breath he bringeth things forth far surpassing her.

Thus Sidney begs the iconoclastic question of the power of the Adversary, which lies smouldering in the ashes of the medieval defense of rhetoric and philosophy against the poets, and which still flared up in the bitter sixteenth-century Protestant suspicion of, and attempts to control and repress, secular art. There may be bad poets, but poetry, for Sidney, is divine. In it, he who will can hear "the planet-like music" of the cosmos. Sidney ends with an anathema against those who cannot or will not hear it, and his last witty words are something more than a light thrust; he finally invokes perhaps the oldest and strongest defense of all poets, for which there is no refutation:

when you die, [may] your memory die from the earth for want of
an *Epitaph*.[18]

Genius and the Poet: Bernard Silvestris, Alan de Lille, Boethius, and Boccaccio

As I have suggested, the Elizabethan poetic inheritance from the
Middle Ages, as claimed by Sidney and Spenser, is to be found openly
acknowledged, in fine details, as in the texture of an allegorical description in Spenser, and in generalizations as broad as Sidney's defense
of allegory and the imagination. It remains to be seen what transforma-
tions have occurred, intentionally or unawares, in the assimilative
processes of Renaissance "imitation," the deliberate making over of the
old in the context of the new. Sidney's apology for poetry is filled with
echoes of Boccaccio's, for both the grounds of the attackers and the
evidence for their repudiation—Augustine and Jerome, Plato, Dante,
and Petrarch—were brought forth in the earlier phases of the series of
so-called "renaissances" in France and Italy from the 1150's to the
fourteenth century. From Sidney and Spenser, let us turn back to the
"sources," to the medieval defense of poetry and its allegory, beginning
at a point in the mid-twelfth century when medieval Platonism began
to supply new themes for poets and to stir up new debates. The heart of
the issue, in philosophy, theology, and poetics, was the claim to superiority of "invisible wisdom." As Richard McKeon summarizes it:

> The Platonic tradition . . . set the Fathers the puzzling task of
> explaining how skepticism and idealism . . . logic-chopping and
> mysticism, had all been derived from the teachings of Plato.[19]

Socrates' *daimon* had already undergone several metamorphoses in
pagan literary tradition before reemerging as the dubious medieval
Genius *Pantomorphos* in Bernard Silvestris's huge Latin *prosimetrum* allegory on the creation of the world, the *Cosmographia* or *De mundi universitate*, a work which McKeon says "treats Christian themes in almost
wholly pagan terms."[20] Helen Waddell compares the "great imagina-

18. Smith, *Sidney*, pp. 164; 169; 155, 158; 157; 207.
19. McKeon, "Poetry and Philosophy," p. 219.
20. Brian Stock's study of Bernard's *Cosmographia* cited above (note 2), which appeared
after this chapter was written, provides a full analysis of the medieval scientific and
philosophical concepts in Bernard's poetic myth. Stock's interpretation of the *genii* focuses
on the sexual images of divine creativity rather than on the role of the deity ("Pantomorphos

tive prose" of Bernard to Shelley's *Defence of Poetry*, and his poetry is "the dream of the *Faerie Queene*, of *The Tempest*, of *Hyperion*."[21] As Curtius describes him, Bernard's Genius is "a scribe, a tutelary spirit, and a vegetation god."[22] I shall enter no further into the dispute that has recently been renewed over Bernard's theological orthodoxy, whether or not he is a pagan humanist nurtured on pseudo-Platonic texts ("Apuleius" and *Aesclepius*) or simply a radical Christian Platonist. Curtius says his work is "bathed in the atmosphere of the fertility cult, in which religion and sexuality mingle."[23] This exotic description may indicate Curtius's bias, but it goes far to account for the fame of Bernard and the long life of the strange figure of the old man, writing, which he took from Isidore of Seville's *Etymologiae* and from Horace, Censorinus, and Hermes. Bernard's cosmic allegory, written around 1150, was immensely popular and widely known; twenty-five manuscripts still survive. It is one immediate source of Alan de Lille's *De Planctu Naturae*, and its imagery fully develops the triple symbolic associations between the creative rod of authority, the pen, and the phallus, which Genius implies in virtually all subsequent versions of the type. Bernard's Genius is the god of universal generation whom the goddess Natura, seeking the means to "crown her creation with man,"

or Omniformis") as artist; see *Myth and Science*, ch. 4, especially pp. 167–78. J.A.W. Bennett, citing Bolgar, calls it "that fascinating amalgam of 'the Chartrian tradition, Christian piety, and natural science,' neo-Platonic cosmology and Aristotelian dialectic" (*Parlement of Foules*, pp. 196–97).

21. In *The Wandering Scholars* (London, 1927; repr. New York, 1961), pp. 124, 128.

22. Curtius, *European Literature*, pp. 112–18.

23. The allegorical significance of Genius in Spenser and his "sources" is discussed by C. S. Lewis in *The Allegory of Love* (London, 1936), appendix 1, pp. 361–63; R. H. Green, "Allan of Lille's *De Planctu Naturae*," *Speculum* 31(1956): 674–94; and George Economou, "The Character Genius in Alan De Lille, Jean de Meung, and John Gower," *Chaucer Review* 4 (1971): 203–10. Two articles by E. C. Knowlton provide broader surveys of the tradition: "The Allegorical Figure Genius," *Classical Philology* 15 (1920): 380 ff., and "Genius as an Allegorical Figure," *Modern Language Notes* 39 (1924): 89 ff. A full bibliography of modern studies of both Bernard Silvestris and Alan de Lille is provided in the notes of the brilliant essay of Winthrop Wetherbee, "The Function of Poetry in the *de Planctu Naturae*," *Traditio* 25 (1969): 87–125, which strongly influenced my ideas in this chapter; his *Platonism and Poetry in the Twelfth Century* (Princeton, 1972) appeared after this chapter was written.

The *De Planctu* was translated as *The Complaint of Nature* by Douglas M. Moffatt, Yale Studies in English 36 (New York. 1908); translations which appear here are from Moffatt. The Latin text is in T. Wright, *Anglo-Latin Satirical Poets of the Twelfth Century* (London, 1872), 2: 430–522, where the *Anticlaudianus* is also to be found, pp. 268–91. Bernard's *De Mundi Universitate* was edited by C. S. Barach and J. Wrobel (Innsbruck, 1876); it remains untranslated. See also T. Silverstein, "The Fabulous Cosmogony of Bernardus Silvestris," *Modern Philology* 46 (1948): 104–16.

encounters at the outermost edge of the created cosmos. He is writing, and perpetuating the natural species, by energizing the impulse to fulfillment in each kind by procreation in the physical world. Genius's energy puts in order and assigns forms to the mindless flux of animality; with his drawing (*pictoris et figurantis addictus*) he regulates and perpetuates the species in nature by "serial law" in order to realize the symmetrical, harmonious cosmic order of all forms. The creative power of sexual procreation relates natural order to divine order; Genius, with his pen, presides over the union of form and matter and gives impetus to sexual union, by design.

It has recently been argued that in his successor Alan's *Complaint*, Bernard's Platonic myth of creativity becomes ambiguous and is undermined by irony. Given Alan's wearisome rhetorical style, his long descriptions, and the strained rigidity of the speeches of his characters (chiefly, the Dreamer, Natura, and Genius), it is very difficult to determine the extent to which ironies may be intended; the cues to the reader left by Jean de Meung in his part of the *Roman de la Rose*, where we next encounter Genius, are less problematic to find and to read. In Alan's *Complaint*, the dreaming poet sees the figure of Genius in the final episode of the poem. There, summoned by Natura, her alter ego and priest Genius appears and pronounces excommunication (his anathema) on all servants of *Venus scelestris* (the lascivious Venus); the attending Virtues throw down their torches, which slowly die, and the poet passes from vision into sleep. In the plot of the dream, Natura has described the outrages (e.g. sodomy) committed against her by men, and Genius has lamented the betrayal of all his works by Falsitas. It is clear enough that the theme is the aftermath of the Fall; human nature has become perverted sexually and alienated in irrationality. As the Dreamer hears her complaint, the images for the prolific generosity of Natura (personified as Largitas) turn to extremes of monstrous growth, or shrink to distorted minutiae. The end of the poem is bitter: licentious Venus, Cupid (now perverted), and their allies the Vices, are so powerful and so contaminating that there is no escape from them except through abstinence; the sentence of Genius's anathema is celibacy, both physical and imaginative. The dream ends with a futile answer to its repeated question, why is nature perverse?[24]

Alan's themes, Genius's and Natura's original ideal powers, and the

24. *De Planctu*, prosa 9. 178–202, 214–42; metrum 1. 10–15, et passim; metrum 4; prosa 4. 2–12.

ultimate ambiguity of all fallen human creative powers, sexual and imaginative, are presented in the *De Planctu* by symbolic images described at great length and with turgid, complex suggestiveness. The allegory is as heavy as it is ornate, and it is often far from clear what Alan's chromatic distinctions mean. According to R. H. Green's interpretation of the allegory,

> Genius is Nature's alter ego who exercises her office among men; he is human nature, an aspect of universal nature represented by Nature herself. He has been driven from human society by the unnatural passion of men in their choice of *antigenius*; he shares the suffering of Nature because he is in fact the part of nature which has been perverted.

Green's difficulty in explaining what he means continues:

> In a sense he too is the *Venus caelestis* in human nature which has been rejected. . . . The place of Genius in the context of Alan's fable . . . demands that he, like the chaste Venus, represent much more than mere physical generation.[25]

The known sources of both Bernard's and Alan's Genius, as C. S. Lewis noted in his brief excursus on Spenser's Genius in the *Allegory of Love*, are the *Cebetis Tabula* and Claudian's *De Consultatu Stilichorius II*.[26] In the first-century A.D. *Table of Cebes*, there is a tablet in the temple of Chronos which is explained by an old man, who has a paper in one hand. Before human souls enter the Gate of Life, they are given warning by the old man's reading of the tablet, concerning the destiny that waits for them in the world. The crowd shrinks away from him in fear of his words. In Claudian's *Second Panegyric*, the *senex* appears again, writing out the laws of life and death in the universe, but he is not there named Genius. In Bernard, he is a scribe or "maker," assigning forms to the creatures:

> Persona deus venerabili et decrepite sub imagine senectutis occurrit. Illic Oyarses idem erat et genius in artem et officium pictoris et figurantis addictus. In subteriacente enim mundo rerum facies universa caelum sequitur sumptisque de caelo pro-

---

25. Green, "Alan of Lille's *De Planctu*," pp. 672; 671 and n. 50. Green does not say what Genius's "much more" significance may be.

26. Stock, in *Myth and Science*, p. 170, n. 4, cites Censorinus's *De Die Natale*, ch. 3, Apuleius's *De Platone* and *De Deo Socratis*, as well as Hermes' *Asclepius*, 19.

prietatibus ad imaginem quam conversio contulit figuratur [In the
form of a venerable old man the god appears. Here was a celestial spirit, a genius dedicated in the art and office of artist and
maker of figures. For in the lower world, the universal appearance
of things follows the heaven, and is shaped with borrowed pro-
perties from heaven, according to the image which his conversion
confers].[27]

But in Alan's *Complaint,* whatever Genius does in his allegorical role
as a creative spirit is arbitrarily either perverted or enhanced by his
two attendants, the antinomian daughter figures Veritas (who assists)
and Falsitas (who thwarts), undermining each other in endless conflict.[28] Genius is an old man with a delicate young face; his garments
flame in changing colors in which a constant montage of images momentarily appears, then suddenly dissolves. In his right hand he
carries a papyrus reed, and in his left a parchment; as in Bernard,
Genius is constantly writing, decorating the parchment with personified
images of human activities. It is a familiar catalogue: Helen as quasi-
divine beauty, the "lightning-flash of boldness" in Turnus, Ulysses'
foxlike strength, Plato, Capaneus, Cicero, Aristotle, symbolic *figurae*
which epitomize power, cunning, eloquence, and subtlety as Genius
inscribes them on the parchment with his right hand. But when his arm
grows tired, he allows his left hand to take over "the task of inscription." Then appear, "in limping imagery," the "shadowy ghosts" of
Thersites, Sinon, Ennius, Paris: treachery, baseness, voluptuousness,
incoherence. When Genius is about to speak, the dreaming poet sees
him remove his common robes, which, as Winthrop Wetherbee reads the
allegory, "testify to his involvement with mortality."[29] Restored by
Natura's kiss, Genius becomes enlarged, elevated to the figure of archetypal priest of Natura and guardian of fertility. In his role as artist and
poet, Genius explains, he has become lost *in infernum tristiae,* an "exile
in the inferno of sorrow," because he is helpless to control the interpretation or "fix" the images of what he makes. Veritas and Falsitas variously distort or enhance his work, which at best was only partly under
his power to control because of his ambidexterity, his two-handedness.
Genius's pen inscribes the parchment, but even the first reading of his

27. *De Mundi Universitate,* 2, prosa 3. 90–95, translation mine.
28. *De Planctu,* prosa 9. 138–66.
29. *Wetherbee,* "The Function of Poetry," p. 116.

images is randomized or made ambiguous. If Alan's allegory of art is rhetorically labored, it is also tendentiously Neoplatonic: what once, ideally, was pure form and true *figura*, is perceived when the Eternal Mind greeted matter

> formarum speculum meditantem aeternalis salutavit idea, eandem iconiae interpretis interventu vicario osculata [as it was considering the reflection of forms, kissed it by the intervention and agency of an image].[30]

It has become debased, corrupted by human desire, abuse, excess. Thus the complaint of Genius echoes that of Natura, for he too has been overwhelmed by human vice; like Natura and Largitas (natural fecundity and plenitude) Genius is betrayed by the *falsitas* which deforms all images, turning Venus to lasciviousness, Cupid to cruel Jocus, Natura to perversion, and her generosity to prodigality or avarice under the pressure of human desire, the irrational will.

In this reading of the dream, there is no way to distinguish between true and false in poetic fiction, for the archetypal figure of the poet, Genius the maker, Natura's priest, is exhausted and alien; in Alan's allegory, there is falseness in the very source of poetry. Natura, betrayed, cannot enforce the orderly carrying out of her laws, nor make the created natural world conform to its divine prototype. In her distraught complaint she is the converse of Chaucer's Kind and Spenser's Nature. Her mythic agents and powers, the benign Venus, Hymen, and Cupid, whom she entrusted with the regulation of human fertility, have become themselves debauched. Now *Venus scelestris*, an adulteress *cum antigamo* (*antigenio* in two MSS), perverts sexual procreation, and her children, Cupid and his counterpart Jocus, have become agents of the irrational. Both debase language. Cupid's half-brother Mirth (Jocus) was begotten on Venus by Antigamus in 'illegitimate fornication," the joy of sloth and pleasure, unrestrained licentiousness, expressed in terms of art:

> dialecticis conversionibus se invertens, rhetoricis coloribus de-coloratis, suam artem in figuram, figuramque in vitium trans-ferebat [destroying herself in grammatical constructions, perverting herself in dialectical conversions, she changes her art into

30. *De Planctu*, prosa 9. 143–46.

artifice, by gaudy colors of rhetoric, and her artifice into vicious-
ness].[31]

When she is asked to explain what has become of love (Hymen,
Venus, and Cupid), Natura's "Song of Cupid" expresses the corruption
of the meanings of words by rhetorical *antiphrasis*, the paradoxical
explanation of the inexplicable, "to conceive of a subject unknown":

> inexplicabilis naturae haec exeat explicatio, . . .
> de ignoto notitia:
> Pax odio, fraudique fides, spes juncta timori . . .
> Est amor, et mixtus cum ratione furor . . .
>
> > Dum furit iste furor, deponit Scilla furorem
> > Et pius Aneas incipit esse Nero
> > Fulminat ense Paris, Tydeus mollescit amore,
> > Fit Nestor juvenis, fit Melicerta senex,
> > Thersites Paridem forma mendicat, Adonim
> > Davus, et in Davum totus Adonis abit.

> [Love is peace, joined with hate, faith with fraud, Hope with fear,
> fury with reason. . . . While (Cupid's miraculous) fury rages,
> Scylla puts aside her madness, good Aeneas begins to become Nero,
> Paris flashes his sword, Tydeus is gentle in love, Nestor becomes
> young and Melicerta old, Thersites begs Paris for his beauty,
> Davus begs Adonis, and into Davus goes all of Adonis.][32]

The extreme pessimism of the dream's conclusion seems to foreclose
any possibility for the regeneration of human reason, or, in art, rediscovery of cosmic order. Having delivered his anathema, cursing men,
Genius goes back to exile in "the inferno of sorrow." "An impossibly
complex maze of *phantasia*" separates human consciousness from whatever guidance Genius once ideally exerted as intermediary spirit between man and the divine. Rational process (dialectic) and poetic
inspiration, since the Fall, can only work back through the maze in the
mind to perceive a futile and hopeless dead end: not an infinite, but a
finite regress to the helpless figure of Genius, languishing *in infernum
tristiae*. The only link between human and divine perceived by the
Dreamer is "enfeebled by ceaseless struggle with the inner tumult and

31. Ibid., prosa 5. 215.
32. Ibid., metrum 5. 1–3, 23–28.

perverted impulses of men," suspended between memory of lost Paradise, and awareness of the abyss to come, impotent to restore and "reawaken man to a consciousness of himself."[33] Genius pronounces the order of excommunication out of the secret places in his mind [*sub haec verborum imagine praetaxatam*] and withdraws.[34]

There is no consolation for the Dreamer-poet. On the contrary, for fallen man the allegorical universal powers of Natura's vision (the benign Venus and Genius) offer no hope of regeneration or of human fulfillment reconciled and restored to her cosmic order, for primordial chaos has reasserted itself in self-destructive human desire. First presented equivocally as neither tragic nor in anti-intellectual satire, the dogmatic themes of *De Planctu*—the estrangement of the imagination and the degradation of physical nature—are later brought into a new kind of synthesis and reconciliation in Alan's sequel, the *Anticlaudianus*. In the new allegory, Natura creates a new man, who leads his armies, with Natura at their head, in victorious conquest over the armies of Vices of his forebears. After the psychomachia, Natura and *homo novus* are reunited in the renovated paradise, seen as lost in Genius's memory at the ending of *De Planctu*:

> enim mens mea hominum vitiis angustiata deformibus, in infernum tristitiae peregrinans, laetitiae nesciat paradisum [for my mind, tormented by the misshapen vices of men, wandering in the depths of sorrow, does not know the paradise of joy].[35]

The immense fertility of Bernard's and Alan's multicolored symbolic images and personifications of Natura, Venus, Genius, and Cupid, however stale the allegory and however turgid the Latin rhetorical *flores* that present them, is witnessed by their prolific influence, in imitations and wholesale borrowing, and by their extraordinary longevity in vernacular literary tradition. From the *Roman de la Rose* to the *Parliament of Fowls* to the *Faerie Queene*, they remain alive as learned allusions, and the prolonged echoes of later Spenserians transmit them down to the nineteenth century. Natura, as Curtius and Lewis suggested long ago, is the first of the new postclassical mythologies strong enough to rival Venus.

As for the later medieval development of Genius himself, the symbolic

33. Wetherbee, "The Function of Poetry," pp. 118, 119.
34. *De Planctu*, prosa 9. 211–12.
35. Ibid., prosa 9. 188–91.

analogies between sexual and artistic creative power made explicit in the descriptions of his wand and scroll in the Latin poems become more sophisticated in the *Roman de la Rose,* and thereafter become increasingly debased. Almost inevitably, perhaps, in the derivatives of Jean de Meung's ironic Genius, his role as a poet and the fading images he makes—the defense against Death in the garden—are superseded by the phallic power he wields. In Jean de Meung's ending of the *Roman,* Genius's fragile reed pen becomes the bright candle Venus places in his hand ("certainly not of virgin wax"), and "the imagery of inscription" becomes obscene with satiric double entendres. He anathematizes not sex but celibacy with the image of his pen:

> Shame on the thriftless ones of whom I speak,
> Who never deign to set themselves to work
> To write their names upon the tablets fair
> Or stamp their likenesses, which might endure
> . . . those who with their stylets scorn to write
> Upon the precious tablets delicate
> By means of which all mortals come to life
> Which Nature never lent us for disuse
> But rather that we all should scriveners become.[36]

The degeneration of Genius as Venus's voluptuary priest continues into the sixteenth-century French descendants of the *Roman,* where he is still associated with the powers of sexual initiation and excommunication in Martin Le Franc's *Le Champion des Dames* (1442), Jean Lemaire's *La Concorde des deux langages* (1511), and Ronsard's *Bocage Royale II* (1560). The parallel tradition in Gower's *Confessio Amantis,* and, in French, Marot's *Temple of Cupid* (1515) and Molinet's reallegorization of the *Roman de la Rose cler et net* (1500), reflects the "moral" reading of the *Roman,* a chastely sophisticated interpretation of the psychology of virtuous love.

In the *Roman* itself, the power of Jean de Meung's irony overwhelms his Genius's final sermon, with its antithetical exempla of the garden of Mirth and the Elysian garden of Natura and the Lamb, the Fountains Perilous and the triple well of Paradise. Where Alan's poem ended with an anathema against both sex and poetry, Jean's Genius ends his

36. *The Romance of The Rose,* by Guillaume de Lorris and Jean de Meun, trans. Harry W. Robbins, ed. Charles W. Dunn (New York, 1962), ch. 91, ll. 49–53, 101–06, pp. 414–15 (chapter and line numbers refer to the translator's numbering).

sermon in mockery, "What's this I pipe to you? High time it is I put my pipe away,"[37] and the throwing down of his torch ignites the audience. The flame sets fire to all the world, and Venus eagerly spreads it among women, rejoicing as Genius vanishes. The conquest of the Rose immediately ensues, in all its erotic explicitness.

The sacred image of God as author, of which the profane Genius has become a parody in secular poetry, was brilliantly summarized in Richard de Bury's exegesis in defense of literature:

> Our Savior exercised the office of a writer, when, stooping down, He wrote with his finger on the ground (John, viii). . . . O singular serenity of writing, in the delineation of which the artificer of the world, at whose tremendous name every knee is bent, bowed down [when] the finger of God was applied to perform the office of a pen! We do not read that the Son of God sowed or ploughed, or wove or dug, or that any other of the . . . arts were becoming to the divine wisdom, humanized, excepting to trace letters by writing. . . . God himself inscribes the just in the book of the living. Moses indeed received stone tablets written upon by the finger of God. Job exclaims, "Let him who gives judgment write a book!" The trembling Belshazzar saw fingers writing on the wall, Mene Mene Tekel Upharsin. . . . The King of kings, and Lord of lords, Christ himself had writing upon His garment and upon His thigh; as without writing, the perfect regal ornament of the Omnipotent cannot be apparent.[38]

For the twelfth-century Chartres Platonists as for their humanist descendants for the next four hundred years, from Boccaccio to Sidney, poetry is the language in which man communicates with the divine. The limits of poetic expressiveness measure man's power to perceive the divine in himself and in the order in nature, and his desire to achieve harmony with it. But in Alan's *Complaint*, lascivious *Venus scelestris* and Genius's "emanation," Falsitas, have corrupted Nature's arts, both sexual and creative, which can no longer communicate the cosmic order her creation once revealed. Natura blames language itself— "false orthography, bizarre rhetoric, corrupt grammar, prostitute logic" —in her long denunciation of the psychological, intellectual, and sensual perversions of fallen man. In order for the poet to understand her

37. Ibid., ch. 94, ll, 290–91, p. 437.
38. *Philobiblon*, ch. 16, pp. 68–69.

at all, his own "fantasy" must be emptied out of the Dreamer's sick mind ("I vomited my illusion"), before he can be brought to recognize and understand Natura's vision.[39] It is in the Dreamer's role as a poet that Natura has sought him out, to become her *secretarius*. It is at this point in the allegory that the *Plaint of Kind* becomes most problematic, and Alan's Natura no longer corresponds with Chaucer's Kind and Spenser's Nature. The dreamer's question—how can he learn to tell true from false in poetry [*figmentum poetarum*]?—causes Natura's mood to change:

> Tunc illa, authenticae serenitatis vultum vultus tumultuose figurans. [Her first calm look then became much disquieted.][40]

She is outraged that the question of secular poetic truth is even raised. The myths of the loves of the gods disgust her.

If, for the Chartres Platonists, the defense of poetry is that the image of the natural world in a poem reflects the image in the mind of God, it would seem that Alan de Lille is ironically undermining that apparently secure position by raising the question of poetic ambiguity. In *De Planctu*, postlapsarian man is corrupt in both mind and body; worse, in the sickening image of the Dreamer it is the imagination itself that deforms the body and yields to lust. In their capacity to perceive and transmit images of desire, or even of nature itself in the fallen world, poets are suspect. Grasping for Natura's allegorically embroidered gown, they have torn it at the very point where man himself is figured. This is the part of Alan's allegory that Chaucer omits, and where Spenser substitutes an extraordinary stanza of his own, in which Natura's gown is compared to the perfect disguise worn by Christ (Luke 9:28f.) when he appeared transfigured to the three apostles on Mount Tabor:

> For well I weene
> That on this same day, when she on Arlo sat,
> Her garment was so bright and wondrous sheene,
> That my frail wit cannot devize to what
> It to compare, nor finde like stuffe to that:

39. *De Planctu*, prosa 3. 270–76: "When Nature unveiled to me through these words, the face of her being, [and] . . . as by a key, unlocked ahead for me the door to her acquaintance, the little cloud of stupor which had lain close on my mind, lifted. And, as by some medicinal potion, the sick stomach of my mind cast out all the remnants of its illusion."
40. Ibid., prosa 4. 192.

> As those three sacred saints, though else most wise,
> Yet on Mount Thabor quite their wits forgat,
> When they their glorious Lord in strange disguise
> Transfigur'd sawe; his garments so did daze their eyes.
>
> [*FQ* VII, vii, 7]

Natura's gown is, as I have said, a significant variable in the evolution of her allegory; the tear in it is conspicuous in most medieval versions, except for Chaucer's. The meaning of that tear provides a paradigm in allegorical ambiguity, as Boccaccio makes quite clear. In his great defense of secular allegory and pagan myth in the *Genealogy of the Gods*, Boccaccio borrowed the figure of Alan's Natura (by then widely familiar in the *Roman de la Rose*) and conflated it with the older one of Boethius's Philosophia to make a new goddess, both creative and wise. Boccaccio's Lady Philosophy, "like the Empress of all the World," presides over a celestial House of Wisdom.[41] She sits, not on a hill of flowers, but on a lofty throne, arrayed in royal robes, crowned with a gold crown, holding in her right hand a sceptre, and in her left several books. Her other prototype, Boethius's Philosophia, had the flashing eyes of youth, yet (like Genius)

> she seemed so old she could not be thought of as belonging to our age. . . . Her height seemed to vary: sometimes she seemed of ordinary human stature, then again her head seemed to touch the heavens.

In Boethius, her delicately woven gown, unlike Natura's, is darkened by time and neglect; it too, is torn and is embroidered with the Greek letters θ and π (for Theory and Practice, which evolve into two goddesses attendant on Natura in Bernard) and a design of ladderlike stairs

> ascending from the lowest level to the highest. This robe had been torn, by the hands of violent men, who had ripped away what they could. In her right hand, the woman held certain books; in her left hand, a scepter.[42]

41. *De Genealogia Deorum*, in *Boccaccio on Poetry*, ed. and trans. Charles G. Osgood (Princeton, N.J., 1930), 15.5, p. 33 (hereafter cited as Osgood, *Genealogy*).

42. Boethius, *The Consolation of Philosophy*, ed. H. F. Stewart and E. K. Rand (Cambridge, Mass., 1918), prosa 1; English trans. Richard Green, *The Consolation of Philosophy* (New York, 1962), p. 3–4. (Hereafter, references cited as *Consolation* are to Green; Latin quotations are from the Loeb text.)

Both Boethius's and Boccaccio's sacred mistresses of all knowledge, associated by elaborate background imagery with the seven liberal arts, philosophers, and poets, are collateral descendants of the biblical allegory of Wisdom, personified abstractly but not described in Job 28, Proverbs 9, and Ecclesiastes 7–10.[43] From this figure develop a whole series of goddesses: Prudentius's Wisdom (*Psychomachia* 823–915), Philosophia in Macrobius's *Somnium Scipionis*, Calliope in Fulgentius, Natura in Alan. In Boethius and in Boccaccio, as in Alan, the allegorical gown —Natura's elaborately pictorial dress, Philosophy's flowing goddesslike splendor of robes—is torn by men who fall upon her in violent haste to tear away a few shreds, and, as Boccaccio describes it,

> then they rush forth from the sacred house, and set themselves up
> as scholars and prophets, lords of all wisdom, blowing up a huge
> cloud of reputation.

Finally, according to Boccaccio, these tearers of Wisdom-Natura's gown rise up like a conspiracy to denounce poetry—in schools, in public squares, in pulpits:

> They say poets are liars—propping themselves up with Plato's
> authority . . . that poets ought to be turned out of town, and that
> the Muses, their mumming mistresses, as Boethius says, being sweet
> with deadly sweetness, are detestable . . . and should be driven
> out with them and utterly rejected.[44]

Boccaccio begins his defense of poetry with the symbolic tearing of the gown, which Spenser replaced with the perfect one of Christ's transfiguration, and which Chaucer avoided by referring enigmatically to Alan. In the dramatic scene in Boccaccio's defense, his Philosophy's complaint is the antithesis of Natura's: those who now attack the poets are the ones who have torn her gown. In Alan, Natura bewailed the poets themselves, who degrade the image of human love, and debauch the imagination. In the *Parliament of Fowls*, the serene Chaucerian goddess who presides over the nuptials in the garden is subject to no such outrage, and her judgment is celebrated by a song: this is the

43. "Wisdom hath builded her house, she hath hewn out her seven pillars; she hath killed her beasts; she hath mingled her wine; she hath also finished her table. She hath sent forth her maidens; she crieth upon the highest places of the city, Whoso is simple, let him turn in hither." (Proverbs 9:1–4).

44. Osgood, *Genealogy*, 14.5, p. 36.

natura triumphans of Alan's sequel, not the ruined Natura of the *Plaint of Kind.*

Chaucer's *Book of Fame* and the Allegory of Poets

Chaucer's dream visions are at once synthetic "imitations" and independent experiments in allegory, in which heterogeneous visionary themes are brought together in the mind of the Dreamer. The purpose of elegy in the *Book of the Duchess* and the Valentine occasion of the *Parliament of Fowls* provide for each a kind of centripetal coherence which is not easy to find in the *Book of Fame.* In its first two books, Venus's temple, the grief of Dido, and the highly comic exploration of the upper atmosphere seem rather to be developing centrifugal energies in the dream; nowhere in it, as Bennett says, "should we be content with a literal reading." He also interprets the poem, very persuasively, as "the discovery of new poetic *matiere.* In one sense, the whole work is a vindication of poetry."[45] In a very elliptical sense, it may be. But the *Book of Fame* is also the most enigmatically allegorical of all Chaucer's allegories; the Dreamer is continually duped, and the goddess whom he sees at last is a parody of the images of authority that poets seek. In Book III, in the concluding episode, what seems to be getting out of control is not poetry but scepticism:

> Loo! how shulde I now telle al thys?
> Ne of the halle eke what nede is
> To tellen yow that every wal
> Of hit, and flor, and roof, and al
> Was plated half a foote thikke
> Of gold. . . .
> But al on hye, above a dees,
> Sitte in a see imperiall,
> That mad was of a rubee all,
> Which that a carbuncle ys ycalled,
> Y saugh, perpetually ystalled,
> A femynyne creature,
> That never formed by Nature
> Nas such another thyng yseye.
> [*HF* 1341–46; 1360–67]

45. J.A.W. Bennett, *Chaucer's Book of Fame* (Oxford, 1968), p. xi.

The Muses abolished by Boethius's Philosophia, recalled and defended by Boccaccio's, are restored again to ambiguous positions of
honor around the throne of Chaucer's weird montage of goddesses—
Fortuna's sister, Virgil's Rumor, Boethius's Wisdom:

> For alther-first, soth for to seye,
> Me thoughte that she was so lyte
> That the lengthe of a cubite
> Was lengere than she semed be.
> But thus sone, in a whyle, she
> Hir tho so wonderliche streighte
> That with hir fet she erthe reighte,
> And with hir hed she touched hevene
> Ther as shynen sterres sevene . . .
> But, Lord! the perry and the richesse
> I saugh sittyng on this godesse!
> And, Lord! the hevenyssh melodye
> Of songes, ful of armonye,
> I herde aboute her trone ysonge,
> That al the paleys-walles ronge!
> So song the myghty Muse, she
> That cleped ys Caliope,
> And hir eighte sustren eke,
> That in her face semen meke;
> And ever mo, eternally,
> They songe of Fame, as thoo herd y:
> "Heryed be thou and thy name,
> Goddesse of Renoun, or of Fame!"
>
> [HF 1368–76; 1393–1406]

Instead of pictorial animals on a figured gown, the description of Fame
scans the mythological animal imagery of her attributes: on her feet,
partridge wings; she has upstanding ears, many tongues, and as many
eyes as feathers on a fowl:

> Or weren on the bestes foure
> That Goddis trone gunne honoure,
> As John writ in th'Apocalips.
>
> [HF 1383–85]

In John's vision (Revelation 4, 5), the throne he sees is not *a rubee all, /
Which that a carbuncle ys ycalled*, but like an emerald surrounded by a

rainbow, out of which proceed lightnings, thunderings, and voices, and in front of it, the seven lamps of burning fire are the seven spirits of God:

> And before the throne there was a sea of glass like unto crystal, and in the midst of the throne, and round about the throne, were four beasts full of eyes before and behind. . . . And the four beasts had each of them six wings about him; and they were full of eyes within: and they rest not day and night, saying Holy holy, holy, Lord God Almighty, which was, and is, and is to come.
>
> [Rev. 4 : 6, 8]

The voices of the spirits prepare John for the vision of the Book in the right hand of "him that sat on the throne,"

> written within and on the backside, sealed with seven seals. And I saw a strong angel proclaiming with a loud voice, Who is worthy to open the book and to loose the seals thereof? And no man in heaven, neither in earth nor under the earth, was able to open the book.
>
> [Rev. 5 : 1–3]

But in the throne room of Fame there are no mysteries withheld from the Dreamer; there is no Sacred Book. He sees all there is to be seen: the seven worthies, first, helping Josephus hold the fame of the Jews on his shoulders, and as the music rises the enumeration of the poets, Fame's historians, finally ends with the Claudian of Alan's *Anti-claudianus*. He stands on his pillar of sulphur, looking as if he were mad, bearing up the fame of hell; he is there as creator of Pluto and Prosperpine, *that quene ys of the derke pyne*. The break at this point in the narrative of poets is sudden, and the simile it turns on is as ambiguous as the allusion which links the sacred symbols of John's Apocalypse to the chanting Muses and their profane parody of a hymn to Fame. The tone changes abruptly:

> What shulde y more telle of this?
> The halle was al ful, ywys,
> Of hem that writen olde gestes,
> As ben on treës rokes nestes;
> But hit a ful confus matere
> Were alle the gestes for to here,
> That they of write, or how they highte.
>
> [*HF* 1513–19]

The Dreamer's summary dismissal of *ars poetica*—Homer and Virgil, Statius and Ovid, Lucan, Guido, Dares, and "Lollius"—in a crowded chattering rookery of confused "olde gestes" is as sardonic as Natura's contempt for the poets in *De Planctu*. That break came when Alan's Dreamer asked about truth in poetic mythology, and Natura angrily replied

> What! in your questioning, do you dignify, as a doubt, a question unworthy even of the form of a doubt? Do you attempt to give faith to the dreams of poets, which the art of poetry has portrayed? . . . Do you not know how poets expose naked lies to their audiences with no protective covering, so they can intoxicate their ears, and bewitch them with the honey sweetness of sound?[46]

Natura continues, contrasting the sacred poetics of divine reason with the wanton darkness of lustful imagination: the sounds of the lyre are false. It is at this point that the Dreamer asks why Natura's gown is torn and learns of the *raptus Naturae*, the assault by fallen man.

The irascible humility of Chaucer's Dreamer and his denial of any knowledge of his own, except what he can remember or borrow from his old books, should be read against the double face of the book itself—not sealed with seven seals, but a *ful confus matere*, an ambiguous witness of the secular world distorted beyond recognition as a mirror of its prototype. Only the sacred book, *biblia*, which records the creation of the sacred world, the world that is lost until Apocalypse, only that Word can be trusted and loved. Following Augustine, who used the image of the Egyptian woman, tamed and shorn, whom Moses made worthy to serve in his house, Richard de Bury defended the reading of secular poets without using exegesis to baptize them. The worst vice is ignorance, as it was for Socrates. So, since even sacred poetry alludes to fictions, de Bury says, "One can read any poet, and make study grateful to God, the circumstances of virtue being observed." Quoting the Venerable Bede, de Bury continues:

> Some read secular literature for pleasure, being delighted by the fictions of poets and the ornaments of their words; but others study

46. "An interrogatio em quae nec dubitationis faciem digna est usurpare, quaestiones quarerendo vestis imagine, an umbratilibus poetarum figmentis, quae artis poeticae depinxit industria, fidem adhibere conaris? . . . An ignoras quomodo poetae, sine omni pallationis remedio, auditoribus nudam falsitatem prostituunt, ut quaedam mellitae delectationis dulcedine velut incantatas audientium aures inebrient?" (*De Planctu*, prosa 4. 194 ff).

them for erudition, that by reading the errors of the Gentiles, they
may detest them, and that they may devoutly carry off what they
find in them useful for the service of sacred erudition; such as
these, study secular literature laudably.[47]

After the denunciation of poetic fiction during the earlier Middle Ages
("A mouth that lieth destroyeth the soul. . . ."), de Bury's doctrine is
the mildest of compromises. But it gives small comfort to poets, provides
no defense for "makers," and leaves the creative imagination still
vulnerable, its pleasure rebuked. In support of his premise that "the
love of books is . . . the love of wisdom, which has been proved to be
ineffable," he expounds the Greek word *philosophia*, with a quotation
from Plato's *Phaedo*, to affirm that such love transcends the flesh:

This love is also called by a Greek word Philosophy, whose virtue
no created intelligence comprehends, wherefore it is believed to be
the mother of everything that is good (Wisd. vii); for like a heavenly dew it extinguishes the heat of carnal vices, . . . by entirely
expelling idleness, which being removed, every particle of concupiscence will perish. Hence Plato says, in Phaedo, "The philosopher is manifest in this—that he separates the soul more widely
from communion with the body than other men."[48]

What de Bury, Abelard, and Hugh of St. Victor share is the conviction that only Scripture is the Word; secular poetry, both ancient
and modern, is dangerously ambiguous. The vernacular is tainted and
poets suspect, capable of distorting the power of language and deluding
men. Secular love poetry, seductive visions, and erotic dreams are
doubly corruptive because since the Fall all human creativity, sexual
and artistic, as Allan's Natura explains, is corrupted by Adam's choice.
Genius, carrying pen and scroll as priest, poet, and lover of Natura,
is himself ambidextrous, but not impotent. He foresees, in despair, but
he cannot control the use to which his images are put. The ironic
Genius of Jean de Meung's *Roman* turns his creative reed into an ob-

---

47. *Philobiblon*, ch. 15, pp. 60–61; Bede, *Distinctione* 37. De Bury may also have been thinking of Bede's commentary on Pope Boniface IV's ceremonial purging of the pagan gods from
the Pantheon in Rome in 615 A.D., when it was dedicated to the Virgin and became Santa
Maria Rotunda. Bede cites eyewitness reports of the demons seen flying out of the dome during the purification rites. See Bede, *The Ecclesiastical History of the English Nation*, trans. John
Stevens (London, 1910), ch. 4, p. 71.
48. *Philobiblon*, p. 63.

scene phallic joke. He writes on the scraped skin of a dead sheep, as Alan's Dreamer bitterly remarks. As guilty as the tearers of Natura's gown, the new poets, even Alan himself, are corrupt—makers of secondary worlds, misleading illusions. In this reductive Platonic moral critique, all poetry, all fictitious art—painting, sculpture, myth— is not an *integumentum* which veils truth ("the secret, sweeter kernel of truth within"), but a seductive, pseudo-intelligible maze of chimaeras and unicorns, lying Odysseus and suicidal Dido, a labyrinth of reflections of self-indulgent fantasy, the food of devils (*dæmonum cibis*). This is the attack on poetry to which Boccaccio responds, as we shall see, in the *Genealogy of the Gods*, in order to redefine and defend allegory by arguments repeated from Dante to Sidney, who could not give up the imagination which sees God. Answers must be made to the perversions of Venus and Cupid, and to Genius, whose anathema to the dreaming poet in Alan's vision is reason and celibacy: the only way to escape the subversive maze is not to enter it at all, to stay away from illusion and its desires altogether. Such ascetic and puritanical doctrine is already subtly undermined in Alan by the fact that it is delivered by an allegorical figure in an allegorical poem to a fictional Dreamer pretending to be a sleeping poet. Like the paradox of Epimenides of Crete, "All Cretans are liars," such poetic denunciation of poets, "All Poetry is corrupt," leaves the fiction itself ambivalent, if not intact. One cannot step behind a mirror if the mirror itself is an illusion.

The *Book of Fame*: Chaucer's Dante

In the evolution of Alan's allegory in the later Middle Ages, the book of Natura became the book of the poets, and the image of the book itself—held by Wisdom, dedicated to Fame, inscribed by Genius—is a symbol of the poetic imagination become concrete. What it says cannot be trusted; that it *may* be true is always possible. That poets know what they say is dubious: Veritas and Falsitas take charge, and in Chaucer's great Ovidian image, what once was Natura–Philosophia in her robes is transfigured into the grotesque and terrible figure of Fame. In her house, Fortune's wheel whirls on an eccentric cam; below it, the labyrinthine daughter-house of Tidings spins out language, out of control. The theme of the third book of Fame is cacophony: all the meaningless babble of languages, from Nimrod's arrogant attempt to speak to God down to the mindless pride of harpers and jongleurs—like gargoyles and baboons, as many as snowflakes in a storm—crowding the window niches of Fame's temple, playing on their instruments:

> alle maner of mynstralles,
> And gestiours, that tellen tales
> Both of wepinge and of game, . . .
> And countrefete hem as an ape.
>
> [*HF* 1197–99; 1212]

All reiterate the theme: "as craft countrefeteth kynde" [*HF* 1213]. Fallen art imitates fallen nature. In the *Complaint of Nature*, Alan's allegorical explanation of the corruption of myth, and of all poetry, is moral first, and then aesthetic. For, as Wetherbee explains Alan's dream, the corruption of man's nature is reflected in the corruption of his art: "the only artist capable of genuine metaphor was Adam in the Garden, giving names to his subject creatures, and therein realizing his true dignity as a man."[49] If Chaucer borrowed from Alan bits and pieces of *countrefete* descriptive imagery in the *Book of Fame*, I think his paradoxical deprecation of his own art may also be reflected, infused with the more profound imitation of Dante. The third book of the *Book of Fame* opens with an invocation to Apollo, god of wisdom and light, and the Dreamer asks for divine aid to *shew art poetical*. His eagle has brought him to the mountain of melting ice (*not of stel*, nor *of glass like unto crystal*). This is his final hallucination, and he promises that if the god will help him "to shewe now / that in myn hed ymarked ys"—to describe, he explains, what he sees in his imagination—then in gratitude, the next time he sees a laurel, he will kiss it, "for hyt is thy tree. / Now entre in my brest anoon!" This is a crux of extreme equivocation in tone, given all the the game and role playing in the 1090 lines that precede it. As Dante vindicated all true poets, followed Virgil, and made Apollo his last Muse, so Chaucer seems to follow Dante.[50]

In the parallel passages in *Paradiso*, I, 23–25, Dante turns toward the sun, at the equinoctial point which is noon in Purgatory, midnight in

---

49. Wetherbee, "The Function of Poetry," p. 103.

50. The range of interpretations of this passage is typical of modern arguments over the poem. Sheila Delany, in *Chaucer's House of Fame, The Poetics of Skeptical Fideism* (Chicago, 1972), surprisingly omits the third invocation, although she discusses those of Books I and II. J. A. W. Bennett, in *Chaucer's Book of Fame*, pp. 100 ff, reads the invocation as reverence to Dante. Muscatine is dubious, in *Chaucer and the French Tradition* (Berkeley, 1957), p. 108; Alan Renoir regards the whole invocation as comic, "tongue in cheek," in *The Poetry of John Lydgate* (London, 1967), p. 55.

Jerusalem, and prays to Apollo, since he needs more than the Muses of Parnassus,

> tanto che l'ombra del beato regno
> segnata nel mio capo io manifesti,
> [that I make manifest the shadow of
> the blessed realm imprinted on my brain].

Dante promises to come to *tuo diletto legno*, "thy chosen tree," where Apollo (divine light, God) will see him:

> e coronarmi allor di quelle foglie,
> che la materia e tu mi farai degno.
> [and crown me, then, with the leaves of which
> the matter and thou shalt make me worthy].

He then goes on to develop the image of the sacred laurel leaf:

> Sì rade volte, padre, se ne coglie,
> per trionfare o Cesare o poeta,
> colpa e vergogna dell' umane voglie,
> [So few times, Father, is there gathered of it,
> for triumph or of Caesar or of poet—
> fault and shame of human wills.][51]

Chaucer's translation of Dante's prayer omits this last glimpse of the coronation "of Caesar or of poet," but the omitted link supplies the poet of Fame with justification both for borrowing Dante's Apollo and for the ironic anticlimax of his own invocation: not a coronation, triumphant access to godlike power, but an almost capering kiss of the trunk of a tree:

> Thou shalt se me go as blyve
> Unto the nexte laure y see,
> And kysse yt, for hyt is thy tree.
> Now entre in my brest anoon!
>
> [*HF*, 1106–09]

Chaucer thus enters the last part of his most tendentiously ambiguous poem with a passage of Dante to spare, the unused *colpa e vergogna dell' umane voglie*: his own consciousness, suppressed by his narrator for the

51. *The Paradiso of Dante Alighieri*, trans. P.H. Wicksteed (London, 1899; repr. 1946), 1: 22–29.

sake of self-satire, of the guilt and shame of human will. The poet knows both what he omits and what he alters. He is the recording witness of both his own absurdity and all human corruption. The mortal pity of all man's attempts to love, to be true, to sustain visions—not his final Paradise—these are Chaucer's special themes. Better than most men, he is the witness of human limitation in his own person, as his own dreamer who longs for what he knows cannot be: he sees into the void that separates imaginable beauty and human truth. His art, the *craft* that *countrefeteth kynde*, fills that gap with fictions, the works of the poets and musicians in Fame's House: *Virgile, Ovide, Omer, Lucan,* and *Stace.*

The third book of the *Book of Fame* is surrealistic satire, a defense of *art poetical* profoundly sceptical, that extends to questioning of all secular knowledge. In the babble of its last episode lies bitter doubt of everything contained in all old books, becoming comedy in the narrator's stupefaction. By turns delighted, stunned, awed at the cacophony of endless noise, music, unintelligible lies and truths in the writers and singers swarming around the Temple, he traces the desire for his *tydyings* further back into the daedal maze. Following the sound waves, just as the Eagle in Book II described their rising into the outer sky in circling rings, he finds their madhouse of emanations in the wicker house, the carousel of Aventure. Aventure [Chance] is the mother *of tydynges, | as the see of welles and of sprynges,* so the image of the circles in the water of the Eagle's learned discourse turns his science back into the primitive nature of its source, the mythopoeic mutability of the voice of waters and the shapes of clouds. In the wicker house, the illusions of art are revealed to be fortuitous effects of collision at the thousand holes in its roof. Sounds pour forth among vapors and winds, breath, in a cloudy dissolving stream of imagery of noise which is ultimately reducible only to silence. The poem has nowhere further to go, since all possible exits are blocked, filled with lies compounded with *sad sothes,* copulating, compromising, to escape into the air:

> And somtyme saugh I thoo at ones
> A lesyng and a sad soth sawe,
> That gonne of aventure drawe
> Out at a wyndowe for to pace;
> And, when they metten in that place,
> They were achekked bothe two,
> And neyther of hem moste out goo

> For other, so they gonne crowde,
> Til ech of hem gan crien lowde,
> "Lat me go first!" "Nay, but let me! . . .
> We wil medle us ech with other,
> That no man, be they never so wrothe,
> Shal han on [of us] two, but bothe
> At ones. . . ."
> Thus saugh I fals and soth compouned
> Togeder fle for oo tydynge.
>   Thus out at holes gunne wringe
> Every tydynge streght to Fame,
> And she gan yeven ech hys name,
> After hir disposicioun,
> And yaf hem eke duracioun,
> Somme to wexe and wane sone,
> As doth the faire white mone,
> And let hem goon.
>
>   [*HF*, 2088–2117]

The dream ends in incoherence, with twenty thousand *wynged wondres, o, many a thousand tymes twelve*, of lies flying about the Dreamer's head, and men pushing him, running and stamping *as men doon aftir eles*, a primordial swarm, shapeless, mindless, in which the Dreamer begins to drown, at the moment he sees the man, nameless, *But he semed for to be | A man of gret auctoritee*. The dream has undermined the credibility of any voice that speaks in it, and the *man of gret auctoritee* has nothing left to say that will not be quickly blown through the walls and twisted into the mass of blur between the whirling wicker house and the golden temple on the melting mountain. Fiction falsifies itself in the House of Fame, and Chaucer's dream comes to a dead end.

The dreaming "I" whose hallucinations have to be taken at risk, at face value, is not the only role the medieval poet can play in his poem, but it is, in a sense, the easiest and most familiar. The more difficult role is that of the narrator who is not asleep, who takes responsibility for his poem and accounts for its worth. The ambiguity of his word, and its hypothetical relation to truth and *auctoritee* remain open to doubt and are never escaped.

> Now I quite acknowledge that these allegories are very nice, but
> he is not to be envied who has to invent them; much labor and

ingenuity will be required of him, and when he has once begun, he must go on and rehabilitate Hippocentaurs and dire chimaeras. [I have no time for this, for] I must first know myself, and while I am still in ignorance of my own self it would be ridiculous to be curious about that which is not my concern . . . am I a monster more complicated and swollen with passion than the serpent Typho?[52]

As some of the Chartres Platonists argued, anticipating Boccaccio and Sidney, if Plato had not had the soul of a poet, he would not have feared poets enough to consider banning them. Both elements, the sceptical and the mystical, were transmitted through the debates of twelfth-century Platonism on the authority of Augustine himself, who found in Plato "the most nearly in accord with Christianity of all philosophies."[53] Chaucer did not know the *Phaedrus* directly, of course, but he knew the Chartres Platonists and enough of Socrates from postclassical sources to drop his name lightly in another dream context, to the Black Knight who has lost his queen in the *Book of the Duchess*:

> "A, goode sir," quod I, "say not soo!
> Have som pitee on your nature
> That formed yow to creature.
> Remembre yow of Socrates,
> For he ne counted nat thre strees
> Of noght that Fortune koude doo."
>
> [*BD* 714–19]

The *Book of Fame* is a great poem, but its power is strange and mixed. Its most vivid passages are not those which acquire their resonance from other poets—the parodic imitations of Virgil, of Dante, of Ovid, and the set pieces of decorative description. Rather, the poem comes alive in its protean voices, the satiric dialogue of the Dreamer in colloquy with the Eagle, in addresses to the audience, and in the montage of speakers overheard and personified ideas in the sonorous limbo of Aventure. The Socratic ironies of the narrator's detachment undermine his mock reverent imitations of *auctoritees* and determined pursuit of the

52. Plato *Phaedrus* 229D, E; trans. Rafael Demos, in *Plato* (Cambridge, Mass., 1927), p. 287; cf. text and commentary in R. Hackforth's edition (Cambridge, Eng., 1952), pp. 24–26.
53. St. Augustine, quoted by McKeon, "Poetry and Philosophy," p. 220.

secrets of *art poetical* which enrich its surface. Whenever he seems to
have the truth he is seeking within his grasp it begins to disintegrate
or is cast into doubt by a sceptical afterthought: *But men seyn, "What
may ever laste?"*

The archetypal image of Natura's priest, Genius, never appears
directly in Chaucer's poems, nor is his ancient association with the
power of the poet to make images revived again until Spenser, who
invokes not only his prolific sexual creativity, but his visionary power
as well. In the Garden of Adonis (*FQ* III, vi), he is "Old Genius, the
which a double nature has," whom Spenser distinguishes from his
antitype, the Genius of Acrasia's Bower:

> They in that place him Genius did call:
> Not that celestiall powre, to whom the care
> Of life, and generation of all
> That lives, pertaines in charge particulare,
> Who wondrous things concerning our welfare
> And strange phantomes doth let vs oft foresee.
>
> [*FQ* II, xii]

Bernard's Genius has become symbolic of the ambiguity of all creative
energy, in Alan's *De Planctu Naturae,* and explicitly of that art whose
mastery Chaucer's Dreamer seeks in the Temple of Fame; for Genius
never stops making images, copying the names of the good and evil
celebrated by the poets who made them *figurae,* immortal.

As Curtius and, more recently, Peter Dronke have shown, there is
still much to be learned from the history of classical topoi as they are
borrowed and altered in the evolving medieval tradition. Dronke
argues for originality, imaginative and symbolic uses of commonplaces,
in medieval Latin poems:

> However much less we may know about their functions than
> about allegory and *figura,* the existence of "unfixed" meanings
> must be reckoned with. From the very first . . . literary . . .
> Christendom was a world that inherited and furthered symbolic
> modes of expression. While these . . . are not to be found in
> every medieval literary text, and not necessarily in every text that
> is imaginatively outstanding, to exclude the possibility of their
> presence would be to falsify historically.[54]

54. *Poetic Individuality in the Middle Ages, New Departures in Poetry, 1000–1150* (Oxford, 1970),
p. 196.

The earthly paradise, heavenly ascent, the underworld, metamorphosis, the Muses, and the gods, are common property of European poets from the sixth century to the twelfth in Latin, and from the twelfth to the eighteenth in the vernaculars. Their origins are in the surviving fragments of the first six centuries of the Christian era, when the inheritance from the pagans and the Greeks was transmitted into Christian Latin rhetoric and poetry; the new voices of authority emerge from the falling world of Rome. Awareness of their debt can again be documented in England from Richard de Bury, contemporary with Boccaccio and the new humanists in Italy:

> What would Virgil, the greatest poet of the Latins, have done if he had not at all plundered Theocritus, Lucretius, and Homer, or ploughed with their heifer? What could Horace . . . have pored over but Parthenius and Pindar, whose eloquence he could in no way imitate? What Sallust, Tully, Boethius, Macrobius, Lactantius, Martianus, nay, the whole cohort of the Latins in general, if they had not seen the labours of the Athenians or volumes of the Greeks?[55]

As the ghosts of early Latin poetry haunt the new vernacular poets of the later Middle Ages, they in turn become ghostly presences in the poems of their successors in the Renaissance. Looking back, however, the temporal perspective foreshortens. Harrington's conception of Ariosto, in the 1591 Preface to his *Orlando*, is a case in point. As Wellek comments,

> Homer and Ariosto (like Ovid and Shakespeare in Meres) are [imagined] as living at almost the same time, with no consciousness of the gulf of ages and poetical traditions [between them].[56]

It has recently been said that Boethius is the founder of the European tradition of introspective poetry:[57] the *Consolation*'s dialogues express the medieval Christian's basic anxieties of self, the enigmas of personality, and unreconcilable elements implicit in the fusion Boethius attempted, the synthesis of classicism and Christianity. In Boethius's dialogues with Philosophy, the poet introspects, and the subject of his

---

55. *Philobiblon*, ch. 10, p. 54. Cf. his sad meditation on the destruction of old books ("the [lost] Georgics of Noah . . . the Antidotes of Aesculapius, the Argonautics of Jason") in ch. 7, pp. 39–41.

56. René Wellek, *The Rise of English Literary History* (Chapel Hill, 1941), p. 12.

57. J. B. Morrall, *The Medieval Imprint* (London, 1971), p. 64.

vision is himself. There is no hero, no victory, and the Muses are banished at the outset. The literal imprisonment of his body becomes the
metaphorical bondage of his soul, enslaved to its passions, its blindness,
its despair. From Boethius and his immediate model, Martianus Capella's *Marriage of Mercury and Philology,* medieval secular poetry found
means to explore not only epic themes—the battle deeds and conquests
of famous heroes and lovers—but also quests in private dreams, the
individual doubts and ecstasies of the self face-to-face with enigmatic
universals. This view, which too narrowly excludes Augustine, Plato,
and the biblical visionary tradition, echoes, I think, Vico's and Freud's
dubious regard for artistic work as a kind of defense against the flux,
and it seeks a psychological "defense" of allegory in place of the discarded image of the divine on which Boccaccio's and Sidney's Renaissance defenses depend. Like the "work" of the dreamer, condens-
ing, joining contraries, making concrete imagery and elaborate
metaphors to solve problems of both inner past and external present
experience which the waking mind evades, the artistic processes of
dream symbolism—of the imagination ceaselessly at work—are indeed
the basic forms of fictional creation in poetry. But of course, symbol
making is a constant, not restricted to dreams and poetry. As Plato saw,
men cannot think without making sensations into symbols, which are
then combined and manipulated in what he calls reasoning. The mind
masters form and substance simultaneously in the act of perceiving and
making meaning. Plato's idea is transmitted in Aristotle, Boethius, and
hence in Chaucer: "With a single glance of the mind it formally, as it
were, sees all things."[58] Fiction making and symbolizing may be, as
Freud believed, as vulnerable to analysis as are memories and dreams;
they may be read as the defenses erected by poets against their anxieties, artifacts which less articulate men seek out to deflect their own
turbulence. But the poet, in his fictional vision, has the freedom to
exercise deliberate artistic control. Chaucer's mastery of the waking
Pilgrims, and of his allegorical Dreamers, and the narrator and reader
of *Troilus and Criseyde,* exhibit the authority Sidney claims for the poet,
"who nothing affirms, and therfore never lieth": a definition even more
Chaucerian, I think, than "Renaissance," for the paradox of authority
transcends the paradox of imitation.

58. Boethius, *Consolation* V, prosa 4, Green, p. 111; cf. Aristotle *de Anima* 432ª, 17: "The
soul never thinks without a mental picture;" 431ᵇ, 2: "The thinking faculty thinks of its
ideas (*eidos*) in terms of images (*phantasma*)." trans. Philip Wheelwright (New York, 1935).
Langland's *Imagynatyf* and Spenser's *Phantastes* personify this medieval psychological topos.

III

Self-impersonation: The Chaucerian Poetic "I"

> The results of art would be vain if they were all brought about
> by compulsion. Everything which is known is known not ac-
> cording to its own power, but rather according to the capacity of
> the knower.
>
> Boethius, *Consolation*, V, pr. 4

The most problematic aspects of fictional ambiguity in medieval
poetry are apparently genetic, and they arise in the varying relations
implied in the text between the poet, his audience, and the conventions
of the tradition in which he writes. The universal "I," the hypothetical
audience or reader addressed in the poem, and the validating generic
formulae are, however, aspects of the text, not of the poet.[1] Recurring
variant patterns, like the use of occupatio, for example, may become
distinctive marks, theoretically recognizable as an "identity," as a poet
creates his own style by modifying convention to his liking, without a
conscious pursuit of originality. The poet's "I" may perhaps be an
excellent mimic, as has been surmised in the multiple authorship
arguments over the poets of *Sir Gawain*, *Pearl*, and *Piers Plowman*.[2] An
originator, skillfully copied by imitators, or one man, developing his

1. E. Talbot Donaldson was the first twentieth–century Chaucerian to make this point, in
"Chaucer the Pilgrim," *PMLA* 69 (1954): 928–36; the ensuing controversy is described in the
introduction to William R. Crawford's *Bibliography of Chaucer, 1954–63* (Seattle, 1967), pp.
i–xl. See also Lowry Nelson, Jr., "The Fictive Reader and Literary Self-Reflexiveness," in
The Disciplines of Criticism, Peter Demetz, Thomas Greene, and Lowry Nelson, eds. (New
Haven, 1970). Ben E. Parry, in *The Ancient Romances* (Berkeley, 1967), appendix three, pp.
325–29, discusses the "Ego–Narrative in Comic Stories," tracing the evolution of first-person
narration from Homeric seriousness (Odysseus's wonder tales of his wanderings) to the ironic
use of first person in Lucian's *Luciad*, Apuleius's *Metamorphoses*, and Petronius's *Satyricon*.

2. The four anonymous, highly conventional alliterative poems of the single MS, Cotton
Caligula A. x, (*Gawain, Patience, Purity*, and *Pearl*) would seem to provide a test case for stylistic
identification as to separate or common authorship. D. R. Howard (*Speculum* 47[1972]: 550) is
sceptical of the single poet case made by A. C. Cawley and others. The question is, if a single
poet wrote all four, did he begin at the top of his powers (with *Gawain*?) and then slowly fade,
or did he reach mastery of irony last? Or, were there several poets involved in these poems?
The case for Langland's authorship of all three versions of *Piers Plowman* has been made by
George Kane in *Piers Plowman, The Evidence for Authorship* (London, 1965).

special style? With anonymous manuscripts, before printing, such questions have to be taken seriously, as they strongly prejudice interpretation. In the case of Chaucer, the work done by the great Victorian editors has sifted the imitations out, but the Elizabethan reader was confronted by numerous Chaucerian impostors, as well as the various kinds of impersonation Chaucer invented for himself. Then too, a poet may be parodying a style while seeming to play it straight; thus, for example, if in *Sir Thopas* Chaucer obviously burlesques minstrel romance, what is the level of irony in his *Melibee*? As the Monk's tragedies at last exasperate the Knight,

> "Hoo!" quod the Knyght, "good sire, namore of this!
> That ye han seyd is right ynough, ywis,
> And muchel moore; for litel hevynesse
> Is right ynough to muche folk, I guess, . . ."
>
> [B² 2767–70]

so in *Melibee* Chaucer stretches the limits of tolerance for prose homily of the modern reader. It becomes a test case, in which the vexed historicity of the "medieval mind" (what Chaucer's audience patiently "would have enjoyed"), the slyness or true sincerity of the speaker ("Chaucer the Pilgrim"), and the traditional interpretation of medieval moral allegory come together in a knot of ambiguity. I shall comment later on *Melibee* and *Sir Thopas* and their speaker, but first something needs to be said about the more general problem of the fictional "I" in medieval poems.

The unravelling of ambiguity may seem to be a process of clarification, but that something is unravelled may also mean a whole image disintegrates and a pattern is lost. Who are the speakers in Chaucer's poems, and how are the Dreamer, the Narrator, and the Pilgrim to be understood? The Renaissance reader in general relied on Quintilian and Horace, applied the principle of decorum, and assumed that Chaucer's Plowman, his clergy, and his talking animals observed the rules for appropriate speech:

> If the words of a speaker seem inappropriate to his situation, the Romans, both the aristocracy and the populace, will simply laugh. It will make a great difference whether it is a god who is speaking or a hero, a ripe old man or a youth still in flower. . . . Either follow tradition, or else make what you invent consistent.[3]

3. Horace, *Ars Poetica*, ll. 99–135.

In Elizabethan commentaries, Chaucer is always praised for his "consistency" and decorum, but he is also always taken to be the "Chaucer" in the poem. The narrator of *Troilus* is Chaucer himself, and the pilgrimage to Canterbury was accepted as based on fact, even though the pilgrims were understood to be veiled in fiction, by poetic license, in order to protect the poet. Speght's comments on the *Tales*, in his editions of 1598 and 1602, amplify the theme of Puttenham's approval in 1589:

> The Canterbury Tales be but riding rhyme, nevertheless very well becomming the matter of that pleasaunt pilgrimmage, in which every man's part is playd with much decency.[4]

The veil of allegory, however, was far more subtle and flexible, as it was described and used in the Middle Ages, than the heavier Renaissance allegory which succeeded it, and its conventions allowed Chaucer the poet more freedom of maneuver than was apparent to writers like Puttenham, who rewrote the rules from the perspective of the 1580's. After 1400, as I shall try to show, not only Chaucer's sources (both real and "faked"), but many of his subtler stylistic conventions were increasingly dimly perceived.

"Intended" Meaning: *Allegoria, Ironia,* and the Narrator

Medieval allegory, according to the grammarians, is a trope or mode in composition, "the indirect and ironic revelation of thought": *tropus quo aliud significatur quam dicitur,* as Donatus defines it. It is arbitrary, and controlled by intention: "saying something while pretending not to say it," as Anaximenes describes *ironia* (1434a17).[5] Pompeius makes a subtler differentiation between *ironia* and *allegoria* in his *Commentary on Donatus*:

> ironia est, quotienscumque re vera aliud loquimur et aliud significamus in verbis; non ita, ut diximus de allegoria quando aliud dicimus et aliud significamus, non, sed isdem verbis potes et *negare et confirmare.* Sola autem pronuntiatione discernitur.[6]

4. *The Arte of English Poesie* (London, 1589; facsimile edition, Kent, Ohio, 1970), p. 76.
5. Quoted in George Kennedy, *The Art of Persuasion in Greece* (Princeton, 1963), p. 116.
6. "It is irony whenever we say one thing and we mean another in words; not thus, as we said of allegory, when we say one thing and signify another, no, but you can in the same words both deny and affirm. But this is discernible only in the pronunciation." Sextus Pompeius, *Commentum artis Donati*; text in Heinrich Keil, *Grammatici Latini*, (Leipzig, 1868), 5: 310

Allegorical language refers to something quite distinct from the literal meaning of words, whereas "ironic words can both affirm and deny what they state." Allegory thus contains an implicitly subversive element within its system of control, the enigmatic possibilities of *significatio*: irony, enigma, ambiguity. The Nun's Priest appeals, in his *moralitas*, to our grasp of the truth of his fable, slyly assuming the "obvious" meaning of Fox and Cock, which is, of course, very far from obvious, as the Nun's Priest's mockery makes clear:

> But ye that holden this tale a folye
> As of a fox, or of a cok and hen,
> Taketh the moralite, goode men.
> For seint Paul seith that al that writen is,
> To oure doctrine it is ywrite, ywis;
> Taketh the fruyt, and lat the chaf be stille.
> Now, goode God, if that it be thy wille,
> As seith my lord, so make us alle goode men,
> And brynge us to his heighe blisse! Amen.
>
> [B² 3438–46]

In that last moment, the power of allegory slips from the controlled poetic Nun's Priest's "I" to *ye, goode men, that holden this tale a folye*; it is left to God to *make us alle goode men*.

In a famous passage, Northrop Frye remarks that "continuous allegory prescribes the direction of the reader's commentary, and restricts its freedom."[7] Following Frye, Angus Fletcher's "compulsive" theory of allegory similarly restricts the freedom of the audience and of the poet, "in scope of moral attitude and degree of enigma." Fletcher admits that poets vary, but the equivocal *moralitas*, the self-satirizing persona, and deliberate obscurities in *trobar clus* are explained as merely softening and complicating devices of the "controlling rigor" of allegory's intentional, purposive structure. "Allegorical intention is usually under a high degree of authorial control,"[8] but irony leaves

---

ff., s.v. *allegoria* (italics mine). The most comprehensive modern treatment of the genre is the monograph of John MacQueen, *Allegory* (London, 1970). For medieval theory, MacQueen cites Bede's *De Allegoria*, which follows closely the descriptions of allegory of Isidore and Quintilian, "in terms of irony, antiphrasis, aenigma, *charientismus, paroemia*, and sarcasm," which, MacQueen says "we may safely ignore" (p. 50).

7. Northrop Frye, *The Anatomy of Criticism* (Princeton, 1968), pp. 90–91.
8. Angus Fletcher, *Allegory. The Theory of a Symbolic Mode* (Ithaca, 1964).

open to doubt which of several, if any, possibilities take precedence. Fletcher begs the question, in the manner of the Nun's Priest himself, in his conclusion: "Allegory is itself a form of *ironia* . . . or, perhaps, *ironia* is a type of allegory."[9] I suggest that what we frequently find in Chaucer, and find so difficult to describe, is in effect allegorical irony: the literal meaning of words, simultaneously undermined and affirmed.

The indispensable element of the speaker's "delivery" (*pronuntiatio*), which all the Latin grammarians and rhetoricians note as the essence of irony is, of course, largely irrelevant to written texts. The missing elements of voice and gesture are the sources of the majority of the modern disputes over ambiguity and undetermined allegory in medieval poems, both sacred and secular, and those which, like Chaucer's *Melibee* or the anonymous "The Mayden in the Mor" are ambivalent or antinomian.[10] To rely on the scriptural exegetical techniques which Dante recommends for the *Comedy* and Boccaccio uses to rehabilitate the pagans (whose myths he loved and defended) in interpretation of all other medieval fiction may simplify, redefine, and often distort what such exegesis purports to reveal: the controlled correspondence intended by the poet. What the speaker "means" is in the poem, not in the poet's or his friends' advice to the reader (in the case of Spenser's "E. K.," for example). Threefold and fourfold analysis may have to magnify appropriate elements in the text to fit the size of the critical lens, and thus reduce or ignore ambiguities, equally likely to have been "intended," to a deceptively static simplicity. Coeval with the ladder-like descriptions of allegory, vertical and horizontal, are the equally venerable and clear rhetorical recommendations to medieval poets for achieving the spiralling figures which are the subtypes of allegory: in *ad Herrenium*, for example, *ironia, antiphrasis, aenigma, charientismus, paroenimia, sarcasmos, asteimos*. These are modes for making oblique concessions and refraining from making truth claims.

Allegory refers to a reality "other than that indicated by its words": allegorical ironies hover about the same reality, but reveal it from two points of view, thus providing the poet with the means for poetic detachment and for disclosure by *amphibologies* to which the poet alone

9. Compare Fletcher: "Allegory does not admit doubt; its enigmas show an obsessive battling with doubt" (*Allegory*, pp. 322–23).

10. See the brilliant analyses of "Mayden in the Mor Lay" by Joseph Harris, *Journal of Medieval and Renaissance Studies* 1 (1971): 59–87, and Siegfried Wenzel, *Speculum* 49 (1974), 69–74.

holds the key. Polysemous intention, multiplicity of meaning, which the rhetoricians variously classify under *significatio*, generally has five basic forms: hyperbole (exaggeration by over- or understatement); ambiguity (punning); implication (*consequentium*), interruption (calculated surprise) and analogy (simile, metaphor, metonymy, synechdoche). These are general and familiar terms in medieval rhetoric, which describe the implicit parameters of language, and which provide for the curves of literary style; they alter, by inference, the dimensions created by a fictional straight line, the literal meaning of *litterae*. They are the modes of implication, of indirect speech, of "allegorical irony," and are as applicable to the vernacular as they are to Latin.

The sight-lines discovered by Cimabue and Giotto in their studies in perspective create the illusion of the observer as the third dimension of a painting. Giotto's horizons thus conjure an illusion of greater "reality" by inclusion of the spectator in extended space; in contrast, the presence of allegorical irony and *significatio* in fiction complicate and deepen poetic reality by inclusion of the reader in the task of interpreting their extended meanings, beyond the literal line, without defining the horizon. Ambiguity invokes the audience. Hence it is that the most dogmatic controversies in all interpretations of medieval poetry begin, not with debatable sources, "style," or influence, but with "intention": where the literal level, the fable, permits doubt. In order to discuss what a poem means, or once "meant," critical judgments of double meanings—"polysemous textures"—must first be made and agreements reached, based on whether, where, and to what extent a given object or action in a poem is symbolic, a statement ambiguous, or a narrator's voice lightly or heavily ironic. The last is of course the most elusive, and most vulnerable of all to misinterpretation, even *viva voce*, and most liable to distortion and loss in transmission. "The truth of the voice perishes with the sound. Truth latent in the mind is hidden wisdom and invisible treasure."[11] Where it is clear that there are extended meanings or a plurality of meanings intended, as in the *Roman de la Rose*, for example—a hierarchy of allegorical correspondences, typology, parody, and ironic *significatio*—not even the first author could control or foresee the ambiguities that would arise, for contemporaries as well as for posterity. Thus Dante's Letter to Can Grande and Spenser's Letter to Raleigh have themselves finally become dimensions of the

11. "Vox audita perit: littera scripta manet" (*Philobiblon*, p. 16).

Comedy and the *Faerie Queene*, which, in the latter case, complicate the fiction rather than guide the reader.

The narrator's "I" is the primary crux, the point where biography, social history, and historical interpretation intersect in the knot of ambiguity. Where the author's instructions, received tradition, and newly found analogues or "facts" are tangled in conflict, modern psychobiography and old-fashioned historicism seek to resolve, "unravel," apparent contradiction, by finding the latent pattern which will account for all the parts of a whole paradoxically greater than the *litterae* of the poem.

> No biographical information is required to see that a man is a cripple, if you watch him walk; similarly (in allegory), no such information is required to show that a given action is compulsively ordered. The analyst simply has to inspect the rhythm of the action. Thus it is with literary criticism.[12]

The new formalist critics are more sophisticated than the subtlest of their ancestors, the medieval and Reniassance rhetoricians, but I think it requires something more than "simply to inspect the rhythm of the action" of a poem, which does not limp, to see what its allegorical and ironic movements may mean.

The latent power of *significatio*, allegorical and ironic ambiguity, lies in the virtually limitless freedom it affords to the poet to invent antinomies that may admit of no resolution, to permit contradictions to stand, and, as in surrealism (in Hieronymus Bosch, or Dürer), arbitrarily to create new symbols or alter the received meanings of tradition. So Dante transfigured the Rose and Chaucer created a new Criseyde. It may also be that poetic ambiguity, like myth, can reconcile, by means of paradox, conflicting ideas, antinomian values, or kinds of experience, and thus make inexplicability bearable. This is the effect achieved by the greatest elegies and some love poems, which cannot be reduced to their themes of death and sex. I would claim for medieval allegory, and in particular for Chaucer's ironic manipulation of its conventions for multiple perspective, an autonomy for the poet different from the "authorial control" of rigid correspondent meanings. Chaucer's Narrator does not conduct a ritual in which the reader plays a role on cue, agreed upon in advance, as he does for example in the later allegorical

12. Fletcher, *Allegory*, p. 301.

pantomime of a poem like Hawes's *Pastime of Pleasure*. On the contrary, in Chaucer the reader learns at the outset that the Narrator is not *a man of greet auctoritee*, a man to be trusted, a man in control of the fiction. As in the *Envoy to Bukton*, he expects the reader to take part in, and often take over, the task of interpretation.

The Posthumous Evolution of "Chaucer the Poet" in the Fifteenth and Sixteenth Centuries

The successful portrayal of a poetic "I" may be compared to an actor playing a part. The actor must be completely convincing in each of his roles: the audience must feel that he not only believes what he says, but is what he pretends to be. If the actor's own personality intrudes through the character he plays, the artistic illusion is broken.[13]

When an actor dies, his art dies with him. Whether or not they were all once read aloud, the subsequent performances of Chaucer's narrators have been since 1400 through the silent medium of text. What the medieval audience knew, however, and took for granted, post-medieval audiences gradually forgot: that the poetic "I" is to be taken at face value, and that the speaker is in the poem, not to be sought, or found, in the man behind the poem. The poet may, or may not, be identical with the "I" who claims our attention; he may be playing an old familiar role, inventing a new one, or speaking without a mask, *in propria persona*.

While it may have been conventional, as D. L. Sutherland has suggested in the case of Adam de la Halle,[14] and as Nancy Regalado argues for Rutebeuf, for a medieval poet to adopt a specific, public "poetic personality" as a blazon or emblem unique to him, in other cases the conventions of genre may dictate the model for the poet's "I," appropriate to an occasion or a theme. His identity is a fiction, which may come near, or never approach, the poet's own. Courtly lyric establishes the "I" as the lover, although there are some poems in which the speaker is evidently a woman whose poetic anonymity is complete. One of the apocryphal poems published and read as Chau-

13. Nancy J. Regalado, *Poetic Patterns in Rutebeuf* (New Haven, 1970), p. 262.
14. D. L. Sutherland, "Fact and Fiction in the *Jeu de la Feuillee*," *Romance Philology* 13 (1960): 419–28.

cer's in the sixteenth century editions of his *Works* is an example. *The Assembly of Ladies*, printed as Chaucer's by Thynne in 1532, opens with the following stanza:

> In Septembre at the fallyng of the lefe
> The fressh ceason was al togyder doon
> And of the corne was gathered the shefe
> In a gardyne aboute twayne after noone
> Ther were ladyes walking / as was her wone
> Foure in nombre / as to my mynde dothe fal
> And I the fyfthe / the symplest of hem al.

[f.ccxciiii]

A versatile poet may play several roles in succession, and play them off against one another, as Lydgate does in his long career, imitating Chaucer as dreamer–elegist in the *Complaint of the Black Knight* (attributed to Chaucer until 1878), and as garrulous old pilgrim ("Dan John") in the *Siege of Thebes*.

The varying degrees of approximation between the poet's "I" and the autobiographical personality of the poet in Chaucer range on a scale from the first-person of the witty note to Adam the Scrivener and the *Envoy to Bukton* to the enigmatic poet of *Troilus*, who variously reappears (to take responsibility for having written it) in the two Prologues of the Dreamer in the *Legends of Good Women*, and in the third person in the Prologue of the Man of Law, as the author of the whole catalogue of "Chaucer's" works which the Man of Law has no desire to rival. None of these are the "Chaucer" of *Melibee*, the moralist who speaks in prose, when his first attempt at romance, *Sir Thopas*, fails to amuse the pilgrims. As Maynard Mack has shown, the poetic "I" in satire may adopt several modes of address in succession, not necessarily consistently: the naive injured innocent, the fearless scourge, the cynical wit, the conservative defender of old values.[15] The "identity" in poetic performance that is appreciated and valued most, and is most persuasively "authentic" or "sincere," is that "I" who successfully reenacts the whole dream, concludes the passionate love letter, or effects the powerful denunciation of a vice. Medieval audiences did not regard a poet as a hypocrite merely because he didn't dream, slept well, was not in love, or was well known to love gambling and wine. They

15. See Maynard Mack, "The Muse of Satire," *Yale Review 41*(1951–2), 80–92.

did not immediately or always identify the poet with the speaker of the poem.

The study of Chaucer's reputation in the fifteenth and sixteenth centuries, however, reveals the gradual conflation of his various poetic identities into a composite personality, the synthetic "Chaucer" praised by his publishers (Caxton, Thynne, and finally Speght), and venerated by his imitators. The Chaucer of the fifteenth-century "Chaucerians" in Scotland and England gradually assumed the shape and dignity of their collective eulogies, and the several literal selves of his poems blurred into one cumulative, indistinct "Chaucer," the patriarch and *first maker* of the English language. Some further consequences of this process will be discussed in chapter 8, where the editing and printing of the Renaissance folios are surveyed.

Those later readers who possessed or inherited manuscripts undoubtedly formed opinions different from those of the buyers of early editions, who, as we shall see, read much more than "Chaucer's *Works*." Speculation is of course hazardous where so little is known, and the evidence of confusion in both manuscripts and printed texts is abundantly muddled. Caxton's Preface to the second edition of his *Canterbury Tales* (1484) is clear proof, however, that comparisons were made between "good" and "bad" texts, and it also suggests that the disparities among Chaucer's various poetic personae were already being submerged unintentionally in *the sayd Gefferey chaucer first auctour | and maker of thys book*.[16] Caxton's desire to vindicate his text as authentic (echoed by all of his successors), and to praise his author as a *laureate poete*, would suggest why he insists that his "Chaucer" is the work of but one man, *myn auctor*, a true text with all omissions repaired and spurious *versys that he neuer made ne sette in hys booke* excised. Such claims tacitly enforce the reading of all first-person narrative naively, as expressive of the poet himself, as a *de facto* guarantee of the authenticity of the poems. A plurality of fictional selves was as difficult for an editor then, working from many manuscripts, as it is for the modern reader now, reexamining the puzzling early printed texts those publishers produced as "Chaucer's *Works*." There is double jeopardy apparent already, in even so clear a case as "Caxton's 'Chaucer,' " that we too may infer plausible motives and assign causes to satisfy our modern preconceptions of the publisher, the poet, the reader, and his book. To whatever degree that

16. *The Prologues and Epilogues of William Caxton*, ed. W. J. B. Crotch, *EETS* 176 (London, 1928, repr. 1956), p. 91 ("Prohemye" to *Canterbury Tales*, 2d. ed. [1484]).

Chaucer's poetic personalities were distinct from his public role and private life in late fourteenth-century London, empirical reading of the poems is the only modern witness. The *Life-Records* and contemporary anecdotes tell us virtually nothing of Chaucer the man. We know what he did, where he travelled, how much he was paid, and when he died, and we surmise a great deal as to what he read, on the evidence of his works. Of his personal life and personality—as courtier, husband, friend—and his political opinions and religious beliefs, only negative and indirect evidence remains. After his death in 1400, empirical reading of his successors suggests that the multiple role-playing "Chaucer" of the poems, whom modern criticism has rediscovered, gradually merged into that *noble grete philosopher*, as he was for Caxton, Skelton, and Spenser, and that his many poetic selves became one. That neither Skelton nor Spenser was "Colin Clout" was taken for granted by readers, but that Chaucer was distinct from "Geffrey" faded gradually from view.

In English literary history, the genetic fallacy is perhaps nowhere more richly illustrated than in the posthumous evolution of "Chaucer," slowly invented in retrospect, first by younger contemporaries, then by posterity.[17] His is the longest documented case of continuous metamorphosis in English poetry, for the reputation and influence of Milton and Shakspere do not begin until two centuries later, when Chaucer had already become "England's Homer," and few have suffered more the cost of linguistic obsolescence. Until the beginning of the seventeenth century, however, the increasing obscurity of his language at first parallels, and then outruns, the reverence of posterity. An immediate effect of the evolution of the language was the continuous addition of "apocrypha," imitations, some almost parodying Middle English, added to the canon of Chaucer's poems in the eight printings of his works between 1500 and 1598. The dates of his birth and death shifted backward and forward; his epitaph, as Caxton tells us, was provided by a visiting Italian in 1479 and replaced by another in 1556. He acquired posthumous knighthood and armorial bearings, and a curious family history which linked his progeny (the "Woodstock Chaucers") to Alice de la Pole, Countess of Salisbury and Duchess of Suffolk, and thence ultimately to Henry VII. Speght's folio of 1598 opens with a full-page

17. The case for the genetic fallacy is restated by William K. Wimsatt, Jr. in "Genesis: A Fallacy Revisited," in Demetz, Greene, and Nelson, eds., *The Disciplines of Criticism,* pp. 193–227.

engraving and portrait (based on Hoccleve's "memorial sketch") entitled "Chaucer's Progenie," with a family tree tracing the lineal descendants of Sir Payne Roet (based on Leland's and Bale's anti-quarian research). Chaucer is younger, then older than Gower—first his master, then his pupil—in the imagined antagonism between them read out of the *Confessio Amantis'* confused textual history.[18] Finally, and most curiously of all, fiction became fact, as Thomas Usk's prolix prose *Testament of Love* was understood to be Chaucerian autobiography, recording royal censorship and imprisonment; the *Testament,* printed in all the sixteenth-century *Works* as authentic, was not found to be false until Usk's anagram was discovered in it by Skeat and Bradley in the nineteenth century. Its absurd anecdotes and confessions of intrigue were taken to be true by Renaissance readers, and served to corroborate the literal image of the simple man, the naive "I" of the poems, as autobiographical and in earnest, when not very clearly in jest. The Renaissance re-creation of "Chaucer the poet" entailed, to sustain the illusion of Spenser's "old Dan Geffrey," for example, neglect and in-attention to the devices of medieval ambiguity, of rhetorical *ironia*—that which both affirms and denies at the same time—while those of *allegoria* remained very much alive. The medieval poet's indispensable privilege is the convention which leaves unclear the relation of the poet himself to the person who says "I" in the poem, and leaves him free to become other selves. What Elizabethan poets assumed for their own art, they did not attribute to their ancestors'. But, as Spitzer observed, the "Ich-Erzählung" enables the narrator to change roles at will: he may confess, make himself subservient to the audience, and even give up his power to make or break men's fame, by denying the power of the fiction-making itself in the formulae for denial of authority. Abdication of control of response is the price of the use of irony.

All the greater medieval poets of the narrative "I," Jean de Meung, Chaucer, Dante, and Langland, were masters of the ideal of medieval rhetoric, convincing verisimilitude: persuasion. The corollary of poetic *significatio* is artistic freedom, whose abuse is what sent Alan's Genius into the *infernum tristiae,* and deafened the Dreamer with lies in the House of Fame. The paradoxes of allegorical irony (ambiguity) and allegorical verisimilitude (belief) depend upon the fictional contract made with the audience: "It is to be understood that I have dreamed

18. See John H. Fisher, *John Gower, Moral Philosopher and Friend of Chaucer* (New York, 1964).

this dream, and what men see in dreams is—or may be—true." At the beginning of the first book of the *Confessio Amantis*, just before he introduces his Venus and her priest, the severe Genius who is to be his Confessor, Gower carefully sets forth in a marginal gloss how his *woful care, wofull day, wofull chance* of love and fortune are to be understood:

> Hic quasi in persona aliorum, quos amor alligat, fingens se auctor esse Amantem, varias eorum passiones variis huius libri distinccionibus per singula scribere proponit.[19]

The medieval poet's personae of himself and others are projections of potential selves, *figurae:* the poet trusts his audience to observe, and to interpret, their fictionality.

Both Chaucer and, to a lesser extent, Gower, underwent a process of reverse projection and simplification in the course of the evolution of their *Works* in the fifteenth and sixteenth centuries. The speakers in the poems were read out of the texts and into life, so that the fictional opinions, experiences, and attitudes in the poems could be reconciled and understood as the coherent meaning of the poet, thus extrapolated and made "consistent." It became possible to accept not only the prose *Testament of Love,* but eventually the violent anti-Roman allegory of the *Plowman's Tale,* as by the same hand as that of the *Pardoner's,* without differentiating between the crude polemic of a pseudo-Chaucerian and the art of the Pardoner's charisma, as Chaucer the Pilgrim describes it. The satire in the *General Prologue* was easily understood, but the *Monk's Tale* was read, not as a further evaluation of the Monk, but as "Chaucer's" kind of tragedy.

The obsolescence of the language is not enough to account for the Elizabethan blindness to what they praised, as indeed the *Plowman's Tale was* praised, and echoed verbatim by Spenser, in the *February* and *July* eclogues of the *Shepherd's Calendar,* as part of his imitation in homage to "Tityrus." It would seem that Renaissance readers did not assume that medieval poetry need be read with the subtlety and attentiveness to complex implication that their own art demands. The finer manipulations of tone and perspective in Chaucer's poems were not expected and rarely understood. Given the grotesque distortions of the printed texts,

---

19. "Here, as if in the person of others, those whom love binds, feigning himself to be the Lover, the author proposes to write of their various passions, one by one, in the various parts of this book." *Confessio Amantis,* I, 60 ff. (marginal gloss), in *John Gower's English Works,* 2 vols., *EETS* 81 (London, 1900), 1:37.

from the end of the fifteenth century onward, that the poems were mis-
read is not at all surprising. Perhaps a single example of the corruption
of the Renaissance texts will suffice, at this stage, to illustrate the point;
in chapter 8 more evidence will be presented to show what the sixteenth-
century reader read.

In the 1532 folio text of *Troilus and Criseyde*, printed by William
Thynne and reprinted throughout the century, the seventh stanza of
the Proem to Book I reads as follows:

> And byddeth eke for hem that ben at ease
> That god hem graunt aye good p*er*seueraunce
> And *sende hem grace* her loues for to please
> That it to loue be worshippe and plesaunce
> For so hoope I *my selfe best to auaunce*
> To praye for hem / that loues servauntes be
> And write *her wo* / and lyue in charite.
>
> [I, 43–49 (italics mine)]

Aside from relatively minor spelling variants, the major differences
between this stanza and the modern text, as edited by Root, are three,
and in each case the folio text is without any manuscript support. That
is to say, the variant readings of the manuscripts concern other words in
the stanza, and none agree with the reading of the folio. In 1. 45,
Thynne's *sende hem grace* replaced Chaucer's *sende hem myght*; in 1. 47,
my selfe best to auaunce replaced *my soule best avaunce*; in 1. 49, *her wo*
replaced *hire wo*. (The modern text in 1. 45 reads, *hire ladies so to please*,
where the folio and one group of manuscripts have *loues* for *ladies*.) In
short, then, in 1532, the Narrator asks prayers for *grace*, rather than
myght, for lovers; more shockingly, he hopes to advance himself, not his
soul, and finally, he writes *her wo* (not that of love's servants), which
may very likely have been understood to mean Criseyde. She is indeed
the Narrator's fallen heroine, but the tragedy that is the poem's theme
belongs to Troilus, not to his betrayer.[20] The accumulation of such
minutiae, begun long before 1532, accelerating throughout the century,
is one cause of the fading meaning of the poems.

The broader, and hence hazier, elements of Renaissance prejudice
and preconception of what a poet, living in the barbarous age of the

---

20. *Hire* as 3 pl. form of the pronoun is already virtually obsolete in the fifteenth century;
Caxton's later texts substitute *thei, theim, their* for his earlier forms *thei, hem, hir(e)*.

reign of Richard II, could be expected to be able to say are probably more important dimensions of the Elizabethan "Chaucer" than the gradual double warping of his language and the text. It seems clear that the brilliant re-creation of Chaucer's world in Shakspere's *Richard II* and *1 Henry IV* remained unrelated to the attitude of Elizabethan critics writing about the evolution of English poetry from its primitive beginnings: from the age of the *Book of the Duchess* and its Dreamer's Black Knight to that of Shakspere's John of Gaunt is a shift from darkness to light. This paradox is apparent in Sidney's judgment in defense of Chaucer in the *Apologie for Poetrie*, which mingles wonder with condescension:

> Truly, I know not whether to meruaile more,
> either that he in that mistie time could see
> so clearly, or that wee in this cleare age walke
> so stumblingly after him. Yet he had great
> wants, fitte to be forgiuen in so reuerent antiquity.

IV

The Imaginary Audience

Lectoribus auctor recipit opusculy huius auxesim.

Skelton, *Speke Parrot*

Adam scriveyn, if ever it thee bifalle
Boece or Troylus for to wryten newe,
Under thy long lokkes thou most have the scalle,
But after my makyng thou wryte more trewe;
So ofte a-daye I mot thy werk renewe,
It to correcte and eek to rubbe and scrape;
And al is thorough thy negligence and rape.

Chaucers Wordes unto Adam, His Owne Scriveyn

As in the case of the distinction that should be observed between the poet and the poetic "I" in any poem, so also in the case of the audience, there may be two: the audience of contemporaries in any given period who read (or hear) the poem, and an imaginary audience addressed within the poem. Our difficulties in interpretation arise from the unobtrusive universals, "I" and "ye," of direct and indirect address, especially in complex or ambiguous contexts where the implications of allegorical *ironia* and *significatio* must be inferred from the literal level on a scale ranging from clear to deeply veiled allusion. We try to deduce the medieval audience chiefly by interpreting social history, by inference from symbols, and by imaginative projection, back into a Rankean version of "how it really was," in short, by hypotheses and by abstraction.

Now, abstraction, as Whitehead put it, is "the omission of part of the truth." So is exaggeration, of selected aspects of any pattern, an omission of part of the truth. "Highlighting" is perhaps inevitable in the perceiving of recurrent images or stylistic traits abstractly as historical patterns, "characteristics" of medieval or Renaissance art. In order to see them at all, some distortion, omission, or emphasis is perhaps necessary if we are to surmount the limitations of our knowledge of the past. Historical fragments and lacunae invite imaginative response and offer tangential possibilities for adding to the truth, supplying the missing details to fill in a plausible design. As many recent critics claim, with almost too glad confidence, there is much to be gained by analogy, for example, with medieval architecture, sculpture, and the history of music, and the socio-political backgrounds against which medieval poetry was written and read. Clearly, the medieval audience and patron did accept and prefer certain artistic styles (polyphony, Perpendicular, marginal grotesques) which invite analysis. So we proceed analogically, comparing the arts by suggestion, looking from effect to cause. My analogy between Giotto's perspective and the effects of irony's appeal to the audience is an obvious example. If we could rediscover the audience, we could theoretically interpret more of what a poem "means." But it is a fact, and an anachronism of dubious value, that modern readers know considerably more about the pagan gods, for example, than did the medieval and Renaissance writers who received them from antiquity before us. We may add too much, or not enough, of seemingly relevant evidence; other difficulties that arise in analogical criticism will be explored in chapter 7.

The question of Chaucer's audience, those upon whom allegory and irony made their original demand to be understood, is a hard historical question, harder for us than for our Elizabethan predecessors, who found relevant "medieval" analogies comparable to some of our own. The following brief sketch is intended simply to suggest kinds of critical historicism relevant to other dimensions of the "waning of the Middle Ages," which will then be set aside, because they do not lead to adequate answers to the questions all to some extent share: how were the *Canterbury Tales*, the dream-visions, and *Troilus and Criseyde* read in Adam the Scrivener's laborious first copies? As Skelton's epigraph says, "By his readers an author receives an amplification of his little poem."

Historicity in Interpretation: Renaissance and Modern Analogies

Roger Ascham, John Fox, and many ardent sixteenth-century reformers read Chaucer's anticlerical satire as prophetic of the dawn to come. Modern literary Marxists, armed with a secular theory of history, reread Chaucer, Langland, and the sayings of John Ball, and examine medieval sermon literature and fabliaux, seeking to go beyond the context of doctrinal heresies and schismatic struggle in the medieval Church in order to find economic and social tensions, and emergent scepticism, in the State outside the Church. Gabriel Harvey, Dr. John Dee, and other Elizabethan humanist intellectuals were fascinated by Chaucer's knowledge of alchemy, magic, and the stars; modern Freudian and Jungian critics use psychohistorical techniques to penetrate unconscious symbolic structures, in water imagery, animal figures, and conventional dream vision poems, holding as a constant—or perhaps unaware of— the traditional Latin literary formulae that connect medieval dreams, for example, not to poetic identities but to classical antiquity, formulae ultimately traceable, perhaps, to primitive shamanism. (The idea of the flight of the mind through the universe, for example, was a common-place in classical literature known long before Macrobius's version of Cicero's *Dream of Scipio,* where Lewis traced it, in Homer, Pindar, Plato's *Theatetus* and *Republic,* Euripides, Xenophon, Horace, and Ovid's *Fasti.*)[1] Spenser and his annotator "E.K." were strongly affected by the medieval image of an archaic, fallen world; modern literary historians, more cautiously following Huizinga, point to the terrors of the age, the Black Death, mystical hermits and cults, to authenticate prevalent literary and artistic themes of *danse macabre* and *contemptus mundi,* in which are seen the abnegation and disintegration of the self.

Each partial view corroborates, but does not quite match, the others' attempt to distinguish "medieval" from Renaissance. But were the later medieval centuries, I wonder, in fact more chaotic and terrifying, more violent and haunted by witches, than the sixteenth? Giordano Bruno, who belonged to the select London intellectual circle of Sidney, Fulke Greville, and Elizabeth's Dr. Dee in the early 1580's, was burned at the stake in 1600 at Geneva. Were the Wars of Religion less, or more dis-ruptive and inducive of scepticism, than the Babylonian Captivity, the Great Schism, and the periodic *chevauchées* across the north of France, which became in retrospect the Hundred Years' War? The decadence of every age appalls its moralists; the *psychomachia,* as Mircea Eliade and Geoffrey Kirk have shown, is a topos of preclassical antiquity. We shall have difficulty distinguishing Chaucer's audience, and his Renaissance reader, by highlighting as typically "medieval" or "Re-naissance" what is, in fact, commonplace.

Deliberate enlargement, "highlighting," is perhaps equally helpful and harmful for literary history. Brilliant theoretical simplifications give us the sense of discovering light in darkness, an escape from his-

1. See the citations in Roger M. Jones, "Posidonius and the Flight of the Mind," *Classical Philology* 21(1926): 97 ff.

torical ignorance, but where there is overlap and contradiction, as in interpreting any transitional period, obscurity remains. From the middle of the twelfth century to the end of the sixteenth, the vague chronological boundaries for the beginning of Renaissance consciousness and the final decay of the Middle Ages, major events and personalities cast shadows over more minute particulars: the subtler shifts in attitude, hardly worth mention in the chronicles, which coalesce, and collectively comprise change. It is worth examining minor alterations in literary conventions in the poems themselves, as they cumulatively become taken for granted, in search of evidence that mutation is occurring, or an older model is gradually becoming obsolete. The great medieval themes of plague and apocalypse retain their power, and it is of course also true that in each reign, from the fourteenth to the sixteenth century, men were increasingly conscious of the immediate past as a "transitional" era. But so is every age, except the first and the last, and on literary evidence alone one could argue that the Middle Ages were not so much more naive, chiliastic, or apocalyptically mindful of human sin and despair than the eras of Spenser, Bunyan, or Swift. Huizinga's vivid periodization of the fifteenth century as an age of blood and roses distorts both the fourteenth and the sixteenth, and overdramatizes the Dance of Death as a dominant cultural symbol. On the contrary, to right the balance, it is equally likely that medieval poetry was as rich in satire and innovations in irony and comedy as its Renaissance posterity. From this point of view, what men laughed at in private, we may come somewhat closer to Chaucer's audience than through the public record of sensational events.

The Appeal to the Medieval Reader

Medieval allegory and romance are already beginning to develop new modes and variations by the beginning of the fourteenth century, in the increasingly sophisticated uses of poetic irony, to undermine the illusion of serious treatment of traditional themes, and to complicate the treatment of affirmed beliefs.

> This storie is also trewe, I undertake,
> As is the book of Launcelot de Lake,
> That wommen holde in ful greet reverence.
>
> [B² 4401–03]

So, in an aside, remarks the Nun's Priest, one of Chaucer's most enigmatic moralists.[2] In a parallel allusion, the prolix occupatio of the Squire,
the ironic attitude is more difficult to assess, because it suggests a different kind of ambivalence toward Lancelot's romance: the tone is not
dry, and not sceptical, but rather the youthful hyperbole characteristic
of the Squire, unwittingly self-satirized:

> Who koude telle yow the forme of daunces
> So unkouthe, and swiche fresshe contenaunces,
> Swich subtil lookyng and dissymulynges
> For drede of jalouse mennes aperceyvynges?
> No man but Launcelot, and he is deed.
> Therfore I passe of al this lustiheed;
> I sey namoore, but in this jolynesse
> I lete hem, til men to the soper dresse.
>
> [F, 283–90]

If Chaucer gently ridicules the Squire's enthusiasm for romance, he
travesties both romance sentiment and the Petrarchan conceits of the
balade in *Rosemunde* in the conventional first-person singular:

> Nas never pyk walwed in galauntyne
> As I in love am walwed and ywounde,
> For which ful ofte I of myself devyne
> That I am trewe Tristam the secounde.
> My love may not refreyde nor affounde;
> I brenne ay in an amorous plesaunce.
>
> [17–22]

The complex ironic modulations in Chaucer are of course not unique,
nor are they restricted to comedy and satire in medieval poems. The
hammering ironies in *Piers Plowman*, and *Sir Gawain and the Green Knight*'s
extraordinary delicacies of tone are well enough known to support the
case that allegorical irony and ambiguity are not the exception, but
more and more becoming the rule. Our difficulty lies in determining the
degree of complicity of the medieval audience, the extent to which
ironies now apparent to us were perceived then as "intended." The later
Renaissance reader, for whom all medieval poetry was increasingly
difficult and remote, will not be considered here except indirectly, as the
inheritor of the role of the audience.

2. For an interpretation of this tale and Spenser's *Muiopotmos*, see Judith Anderson, " 'Nat
Worth a Boterflye,' " *Journal of Medieval and Renaissance Studies* 1 (1971): 89–106.

Thus, in addition to the silent text are the secondary unstated assumptions, the ground of the reader's agreement to differentiate subtle *significatio*—hyperbole, understatement, puns, structural wit in juxtaposition, reversal, sudden interruption—and the reader's implicit comprehension of the serial hierarchy of meanings in *allegoria*. The poet tacitly controls the fiction making process. He attempts to determine how his fiction should be read, but the poet's control is never absolute, and his autonomy breaks at the point where his reading becomes silent. The essential element in allegorical irony (*pronuntiatio*) is taken over by the reader. In all ambiguity, open questions remain open, *de facto*, for the poet cannot explain his implied meaning without literally destroying it: the reader's wit is indispensable for his own wit to work.

The "ye" addressed in later medieval poetry is simultaneously an audience of listeners and a reader. The conceptions of a real "audience" of persons and of an ideal "reader" are both equally abstract, in Whitehead's sense, and necessarily subjective. They are as unique to each poem as the voice of its narrator, which is their definitive source. The reader addressed, or the listeners urged to "heed well," are reflexive of the speaker and imagined by the poet as the third dimension of the fiction. The allegorical agents or mimetic characters addressed within a narrative exist in secondary reality, in time and space which are devised, elastic, and absolute, whereas the poet's ultimate audience is relative and indeterminate, changing in time and place, in each subsequent individual reading of the poem. There are formulae for establishing the sphere of reference of a fiction, as in Bunyan's blunt "I laid me down in that place to sleep, and / behold, I dreamed a dream." But every poem sets forth its own dimensions, which only the most generalized theory can explain. For allegorical ironies—which "affirm and deny at the same time"—as for all forms of *ironia* and *significatio*, only the uncertainty principle holds in every case: verification can never be absolute, because in the very act of apprehension of the evidence, the observer has intervened. In physics, subjectivity is a variable. In poetry, the reader is a construct of the poem and subject to the same constraints in interpretation that apply to the imagined speaker, the "I" who addresses "ye."

Medieval Oral Formulae: The Listener and the Reader

Reading, in the Middle Ages, was probably more often than not a public activity, or at least not silent. The famous story of Augustine

(*Confessions*, 6.3) watching Ambrose reading to himself silently, expresses wonder: "You could see his eyes move, but you could hear nothing." In the twelfth century and thereafter, however, it becomes possible to imagine readers as a silent audience, an abstraction. At first the audience of "readers" was a clerical and courtly elite; many of the jongleurs were themselves illiterate, as were many priests. Both the higher clergy and the poets frequently denounce failures in memory and improvisations committed by humbler men, as well as bewail the circulation of imperfect texts.

The uses of the apostrophe to the audience the poet is addressing in the admonitory formulae for beginning and ending poems (invocation, denial of authority, the modesty topos) begin to develop and change in the period just before and immediately after the invention of printing. The existence of large commercial scriptoria in the thirteenth and fourteenth centuries implies not only private ownership of manuscripts, but also silent reading, in the earlier process of copying texts. However, printed editions, estimated as between three and five hundred copies, on average,[3] made possible multiple copying and individual possession of books on a scale unimaginable before 1450. When Caxton addresses the future reading public in the prologues and epilogues he provides for his and his authors' books, he is facing the new, unknown audience of strangers, which expanded the traditional outer dimension of the private lyric, the most personal confession, and emotional visions and prayers.[4] In antiquity and in the Middle Ages, men's thoughts were "published," but mechanical "publication" brought about growth of such magnitude that quantitative change became qualitative. Just as the accidental luck of Columbus changed the conception of the size and shape of the ocean and the earth, by 1500 printing had already begun to alter irreversibly the conceptions of the relations that may obtain between minutiae, the poetic "I" and "ye."

The psychological dimension of the imagined audience is as critical a concept in medieval poems as it is in later ages, and no less difficult to rediscover and evaluate than the speaker who professes to invoke his muse, address his audience, or allow himself to be overheard. Conditioned by print and silent reading, and highly aware of historical con-

3. See H. S. Bennett, *English Books and Readers, 1475–1557* (Cambridge, Eng., 1952), pp. 224 ff.

4. See W. J. B. Crotch, ed., *The Prologues and Epilogues of William Caxton, EETS* 176 (London, 1928, repr. 1956) for texts of Caxton's editorial introductions.

ditioning and limitation, modern criticism has become ingenious in attempting to compensate for known bias and inevitable ignorance, especially in the face of ironies. And, as some modern agnostics remain sadly convinced of original sin, without any hope of redemption, so medievalists, conscious of the inscrutability of even the monuments that remain undestroyed, seek to find in abstraction what the loss of the evidence denies: certainty as to "what it really means." Sensitivity, and analogues, have to be made evidence by default.

One way we may overcompensate in interpretation is by favoring "oral" aspects of both speaker and audience in medieval poetry, attributing effects and patterns of hypothetical intention to "oral delivery," which occasionally begins to seem a configuration of mind, as "black letter" seemed to be an aspect of Middle English for the eighteenth century (to Urry's incensed critics, "Chaucer *wrote* black letter"). Of course, the public reading of poems is one dimension of medieval poetry, and an aspect to be considered in poetics, for which there is abundant contemporary evidence. But Chrétien de Troyes describes ladies as his readers, "in their chambers," in the 1160's,[5] more than two centuries before Chaucer's Monk offers a life of St. Edward (*Or ellis, tragedies | Of which I have an hundred in my celle*), and the Nun's Priest mocks the ladies' love for Chretien's *Lancelot*. Chaucer's self-portraits as a solitary reader are a cliché; the Clerk, and the Miller's Nicholas, who also read in bed, counterbalance the reading aloud of Jankyn's Book to the Wife of Bath, and the "Siege of Thebes" in *Troilus*. Like Dante's Letter to Can Grande and the *Convivio*, the formulaic clues to the "oral tradition" can be overinterpreted, in criticism or in defense of digressive poetic structure, encyclopaedic narrative, and "borrowing" of conventions in medieval fiction. As C. M. Bowra observed of the impact of Parry's discoveries of the Homeric oral formulae,

> A literate poet composes with single words which he chooses for their individual worth to him, and we judge him by his choice and combination of them. A formulaic poet composes with formulae, and it is by his choice and combination of them that he is judged.

5. Ritchie Girvan, "The Medieval Poet and His Public," in C. L. Wrenn and G. Bullough, eds., *English Studies Today* (Oxford, 1951), p. 90: "Gaimar wrote L'Estorie des Engleis at the request of Constance, wife of Ralph Fitz Gislebert, his patroness, and tells us that an Anglo-Norman poet, David, wrote a metrical history of Henry I by order of Adelaide of Louvain, which Constance valued so highly that she paid a mark of silver for a transcript to read in her private chamber."

A new combination of old formulae may lead to an entirely un-
foreseen result; many formulae change their tone with the context,
and something new may always emerge.[6]

Such modern wisdom is affirmed by the narrator of *Troilus*, speaking of
the old formulae of love, and of poetry, to his double audience:

> Ek scarsly ben ther in this place thre
> That have in love seid lik, and don, in al,
> For to thi purpos this may liken the
> And the right nought, yet al is seid, or schal;
> Ek som men grave in tree, some in ston wal,
> As it bitit; but syn I have bigonne,
> Myn auctour shal I folwen, if I konne.
>
> [II. 43–49]

The poet of *Troilus* is speaking as a writer, by the implication of parchment and ink (*som men grave in tree, some in ston*), who is engaged in re-
creating the illusion of his lovers' speech to his imaginary audience of
lovers, whose sympathies he needs:

> Ye knowe ek that in forme of speche is chaunge
> Withinne a thousand yeer, and wordes tho
> That hadden pris, now wonder nyce and straunge
> Us thinketh hem, and yet thei spake hem so,
> And spedde as wel in love as men now do;
> Ek for to wynnen love in sondry ages,
> In sondry londes, sondry ben usages.
>
> And forthi if it happe in any wyse,
> That here be any lovere in this place
> That herkneth, as the storie wol devise,
> How Troilus com to his lady grace,
> And thenketh, "so nold I nat love purchace,"
> Or wondreth on his speche or his doynge,
> I noot; but it is me no wonderynge.
>
> [II. 21–35]

As I shall describe it in chapter 7, the definitive dimension of the *Troilus*
narrator is his dependence on the written source, his *olde book*, whose
composite texture of *auctors* (Boccaccio, Dante, "Lollius") is known to
none but the poet himself. The narrator's autonomy lies in his inter-

6. C. M. Bowra, *Homer* (Cambridge, Eng., 1972), p. 29.

mediary role between the book and the audience, the fictive "ye" and *thre, in this place,* who may or may not approve or understand his poem. The interpretation of paradox is beyond the narrator's power to control; his ironic attempts to control the reading of *Troilus* are a source of the poem's great ambivalence.

The various modern oral–formulaic perspectives, which renew the Renaissance association of Chaucer with Homer, as well as the native emphasis on the "English tradition" of Germanic *scops,* and the structuralists' primitive configurations of poetic ritual and symbol, all presuppose an originally illiterate audience, which casts a glow of power on the poet. Such analogues are inadequate in several ways, but they are no worse than Huizinga's "violent tenor of life," or the patronizing attitude of earlier apologists for "the Medievals," who condescend to both poets and audiences, conceiving them in terms that suggest manuscript miniatures. For example, C. S. Lewis described the audience of *Troilus,* listening "like children looking at a landscape picture, and wanting to know what happens to the road after it disappears into the frame."[7] In a more recent popular account of *The Discarded Image,* Lewis says

> In the medieval, we are at first hardly aware of a poet at all. The writing is so limpid and effortless that the story seems to be telling itself. . . . The characteristically medieval imagination . . . is not . . . transforming, like Wordsworth's, nor penetrative, . . . like Shakespere's. It is a realising imagination. . . . The efficient cause [of vivid narrative] surely was their devout attention to their matter and . . . confidence in it. They are not trying to heighten it or transform it. It possesses them wholly. Their eyes and ears are steadily fixed upon it, and so—perhaps hardly aware how much they are inventing—they see and hear what the event must have been like.

The poets, and by implication the readers, thus envisaged are characterized by a childlike credulity in fable, which is at odds with the complex prescriptive rhetorical theory quoted in other contexts as the "[medieval] impulse at work" in naive and digressive allegory, "the love of the labyrinthine." These "Medievals" are innocent, clever children only if we ignore what the poems are about.[8]

7. "What Chaucer Really Did to *Il Filostrato*," first published in *Essays and Studies, 17* (Oxford, 1932).

8. C. S. Lewis, *The Discarded Image* (Cambridge, Eng., 1970), pp. 205–06, 208, 210. Per-

The frequency of allusions to the illuminated frontispiece of the Corpus Christi manuscript (ca. 1450) of *Troilus and Criseyde* in the criticism of the past twenty-five years suggests two strong trends in "historical" authentication in interpreting Chaucer's irony, which diverge from the same point, and envision the role of the poet vis à vis his audience in quite different terms. On the one hand, the image of Chaucer reading aloud provides suggestive clues to the style of the narrator and the expectations of his courtly audience, waiting in the garden to be given pleasure and instruction by a subservient figure, the "licensed entertainer" whom the elegant court of Richard II regard with tolerant affection. The other reading of the picture sees the lectern from which the poet speaks as, allegorically, a pulpit, and instead of stressing the cultural history of the aristocratic romance, emphasizes instead the narrator as moral philosopher. The ambiguities in the satiric substrata of allegorical irony in *Troilus* then reveal, "properly read," admonition and mockery of courtly romantic themes, warnings only ostensibly delivered to please the aristocratic audience. In this case, neither poet nor reader can be considered naive, for both must equally discount the literal level of the poem as chaff. Thus, not Boccaccio, Chrétien, and Jean de Meung, but Innocent III, Augustine, and the Fathers are sought as truer authorities for interpretation. Boethius serves either case.

The visual image of the poet in performance, whether he be seen as

---

haps because I have not understood him well, I cannot reconcile three statements Lewis makes concerning Chaucer's originality and his use of authorities in reference to *Troilus*: 1) "The distinction between history and fiction cannot, in its modern clarity, be applied to medieval books, or to the spirit in which they were read" (*Discarded Image*, p. 179); 2) "The poem as we now have it cannot be attributed to a single author" [of Chaucer's reworking of Boccaccio] (*ibid.*, p. 210); 3) "The statement that he is taking something from his sources is . . . almost a proof that he is inventing" (*Allegory of Love*, p. 185, n.1; cf. *Discarded Image*, p. 210). Neither of the first two dicta can be true in the light of the third, which seems to me self-evidently so. While Chaucer's originality cannot be measured by "subtracting one poem from another" (Muscatine, *French Tradition*, p. 124), it is notable that Boccaccio uses the formula of authority only twice, as a perfunctory aside: *Il Filostrato*, I, 46 and III, 90. Chaucer's elaborate and complex manipulations of the formulae *as the boke seyth / myn auctor seyth* are a conspicuous element in the allegorical irony of *Troilus*. The narrator uses the *boke* to make significant maneuvers where none are apparently needed, to supply answers for non-questions, and he struggles to find complicated solutions to seemingly simple problems. It is not unanimously agreed that "what Chaucer did to *Il Filostrato*" was thoroughly to "medievalize it." The questions raised by the *olde bokes* imply profound awareness of the distinctions between history and fiction, and the attribution of the *Troilus* to a single author is as certain as Malory's for the *Morte Darthur*. These issues are discussed in ch. 7.

admonishing or entertaining a sophisticated elite, is a powerful one, which in effect diverts attention, as do Chaucer's narrators themselves, from the fact that the poet is the author of a fiction and neither a jongleur nor a priest. It is Chaucer the poet whom the illuminator of the manuscript posthumously memorialized for the duke of Gloucester, just as Froissart and Christine de Pisan are pictured on contemporary manuscripts presenting their works in bound volumes to their patrons. Froissart kneels before the duke of Burgundy, and Christine kneels before the French queen, with the book in outstretched hands. There is no ambiguity in either image that the transmission of the *Chroniques* and the poems is not chiefly written, however often both books must have been read aloud. The various poetic identities suggested by stress on oral presentation—the court entertainer, obsequious diplomat, and covertly sermonizing satirist—magnify one pose, and in effect simplify the ambiguity of Chaucer's speakers and his audience. The result arbitrarily reduces both his artistic autonomy and his originality to levels misleadingly close to those which he satirizes himself in the daisy-picking Dreamer and the virtually inarticulate Pilgrim.

In *Troilus and Criseyde*, Chaucer probed more deeply than any of his contemporaries, except Langland, the indeterminate depths of ironic implication, chiefly by means of his surrogate voice, appealing constantly for understanding from the lovers who ultimately "read" the double meaning of his *tragedye*, but who are tacitly held back from interpretation while the narrative is being unfolded for them. The audience and the Narrator, and the old books on which he constantly relies for the truth in *Troilus and Criseyde*, extend the limits of medieval secular poetry as far as Dante extended the sacred cosmos in the *Comedy*. Both poems revolutionized the possibilities for the vernacular. As a reflexive dimension of the poem, the imaginary audience perfected in *Troilus* will be discussed further in the later history of the poem and its Renaissance imitation in chapter 7. The *Canterbury Tales* epitomize as well some of the possible manipulations of the imaginary audience, envisaged by a speaker, to which we will now briefly turn.

The Canterbury Pilgrims: Performance and Audience

The device of the Pilgrim poet subordinated by his characters in the *Canterbury Tales* is the brilliant outcome of Chaucer's earlier experiments with conventions: comic identity, suppressed power, and the denial of art. In the earlier dream visions, the poem evolves suddenly, through the agency of fantasies called up by the power of a pivotal book.[9] In *Troilus and Criseyde*, the narrator serves as mediator between the *historial* narrative and the audience, both of which are greater than he—the book for its assumed veracity, the audience for its creation of the meaning received through his agency. The meaning is what "ye loveres" learn. In the *Canterbury Tales*, Chaucer plays the game of storyteller of his thirty storytellers, in a more complicated set of fictional perspectives than he had hitherto attempted. His speakers are all also listeners.

Each poem envisages its own readers, who, ideally, would be under the poet's perfect power to control, alert to his cues and sympathetic but unable to anticipate him or to consider alternatives. The ideal audience, be it reader or listener, is wholly subservient to the poet's authority. The Pardoner, for example, conjures up for himself such an audience for his sample sermon, in the imagined congregation he induces to buy his wares by the charisma of his imagery of the damned. The Pardoner describes how he masters his audiences—"them"—by playing on their guilt and fear of exposure, their vulnerability to judgment, and need to protect themselves; "they" always easily yield, comply with the ritual, the acceptance of which protects him. In exposing the fraudulent Pardoner to his humiliation at the hands of the secondary audience, the fictional pilgrims, Chaucer addresses his third audience, inviting them to appreciate their superiority to both of the audiences within the fiction, the credulous and the cruel, and to witness the defeat of the Pardoner's mysterious power to enslave. Each invites the reader to see the illusion of power broken, and in so doing, exerts his own power over the reader's response. These are continuing tensions in the *Canterbury Tales*, within the field of illusion where the poet, narrator, pilgrims, and reader contend in the task of interpretation.

A variation, the triple audience, is created by the Wife of Bath in her imaginary conversations with her old husbands, interrupted by the fictional audience of Friar, Pardoner, and Summoner. The paired interludes prepare for the *flytyng* to come, in which each *Tale* imagines the listening adversary as protagonist, and employs the audience as a weapon to wound the opponent, finally enlisting its agency to expel the victim, in contempt. Like the Pardoner, both Friar and Summoner are presented as fearful and masterful men in terms of powerful language. The Friar is a seductive and insinuating confessor: *In alle the orders foure*

9. See the extended study of Robert Payne, *The Key of Remembrance* (New Haven, (1968).

is noon that kan | So muchel of daliaunce and fair langage. The drunken Summoner retains the potent verbal curse of his writs, even reduced to three magic words: *Ay 'Questio quid iuris' wolde he crie.*[10]

The dramatic ironies of the *Canterbury Tales* manipulate many such double audiences. The literal levels involve the audience of thirty-odd performers within the fiction, enacting the struggle for control over one another in verbal contests, which the narrator reenacts ironically for the outer audience, breaking the illusion by frequent asides. Chaucer the Pilgrim takes his audience into his confidence: *And eek ye knowen wel how that a jay | Kan clepen 'Watte' as wel as ken the pope.* His comments and apostrophes, like Dante's warnings to the reader to attend the *allegoria*, in effect call attention to the artifice itself.[11] The listening "ye" whom the Pilgrim addresses are invited into complicity in the fiction, and to share his own fictional deference to authority: we would agree, he suggests,

[THE PARDONER.] He was in chirche a noble ecclesiaste.

[THE WIFE OF BATH.] She was a worthy womman al hir lyve;

[THE SHIPMAN.] And certeinly he was a good felawe.

[THE MONK.] And I seyde his opinion was good.
    What sholde he studie and make hymselven wood
    Upon a book in cloystre alwey to poure,
    Or swynken with his handes, and laboure,
    As Austyn bit? How shal the world be served?

The third, outermost audience, the reader of the book of *Tales*, is not under the Pilgrim's control, but is a witness, observing him playing a minor role within the fictional construct. The interpretations of the *Tales* given by the retrospective Pilgrim are distinct from the reactions of the speakers of the *Tales* and the Host to one another. Memory and commentary together form a composite fiction which invites allegorical interpretation, of apparent multiple discrepancies in intention, and moral ambiguities unresolved.

As a continued metaphor develops into *allegoria*, so a sustained series of such tropes develops into ironic discourse: allegorical *ironia* thus can become a role. Quintilian summarizes the figure briefly thus:

10. *Canterbury Tales,* A, 211–12; A, 646.
11. See Leo Spitzer, "The Addresses to the Reader in the *Commedia,*" *Italica* 32 (1955), 143–65.

In the figurative form of irony, the speaker disguises his entire meaning, the disguise being apparent rather than confessed. For in the trope [the single word], the conflict is purely verbal, while in the figure [sentences, paragraphs, whole works], the meaning and sometimes the whole aspect . . . conflicts with the language and the tone of voice [*pronuntiatione*] adopted. Nay, a man's whole life may be colored with irony, as was the case with Socrates, who was called an ironist because he assumed the role of an ignorant man, lost in wonder at the wisdom of others.[12]

If Plato's presentation of Socrates' ironic detachment, his innocent double entendres, and his infinite capacity to doubt be contrasted with Chaucer's development of his naive truth seeker—his "Geffrey"—we see the relative clarity of philosophical doubt against the banal simplicity of self-satire. In Plato, Socrates' witty friends are always discomfited and admit defeat, whereas the Chaucerian narrator, obscured by comic disguise, is at the mercy of powers apparently beyond his control. His fictions are more powerful, more ambiguous, than his self-deprecating explanations. It is left to the verdict of the reader to imagine and ascertain the whole ironic narration, composed of staged and spoken parts, in which the narrator participates. Like Plato's, the poet's detachment is virtually complete.

Within the fiction, the Pilgrim refers to the *Tales* as his book, in the process of developing his ambivalent role as servant, rather than master of the fiction:

> He nolde his wordes for no man forbere,
> But tolde his cherles tale in his manere.
> M'athynketh that I shal reherce it heere.
> And therfore every gentil wight I preye,
> For Goddes love, demeth nat that I seye
> Of yvel entente, but for I moot reherce
> Hir tales alle, be they bettre or werse,
> Or elles falsen som of my mateere.
> And therfore, whoso list it nat yheere,
> Turne over the leef and chese another tale;
> For he shal fynde ynowc, grete and smale,

---

12. Quintilian, *Institutes* IX, ii, 44–47, trans. W. E. Butler, *The Institutes of Oratory* (Cambridge, Mass., 1953). In *The Word Irony and its Context, 1500–1755*, (Durham, N. C., 1961), Norman Knox reviews later interpretations of Cicero's and Quintilian's terms.

> Of storial thyng that toucheth gentillesse,
> And eek moralitee and hoolynesse.
> Blameth nat me if that ye chese amys.
> The Millere is a cherl, ye knowe wel this;
> So was the Reve eek and othere mo,
> And harlotrie they tolden bothe two.
> Avyseth yow, and putte me out of blame;
> And eek men shal nat maken ernest of game.
>
> [A 3170–86]

After the Prologue, the Pilgrim exerts no authority over the narrative, and it records, with increasing vividness, animosities and interruptions breaking the conventions of courtesy and order between speaker and audience. The telling contrast is, of course, with the balanced formal symmetries of the *Decameron*—ten speakers, ten days, a hundred Tales, with appropriate cadenzas which emphasize the firm, underlying structural plan. Boccaccio's various unities of social class, theme, and style create a set of relatively static tableaux; in the *Tales*, Chaucer dramatizes conflicts in the audience and in the tensions between what it wants and what it gets. The inadequacy of the speaker's art is pronounced and repeated when the Monk and "Chaucer" are cut off, the Pardoner is silenced, and *ad hominem* replies are made. At the outset, the Host assumes a major role as critic in his belligerent demands and clumsy verdicts. The dynamic rhythm of the Fragments seems to be building on various strong reciprocities between speaker and audience. The pilgrims again and again resist the rhetorical persuasion of the greater tellers and deny the illusion of their power. The contest develops, proceeding from the Knight's romance (followed by its superb double parody in the *Miller's* and *Reeve's Tales*), to the astonishing arrival of the Canon and his Yeoman, in thematic fugues on kinds of illusion, the majority of which depend on the charisma of language itself to threaten and deceive. The *Tales* turn on the fundamental duplicity of words and the risks of playing with linguistic illusion. The Miller's climactic cry "Water!" and the Reeve's Cambridge yokels play on dialect and comic delivery (*pronuntiatio*); the Nun's Priest, Canon's Yeoman, and Manciple exploit credulity and misinterpretation; the *Tales* of the "marriage-group" respond in an echoing extended conversation. So too, the disparity between speaker's intention and hearer's understanding functions within the *Tales*, as in a larger sense it qualifies and undercuts the presentation of the whole by the naive Pilgrim to "ye," the reader to whom he must surrender and appeal for judgment. The ultimate revelation of this theme is the poet's *Retraction*, which envisions the symbolic reading of his whole life, the only judgment that matters to a Christian.

The *Canterbury Tales* flatter the worldly reader by exposing the narrator's intention and his incompetence simultaneously. He explains what he is trying to do and presents speakers far more artful than himself, whom he in turn silently undermines by devising their exposure through *ironia*, that which affirms and denies at the same time. Thus, the invented audience within the fiction provides a deceptive picture of the subordinate poet at the mercy of the "facts" (the mimetic journey) and of the pilgrims themselves, in constant verbal contest for *maistrye*, on a sharper and clearer level within the *Tales*. The Pilgrim suggests a critique of the *Tales*, but is himself subject in turn to the greater freedom of the audience outside the narrative, which, like the one within, agrees to grant the fiction more than face value. It is left to us, as in all forms of irony, to err or to "see," in making ultimately private judgments. In the lyric to Bukton, the "Wif of Bath" is at once her Jankyn's widow, she who routed the Friar, and Chaucer the Pilgrim's garrulous old dancer; she shifts from dramatis persona to ironic allegorical symbol simply in terms of the audience. As Bukton is advised to consult her, so the authority Chaucer exercises over her in her Prologue falls to the reader: her maker surrenders his autonomy, while preserving her ambiguity.

In one of his most "Chaucerian" comedies, *A Midsummer Night's Dream*, Shakspere extends the three-dimensionality of the imagined audience, and burlesques the role of the playwright–maker, in Peter Quince the carpenter's production of Pyramus's tragedy. The building of Wall out of a plank and finding a lantern for the Moon destroys the illusion of the play within the play and reexerts the external power of the playwright. For the audience is invited to imagine not itself, as spectators of the Theban tragedy, but the spectators of the inner audience, the duke of Athens and Hippolyta. Shakspere's extended dramatic illusion can enclose the dream world and the satyr play within the "real" world of Athens by a series of tacit agreements as to the fictionality of all speakers, which the audience in complicity accepts. As in the *Canterbury Tales*, the complicity of the audience then is the given, and while the poet has the power to fabricate, abbreviate, or distort the illusory "reality"—be he Peter Quince or Shakspere—he must share control over the meaning of his fiction with the audience. They are present to be pleased, persuaded, taught, and, also, to judge. As the reader submits to the poet, so the poet submits to the reader, and to time.

Since Socrates' playful undercutting of the pretensions of Ion, the double power of the poet as maker and seer has been contaminated: as public figures, poets are of philosophical suspicion and concern, ethical as well as aesthetic. To the artless question of whether an artist can make as "good" a table as a carpenter, Ion must concede that poetry is an illusion and that poets make lies. Unlike the "making" of Shakspere's Peter Quince, whose dramatic performance is temporal, the poetic lie outlives the poet. Horace paints an exhilarating satiric picture of the rhapsode, long haired and wild eyed, whose ecstatic excesses give poetry a bad name. He is hardly a threat, but the demonic voice may be. The question raised is anxiety over the disputed role poets should play in society—Plato's question—which implies power over the audience, and ethical responsibility. Horace's advice to the Pisos, while light in tone, is serious in intent: "Be sure, before you publish,"

> put your manuscript back in the closet, and keep it for nine years. One can always destroy what one has written, but a word once published can never be destroyed.[13]

Plato's *Ion* is relevant to Elizabethan, not medieval, poetry; but the basic issue of the poet's power, as I have argued in chapter 2, is a constant: explicit in Dante and Shakespere, implicit in Chaucer and Spenser. If Angus Fletcher is right, "the search for pure power is at the heart of all allegorical quests, and goes on in spite of its fundamental irrationality."[14] But the converse is the case in Chaucer's extraordinary rational refusals of power, his profoundly ambiguous ignorance, and his subservient deference to all "authority." The conversion of fear of power into respect for authority reflects the internalizing of control by various devices of symbolic reduction and compression. When these emerge in the rigid agencies of allegory, interpretation is predetermined, and agreements on meaning may finally be reached. The latent powers

13. Horace, *Ars Poetica*, ll. 388–90.
14. Fletcher, *Allegory*, p. 338.

of the modes of irony, however, give both poet and reader contending freedoms and protean power to transcend or destroy the illusion of truth in a fiction.

The ambiguity of the audience, "ye" and "thee," is potentially twice as great as that conferred by the indeterminate voice of the speaker. The poet may be addressing either the projected reality inside the fiction, or the contemporary audience, or both. The advantages of allegorical irony, in such fluid circumstantial possibilities, extend the medieval poet's freedom beyond the static, ladderlike correspondences of *litterae*, the literal meanings of words, and their various *figurae*. Within the continuum of the poem, he may introduce not only traditional figures like Natura or Dido, signifying by common agreement fecundity and suicidal passion, but also dynamic and elastic possibilities for re-creation such as the spellbound Dreamer of the *Book of the Duchess*, the ironically flawed Gawain, or Piers the Plowman. In foursquare personification, as little ambiguity as possible is allowed to infiltrate the fiction. Although we may ask of a fragment, is this dove Venus's or Mary's?, in larger contexts symbolic action is defined and delimited so that transmitted meanings will come through fully and clearly. As soon as allegorical irony arises, symmetry is threatened and the fiction is penetrated by the reader. He must pick through the chaff, or in Langland's finer image, remove the bitter bark for the sweet kernel within.[15] For allegorical irony, "that which affirms and denies at the same time," another kind of metaphor suggests itself. The medieval *speculum* is a symbolic image for an imaginary curving mirror, in which the audience could see the "narrator" and his "audience" in the fiction, whose surface separates the illusion from the contingent present. Subsequent readings of medieval poetry begin with fragments of a broken mirror.

The relations suggested between illusion and truth, and the ambivalent awareness of *ars poetica* as fiction, are the final elements to be considered in this investigation of Chaucerian ambiguity, which only the greater poets among his Renaissance successors learned to imitate, and attempted to surpass. *Auctoritee, the book seyth*, and *myn auctor*, terms which begin to fade and become archaisms after 1500, are the alternating third terms in the fictional contract that is established between

15.
> Als on a walnet, wiþoute is a biter barke,
> And aftir that biter barke, be the shel awaye,
> Is a kernille of conforte, kynde to restore (B xi. 251–53).

the medieval poetic "I" and the audience. The validity of the dream, the historicity of an event or a story, are established within certain conventional limits. These formulae too are open to ironies, like the clouds over the house of Aventure in the *Book of Fame* or any *Legends of Good Women.* Chaucer opens his Prologue to that poem with a Socratic invitation to believe the book—there is, after all, no other way to know —for what it might be worth:

> A thousand sithes have I herd men telle,
> That there is joye in hevene and peyne in helle,
> And I acorde wel that it be so:
> But natheles, this wot I wel also,
> That there ne is non that dwelleth in this contre,
> That eyther hath in helle or hevene ybe,
> Ne may of it non other weyes witen,
> . . . .
> But as he hath herd seyd, or founde it writen;
> But wherfore that I spak, to yeve credence
> To bokes olde and don hem reverence,
> Is for men shulde autoritees beleve,
> There as ther lyth non other assay by preve.
> For myn entente is, or I fro yow fare,
> The naked text in English to declare
> Of many a story, or elles of many a geste,
> As auctors seyn: leveth hem if yow leste!
>
> [G. Prol. 1–9; 81–88]

V

Auctoritee and Modesty:
Chaucerian Denials of Art

> The novelistic fiction of a written source (*li livre*, in Marie de France), which should testify to the veracity of the author, while his mind is left free to fabulate, requires only an indication of the book's existence. One does not need to know the source of a Source.
>
> Leo Spitzer

Spitzer's witty apothegm on Marie's *Fables* is clearly and broadly true of medieval vernacular fiction; *li livre* (like the formulaic *dicitur* of the Latin Fathers) adds an aura of authenticity to what would otherwise be only the word of an author. The "fiction of a written source" explains the omnipresent formulae, remnants of oral tradition, which fill minor medieval fiction with meaningless references to *myn auctor* and *the book seyth*, which become increasingly obsolete, and finally archaisms, in the later Renaissance. Trivial in themselves, stylistic conventions such as these become more significant when they are seen as elements in a larger pattern, the fable freely being formed in the mind of the author. Then their veracity and origin, whether or not the "source" is named, may become not only interesting, as in the case of Natura's gown, but indicative of how the fable may be read. One may need to know "the source of a Source."

The greater allegories reveal their patterns slowly, gradually opening up the latent meaning in figures of archaic simplicity. After we see the knight and the lady riding across the plain, we see that she is followed by a lamb; soon after the dreamer awakens in the dark wood, his path is blocked by a lion and a leopard. It is by means of dramatic and poetic treatment of symbols of power and symbolic authority that interpretation of *allegoria* and *ironia* is transmitted from the poet to the reader. To the degree that literary and figurative images of authority are ambiguous, the degrees of allegorical irony intended are deliberately obscured. The poet may tell us exactly what the lion and the lamb mean, as Bottom the Weaver reassures the Athenian ladies in Peter Quince's play, and perhaps many readers would prefer to be told.[1] Chaucer very frequently alludes to his *auctors* by name in both comic and serious contexts, but very rarely without a covering haze of irony. Chaucer's characterization and his deepening of the fictional context by means of allusions to authority and the modesty ploy are among his most subtle devices of style; but, like the play on superfluous final *-e* in rhyme and the metrical pratfalls of *Sir Thopas* (which some modern editors italicize to aid the reader), these aspects of Chaucerian irony also depend on an accurate text. In the case of the *Canterbury Tales*, the hazards of transmission were more severe than for any of the other major poems; the Elizabethan reader inherited fragments, restored to a semblance of unity. After 1400, the *Tales* had been variously reassembled, in copies of earlier copies; the integrity of their order, as well as of their language, was already disintegrating when Caxton made his first two attempts to edit them in 1478 and 1484. The efforts of sixteenth-century publishers, as will be seen in chapter 8, increased the confusion by rearrangements, added links, and new *Tales*. Nevertheless, even in these corrupt texts, in which the spurious and the genuine are jumbled together, the Chaucerian manipulation of medieval formulae is apparent and can be examined in the light of later imitation.

The *Canterbury Tales*: Allusion and Allegorical Irony

> lordynges alle, I yow biseche,
> If that yow thynke I varie as in my speche,
> As thus, though that I telle somwhat moore
> Of proverbes than ye han herd bifoore
> Comprehended in this litel tretys heere,
> To enforce with th' effect of my mateere,
> And though I nat the same wordes seye
> As ye han herd, yet to yow alle I preye
> Blameth me nat; for, as in my sentence,

1. Conventional marginal glosses, both scribal and authorial, annotate medieval vernacular as well as sacred Latin texts (*Glosynge is a glorious thyng, certeyn,* | *For lettre sleeth, so as we clerkes seyn*, as the Summoner's friar explains). The glossing of Gower's *Confessio Amantis* and Lydgate's *Troy Book* is fuller and more elaborate than the marginalia found in the Chaucer MSS, which later sixteenth-century editors adapt to supplementary annotation. See W. R. McCormick, *The Manuscripts of the Canterbury Tales* (Oxford, 1933) and John M. Manly and Edith Rickert, *The Text of the Canterbury Tales*, 8 vols. (Chicago, 1940).

Shul ye nowher fynden difference
Fro the sentence of this tretys lyte
After the which this murye tale I write.
And therfore herkneth what that I shal seye,
And lat me tellen al my tale, I preye.

[*Melibee*, B² 2142–56]

Chaucer's modest appeal to the authority of Harry Bailly and the pilgrims, in effect excusing and admitting the tedium of his proverbial *tretys lyte*, the *murye tale* of *Melibee*, uses the simple formulaic language of anonymous apology until the last line. Its fleeting reinforcement of the speaker's role as the teller of the interrupted *Sir Thopas* plays to the audience with a plea that makes his present serious tone equivocal. The *moral tale vertuous*, unlike those of *Mark, Mathew, Luc*, and *John*, which need no defense, is an evangelical sermon–debate on vengeance and nonviolence in more than nine hundred lines of bad prose. That *Melibee* is edifying is beyond question, and every possible means of explaining the allegory as it proceeds is repeated until there can be no mistake of the intended moral meaning. While Melibeus is away, his old foes break into his house, beat his wife, and wound his daughter Sophia,

wyth fyve mortal woundes in fyve sondry places,–/
this is to seyn, in hir feet, in hire handes, in
hir erys, in hir nose, and in hire mouth, and
leften hire for deed, and wenten awey.

[B² 2161–65]

The remainder of the *Tale* consists of the wisdom of the wife, Prudence (an oblique antitype to the Wife of Bath), who teaches her husband the meaning of forgiveness. In *Sir Thopas*, every nuance of medieval romance is parodied; in *Melibee*, the bottomless well of homiletic prose is plumbed. Taken together, the two *Tales* project the poet as if in a pair of carnival mirrors, one convex, the other concave; both images absurdly stretch and flatten their subjects, which are traditional themes worth serious treatment, the quest romance, the moral dilemma. The very strength of the model makes each a legitimate means for satire; but the allegorical irony is directed not at romance, nor wisdom, but *through* them, to the impotent poet who is unable to master his art. The preposterous *Sir Thopas* and stupifyingly prolix *Melibee* turn good subjects into bad art, in a grotesquely comic master performance whose illusion transmutes gold into dross.

The characterization of the Parson, whose only *lore* is *Cristes*, in the *General Prologue* bears no such signs of ironic intention, nor does his own Prologue equivocate. His sarcastic denunciation of poetic *geeste, rum, ram ruf, by lettre*, is entirely consonant with the strong lines of the Pilgrim's *effictio*, and his prose sermon is to be taken straight. The Parson is *nat textueel*, and puts himself *under the correccioun of clerkes*; as in the similar case of the Second Nun, the relation of speaker, *Tale*, and source of *auctoritee* is not ironic, but allegorically formal, systematic, and overtly didactic. Neither *Tale* supports Fletcher's hypothesis that "at the heart of any allegory will be found the conflict of authorities."[2] The conversion of St. Caecilia's Romans in the *Second Nun's Tale* is not a true psychomachia between Satanic powers and her divine light; when Almachius, the prefect, asks *"Ne takestow non heede of my power?"*, it is purely human power to enforce the social code of sacrifice to Jupiter, against which Cecilia's *auctor*, Christ, makes her own sacrifice mock the merely human:

> "Youre might" quod she, "ful litel is to dreede,
> For every mortal mannes power nys
> But lyk a bladdre ful of wynd, ywys."
>
> [G 437–40]

The "conflict of authorities" seems to work at the same relatively simple level of symmetry in the *Physician's Tale*, where the dogmatic exempla of sacred and profane relationships link father–child, master–slave, governess–youth, judge–accused, in an apparently clear pattern of true and false dichotomies. The illusion of order is here, however, undermined ironically, not by Virginius's sacrifice of his innocent daughter, but by the uprising of the mob in the courtroom who seize authority and try to kill their judge. The *Physician's Tale* is further complicated by the ironies of his portrait in the *General Prologue* (11. 411–444). The list of fifteen medical and scientific texts, and his dubious *magyk natureel*, the sources of his power, are evaluated by the one book which suffices for the Parson's authority and which the Physician is said not to read: *His studie was but litel on the Bibel*.

The invocation of authorities by allusion is a means of characterizing within the *Tales* analogous to the hints Chaucer drops in the *General*

2. Fletcher, *Allegory*, p. 22.

Prologue: the Clerk's favorite *Aristotle* shifts subtly to his "pseudo-Petrarch"; the Man of Law's massive catalog of casebooks anticipates his case against "Chaucer," the canon of his poems. The Monk's preference for the new world of experience over the old text of Augustine deepens the irony of his conception of *tragedye*, of which he has *an hundred in my celle*:

> Tragedie is to seyn a certeyn storie,
> As olde bookes maken us memorie,
> Of hym that stood in greet prosperitee
> And is yfallen out of heigh degree
> Into myserie, and endeth wrecchedly.
> And they ben versified communely
> Of six feet, when men clepen *exemetron*.
> In prose eek been endited many oon,
> And eek in meetre, in many a sondry wyse.
> Lo! this declaryng oghte ynogh suffisc.

[B² 3162–72]

Variations on the straightforward formulae associating speaker and sources of authority are common features of every *Tale*, for invocations of authority are of course structural components and evidence in all kinds of debate; a citation is an assertion of power. The *auctors* underline Theseus's Boethian answer to Egeus's proverbs, and Nicholas's and the clerk of Orleans' tables of stars and tides in the *Knight's*, *Miller's* and *Franklin's Tales*. The comparison of sources and *auctoritees* balances the comic *debats* between Chantecleer and Pertelotte, Pluto and Proserpine, and unbalances Dorigen's self-torturing lament to Fortune in the tales of the Franklin, the Merchant, and the Nun's Priest. In these contexts the speaker's characteristic allusions to "authority" need not in themselves be equivocal; the implications of any allusion may be made to seem suspect by other means. The *auctors* and sources cited are usually the sources used.

As has been suggested, the citation of a named source for verification is basically a more sophisticated and concrete version of the standard minstrel formula (*myn auctor seith*) for padding a line, or making an easy rhyme, without making a commitment to anything more than a platitude. Oakden's study of alliterative poetry lists roughly one hundred variants of the tag *as þe boke tells / says*, and catalogs more than 220 examples of its occurrence in poems from early Middle English to the fifteenth century, starting with Wulfstan's *Homilees þaet þe bec seggað*.[3] In prose, the unobtrusive narrator in *Morte Arthure* cites *the Frensshe book* some seventy times, without irony and unselfconsciously; Malory's "author" is still using the old convention in order to alter the disbelief of his imaginary audience, to make the Arthurian world not less, but more credible. He is calling attention, not to its fictionality, but to its historicity, so he invites not "willing suspension of disbelief," but faith.[4] In Malory, the authority formula is still potent as a device for justification.[5]

Modesty Topoi in Chaucer and Lydgate

Variations of the authority formula may, however, become forms of allegorical irony. For example, occultatio, "insinuation, allusive suggestion, concealment," is a figure closely related to the more familiar modest demurral, occupatio, "denial of authority," "pointed refusal to mention"; occultatio is the recommended rhetorical device for foreshortening a narrative while preserving the illusion of amplitude, as well as veracity.

> But, sires, by cause I am a burel man,
> At my bigynnyng first I yow biseche,
> Have me excused of my rude speche.
> I lerned nevere rethorik, certeyn;
> Thyng that I speke, it moot be bare and pleyn.
> I sleep nevere on the Mount of Pernaso,
> Ne lerned Marcus Tullius Scithero.

3. J. P. Oakden, *Alliterative Poetry in Middle English, The Dialectal and Metrical Survey*, 2 vols. (Manchester, 1930–35; repr. in one vol., New Haven, 1968), pp. 387–89.

4. Cf. P. J. C. Field, *Romance and Chronicle* (London, 1970), p. 145.

5. Cf. Wordsworth's dream, *Prelude* V, 1–140, where he falls asleep by the sea reading *Don Quixote*, fusing his anxiety with the romances of the hallucinated Knight; Wordsworth's explanation of his dream's ambiguities (141–91), like Coleridge's for *Kubla Khan*, attempts to maintain the medieval dream-book convention, which becomes next, by metamorphosis, the "reality" of Browning's *The Ring and the Book*. Browning's research into the historicity of his "square old yellow book" established the Franceschini affair as Browning recreated it. Finding his imaginative liberty under conditions of utmost restraint in his ideal of "verisimilitude," Browning's justification of art is "That Art remains the one way possible/Of speaking Truth." The book becomes not "history," as Browning wanted it to be, but "an idealized reading of life," an allegory: "The thing's restorative/I' the touch and sight . . . word for word." See the commentary of W. C. DeVane, *A Browning Handbook*, 2d. ed. (New York, 1955), pp. 318–48.

Colours ne knowe I none, withouten drede,
But swiche colours as growen in the mede.
Or elles swiche as men dye or peynte.
Colours of rethoryk been to me queynte.

[F 716–26]

The Franklin's elegantly humble denial of art includes all three of
Cicero's names, and the Muses by metonymy; his flowers are *flores* by
both synechdoche and pun. Similarly, in Lydgate the modesty topos is
a stylistic trademark: his fictional narrators invariably claim to be
following plainly marked, well-known paths, and he pauses every
twentieth line, on average, to reiterate *myn auctor seith*, in repeated
ironic denial of his own worth:

For in makyng, [Chaucer] drank of the welle
Under Pernaso, that the Musis kepe:
On which hylle I myght never slepe,
Unnethe slombre, for which, alas, I pleyne.

[*Troy Book* III, 554–57]

The pedantic self-deprecation of both the Franklin and Lydgate's
narrator are equally fictitious and rhetorical, and both invite speculation on deceptive poetic artifice itself, and on the validity of their
claims of innocence.

A more interesting case of denial of authority is Lydgate's treatment
of the wedding of Oedipus in his *Siege of Thebes* (I, 817–46), in which
ironic refusal to elaborate (occupatio) and oblique allusion to an
auctor (occultatio) again combine. Here, the theme itself, the inces-
tuous wedding of Oedipus, is threatening:

I can not seyn nor mor thereof devise.
Demeth зour-silf that prudent ben and wise,
And Edippus hath among in mynde,
Of whom the weddyng, like as зe may fynde,
Vnhappy was and passing odious,
Ifortuned and vngracious.
I am wery more therof to write.
The hatful processes also to endyte
I passe ouer, fully of entent;
For ymeneus was not ther present,
Nor lucyna list not ther to shyne,

> Ne ther was none of the musys nyne
> By on accord to make melodye;
> For ther song not be heuenly Armonye
> Neither Clyo nor Calyope,
> On of the sustren in nombre thries thre,
> As they dyde whan philolidgye
> Ascendid vp hegh aboue the skye
> To be weddid this lady vertuous
> Vnto hir lord þe god mercurius;
> As Marcian ynamed de Capelle,
> In his book of weddyng can ʒou telle,
> Ther concludying in this mariage
> The poete, that whilom was so sage,
> That this lady, called sapience,
> I-wedded was vnto eloquence;
> As it sat wel, by heuenly purueaunce,
> Hem to be ioyned be knot of Aliaunce.
> But both two, sothly, of entente
> At the weddyng in Thebes were absent.

The same rhetorical tactics and strategic allusion express the contempt of Chaucer's Merchant for the disgusting marriage rites of January and May, in his brilliant occupatio:

> And certeinly, I dar right wel seyn this,
> Ymeneus, that god of weddyng is,
> Saugh never his lyf so myrie a wedded man.
> Hoold thou thy pees, thou poete Marcian,
> That writest us that ilke weddyng murie
> Of hire Philologie and hym Mercurie,
> And of the songes that the Muses songe!
> To smal is bothe thy penne and eek thy tonge,
> For to descryven of this mariage.
> When tendre youthe hath wedded stoupyng age,
> Ther is swich myrthe that it may nat be writen.
> Assayeth it yourself, than may ye witen
> If that I lye or noon in this matiere.

[E 1729–41]

The Merchant's contempt extends even to his *auctor* Martianus Capella

(*Hold . . . thy pees!*), and his denial of the power of art to *descryen swiche myrthe* pointedly scorns (by omission) the Miller's tale of the marriage of Alison and old John, the dotard husbands described by old Alice of Bath, and in effect satirizes all the authorities in his audience who have spoken of *swich myrthe* and *jolitee*. The Merchant's frequent allusions to the Wife form a running private mockery parallel to his *Tale's* profane parodies of the Song of Solomon, which extend the satire of *auctoritee* far beyond the immediate fictional context.

The contrast between Lydgate's expanded and Chaucer's condensed use of occultatio suggests the difference between the silent assertion of Chaucer's autonomy, by controlled refusal and multiple allusion, and Lydgate's voluble inability either to follow his *auctoritee* or to avoid its mastery of him. His savage irony, which Thomas Warton praised as "something Chaucer cannot surpass,"[6] is directed at the obscene marriage of Oedipus contaminating his *historiale* theme: he detours into the allegory of Martianus's "Wedding of Mercury," but cannot escape from his own conspiracy in the suppressed knowledge of the unspeakable. Fictionally he has become, in Tertullian's sense, incriminated, as both priest and poet. But the Merchant is not averse to describing his immoral wedding; Chaucer abbreviates the ceremony itself, and expands the detailed reenactment of the wedding night. The physical and concrete verisimilitude of the Merchant's rhetorical treatment of sex (with its pornographic allusion to *the cursed monk, daun Constantyn's . . . book De Coitu*) heighten the tensions between the Song of Songs and its singer, and the garden, framed by allusions to the *Romaunce of the Rose*, Priapus, and Pluto's rape of Proserpine. The Merchant's ironies employ both the inner and outer audiences, the pilgrims and the reader, whom Lydgate similarly affects to address, to fear, and to edify. The *Siege of Thebes* is awkwardly appended to the *Canterbury Tales* by its own Prologue, in which Lydgate attempts to maintain the fictional pretext, in his conversation with his grosser Harry Bailly, but his departure into the imaginary company is remarkable mainly for its self-conscious conjunction of fiction with fact.

> I answerde, my name was Lydgate,
> Monk of Bery nyȝ fyfty ȝere of age
> Come to this toune to do my pilgrimage,

6. Thomas Warton, *The History of English Poetry*, 2d. ed. (London, 1774), 2:51–100. Warton discusses Lydgate's style at length; his remark on "Oedipus" is in his *Observations of the Fairy Queene of Spenser* (1754), p. 229.

> As I haue hight, I haue therof no shame.
> "Daun Iohn," quod he, "wel broke ȝe ȝoure name!
>
> [Prol. 92–96]

The great difficulty in imitating Chaucerian ironic detachment is
clearly apparent in Lydgate's uses of his favorite topoi. Although it is
demonstrably different in kind, Henryson's later imitation of Chaucer's
narrative voice remained virtually undetected for two centuries;
Lydgate's surprisingly proud avowal of his own has been, since Warton,
to his disadvantage.

In the *General Prologue*, the Man of Law is described as a reluctant
speaker whose words are worth money and whose opinions are pro-
fessionally measured. His prologue changes the terms of the modesty
topos, and its inconsistencies suggest Chaucer's revisions still in progress. The last seven lines of the Man of Law's preliminary address vary
the "denial of the Muses":

> But of my tale how shal I doon this day?
> Me were looth be likned, douteless,
> To Muses that men clepe Pierides—
> *Methamorphosios* woot what I mene;
> But natheless, I recche noght a bene
> Though I come after hym with hawebake.
> I speke in prose, and lat hym rymes make.
>
> [B¹ 90–97]

The Man of Law's promise of "prose" must refer, of course, to a tale
other than the Constance legend, which is now certainly his. From
line 46 to line 90, the interpolated list of Chaucer's own works, *nat
worth a bene*, shifts self-parody away from outward satire and turns it
inward, toward a lighter comic mockery which is not immoral but sly,
impudent to the art of fiction itself. The Man of Law's occupatio, which
is again occultatio (deferring to other *auctors*), prolongs his narrative by
citing all the evidence for the impossibility of going on, the Chaucer
canon, and introduces "Chaucer the poet" as a contemptible rival into
the fiction, thereby inverting both the authority and modesty conventions at once. It is a trick, like a brilliant practical joke, which can be
played successfully but once.

> But natheless, certeyn,
> I kan right now no thrifty tale seyn

That Chaucer, thogh he kan but lewedly
On metres and on ryming craftily,
Hath seyd hem in swich Englissh as he kan
Of olde tyme, as knoweth many a man;
And if he have noght seyd hem, leve brother,
In o book, he hath seyd hem in another.
For he hath toold of loveris up and doun
Mo than Ovide made of mencioun
In his Episteles, that ben ful olde.
What sholde I tellen hem, syn they been tolde?

[B¹ 45–56]

Making the same point—there is nothing left to "make" since Chaucer ascended Parnassus—Lydgate affected simple irony, the deprecation of his own art. In the *Man of Law's Prologue*, Chaucer invites the audience to break the illusion, for the witty disparagement of "Chaucer's" old books calls attention to the fictionality of the Man of Laws, and of "Chaucer," and thus affirms the omniscience of the maker of all the pilgrims. It also risks a complex maneuver for the teller of *Thopas* and *Melibee*, which, as we have seen, he achieves by a second double-blind test of satire.

The Wife of Bath

The Chaucerian archetype of all ironic invocations of authority, and the antitype of the humble figure of the modesty topos, is the Wife of Bath. Modern criticism has rightly condemned those sentimental readers who regard the Wife as no more than a dear Old Bawd, comic but harmless, and who sympathize with the autobiographical "life" of her Prologue.[7] It is, however, equally simplistic and reductive, I think, to argue that she is not in any sense a "character," only an allegorical personification, an abstract argument about which, given the "sources" of her satire, there need be no further debate. Her character fuses, encompasses, and transcends the *Roman*'s Duenna and Juan Ruiz's Trotaconventos; she personifies Carnality (and, one might argue, subtypes of Gluttony, Avarice, Pride, and Sloth). Her diatribe em-

7. See e.g. D. W. Robertson, *A Preface to Chaucer* (Princeton, 1962), pp. 317–31; Bernard Huppé, *A Reading of the Canterbury Tales* (New York, 1964), pp. 107–35, 187–90, whose views contrast with those of Lumiansky, C. S. Lewis, and the followers of Kittredge, Lounsbury, et al.

bodies both medieval clerical misogyny, and the paradoxes of *Frauendienst*. All are true. "Who peynted the leon, tel me who?" *Men may devyne and glosen, up and doun*, but Alison is not reducible to an abstraction. The brilliant manipulations of her soliloquy, with its constantly shifting audiences and reiteration of the insistent *I* and *me* and *mine*, reaches out to the future (*Ye wise wives, that kan understonde | Thus sholde ye speke*), back into the past (*Thou, olde dotard, Sire olde fool*), and loses its way, while dominating the fictional stage and those who dare interrupt her. The heavy irony of her citations of Jerome and *Ptholome's Almagest* is leavened by the colloquial, vividly concrete images of cat and mouse, bread and red stockings, moths and wine, which are not arbitrary external ornaments of allegorical personification, but symbolic images unique to the Wife of Bath's identity. The symbolic dimensions of the Wife's Prologue magnify and distort the dominant sexuality that the *litterae* present as her theme. The inexhaustible energy and desire she manifests are sublimations more profound than the naturalistic egotism typified in the Miller's young Alison; the difference is not that between cat and kitten, but between the sense of touch and synaesthesia: sex is, in her, synergesis. The Wife's soliloquy on power simultaneously affirms and denies her freedom, for she is created by allegorical ironies, and is a tissue of allusions.

> But now to purpose, why I tolde thee
> That I was beten for a book, pardee!
>
> [D. 711–12]

The crisis of the action in the Prologue, her confrontation with Jankyn's book, finally makes concrete the abstract allegorical argument which her imagined life signifies, binding together the symbols of authority and rebellion, will and constraint, self and other. Alison's passionate refutation of Authority—the voices of the *olde bokes*, old men, old Law—in the 828 lines of her Prologue (excluding the interruptions) comprises more than forty references, by name, to exempla and *auctors*, in addition to the colloquial proverbs applicable pro and con to her case, all of which turn against her. Her victims are not merely men, and her enemies not only the common lot of experience—poverty, age, disease—which all men dread; the contest she is endlessly engaged in is against all that denies her vitality, her physical appetite, or so she says. The issues at stake, however, in the struggle for power—for control over her, or her freedom—are profoundly ambiguous univer-

sals: antinomian, Darwinian. The instinctive, anarchic, self-destructive compulsion in men creates its antithesis, the rule of law: affirmation of the self begets denial of the self. The adversary of Alison is
auctoritee itself; the insatiable *I* generates its negation. So, the Book
would destroy her mythical mother, Eve, to whom she owes her image.

> I bar him on honde he hadde enchanted me—
> My dame taughte me that soutiltee.
>
> [D. 575–76]

There is no resolution to the paradox of self-generating antinomies. To
satisfy the Wife, the whole of the fragile, fallible wisdom witnessed in the
symbolic Book must be cast into the fire so she can get the *maistrye*. At
the climax of the scene, as she lies on the floor *as I were deed,* Jankyn the
clerke capitulates, seals his submission by a kiss, and sets her free to live
again.

> He yaf me al the bridel in myn hond,
> To han the governance of hous and lond,
> And of his tonge, and of his hond also;
> And made hym brenne his book anon right tho.
>
> [D. 813–16]

But she is the sole survivor; he is dead within a year, and she is beyond
fertility. The implication that she is sterile is an even deeper irony
than her animal ignorance, which is also, like Eve's, absolute:

> What wiste I wher my grace
> Was shapen for to be, or in what place?
>
> [D. 553–54]

If her character had been left at that, all the power of the satire would
be unequivocally focussed upon her, and all the negations, the *auctoritees*, affirmed. Chaucer's detachment reveals to us, however, the deeper
paradox of self-love: that it is the necessary source of love of other, and
the ground of the Second Commandment.

> Therfore I made my visitaciouns
> To vigilies and to processiouns,
> To prechyng eek, and to thise pilgrimages,
> To pleyes of myracles, and to mariages,
> And wered upon my gaye scarlet gytes.

> Thise wormes, ne thise motthes, ne thise mytes,
> Upon my peril, frete hem never a deel;
> And wostow why? for they were used weel.
>
> [D. 555–63]

There are only glimpses of such characterizing monologue techniques in earlier English poetry, as soliloquy develops out of *debàt*, in *The Owl and the Nightingale*, and in French, in Rutebeuf and Jean de Meung's *Roman*. The later debasements of the Wife of Bath, both obscene and sentimental, in the *Twa Marrit Women and the Wedow* and the misogynist satires of the fifteenth century illustrate how complex and rare Alison is as a symbolic fiction which is at once a philosophical argument, a paradox, and a fully conceived and developed dramatic voice. The growth of her Prologue, were it recoverable, would perhaps reveal several stages in the evolution of Chaucer's narrative art. That her character grew after line 162 of the Prologue is demonstrable. She does, as she threatens the Pardoner, *telle ensamples mo than ten*, and in the process of development she was given a tale more appropriate than the Shipman's, which presumably she was once meant to tell. Good as it is, her *Tale* nevertheless is, in style, closer to Chaucer's less ambitious work. The *Shipman's Tale* has the swift, coiled-spring punning wit of the best Boccaccian fabliaux: the *Wife of Bath's Tale* is looser in style, and its ironies are relatively gentle. The use of occultatio, for example, to frame the Ovidian exemplum of Midas's ears, is of the plainest, least subtle kind. Any speaker can use these impersonal formulae, which have no identifying marks; they defer to an *auctor* by perfunctory cross-reference:

> Ovyde, amonges othere thynges smale . . .

> The remenant of the tale if ye wol heere,
> Redeth Ovyde, and ther ye may it leere.
>
> [D. 952, 981–82]

In the old hag's sermon on *gentilesse*, there is a paraphrase of Dante, duly footnoted:

> Thenketh how noble, as seith Valerius,
> Was thilke Tullius Hostillius,
> That out of poverte roose to heigh noblesse.
> Reedeth Senek, and redeth eek Boece.
>
> [D. 1165–68]

The neutral impersonality of the device—in effect, name-dropping—
is disjunctive; it breaks continuity, as becomes more apparent in its
frequency in other contexts. In the *Legends of Good Women*, Chaucer
uses it as an exit line:

> What shulde I more telle hire compleynyng?
> It is so long, it were an hevy thyng.
> In hire Epistel Naso telleth al;
> But shortly to the ende I telle shal.
>
> [Legend of Ariadne, F. 2218–21]

> Wel can Ovyde hire letter in vers endyte,
> Which were as now to long for me to wryte.
>
> [Legend of Medea, F. 1678–79]

> But who wol al this letter have in mynde,
> Rede Ovyde, and in hym he shal it fynde.
>
> [Legend of Dido, F. 1366–67]

While these formulaic *explicits* by *auctoritee* are marvels of brevity in
comparison with Lydgate's, they are anonymously perfunctory in
contrast with Chaucer's use of the figure in the *Book of Fame*, where
the narrator's voice is developing distinctive overtones. In that poem,
the curious conflated account of Dido's romance in the first book is
prefaced and followed by an occupatio and occultatio, signals which
conventionally detach the narrator from responsibility for or involvement in the authenticity of the fictional *matere*:

> What shulde I speke more queynte,
> Or peyne me my wordes peynte
> To speke of love? Hyt wol not be;
> I kan not of that faculte . . .
>
> [245–48]

> And al the maner how she deyde,
> And alle the wordes that she seyde,
> Whoso to knowe hit hath purpose,
> Rede Virgile in Eneydos
> Or the Epistle of Ovyde,
> What that she wrot or that she dyde;
> And nere hyt to long to endyte,
> Be God, I wolde hyt here write.
>   But wel-away! the harm, the routhe,

> That hath betyd for such untrouthe,
> As men may ofte in bokes rede,
> And al day sen hyt yet in dede,
> That for to thynken hyt, a tene is.
>
> [375–87]

As in the *Wife of Bath's Prologue*, in the *Book of Fame* the continuous stream of interruptions of the narrative for such addresses to the reader, exclamations, proverbs, and parables reveals the ambiguity of the Dreamer's passive role as servant of his *auctor*, limited to observation of what another hand *peynted on the wal*:

> In such wordes gan to pleyne
> Dydo of hir grete peyne,
> As me mette redely;
> Non other auctor alegge I.
>
> [311–14]

But in the Virgilian passage we are directed to consult, there is no lament for Dido; all too often, the "source" is not a Source. Allegorical irony covers many literary truth claims; but the falsification of a fictional source leads to deeper questions of authority and of the parabolic relation between the visionary imagination and truth:

> Small matter, maybe, if they receive from other hands something to contaminate. But they hand to others what they have contaminated, for idolmakers are accepted into the ranks of the clergy.[8]

Tertullian, in the third century, foresaw the Pardoner.

8. Tertullian, "On Idolatry," 89; English text in S. L. Greenslade, trans. and ed., *Early Latin Theology* (London, 1956), pp. 78–110. The imagery of the mortification of the flesh in the Pardoner's sermon is based on commonplaces, but he shares with Tertullian the power to evoke disgust: "The God of the 'physicus' is his stomach, his paunch is his altar, his cook his priest, the smell of cooking is his Holy Spirit and a belch its prophecy. During their 'agape' young catholics copulate, the older ones fix their minds on large platters of roast meat. They measure holiness by conviviality, by a keen palate, by a taste for costly food and fine wine. As materialists they cannot understand spiritual matters. Tomorrow we may die: let us therefore fast to prepare ourselves. (We) fast in training for a contest—not against flesh and blood, but against the powers of this world, against evil spiritual influences (Eph. vi, 12) . . . A fat Christian will please the lion or the bear which devours him more than he pleases God." See Timothy D. Barnes's *Tertullian, A Literary and Critical Study* (Oxford, 1971), for a full account of the evolution of Tertullian's works and beliefs, and their ramifications in Clement, Origen, and Jerome. In *The War Against Poetry* (Princeton, 1970), Russell Fraser alludes in passing to Tudor and Elizabethan iconoclasts' uses of Tertullian as an authority for censorship and the repression of art.

VI

Apologies for Poetry : Originality and Counterfeit Art

> Now, for the Poet, he nothing affirmes, and therefore neuer lyeth. For, as I take it, to lye is to affirme that to be true which is false. So as the other Artists, and especially the Historian, affirming many things, can, in the cloudy knowledge of man-kinde, hardly escape from many lyes. But the Poet . . . neuer affirmeth. The Poet neuer maketh any circles about your im-agination, to coniure you to beleeue for true what he writes. Hee citeth not authorities of other Histories, but euen for his entry calleth the sweete Muses to inspire into him a good inuention.
>
> Sidney, *Defense of Poesie*

The problems raised by discoveries of falsification are common to art and poetry. At fifteen, the apprentice Michelangelo sold fake Roman statuary of his own making, copies he had secretly antiqued and claimed to have found half-buried in the mud. Comparable poetic lies cost practically nothing to make, in time and energy, and are far more difficult both to detect and to understand. Their true cost is the need for repeated defenses of poetry, claims of immunity, apologies. Plato underlies three of the great attempts to justify the poetic imagination and defend its autonomy, Shelley's, Sidney's, and Boccaccio's extra-ordinary challenge to the fourteenth century and the future, *The Genealogy of the Gods*. Boccaccio summarizes, in chapters 14 and 15, the medieval tradition of ambivalent fear and reverence for the pagans, which extends from Pliny and Macrobius on dreams to Dante and Petrarch on mythological allegory: the humanist unification of Apollo and Divine Light. At the end of his Preface, Boccaccio "as Plato advises, . . . invoke(s) God's help," then he concludes with a pro-phetic analogy from the pagan gods whom he is proudly resuscitating,

> torn limb from limb and scattered among the rough and desert places of antiquity, and the thorns of hate; wasted away, sunk

almost to ashes . . . here I am setting forth . . . [to] fit them together, like another Aesculapius restoring Hippolytus.[1]

Humility: Later Medieval and Early Renaissance Conventions

Ambiguous and ironic allusions to authority are often covering fictions, pretending imitation; occupatio and occultatio, *I cannot say, myn auctor seyth*, and similar figures are easy to use deceptively to disguise innovation and obscure originality. Such standard tactics and fabricated sources are taken for granted in medieval poetry; they can often be explained by the obvious short answers, while the unstated questions— why they came to be, and lasted so long—remain unasked. Of course, plagiarism did not exist in the Middle Ages, in that it had not yet been banned. In all art, imitation is a most ancient, respected, and valued form of composition, and, until written texts become common, the anonymity of the fictional "I" virtually precludes "authorship" in the modern sense. So also, one may cite a literary source in innocence, believing it to be extant or true, or adapt and remodel another work without intentional dishonesty. Eight of the Canterbury pilgrims, however, use variants of the verb "counterfeit" as a pejorative.[2] The word occurs as a satiric or negative term in an equal number of contexts elsewhere in Chaucer, with transferred meanings of rebuke or falsehood. It seems clear that to claim *ars poetica* is far more hazardous and difficult than to disclaim it or avoid it:

> For out of olde feeldes, as men seyth,
> Cometh al this newe corn from yere to yere,
> And out of olde bokes, in good feyth,
> Cometh al this newe science that men lere.

Speght chose this passage from the *Parliament of Fowls* as the epigraph for the title page of his highly contaminated edition of 1598, the Chaucer's *Works* which inspired Francis Thynne's *Animadversions* on corrupt texts. But what is *al this newe science* worth? Why does originality entail evasion?

To disclaim originality (*as the boke seyth*) and to belittle oneself are

---

1. Osgood, *Genealogy*, p. 13.
2. The Nun's Priest, Pardoner, Clerk, Squire, Manciple, Man of Laws, Merchant; it is used by the Narrator for the Prioress, and by the Narrators of *Book of the Duchess*, *Troilus*, *House of Fame*, and in *Boece*.

conventional means to evade responsibility for both artistic truth and poetic success or failure. The formulae disarm criticism and permit silent experiment or revision, while seeming to follow a pattern or fulfill a commission assigned, as in Gower's *Confessio* and Lydgate's *Troy Book*. As such, both true and false disclaimers (*myn auctor seyth*) are simply variants of the modesty topos, which prevail in secular medieval fiction and which gradually turn into the converse, pride, in the Renaissance. The traditional, evasive modesty topoi and poetic anonymity are both already beginning to fade out well before 1500: so Lydgate names himself in the *Siege of Thebes*, imitating the example set by Chaucer in the *Book of Fame*. The fifteenth-century Chaucerians extend the precedents set by Chaucer and Gower; gradually, claims to authorship and names of models begin to seek fame and invite praise. While the modest pose may be maintained (in Hawes and Lydgate), the new self-impersonation is not always self-effacing, nor typically ironic: in Douglas, Skelton, and Wyatt, the poetic "I" becomes not more open and trustworthy, but less humble, and the personae of the lover, the satirist, and the moral adviser develop a perceptibly wider range of attitudes toward authority, both their own and others'. After about 1500, we find increasingly common condemnation of the inadequacy and poverty of the language itself taking the place of self-deprecation by the poet. "Blame not me!" if my words are unable to express my love or your beauty. Skelton, in *Phyllyp Sparow* (ca. 1505), makes the complaint mockingly explicit in "Jane's" apology:

> Our naturall tong is rude,
> And hard to be enneude
> With pullysshed termes lusty;
> Our language is so rusty,
> So cankered, and so full
> Of frowardes, and so dull,
> That if I wolde apply
> To wryte ornatly,
> I wot not where to fynd
> Termes to serve my mynde:
>
> . . . .
> Wherfore hold me excused
> If I have not well perused
> Myne Englyssh halfe-abused;

> Though it be refused,
> In worth I shall it take,
> And fewer wordes make.[3]

Failure is deflected from the poet to his medium: his success lies in overcoming the limits of words by his art. In the famous stanza at the ending of *Troilus*, Chaucer's narrator returns to the theme of mutability in language and custom which we considered briefly in chapter four. He confesses his anxiety with the deference that characterizes his stance toward his audience, his *auctors,* and Time itself:

> And for ther is so great diversite
> In Englissh, and in writyng of oure tonge,
> So prey I god that non myswrite the,
> Ne the mysmetre for defaute of tonge.
> And red wherso thow be, or elles songe,
> That thow be understonde, god I biseche.

> [V 1793–98]

Here, it is not that the language is deficient or unable to express his meaning; the speaker fears it cannot last as he has written it—it may be imperfectly copied and imperfectly understood. Its mutability is inevitable, and the intelligibility of the poem is already out of his hands.

The compulsive aureation of English in the fifteenth century and its controversial aftereffects in the sixteenth shift the focus of humanist criticism to the capacity of the language to fulfill the demand of the poet, who is conceived in Sidney's *Apologie* not as the servant of nature, but as the confident maker of a golden world. Chaucer's *craft* that *countrefeyteth kynde* undergoes a metamorphosis, and the new voices of the fictional "I" are already audible in Wyatt in the 1540's:

> I am as I am and so will I be
> But how that I am none knoweth truly.
> Be it evil, be it well, be I bound, be I free,
> I am as I am and so will I be.

> . . . .

> Who judgeth well, well God him send;
> Who judgeth evil, God them amend;
> To judge the best, therefore intend

3. ll. 774–83; 813–18. Text in *John Skelton, Poems*, ed. Robert S. Kinsman (Oxford, 1969), pp. 50–51.

For I am as I am and so will end.

. . . .

Praying you all that do this read
To trust it as you do your creed,
And not to think I change my weed,
For I am as I am however I speed.

But how that is I leave to you;
Judge as ye list false or true;
Ye know no more than afore ye knew;
Yet I am as I am whatever ensue.

And from this mind I will not flee
But to you all that misjudge me
I do protest as ye may see
That I am as I am and so will I be.[4]

As in the later Middle Ages, however, the problem of authority in the
Renaissance is not limited to poetic fictions: it is the burning theme of
religion, politics, and the rewriting of history as "true"; as such it will
concern us again in reconsidering Spenser's relation to Chaucer.

The Problem of Certainty: Solomon's *Trouthe*

For the medieval secular poet, the ambivalence of authority lies as
much in the received truths of the past as in the unstable present,
the common field of satire. The question passes from poet to poet: who
knows, if Homer made lies? As in the case of Renaissance politics,
where decision making is coming to be more and more the manipulation
of power through deceptive psychological strategies, so poetic autonomy is beginning to be asserted in vernacular art, first in Italy by Dante,
Petrarch, and Boccaccio, and, after them, in all Europe. It is an epi-
phenomenon of reverence for authority. Chaucer was probably among
the most widely read in modern languages of his contemporaries; his
attitudes toward antiquity, toward the latent possibilities for betrayal
in fiction, and toward the imagination's problematic "originality"
are outgrowths of experiments in translation. That he speculated on the
plurality of languages, in the constant practice of translation, is self-
evident. The translator of lyric and of allegory is immediately con-

4. Text in E. M. W. Tillyard, *The Poetry of Sir Thomas Wyatt* (London, 1949), pp. 126–27.

fronted with the most acute linguistic dilemmas of multiple implication
and unity of meaning: he is constantly made conscious of fundamental
dichotomies in the truth of his own words, inherent in language itself.
The integrity of language belongs to ethics, and its ambiguity belongs
to rhetoric; the poet is responsible for both.

> "Trouthe is the hyeste thyng that man may kepe"
>
> [*FranklT*, F. 1478]

> My maister Bukton, whan of Crist our kyng
> Was axed what is trouthe or sothfastnesse,
> He nat a word answerde to that axing,
> As who saith, "No man is al trewe," I gesse.
>
> [*Buk* 1–4]

Even in the relatively shallow contexts of the satiric poem to Bukton
and the crisis of the *Franklin's Tale*, where domestic melodrama is
tinged with the comedy of excess, the conception of *trouthe* carries moral
weight deeper and more ambiguous than the easy issue of marital fidelity.
Christ is silent, asked what *trouthe* is. The hesitant narrators of Chaucer's dreams, and of *Troilus*, make humble apologies; they can give no
final answers to the questions their stories raise. The Black Knight's
lady is dead:

> "Nay!" "Yis, be my trouthe!"
> "Is that youre los? Be God, hyt is routhe!"
> And with that word ryght anoon
> They gan to strake forth; al was doon,
> For that tyme, the hert-huntyng.
>
> [*BD* 1309–13]

The formel eagle in the *Parliament* successfully resists choice; Troilus
rises beyond his betrayal, and abjures human love. Chaucer makes few
claims to *art poetical* or moral wisdom and rarely lets any affirmation
stand without ambiguity. The characteristic stance of his ingenuous
narrator toward the audience, his dream, and his book is to deny his
own knowledge and to evade or shrug off responsibility for such dubious
wisdom as may be found in books or dreams.

> And with the shoutyng, whan the song was do
> That foules maden at here flyght awey,
> I wok, and othere bokes tok me to,

To reede upon, and yit I rede alwey.
I hope, ywis, to rede so som day
That I shal mete som thyng for to fare
The bet, and thus to rede I nyl nat spare.

[*PF* 693–99]

The insomniac in the *Book of the Duchess* asks for someone to reach him something *to drive the night away*, for reading is a better pastime than *play either at ches or tables*; poetry is put into complex equation with a dubious catalogue of *smale thinges*:

And in this bok were written fables
That clerkes had in olde tyme,
And other poets, put in rime
To rede, and for to be in minde,
While men loved the lawe of kinde.
This bok ne spak but of such thinges,
Of quenes lives, and of kinges,
And many othere thinges smale.

[*BD* 52–59]

Tertullian, attacking art in *On Idolatry*, had invoked a golden age when *men loved the lawe of kind*: before the Fall, before the devil invented art. According to the early iconoclasts and their later medieval and Reformation descendants, Satan invented the makers of statues, and through him the creative impulse was debased, from sacred to profane: even in Sidney's *Defense*, the erected wit still sees God and imagines perfection which the infected will cannot attain. For iconoclasts the creative energy of art, like sexual energy its twin, counterfeits *kynde* and arouses fears: its symbols and their effects are "unclean" and spread contagion. In the *Genealogy of the Gods*, Boccaccio's arguments constantly show, in their very defensive fervor, that the intrinsic ambiguity of art was only partially cleared by the early answers to Tertullian. He cites abbreviated passages from Augustine, edits Jerome, and quotes Plato and Saint Thomas out of context for the defense of poets and of ancient myth.[5] All of his arguments are haunted by Virgil and Cicero, and by Solomon's worship of images:

But remember, he that toucheth pitch shall be defiled. . . .

5. Osgood, *Genealogy*, 15. 9, passim: see Osgood's n. 2, pp. 194–95.

Solomon is . . . convincing proof of human weakness. He enjoyed at God's hand, all wisdom, . . . wealth, great empire, held the Gentiles in just tribute, built a wonderful temple to God, wrought many good works; and yet in his old age forgot the Giver of so many honors, went up into the mountain of offence, and adored the Egyptian idol Moloch on bended knee. And will you prove stronger or more circumspect then Solomon?[6]

As a practicing poet, but no controversialist, Chaucer accomplishes his own defense socratically by averring that he is defenseless and letting *auctoritee* speak. He subtly exploits the paradox of Solomon—his proverbial *trothe* and his vulnerability to human desire and deception—by constant quotation and allusion, just as he uses all such *auctoritees*, for ironic *trouthe*. Solomon serves as the voice of wisdom and authority in *Melibee* (forty-two citations), the *Parson's Tale* (eighteen), and twice he is named by the Wife of Bath, for the "refreshment" of polygamous marriage and as an authority in Jankyn's misogynist Book. He is in Venus's Temple in the *Knight's Tale* with Medea and Circe and the victims of carnality borrowed from Jean de Meung's *Roman*, and Nicholas cites him in the *Miller's Tale* as authority for craft: *Werk al by conseil, and thou shalt nat rewe (thus saith Salomon, that was ful trewe)*. The Song of Songs and Solomon's "true words" echo discordantly in the *Merchant's Tale*, satirized first in Placebo, then Pluto, and finally in Proserpine's voice:

> What rekketh me of youre auctoritees?
> I woot wel that this Jew, this Salomon,
> Foond of us wommen fooles many oon . . .
> . . . .
> I preye yow take the sentence of the man;
> He mente thus, that in sovereyn bontee
> Nis noon but God, neither he ne she.
> Ek! for verray God, that nys but oon,
> What make ye so much of Salomon?
>
> [E. 2276–78; 2288–92]

"Solomon's truth" comes to mean whatever the speaker wants. He is simultaneously David's son, an idolator, and "author" of Proverbs, Ecclesiastes, and the Song of Songs.

6. Ibid., 15. 9, p. 128.

Chaucer's allegorical ironies neither negate, nor affirm, nor despair of *trouthe*, but preclude certainty that any human action accomplishes its end or that human images or words for *trouthe* last:

> For, as that seith Salomon, "whoso that hadde
> the science to knowe the peynes that ben
> establissed and ordeyned for synne, he wolde
> make sorwe." "Thilke science," as seith Seint
> Augustyn, "maketh a man to waymenten in his
> herte."
>
> [I. 228–30]

In effect, Boccaccio's learned and aggressive tactics in defense of poetry are more naive and more conservative than Chaucer's constant doubting of all human authority and abdication of predetermined poetic meanings. His poems are inquiries into *trouthe*.

The Myth of Aesculapius: Plato, Boccaccio, and Spenser

Metaphysical illusion, relativity, and self-deception fascinate Chaucer's sceptics. In the Boethian "Balades de Visage sanz Peinture" entitled *Fortune*, Fortune scorns human pretense to defy her mutability:

> Lo, th' execucion of the majestee
> That al purveyeth of his rightwysnesse,
> The same thing "Fortune" clepen ye,
> Ye blinde bestes, ful of lewednesse!
> The hevene hath propretee of sikernesse,
> This world hath ever resteles travayle.
>
> [*Fort*, 65–70]

In general, this roule may not fayle, Fortune's mocking refrain to "le Pleintif," is logically ludicrous and vindicates the plaintiff's case against her: under Fortune's rule, the world has become absurd. His hero is Plato's:

> O Socrates, thou stidfast champioun,
> She never mighte be thy tormentour;
> Thou never dreddest hir oppressioun,
> Ne in hir chere founde thou no savour.
> Thou knewe wel the deceit of hir colour,

> And that hir moste worshipe is to lye.
> I knowe hir eek a fals dissimulour;
> For fynally, Fortune, I thee defye!
>
> [*Fort*, 17–24]

Socrates went to his death for refusal to repudiate his own integrity, his freedom to doubt; he refused to recant his impiety to the state religion. The only other voice he trusted and did not doubt was that of his own *daimon*, who never prophesied but only warned him against taking action. The radical Christian transformation of Plato's divine reason into divine law by revelation proscribed Socrates' doubt and magnified *daimon* into the demonic, the terrible angels of justice in Apuleius, Augustine, and Dante.[7] Satan's rebel angels, consigned by God to Chaos, constantly escape into the world to spread Satan's torment to men's minds, first in pagan oracles, then in lust and passions, and always in the illusions of art. For Christian true believers, engaged first in the labor of conversion and then in defense of the faith, Tertullian's warnings and Jerome's dicta (in the epistle to Pope Damasus: "The songs of poets are the food of devils!")[8] condemn artistic illusion. Fiction is false, and irony breeds dread. The imagination is the source of uncertainty, of heretical vision, ecstasy, and doubt. Beneath the abyss of doubt lies Hell, the soul's oblivion, the ultimate death of the self in denial of God. Impiety, for Socrates, held no such terrors. He maintains his perfect calmness to the end, convinced that only after death will Wisdom reveal herself in her purity to her lover.[9] " 'Crito,' he said, 'I owe a cock to Aesculepius; do not forget it.' "[10] Such ironic composure is not an option for a Christian. The Socratic refusal to pretend to be wise tears to shreds all definitions of piety, honor, and truth. Socrates answers the priestess of Delphi, who has said there is no man wiser than he, thus:

> It cannot be that (the oracle) is speaking falsely, for he is a god and cannot lie, . . . (So I went to a wise man, and questioned him, and went away, thinking to myself) "I am wiser than this man;

---

7. Ibid., pp. xx–xxii; Osgood's citations of Apuleius's *De Dogmate Platonis* 9.23 and 7.28; Augustine, *De Civitate Dei*, Migne *PL* xli, col. 12–804.

8. Boccaccio's answer (Osgood, *Genealogy*, 14.18, p. 85) cites Fulgentius's *Book of Myths*: "food kept with care, dressed and tasted by the holy doctors of the Church."

9. A. M. Adam, ed., *Apology*, pp. 18–19.

10. *Phaedo*, 22,118A; Demos, *Plato*, pp. 147–233.

neither of us knows anything that is really worth knowing, but he thinks that he has knowledge when he has not, while I, having no knowledge, do not think that I have. . . . I do not think I know what I do not know. . . . I soon found that it is not by wisdom that poets create their works, but by a certain instinctive inspiration, like soothsayers and prophets, who say many fine things, but understand nothing of what they say. The poets seemed to me to be in a similar situation. And at the same time I perceived that, because of their poetry, they thought they were the wisest of men. . . . So I went away again.

It is absurd that he should be tried and convicted as a maker of new gods (*Euthyphro*, 2); he finally understands the oracle, and expounds it at his trial:

Gentlemen, I believe that the god is really wise, and that by this oracle he meant that human wisdom is worth little or nothing. . . . He only made use of my name, as though he would say to men, 'He among you is the wisest, who, like Socrates, knows that his wisdom is really worth nothing at all.'[11]

For a Christian poet, certainty and truth, the integrity of the meaning of words, are not free or playful, but bound to concepts of ultimate consequence. That language is inherently deceptive, polysemous, requires that the poet make sure, as Horace advised, before he publishes, and that he clarify all that can be made clear. Therefore, the modes of irony carry higher risks and greater power than all others, and their symbolic value lies in their capacity to express antinomy, mystery, what is beyond explication. The danger is ambiguity, symbols which may or may not be "true" if conflicting readings remain unresolved. Hence, "originality" *is* suspect and *ironia* a risk. Poetic obscurity can be defended, as Boccaccio defends it, by analogy with "Holy Writ, . . . full to overflowing with obscurities and ambiguities," and by the incomprehensibility of nature:

Why do they not say that the Holy Spirit wove obscure sayings into his works?; to a half-blind man, even when the sun is shining its brightest, the sky looks cloudy . . . for surely, it is not one of the poet's functions to rip up and lay bare the meaning which lies

11. *Apology*, 8.22; 9. 29.

hidden in his inventions. Rather, where matters truly solemn are too much exposed, it is his office to protect as well as he can, and remove them from the gaze of the irreverent.

Nor can poets be called liars, for poetic fiction is not "intended" to deceive:

> Poets are not constrained . . . to employ literal truth on the surface of their inventions . . . if the privilege of ranging through every sort of fiction be denied them, their office will altogether resolve itself into naught.[12]

The office of a true poet, which is the crux at issue for Boccaccio's defense, is the old definition of Isidore of Seville, Raban Maurus, and Vincent of Beauvais in turn, in virtually the same words:

> Officium autem poetae in eo est, ut ea quae vere gesta sunt in alias species obliquis figurationibus cum decore aliquo conversa transducat.[13]

The difficulty still lies in the *figurae*, in all their multiplicity, especially those of the pagan poets, who, Boccaccio concedes,

> with all their knowledge of the liberal arts . . . and philosophy, could not know the truth of Christianity, for that light . . . had not yet shone forth.[14]

Using fourfold exegetical interpretation, Boccaccio then clears Virgil of the charge of having lied about Dido's passion and stands his ground:

> There are certain pietists who, in reading my words, will be moved by a holy zeal to charge me with injury to the most sacrosanct Christian religion, for I allege that the pagan poets are theologians —a distinction which Christians grant only to those instructed in sacred literature. These critics I hold in high respect and I thank them in anticipation for such criticism, for I feel it implies their concern for my welfare. But the carelessness of their remarks shows clearly the narrowness of their reading. If they had read widely, they would not have overlooked . . . the *City of God*.[15]

12. Osgood, *Genealogy*, 14.12, p. 58; 14.13, p. 63.
13. Isidore of Seville, *Etymologiae* 8.7, Migne *PL* lxxxii, col. 308–09.
14. Osgood, *Genealogy*, 14. 13, p. 66.
15. Ibid., 15.8, p. 121; cf. 14.18, *passim*. Boccaccio is referring to Augustine's book 12, on biblical ambiguity.

Boccaccio's vehement sarcasm betrays his own anxiety, in his covert attacks on Jerome, which expose their common love of Virgil and Horace, Cicero and Persius—for which Jerome punished himself, and which Boccaccio kept hidden from his father; for when he was sent to Bologna in the 1330's to study law, his books of the poets were hunted out and burned.[16] The double image, the demonic twin of visionary light in the power of the imagination to imitate and the claim of heretics to "see," drove the iconoclasts to their irrational fear of art. Equally they drove Petrarch and Boccaccio to their fantastically elaborate allegorical readings of Homer and Virgil, to "save the phenomena" by means of selective quotation from the Fathers and commentaries upon commentaries to show what is "concealed within the poetic veil": Dido's suicide is "the triumph of the soul over concupiscence."[17]

Socrates' last words, offering a cock to Aesculapius, the son of Apollo and god of medicine, refer with sublime ironic autonomy to the Athenian custom of sacrifice to the god in gratitude for recovery from sickness. Spenser transforms the ambiguity of Aesculapius' skill in healing Hippolytus—which threatens the immortality of the gods—from benign to Satanic art in the underworld of the first book of the *Faerie Queene* (v, 36–44):

> they be come vnto the furthest part:
> Where was a Cave ywrought by wondrous art,
> Deepe, darke, vneasie, dolefull, comfortlesse,
> In which sad *Æsculapius* farre a part
> Emprisond was in chaines remedilesse,
> For that Hippolytus rent corse he did redresse.

> Such wondrous science in mans wit to raine
> When *Ioue* auisd, that could the dead reuiue,
> And fates expired could renew againe,
> Of endlesse life he might him not depriue,
> But vnto hell did thrust him down aliue,
> With flashing thunderbolt ywounded sore:
> Where long remaining, he did alwaies striue
> Himselfe with salues to health for to restore,
> And slake the heauenly fire, that raged euermore.

The Christian ambivalence toward the fallen world and its corrupt

16. Ibid., 15.10; see Osgood's n. 11, p. 198.
17. Ibid., 14. 13.

inhabitants may tempt the mind into visionary longing for escape, denial, or damnation of art—the tradition that begins with Boethius's abolition of the Muses. Or, one can attempt the more difficult equilibrium of ironic acceptance of the conditional, refusal to despair, even celebration of this world with its promise of renewal. In either case, the imagination's creative power is dangerous and suspect. It is under continual surveillance and scrutiny in so far as it is equally capable of demonic fantasy as of sacred vision. For exactly the same reasons, as Boccaccio's "detractors" aver, the poet is suspect in the City of God and in the rational ideal city of the pagans. For Boccaccio, in his enthusiastic allegorical interpretation, Aesculapius figures forth his own re-creative intelligence, gathering the torn limbs of the old gods and restoring their hidden truths to light. In Spenser, Aesculapius falls again to the temptation of pride, and agrees to heal the fallen Sansfoy; he is essential to the demonic conspiracy of Duessa, Night, and Archimago. The shamanistic power of Chaucer's randy Pardoner stands midway between, reflecting the doubly ironic moral attitude of the poet toward the charisma of his own art, as fascinating and as bitter as his scorn for the debasement of the speakers for the Church. Aesculapius is in hell because of his pity for Theseus's son, for giving him a second life and the possibility of immortality. The analogy for poets, which Spenser saw, is dangerously close; it is also Archimago's power, the power of language, which seems to give access to the dream world, mastery over unknowns. By his art man transcends time and space, leaving behind enigmatic monuments to himself; in poetry, he may arouse emotions, release fears, and express doubts which it would be dangerous for other men to know and feel, given the rhetoric of persuasion and the inherent plasticity of language—like the Pardoner's—which invents lies as seductive and powerful as truth. Such ambiguous considerations are irrelevant to Dante's love for Beatrice, but not for Troilus's love for his Criseyde. Chaucer's knowledge of Christ's *trouthe* and his Socratic stance of ignorance, bent into the comic poses of his wise fools, combine into multiple meanings too subtle and complex to be unwound by Boccaccio's restorative arts, borrowed from Fulgentius, John of Salisbury, and Bernard Silvestris—whose allegorical Genius Spenser re-created as a true, and double maker.

Plato's *Timaeus*, Boethius, and the Medieval Defense of Art

The most widely known of all the dialogues in the medieval Platonic tradition, Plato's *Timaeus* explores the symbolic values of poetic fiction, tracing the recensions of oral narrative backward toward myth, then reversing the process to project Socrates' dialectic upon it. The rational analysis of poetic myth, inquiring into its *allegoria*, makes a stable and seemingly permanently valid interpretation of its content possible, until it is undercut by the irony of Socrates' doubt. Critias begins by telling the story of an aged man ("Critias, at the time of telling it, was nearly ninety years of age, and I was about ten"), who remembers Solon, and the telling of Solon's poems from Egypt:

> if Solon had only . . . made poetry the business of his life, and completed the tale which he brought with him from Egypt, . . . he would have been as famous as Homer or Hesiod or any poet.

Critias recalls how Solon, visiting the city of Sais on the Nile delta, related Athenian history to the Egyptians. He told about Phoroneus, "the first man," and Niobe, and the Deluge, and the survival of Deucalion and Pyrrha. But Solon was brought up short in his tale of the antiquity of the Greeks and the genealogies of Athens by the oldest Egyptian priest. Critias retells his words:

> O Solon, Solon, you Hellenes are never anything but children, and there is not one old man among you . . . there is no old opinion handed down among you by tradition, nor any science . . . hoary with age.

Solon learned then that there was not one Deluge but many, that time after time the earth has been destroyed and purged; that Phaeton and his chariot are a myth which really signifies the recurrent conflagrations of the earth which the Egyptians have been spared, in their Nile valley, and have observed and recorded. The traditions preserved in Egypt are the most ancient, for, the priest continued,

> whatever happened in either your country or in ours, or in any other region of which we are informed—if there were any action noble or great or in any other way remarkable, they have all been written down by us of old, and . . . preserved in our temples. Whereas just when you and other nations are beginning to be provided with letters and the other requisites of civilized life, after the usual interval, the stream from heaven comes pouring down . . . like a pestilence, leaving only those of you who are

destitute of letters and of education and so you have to begin all over again like children, and know nothing of what happened in ancient times, either among us or among yourselves. As for those genealogies of yours which you now recounted to us, Solon, they are no better than the tales of children. . . . You and your whole city are descended from a small seed or remnant of [the fairest and noblest race of men which ever lived], which survived. And this was unknown to you, because, for many generations, the survivors of destruction died, leaving no written word.[18]

The dialogue Critias recalls ("indelible in my memory of his poem") describes Solon's education in Egypt and the rediscovery of the goddess Athena, who founded her city nine thousand years before the great victory and destruction of Atlantis, where Solon's poem had begun. Then Critias and Socrates turn the telling of Solon's tale into a philosophical hypothesis that will transform "the city and citizens, which [were] described in fiction, into the world of reality." What was oral poetic tradition, then poetry, then "indelibly" remembered narrative— the retelling of the memorized fiction of Solon's poem—now becomes at last dialectic, by allegorical interpretation. Socrates calls it "a perfect and splendid feast of reason," soul's entertainment:

And what other [narrative], Critias, can we find that will be better than this, which is natural and suitable to the festival of the goddess, and has the very great advantage of being a fact and not a fiction? How or where shall we find another if we abandon this?

Timaeus the astronomer begins with the generation of the world and the creation of man, Critias receives the men whom Timaeus created, and then

in accordance with the tale of Solon and his law, we will bring them into court, and make them citizens, as if they were those very Athenians whom the sacred Egyptian record has recovered from oblivion.[19]

Because the myths of the *Timaeus*, its *allegoria* and *ironia*, are the most profoundly influential fragment of all Platonic philosophy to survive

18. *Timaeus*, 21B–27B; Demos, *Plato*, pp. 383–415.
19. Ibid.

the fall of Rome and the transition to Christianity, the powerful significance of its myths in the Middle Ages is out of all proportion to the
status any single dialogue has in the larger context of Plato's thought
since the Renaissance. The problematic images of the poet, in the
second, third, and tenth books of the *Republic*, and in the dialectics of
the *Ion* and the *Gorgias*, were not recovered until the twelfth century,
and not available in translation until the sixteenth, when their cumulative impact became immense.[20] Similarly, the importance of Macrobius, Cicero, Pseudo-Dionysus, and Boethius as major sources of
antique thought in Latin are equally disproportionate until the fourteenth century, the revival thereafter of Greek studies, and the new
translations and first editions of the ancients. In England, it was Duke
Humphrey of Gloucester (the owner of the famous *Troilus* manuscript)
who commissioned the early fifteenth-century translation of Boccaccio's
works into French by Italian scholars and, as patron, encouraged the
translation of Greek philosophy into Latin: Aristotle's *Poetics*, Plato's
Republic, and Plutarch's *Lives*.[21]

The ancient iconoclastic distrust of art, both Christian and latent in
Neoplatonism, survived into the Scholastic age, and penetrated, as we
have seen, the Platonism of the twelfth-century Latin poets of Chartres.
The distrust of secular poetry, which aroused fear of the imagination in
all its ambiguous disguises, both sacred and profane, is already deeply
evident in the most influential of all postclassical philosophers, whose
work was written in the first quarter of the sixth century and, once in
circulation, never waned. The symbolic drama of Boethius's banishing
of poetry from his prison cell, at the entrance of the goddess Philosophia,
opens with her words to the Muses, "Who let those whores . . . come
to the bedside of a sick man?" Boethius is also a medieval "source" of
the more ancient myth of Orpheus, which becomes, in his fable, an
allegory of human art's ironic defeat.

In the *Consolation*, Boethius combines dialectic and lyric episodes into
the continuity of philosophical dialogue; his book is both historical
narration and visionary fiction. Philosophy appears as a sudden emanation, in the imaginary setting of his prison cell. However accurate
Boethius's guess turned out to be, it is highly probable he was still under

20. See Bolgar, *Classical Heritage*, pp. 175 ff.; and Raymond Klibansky, *Platonic Tradition*.
The Latin Plato included the *Timaeus* (parts translated by Cicero, Chalcidius, and Macrobius), Aristippus's versions of the *Meno* and *Phaedo*, and parts of Proclus' *Parmenides*.
21. Bolgar, *Classical Heritage*, p. 443, n. 311.

house arrest, with access to his books, when he wrote the *Consolation*, and it is a pseudohistorical fiction made more poignant by the truth. In the conventional opening formulae (metrum 1) the poet, who once wrote songs, is "now driven to take up melancholy measures": "Wounded Muses tell me what I must write, / and elegiac verses bathe my face with real tears." The speaker's solitary state and his theme are elaborated in a series of antitheses; youth falls to age, glory to misery, pride to humiliation, all parallel losses of power working toward the limit of a temporal pattern to provide the timeless dreamlike *now*. For the abolition of false fiction and the driving away of the Muses, the present tense breaks down, without, however, giving up the rational consciousness—closing the poet's eyes. Boethius uses the imagery of eyes to modulate from weeping to vision, from his sad Muses to the flashing eyes of Philosophy, as she glares at them and drives them away.

> The sad hour that has nearly drowned me came just at the time faithless Fortune favored me with her worthless gifts. Now that she has clouded her deceitful face, my life seems to go on endlessly.[22]

Boethius transcends the lyric state of self-consciousness only after the emanation, Philosophy, fixes him with her burning eyes:

> My sight was so dimmed with tears that I could not tell who this woman of imperious authority might be, and I lay there astonished, my eyes staring at the earth, silently waiting what she would do. She came nearer and sat at the foot of my bed.

To bring him to his senses, she dries his eyes with a fold of her robe, saying, "I shall quickly wipe the dark cloud of mortal things from your eyes." So, in a rational state paradoxically achieved through refracted vision, the poet recognizes his own mind. Self-generated, the authority of the vision is "my nurse, in whose house I had lived from my youth." Philosophy, the authority of revealed Reason, is above ambiguity until the final question is raised—as in Alan's dialogue with Natura—the knowledge of evil and the prescience of a benign God. The freedom of the mind to conceive doubt resists Philosophy's explanations of necessity, free will, and divine foreknowledge to the very end, to the dilemma reached in the fifth book.

The human mind, overcome by the body's blindness, cannot discern

---

22. Boethius, *Consolation* I, metrum 1, Green, p. 3.

by its dim light the delicate connections between things. But why does the mind burn with such desire to discover the hidden aspects of truth? Does it know what it is trying to know? And if it does not know, why does it blindly continue the search? . . . When the human mind knew the mind of God, did it know the whole and all its parts? Now the mind is shrouded in the clouds of the body, but it has not wholly forgotten itself.

In this extraordinary evocation of oracular mysticism, Boethius reaches the point where Platonism and Christianity had coalesced in the conception of infinite perfection and divine knowledge, conceived as a shadow in the myth of the cave; the mind cannot transcend itself. The last lyric of the fifth book contrasts the image of man erect, lifting his head to heaven, despising the earth, with "the shapes of living things on earth":

Some . . . with bodies stretched out, crawling through the dust, spending their strength in an unbroken furrow; some soar in the air, beating the wind with light wings, floating in easy flight along tracks of air. Some walk along the ground, through woods and green fields . . . but their faces look down and cause their senses to grow sluggish.

The blind body of an animal conceives of a mind which sees God: it is the visionary power ("unless folly has bound you to earth") of the imagination alone which saves the human from sinking into the ground, in the final mythopoeic image of the clay God formed as the artist of creation, which disintegrates into dust, but for the salvation of divine love.

> You, who look upward with your head held high,
> should also raise your soul to sublime things,
>   lest while your body is raised above the earth
> your mind should sink to the ground under its burden.

Boethius's Hymn to Sacred Love, in the magnificent ninth metrum of Book III, celebrates the binding power of the Maker, who without cause, out of chaotic matter, "makes . . . fashions . . . forms . . . perfects" the image of the beautiful world, "ordering the perfect parts into a perfect whole." The binding power and revolving circles of the world soul embrace God and transform heaven to its own image, and at the highest point of affirmation Boethius reaches, the souls and lesser living forms are

> adapted to their high flight in swift chariots, You scatter them through the earth and sky, and when they have turned back again toward You, by your gracious law, You call them back like leaping flames.[23]

The Hymn's poetic and philosophical authority for sacred Christian poetry was multiplied by countless imitations and variations of its imagery and theme, from the sixth century onward in Latin poetry. Among the earliest poetic fragments in a European vernacular language is the Provençal "Song of Boethius" in a tenth-century manuscript of Latin sermons and parts of the Bible.[24] Boethius's affirmation of divine love in Book III is the ground on which he must stand in the more profound paradox of prescience in Book V, where divine foreknowledge and human freedom are both affirmed. Boethius's Christian belief transcends his Ciceronian logic. Following Augustine, Boethius asserts both halves of his contradiction, and his antinomy of freedom and necessity was transmitted, along with the allegorical goddess Philosophia, who displaced Fortune and the Muses, into the Platonized Christian poetry of all medieval Europe. But, as in the case of the *Timaeus*, myths older than the literary tradition are also transmitted and reestablished, even in the course of their negation and denial. Boethius's Muses were banished only by a fictional pretext; his treatment of Orpheus is more passionate and severe.

The last poem of the third book of the *Consolation* is, in contrast to the hymn to love, a bitter and ironic fable far older and more deeply ambiguous, perhaps, than any of the poems in the *Consolation*, both in its *litterae* and its allegorical reading. Metrum twelve is the myth of Orpheus, the prototype of poets, whose power—the art of his music—controls all nature:

> With his sorrowful music he made the woodland dance and the river stand still . . . the fearful deer lie down . . . with the fierce lion.

The poem opens with the double paradox, freedom and necessity, concealed in its metaphorical eyes and earthly bonds:

23. Boethius, *Consolation* I, prosa 1, Green p. 5; V, metrum 3, Green p. 108; V, metrum 5, Green p. 114; III, metrum 9, Green pp. 60–61.
24. See Auerbach, *Literary Language and its Public*, p. 278.

> Happy is he who can look into the shining spring of good; happy
> is he who can break the heavy chains of earth.

The death of Euridyce is burning in Orpheus, and he cannot be calmed
even by his own music. Refused by the gods, he descends to the gates
of hell, where his new song—his creative energy impassioned by grief
and denial—paralyzes Cerberus, moves the Furies to weep for pity, and
soothes the tormented souls of Ixion and Tantalus: through his singing
the damned are released from their pain. Orpheus has reached super-
human power; he rivals, and then overcomes, the laws of nature
(mortality) and the will of the gods (irrationality). The power of the
harmony he creates by drawing it forth from his lyre masters the
unknowable malice of death and inexplicability, the refusal of the gods
to heed his sorrow. The one condition Orpheus's art cannot transcend,
his own desire, defeats him at the moment of return.

> Love is a stronger law, unto itself. As they approached the edge
> of night, Orpheus looked back at Euridyce, lost her, and died.
> This fable applies to all of you who seek to raise your minds to
> sovereign day. For whoever is conquered and turns his eyes to the
> pit of hell, looking into the inferno, loses all the excellence he has
> gained.[25]

It is precisely the capacity to raise his eyes that distinguishes the
human from chaotic nature, in the crux of the fifth book, where the
irreconcilable positives are both affirmed. Here, the implicit negation
is revealed, in Orpheus's confrontation with the absurdity of death. It
in inconceivable that his art can master nature, or that human ratio-
nality can outwit the antinomian Divine: there can be no return, for the
merely human. The malice of the pagan gods is awkwardly adjusted to
conform to the Christian reading of the fable in Chaucer's gloss of his
translation of the Boethian *moralitas*:

> For whoso that evere be so overcomen that he ficche his eien into
> the put of helle (*that is to seyn, whoso sette his thoughtes in erthly thinges*),
> al that evere he hath drawen of the noble good celestial he lesith
> it, whanne he looketh the helles (*that is to seyn, into lowe thinges of
> the erth*).
>
> [*Bo*, III, metrum 12, 62–70]

25. Boethius, *Consolation* III, metrum 12, Green, pp. 73, 74.

The myth of the love of Orpheus, like the myth of Narcissus which becomes the myth of Eve at the pool in Milton's Eden, seeks to reconcile the explicable love that binds, makes symmetry and cosmic harmony, creates and renews, with its antithetical necessity, the devouring passion and self-destroying power latent in creation itself. Looking into the abyss of the irrational, seeking to know total self-possession, the rational draws back, condemning its own eyes, rather than deny the power of the gods.

The sacred poetic allegory's inherent ambiguity and latent ironies are partially revealed in Bernard's Neoplatonic re-creation of the myths of the *Timaeus* in *De Mundi Universitate*; the poems of Alan, *De Planctu* and *Anticlaudianus*, which more strongly influenced later vernacular poets, reemphasize the antinomian power of the imagination to deceive and to be deceived. Boethius, who provided images for both, had made radical Plato's doubts of art, the validity of the word, and the veracity of dreams, which are instrumental in the maintenance of faith in the supernatural, both divine and demonic. Such doubts must be repressed because only fiction, symbolic reality, survives the passing of time, and it becomes time's only witness by virtue of its very antiquity. So Timaeus began his account of creation, the marriage of Oceanus and Tethys, and the birth of Phorcys, Chronos, and Rhea, with an ironic question, leaving it unanswered because it is unanswerable:

> To know or to tell the origin of the other divinities is beyond us, and we must accept the traditions of the men of old time who affirm themselves to be the offspring of the gods—that is what they say—and they must surely have known their own ancestors. How can we doubt the word of the children of the gods? Although they give us no probable or certain proofs, still as they declare that they are speaking of what took place in their own families, we must conform to custom and believe them. In this manner, then, according to them, the genealogy of the gods is to be received and set forth.[26]

The solutions found by Plato and Boethius for sacred poetry—ironic question, divine paradox—still hold for Dante, who could perceive and transcend the implicit risks in *allegoria*, revive the myths, and address divine Apollo without dread; his imagination's symmetries are

26. Plato, *Timaeus* 21B–27B; Demos, *Plato*, pp. 383–415.

self-contained. But, for the secular poet, does the breath of God, the "divine fervor" of Boccaccio's description of the true poet, vindicate human love, as well as the love of Orpheus for Euridyce? Boccaccio's definition of poetry, in the *Genealogy of the Gods* 14. 7, ultimately comes from Wisdom 7:25, "Vapor est enim virtutes Dei, et emanatio quidam." It echoes again in Sidney, "when . . . the heavenly Maker of that maker [inspires] him with a divine breath." In Boccaccio, the *fervor quidam exquisite inveniendi, atque dicendi, seu scribendi quod inveneris* becomes magnificent:

> This poetry, which ignorant triflers cast aside, is a sort of fervid and exquisite invention, with fervid expression, in speech or writing, of that which the mind has invented. It proceeds from the bosom of God, and few, I find, are the souls in whom this gift is born; indeed, so wonderful a gift it is that true poets have always been the rarest of men. This fervor of poesy is sublime in its effects: it impels the soul to a longing for utterance; it brings forth strange and unheard-of creations of the mind; it arranges these meditations in a fixed order, adorns the whole composition with unusual interweaving of words and thoughts; and thus it veils truth in a fair and fitting garment of fiction.

"Although they give us no probable or certain proofs," we cannot say that a true poet is not inspired when he brings forth "strange and unheard-of creations of the mind"; for Boccaccio reaffirms the freedom of the mind, the autonomous poetic imagination which "expresses in speech or writing what the mind invents." Boccaccio welcomes ambiguity, and all the miraculous permutations of allegorical fiction, and affirms the poet as maker; as for Plato,

> let us never suppose the learned man meant what these "interpreters" say he did; for I can only believe that great poets and their kind are to be rightly regarded not merely as citizens of his state and all others, but as the princes and rulers thereof.

Boccaccio's manifesto comes more than half a century after Dante had already proclaimed his own truly cosmic autonomy; the *Genealogy* vindicates freedoms already anarchically abused by Jean de Meung, exploited by Rutebeuf's allegorical polemics, and soon licensed again in Chaucer's cruel antitype of Orpheus, the wandering Friar:

> Somwhat he lipsed, for his wantownesse,
> To make his Englissh sweete upon his tonge;
> And in his harpyng, when that he hadde songe,
> He eyen twynkled in his heed aryght,
> As doon the sterres in the frosty nyght.
>
> [A 264–68]

Boccaccio goes one step too far, in his defense of poetic fiction, in denying that rhetoric has any part in the arts poets employ, "when they raise flights of symbolic steps to heaven, or make thick-branching trees spring aloft to the very stars—"

> Haply, to disparage this art . . . men will say that it is rhetoric which the poets employ. Indeed, I will not deny it in part, for rhetoric has also its own inventions. Yet in truth, among the disguises of fiction rhetoric has no part, for whatever is composed as under a veil, and thus exquisitely wrought, is poetry and poetry alone[27]

Even if poets never lie, and even if, as they say, their veiling power of invention comes from the bosom of God, there remains the issue of the indelible image, as in Solon's poem. Even if the great polarities of moral speculation (the *psychomachia*), as Angus Fletcher puts it, the "mythic cosmology [be] reduced by dialectic, . . . to dramatic antitheses [and personifications]," the question still remains in the sixteenth century as Plato posed it: "whether the resulting conflict is good for men to witness, since they are bound to share in what they witness." The question lies near the heart of the paradox of *Troilus and Criseyde*.

27. Osgood, *Genealogy*, 14.7, p. 39; 14.19, p. 92; 14.7, p. 42.

VII

The Evolution of *Troilus and Criseyde:*
A History of Imitations

It is not from any sureness in myself that I cause others to doubt, it is from being more in doubt than anyone else that I cause doubt in others. So now, for my part, I have no idea what virtue is, whilst you, though perhaps you may have known before you came in touch with me, are now as good as ignorant of it also.

Meno, 80C

[Pasquill, to Gnato:] What a goddes name, haue ye a boke in your hande? a good felowshyp wherof is it? let me se. *Nouum testamentum*: what, thou deceivest me / I had wend thou couldest haue skillid of nothing but onli of flateri. But what is this *in* your bosom? an other boke . . . did I not say at the first / that it is a wonder to se this worlde: Som wil be *in* the bowels of diuinite or they know what longeth to good humanitie. Abyde, what is here? *Troylus & Chreseid?* Lord what discord is bitwene these two bokes! . . . As god helpe me, as moche as betwene trouth & lesing.

Sir Thomas Elyot, *Pasquill the Playne* (1533), 3–4

Elizabethan Troy

Looking back through the deep disillusion of Shakspere's *Troilus and Cressida* (1603) and Dryden's pathetic tragedy of 1679, we begin to see more clearly Chaucer's *Troilus and Criseyde*, both what it is and what it is not. In retrospect, the deliberately grotesque distortions of Shakspere's bitter satire of love and heroism emerge; the parodic downward curves of the play seem to spiral ever further away from the tragic fullness and light of Chaucer's poem, and reveal the impossibility of the reconciliation he had attempted, achieved, and then denied. Yet the fulfillment of the dream of love at the center of Chaucer's poem (Book III) remains blindingly pure, no matter how debased its after-images finally become. In Shakspere, Troilus has to see his own nightmare, Cressida giving herself to Diomede:

> This she? . . .
> If beauty have a soul, this is not she;
> If souls guide vows, if vows be sanctimonies,
> If sanctimony be the gods' delight,
> If there be rule in unity itself,
> This was not she. O madness of discourse,
> . . . This is, and is not, Cressid!
>
> [5. 2. 133–42]

Shakspere's answer to all of Troilus's hypothetical subjunctives is their negative: beauty has no soul, vows are not sanctimonies nor is sanctimony the gods' delight. No man knows what is. But what Shakspere's Troilus sees and knows is "fact," however it be interpreted: this is, and is not, Cressida.

Of course it is also true, as it was for Spenser and most readers of Thynne's and Stowe's texts of Chaucer's *Troilus* in the sixteenth century, that Robert Henryson's *Testament of Cresseid* had become after 1532 a sixth part of Chaucer's poem.[1] As Hyder Rollins noted more than fifty years ago, only in very lucky, limited, and precise contexts—when Pandarus, or Criseyde's leprosy, is mentioned—is it possible for us to distinguish allusions to the imitation from references to the original, or to their synthesis, although more than a century had passed between the completion of Chaucer's poem and the writing of its great epilogue by the then virtually unknown *sculemaister of Dunfermline*, ca. 1490.

In the last and clearest version of the original story, Shakspere's audience must bear witness to the degradation of the warriors, the generals, and the lovers, which takes place not in the imagination, but before their eyes. Nothing can be saved from the wreckage of this Troy, and the play repudiates ambiguity.[2] The irony of Thersites' taunts

---

1. R. H. Rollins's essay, "The Troilus–Cressida Story from Chaucer to Shakespeare," *PMLA* 32 (1917): 383–429, and his "critique" in Spurgeon, *Five Hundred Years*, 3: App. A, pp. 1–3, are convenient but long out-of-date source studies. For Shakspere, Robert K. Presson's *Shakespeare's Troilus and Cressida and the Legends of Troy* (Madison, 1953), and Kenneth Muir's *Shakespeare's Sources* (London, 1957), 1: 78–96, provide bibliographical summaries; see also M. C. Bradbrook, "What Shakespeare Did to Chaucer's *Troilus and Criseyde*," *Shakespeare Quarterly* 9 (1958): 311–19. Dryden's revision of Shakspere, which reformulates the plot, will be discussed later in this chapter.

2. O. J. Campbell, *Shakespeare's Satire* (New York, 1943; repr. 1963), ch. 6, discusses the

of Ajax implicates even Nestor and Agamemnon: Helen's lust epitomizes all women, for whom men sacrifice one another, knowing full
well the emptiness of "honor."

> [DIOMEDES.]   Hear me, Paris,
> For every false drop in her bawdy veins
> A Grecian's life hath sunk; for every scruple
> Of her contaminated carrion weight
> A Troyan hath been slain. Since she could speak,
> She hath not given so many good words breath
> As for her Greeks and Troyans suffered death.
> [4. 1. 68–74]

It was rumored very early on, according to Herodotus, that the
whole Greek enterprise was absurd from the start, since Helen had
long been gone to Egypt, and the truth of the matter is the capture of
the city entailed only the further horrors of the Greeks' return: Agamemnon, Cassandra, Medea, Orestes, Antigone.

> This was the account I had from the priests about the arrival of
> Helen at Proteus' court. I think Homer was familiar with the
> story, for though he rejected it as less suitable for epic poetry than
> the one he actually used, he left indications that it was not un-
> known to him . . . and I myself am disposed to add my assent to
> their story about Helen when I consider these things: If she had
> been in Troy, Helen would have been given back to the Greeks,
> whether Paris liked it or not. For Priam and his relations were
> really not so mad as to consent to risk their lives and . . . their
> children that Paris might go on living with Helen. Suppose at
> first they did agree to this, yet after not only many of the other
> Trojans fell in battle every time they fought with the Greeks, but
> the sons of Priam himself (if we are to believe the epic poets) kept

hypothetical audience (perhaps the Inns of Court). Campbell's *Comicall Satyre and Shakespeare's Troilus and Cressida* (San Marino, Cal., 1938) calls the play a satire, as does Alice M. Walker in her edition (Cambridge, 1957). See the opposing views of Karl F. Thompson, *Modesty and Cunning* (East Lansing, Mich., 1971), p. 147; G. Wilson Knight, *The Wheel of Fire* (Oxford, 1931), pp. 51–79; Willard Farnham, *Shakespearean Grotesque* (London, 1971), pp. 128–70. All quotations from Shakspere's *Troilus* are from the edition of Virgil K. Whitaker, *The History of Troilus and Cressida by William Shakespeare* (Baltimore, 1958). For Chaucer's *Troilus*, all quotations are from the edition of R. K. Root, *The Book of Troilus and Criseyde* (Princeton, 1945).

falling, sometimes by twos or three or more—when this sort of thing was going on, I expect that Priam would have given her back to the Achaeans, even if he were living with her himself.[3]

When recounting the history of the rape of Medea, Herodotus gives the version of Helen according to the Persians:

Paris, . . . determined to get a wife out of Greece by carrying her off, being assured in his own mind there would be no requital to be made, for the Greeks had made none either. Therefore he carried off Helen. Then the Greeks resolved first of all to send messengers to demand Helen back and ask satisfaction for the rapt. But when they brought forth these claims, the Persians on their part brought forward the rapt of Medea, saying the Greeks had neither given compensation nor yet surrendered her when they were asked, and yet now looked for compensation from them. Up to this time, then (they say), nothing more had happened than carryings off of women on both sides; but hereafter the Greeks were gravely to blame. For their expedition into Asia [the Trojan war] was made before the Persian invasion of Greece. As for the carrying off of women, they are of the opinion that it is wrong; but to insist upon vengeance after they are carried away is silly. . . . Obviously if they had not wanted to have been abducted, they would not have been. When the women were being captured from Asia, the Persians disregarded the matter. But the Greeks gathered together a mighty host and afterwards came to Asia and put down the glory of Priam, for the sake of a Lacedaemonian woman.[4]

3. Herodotus 2. 115–20; text in *Herodotus, The Histories,* trans. Aubrey de Selincourt, re v. and ed. A. R. Burn (Baltimore, 1972). Cf. 119: "I asked the priests if the Greek story of what happened at Troy had any truth in it, and they gave me in reply some information which they claimed to have had direct from Menelaus himself . . . After the abduction of Helen, the Greeks sent a strong force to the Troad . . . ambassadors were dispatched to Troy, . . . and demanded the restoration of Helen together with the treasure Paris had stolen. . . . The Trojans, however, gave them the answer which they always stuck to afterwards . . . namely, that neither Helen nor the treasure was in their possession, but both were in Egypt, . . . being detained by the Egyptian King, Proteus. . . . The Greeks laid siege to the town, and persisted until it fell, but no Helen was found, and they were still told the same story, until at last they believed it . . . Menelaus [went to Egypt], and was most hospitably entertained, and Helen, none the worse for her adventures, was restored to him with all the rest of his property."
4. Herodotus, 1. 3. He comments on his narrative (with "Chaucerian" irony), "I am bound to repeat what is currently said; I am not bound to believe it" (7. 152–3).

The reinterpretation of these events, so long mythologized and revised in Western histories, reiterates the ironic laws of loss of necessary ignorance, and the inevitable reversal of the ends achieved. The circle of necessity turns the war in its downward path, thrusting down the great walls, emptying the seats of power of the heroes, so at last the craven lesson of the *eirons* (Pandarus and Thersites) is enforced, on Shakspere's stage: it is better to keep your head down, be one among the crowd, tempt no gods, affect to mean, and to know nothing at all.[5]

> [THERSITES.] Here's Agamemnon . . . to what, from but that he is, should wit larded with malice and malice forced with wit turn him to? To an ass, were nothing; he is both ox and ass. To be a dog, a mule, a cat, a fitchew, a toad, a lizard, an owl, a puttock, or a herring without a roe, I would not care; but to be Menelaus! I would conspire against destiny. Ask me not what I would be, if I were not Thersites, for I care not to be the louse of a lazar, so were I not Menelaus.
>
> [5. 1. 50–65]
>
> . . . .
>
> Shall the elephant Ajax carry it thus? . . . Then there's Achilles, a rare engineer. If Troy be not taken till these two undermine it, the walls will stand till they fall of themselves. O thou great thunder-darter of Olympus, forget thou art Jove, the king of gods; and Mercury, lose all the serpentine craft of thy caduceus, if ye take not that little, little, less than little wit from them that they have; which short-armed ignorance itself knows is so abundant scarce it will not in circumvention deliver a fly from a spider, without drawing their massy irons and cutting the web.
>
> [2. 3. 2–15]

The comic *alazon*, who boasts to be more than he is, is the object of our contempt; he bears the brunt of scorn as the scapegoat of those who dare. In Shakspere's *Troilus*, hero and fool are indistinguishable:

5. J. A. K. Thomson, *Irony, An Historical Introduction* (London, 1926), ch. 4: "There are two moods in which a man may confront the jealous gods besides . . . helpless acquiescence. He may defy them, or laugh in his sleeve at them . . . Tragic and . . . Comic Irony are in the last resort the same" (pp. 34–35); "Rhetoric is by its nature (emphatic, persuasive) antipathetic to Irony. There is indeed a figure of speech called 'Irony' but this device is in practice so gross and obvious that the truly Ironical man avoids it" (p. 240); "*Eiron* and *Alazon* are correlative terms, like Greek and Barbarian. Each explains the other. The *Alazon* pretends to be something more, the *Eiron* to be something less, than he is. As Cicero puts it (*de Offic.* 1. 30), the former simulates, the latter dissimulates" (p. 10).

[THERSITES.] . . . that young Troyan ass . . . that stale old mouse-eaten dry cheese, Nestor, and that same dog-fox, Ulysses . . . that mongrel cur Ajax, . . . that dog of as bad a kind, Achilles. . . .

[5. 4. 12–15]

[PANDAR.] O world, world! . . . O traitors and bawds, how earnestly are you set a-work, and how ill requited. Why should our endeavor be so loved, and the performance so loathed?

[5. 10. 35–39]

In virtually all comedy, nemesis is sudden, but long foreseen, laughably physical, and perversely cruel: in Chaucer, we laugh at the scalding of Nicholas, the humiliation of Miller Simkin and the Summoner, in evident relief that he—the *alazon*—is not us. But the rejection of Falstaff, the cudgeling of Thersites, the wrath aroused in us by Iago, turn the punishers upon even those whose role is to undercut, deny, debase human wisdom: the *eirons* and the malcontents themselves. There is no way to escape the nemesis incurred by knowing, or seeming to know, more—or even claiming to know less—than is in fact the case. Buffoon and villain fuse in the impotence of Pandar. So, as the comic sport of punishment turns inward, turns toward tragedy, at the point of transition arise those rare works of art which negate both comic and tragic, and affirm nothing: Shakspere's *Troilus*, the paintings of Hieronymus Bosch, the *Dunciad*. In the theater, the pain evoked by the shattering of images cannot be escaped, and the fantasy is exposed for what it is: fear of the meaninglessness of the events portrayed, made mercilessly close, with no escape left open. The possibility of rehabilitation does not exist for Shakspere's "clapper-clawed Trojans" and their counterpart Greeks, nor was there ever anything among them worth saving.[6] Even the great speech of Ulysses—the dog-fox—before the council, describing the causes of the failure of the siege, corrupts the cosmic image of order; the context breaks it down, and it collapses under the weight of its own rhetorical grandeur, in Nestor's echoes.

[ULYSSES.] Take but degree away, untune that string,
　　　　And hark what discord follows. Each thing meets
　　　　In mere oppugnancy. The bounded waters
　　　　Should lift their bosoms higher than the shores,

---

6. See above, n. 3; Goethe remarked that what he had learned from reading Homer is that "our life on earth is already and actually hell."

And make a sop of all this solid globe;
Strength should be lord of imbecility,
And the rude son should strike his father dead;
Force should be right, or rather right and wrong,
Between whose endless jar justice resides,
Should lose their names, and so should justice too;
Then everything include itself in power,
Power into will, will into appetite,
And appetite, an universal wolf,
So doubly seconded with will and power,
Must make perforce an universal prey
And last eat up himself. Great Agamemnon,
This chaos, when degree is suffocate,
Follows the choking.

[1. 3. 109–26]

The affirmation of ideal order is subverted by its speaker and our knowledge of his cunning, and the destructive purpose to which his wisdom is to be put.

[ULYSSES.] My prophecy is but half his journey yet,
          For yonder walls, that pertly front your town,
          Yon towers, whose wanton tops do buss the clouds,
          Must kiss their own feet.

[HECTOR.] There they stand yet, and modestly I think,
          The fall of every Phrygian stone will cost
          A drop of Grecian blood. The end crowns all,
          And that old common arbitrator, Time,
          Will one day end it.

[4. 5. 217–224]

The final echo is Thersites':

What's become of the wenching rogues? I think they
have swallowed one another. I would laugh at that
miracle—yet, in a sort, lechery eats itself.

[5. 4. 33–34]

Priam's city must be invaded and burned, not through the malevolence of the gods, but through the bestiality of men. The wolf at last will eat up himself, and those who would trap him, the makers of walls, the astrologers, even the sculptors themselves—are enlisted in the same destructive enterprise, obeying the same deadly instinct.

> [PANDARUS.] What verse for it? What instance for it? Let me see.
> "Full merrily the humble-bee doth sing
> Till he hath lost his honey and his sting;
> And being once subdued in armed tail,
> Sweet honey and sweet notes together fail."
>
> [5. 10. 39–44]

So much for the lyric symbol of immortality, order, and the sweetness of procreation—wax, honey, and light.

The war becomes the largest and most compelling dimension of Shakspere's play because it magnifies and randomizes the death instinct which the love theme makes concrete: to love Cressida is to love that which it is death to know.

> [TROILUS.] No Pandarus. I stalk about her door
> Like a strange soul upon the Stygian banks,
> Staying for waftage. O, be thou my Charon
> And give me swift transportance to those fields
> Where I may wallow in the lily-beds
> Proposed for the deserved.
>
> [3. 2. 7–12]

None will survive, though some are not yet dead, and the foreknowledge of time's curse is a mockery. The denial of a heroic death for Troilus is Shakspere's pitiless refusal to affirm any conventions in the play, just as the exposure of Cressida's surrender to Diomede before Troilus's eyes exhausts the formulae for faithlessness.

> [THERSITES.] All the argument is a whore and a cuckold,
> a good quarrel to draw emulous factions and bleed
> to death upon.
>
> [2. 3. 68–70]

> Lechery, lechery, still wars and lechery;
> nothing else holds fashion. A burning devil take them.
>
> [5. 2. 190–92]

Fictionality, History, and Truth: The Trojan Myth and
Renaissance Allegory

Shakspere's *Troilus and Cressida* was first copyrighted in 1603, as
The booke . . . , and then in 1609, as *The Historie of Troilus and Cressida.*
. . . In the printing of the First Folio, three pages of the play were
printed, including it among the tragedies, immediately after *Romeo
and Juliet*, but it was then removed, and, unpaginated, placed between
the histories and tragedies in the complete Folio of 1623.[7] Shakspere's
generically indeterminate play, not listed in the Folio's contents, begot
one more changeling, a final mutant in the line of Renaissance glosses
on the medieval Trojan chronicle. Dryden's *Troilus and Cressida: Or,
Truth Found Too Late* (1679) is a reinterpretation of the tragic elements,
an attempt to salvage Shakspere's play, which Dryden in his Preface
self-consciously acknowledges as his source. In the curious genealogy
of the Troilus story, each inheritor in turn alludes to an immediate
antecedent, the "authority," named or nameless, which maintains the
appearance of historical truth.[8] The history of Pandar and his narrators
could perhaps be compared to the evolution of what Curtius called the
"credibility topos"—the *adtestio rei visae*—and its variants, which are
latent in the strange reciprocity that implicates the inner fiction making
with the outer, the defeated go-between and the author of his failure.

Later in this chapter we will reconsider the line of descent from the
"sources" of the Troilus story in the Middle Ages and the Renaissance,
which go back increasingly unclearly from Dryden, based on Shakspere,
to Shakspere, based on the Renaissance "Chaucer," Chapman, and
others, to Henryson, who changed the ending of Chaucer's *Troilus*,
to Chaucer, the *grant translateur*, based on the aggregate of Latin, French,
and Italian versions of Boccaccio and "Lollius." We may notice here
one striking common factor which links them all, through the cumulative changes of three hundred years. Each reinterpretation picks up
and echoes a tone of anxiety, a concern to preserve the distinction

7. Whitaker, *Troilus and Cressida*, pp. 15–16.

8. Curtius, *European Literature*, p. 175, quotes the "motif" in Dares and Dictys as their
characteristic insistence "that everything is strictly true," and also in Macrobius, who cites
it "among the means of arousing emotion." Curtius traces the credibility topos to Aeneas's
account of the destruction of Troy (*quaeque . . . ipsi vidi*). Griffin and Myrick note the Middle
English commonplace in translations, "*as the Frennsh boke sayth*" in their short history of
Boccaccio's Trojan materials for the *Filostrato*. See below, n. 20.

between myth or "fictionality" (as in the Shaksperean Pyramus and Thisbe playlet) and "true history"; the probability indispensable for *Troilus*, in tragedy or tragic satire. Chaucer's Troilus rejects analogy:

> [PANDARUS.] For this nis nought certain the nexte wise
> To winne love—as techen us the wise—
> To walwe and weepe as Niobe the queene
> Whos teres yit in marbel been yseene.

> [TROILUS.] "Freend, though that I stille lie,
> I am nat deef; now pees, and crye namore,
> For I have herd thy wordes and thy lore, . . .
> . . . .
> Nor other cure canstou noon for me.
> Eek I nil nat been cured: I wol deye.
> What knowe I of the queene Niobe?
> Lat be thine olde ensamples, I thee praye."
>   [*Tr* 1. 697–700, 752–60]

The historicity of the story—a credible "source"—is necessary for it to be not a dream—"what might be"—but a revelation of what has to be. In the excellent words of Morton Bloomfield, "We are all part of time's kingdom [and in *Troilus*], we are never allowed to forget it."

> If there are no strong unique facts, there is nothing to lament. We cannot escape into the web of myth and cycle; the uniqueness of the past is the guarantee of its own transience.[9]

Although Dryden's tragedy lies beyond the temporal limits of Chaucer's Renaissance "Progenie" (as Speght used the term in 1598), his play and Shakspere's are, as we shall see, clear evidence of phenomena which concern literary history as problematically as they are definitive enigmas in aesthetics. The ambivalent fictionality of medieval

9. M. W. Bloomfield, "Distance and Predestination in *Troilus and Criseyde*," *PMLA* 72 (1957): 14–26; repr. in R. J. Schoeck and J. Taylor, *Chaucer Criticism, II* (Notre Dame, 1960), pp. 196–210. See also Charles Muscatine's *Chaucer and the French Tradition* (Berkeley, 1964), ch. 5; E. T. Donaldson, *Speaking of Chaucer* (New York, 1970), ch. 5 and 6; Ida L. Gordon, *The Double Sorwe of Troilus, A Study of the Ambiguities in Troilus and Criseyde* (Oxford, 1970); P. M. Kean, *Chaucer and the Making of English Poetry* (London, 1972). The standard study of Chaucer's sources in *Troilus* is Sanford B. Meech, *Design in Chaucer's Troilus* (Syracuse, 1959). A more recent, very thorough reexamination is Gretchen B. Mieszkowski's *The Reputation of Criseyde*, Conn. Acad. Arts and Science, Trans. 43:3 (1971).

narrative comes alive on the Renaissance stage, and forces the audience
to accept its "truth" as patent fiction. As the painted backcloth replaces
imaginary Troy and Cressida's mutability is impersonated by an actress,
in Shakspere and Dryden, the visionary landscape which the audience
is free to invent, in even the most rigid allegories of the precursors,
contracts to a straight line. So, even in the era of literary dearth C. S.
Lewis labelled the Drab Age, the old poetic codes and cues to the
multidimensional landscapes of the *Roman de la Rose* and the *Parliament
of Fowls* still preserve the technical means to make perspective subservient to wonder or fear, too familiar to be improbable. Thus, to
take an example from one of the most crippled and myopic of early
sixteenth-century allegorical poems, Hawes's Lady Fame comes alive
for a moment, surrealistically, accompanied by her beautiful symbolic
pair of greyhounds (with golden collars, engraved in diamonds, "Go-
vernance" and "Grace"), riding to Graunde Amoure at sunrise, across

> . . . a valaye ferre,
> A goodly lady / enuyronned aboute
> With tongues of fyre / as bryght as ony sterre
> That fyry flambes / ensensed alwaye out
> Which I behelde / and was in great doubt
> Her palfraye swyfte / rennynge as the wynde . . .
> Pegase the swyfte / so fayre in excellence.
>
> [*Pastime of Pleasure*, 155–60, 179][10]

In the Induction to *2 Henry IV*, Rumour, of that same long Virgilian
line of phantom women dressed *with fyry flame / Of brennynge tonges*,
(*Pastime of Pleasure*, 176–77) stands on the boards to command the
audience:

> I, from the orient to the drooping west
> Making the wind my post-horse, still unfold
> The acts commenced on this ball of earth.
>
> [3–5]

When Rumour asks,

> What need I thus
> My well-known body to anatomize
> Among my household?
>
> [20–22]

10. *The Pastime of Pleasure by Stephen Hawes*, ed. William E. Mead, *EETS*, O. S. 173 (1928,
for 1927):11.

the answer lies in the living physical presence of the speaker of the lines, whose reality must be suppressed by an effort of willed submission by the audience in order to achieve, against the evidence of reason, dramatic transcendence.

> O for a muse of fire, that would ascend
> The brightest heaven of invention,
> A kingdom for a stage, princes to act
> And monarchs to behold the swelling scene!
>
> [*Henry V*, Prologue, 1–4]

What Shakspere and Dryden must labor to effect, paradoxically against all the advantages of theatrical trompe l'oeil, is the almost effortless opening into imaginary, "historical" Troy taken for granted by Henryson, Chaucer, and their predecessors. That access, invisible in narrative, is at the threshold of the stage. The flickering ambiguity that plays on Chaucer's Criseyde like light, so that she becomes virtually transparent, a cloudy figure for earthly mutability—*this world, that passeth sone as flowres faire*—can no longer be imagined when we see her seduction before our eyes.

The paradox for the artist and the poet in the Renaissance is that for every gain he makes in the mastery of imitation—as the concept itself undergoes redefinition—his task becomes more hazardous, and the fictional illusion more difficult to enter freely, the closer it comes to victory over doubt. Shakspere tests the fiction again and again in the play within the play, the eavesdropper, the unobserved observer, as in the scene of Cressida's yielding to Diomede. Was *this* Criseyde? To sustain allegorical ambiguity, against the increasing temptation to take possession of more and more "real" territory, becomes a challenge that Spenser was one of the last English poets to master. The timid postmedieval allegorists he succeeded (Lydgate, Barclay, Hawes) depended on the compromises between the "fiction" and the fallen world granted by fiat by the Church to the great secular poets of the three last medieval centuries, from Alan de Lille in the twelfth to Gower and Chaucer in the fourteenth. Spenser, in full possession of his own conservative and nostalgic vision, and in competition with the extraordinary staged reality of Marlowe and Shakspere, sought to make the imaginative inner world of his *Faerie Queene* as deep in the dream time and space as medieval allegory could be, and as vivid and sensuously alive with personages as the other world could be in the fictional theater. The result is, in effect, anomaly. Archimago and his Duessa, the master of fantasia and the archetypal emanation of sexual betrayal, are incomparably more powerful figures than their several Shaksperean analogues, among whom we may see Pandar and his Cressida. But Spenser's mythopoeic images are greater by virtue of their fictionality: they do not appear in the light, but emerge, as in Plato's great myths of the mind, as shadows, envisioned by their Narrator.[11]

Analogy and Reinterpretation: The Example of Pandar

The relative frequency with which historical criticism in all the arts finds analogues (much as theology needs parable, and philosophy, myth) arises from the ready simplicity of parallel. Analogy stresses the likenesses of things across any artificial boundary. Then follows the immensely useful evolution from harmony and analogical proportion ("as x is to y, so a is to b") to metonymy and expressive metaphor ("the heart of the issue," "the depth of despair"). However, analogy easily absorbs or plays down unlikeness and obscures the intermediate steps; in criticism, it may become an evasion. Frequently we are content to have explained and understood an image or an idea by finding its analogue in another form, another vocabulary, even another art. Such analogizing is perhaps indispensable, and metonymy inevitable.[12] This seems to be the case especially in studies of artistic evolution in the Renaissance, when the inheritance of medieval allegorical patterns was being superseded, but not abolished, by the successive revolutions in religious thought and the humanist rediscovery of antiquity. After ca. 1500, the tempo of change—revision and disintegration—speeds up. The contrast between the old woodcuts and the new poems in the volumes they embellish—what Rosamond Tuve called "imposed

11. Cf. *Republic*, 7. 514–518C; 10. 614B–621D. The figure of Plato's Interpreter, who scatters the lots from the lap of Lachesis, the daughter of Necessity, to the souls about to be born again, is perhaps another archetypal figure for Spenser's Genius, but not, of course, for Alan de Lille. The *Republic* was not available in the West until after 1400: the first Latin translation is that of P. C. Decembrio (1439); Ficino began his work on Plato in 1463. See Bolgar, *Classical Heritage*, pp. 277, 434, and Appendix 2; and Klibansky, *Platonic Tradition*, passim, for the medieval Plato.

12. By metonymy I mean simply naming a thing by substitution of either one of its attributes or an associated term, instead of the name itself. A representative Elizabethan rhetoric, Richard Sherry's *A Treatise of Schemes and Tropes* (1550), distinguishes five common forms of "metonomia, or Transnominacioum." See the modern reprint, ed. Herbert W. Hildebrandt in the series "Scholars' Facsimiles and Reprints" (Gainesville, Fla., 1961).

allegory"—illustrates the complex problems in "intention" and re-
sidual meanings we confront.[13] The rise of Plato, rediscovered, the
return of Homer, in full texts replacing the crude medieval synopses,
and the rediscovery of the antique forms of the pagan gods, freed from
their medieval fancy-dress disguises, comprise the Renaissance paradox:
the simultaneous survival and rebirth of the ancients, "known" in the
Middle Ages as if in ciphers.[14] The annotations of Speght's *Chaucer* of
1598 not only gloss the "hard words" of obsolete Middle English, but
provide citations and parallels from both the *Iliad* and the *Odyssey*,
in Greek, for the first time in any edition of Chaucer. The legends of
Troy, especially for the English descendants of "Brut," Aeneas' great-
grandson, are a paradigm for Renaissance reinterpretation of both the
Middle Ages and antiquity.

It may be worthwhile, therefore, to consider the problematic implications of analogy, and to make use of some, as an aspect of interpretation before we examine and compare reinterpretations of Chaucer's poems as they gradually become part of received poetic tradition
and beget new poems. *Troilus and Criseyde* in the Renaissance far
outweighs the dream visions and the *Canterbury Tales* as a "source" and
as a precedent, as well as in the numerical total of posthumous allusions
to Chaucer counted by Spurgeon and Rollins.[15] *Troilus* is one of the
great precursor poems, whose influence, conscious and unconscious,
traced and still untraced, is like that of Dante's *Comedy*, immeasurable.
The case of Shakspere's *Troilus*, where we began, serves as a turning
point for digression, for comparisons of one variable, which will then
return us to the evolution of the story, and its mutation.

Let us begin with Shakspere's Pandarus, whose role is diminished
to less than that of Thersites, his counterpart in the Greek camp.[16] In
the pivotal scene four in act 4, Pandarus begs the lovers to accept
reality, the terms of the truce:

13. See her *Allegorical Imagery, Some Medieval Books and their Posterity* (Princeton, 1966), ch.
4; and Charles Muscatine, *Chaucer's Book* (San Francisco, 1963), for comments on the woodcuts in the sixteenth-century editions of the *Canterbury Tales*.

14. "Homer" was transmitted in the Middle Ages in *Ilias Latina*, 1100 Latin hexameters
summarizing the *Iliad*, by Silius Italicus, called "Pindarus Thebanus." See below, pp. 193 ff.

15. Spurgeon, in *Five Hundred Years*, I, xxv–vii; and Appendix A, III, 1–77, attempted a
statistical treatment of Chaucer's literary influence; her "counts" were immediately chal-
lenged. See below, p. 193 and n. 52

16. In the "postmedieval sources," Pandarus plays little or no role, e.g., in Henryson's
Testament, Lydgate's *Troy Book*, Heywood's *Iron Age*, or Peele's *Tale of Troy*.

[CRESSIDA.] Have the gods envy?
[PANDARUS.] Ay, ay, ay, ay; 'tis too plain a case.

[4. 4. 27–28]

His exit line fleetingly recalls the powerful prognostication of Chaucer's
Pandarus, who foresaw the shielding rain that fell all night in seeming
blessing of Criseyde's surrender, and Troilus's sexual initiation,[17] but
this Pandar has only hyperbole, and he cannot even make himself weep.

[PANDARUS.] Where are my tears? Rain, to lay this wind,
        or my heart will be blown up by the root!

[4. 4. 52–53]

Pandarus makes only one more appearance in the play before the
Epilogue. In act 5, scene 3, he brings Cressida's letter to Troilus, but
his speech (11. 101–06) is nothing but a catalogue of his diseases, and
he never learns what Cressida said.

. . . and I have a rheum in mine eyes, too, and
such an ache in my bones that, unless a man
were cursed, I cannot tell what to think on 't.

This is the imagery of Pandarus's curtain speech, which is acid, obscene,
and malevolent. He wills the corruption of both sex and old age as the
play's legacy to the audience, as Shakspere inverts the moral theme of
the *Testament of Cresseid*, the curse which blasts her beauty and brings
self-recognition of her guilt. This is perhaps the closest point of tangency
between the Henryson version—the Renaissance tradition—and
Shakspere, as we shall see. The symbolic disease which kills Henryson's
Cresseid becomes Pandarus's curse on the audience, and on himself, the
price of their witnessing of his failure. There is, of course, no Pandarus
in the *Testament*: not even Calchas curses, and the gods have all the
power. They are their own intermediaries.

Pandarus was a go-between from the start, and always punished for
his success. As a Trojan named in the war, he first appears in Homer,

17. Cf., *Troilus and Criseyde*, 3. 624–30:
        The bente moone with hire hornes pale,
        Saturne, and Jove in Cancro joyned were,
        That swych a reyn from hevene gan avale,
        That every maner womman that was there
        Hadde of that smoky reyn a verray feere;
        At which Pandare tho lough, and seyde thenne:
        "Now were it tyme a lady to gon henne!"

Iliad 4. 87–140, where Athene, disguised as a young warrior, comes to the Lycian archer Pandaros, "a man blameless and powerful" (4. 89) but "with a fool's heart in him" (4. 104).[18] Hera and Athene make use of him to violate the truce between Trojans and Greeks: he is persuaded to shoot an arrow, which deeply wounds Menelaus. So the jealous gods intervene to break the stalemate, and in the melee that follows (in Dictys' account and in Homer), Pandaros pays the penalty "for that cursed manner of fighting" by losing his life to Diomede (*Iliad* 5. 288–96). Pandaros's desire for glory is the means used by the gods to punish men, ultimately, for Paris's choice of Venus's beauty: sexual desire.

Much later, in the conflation of "Dares" and "Dictys" in Benoit's *Roman de Troie* (1155) and Boccaccio's *Il Filostrato* (1340), there is etymological word play, in French and Italian, on Pandar's Greek name ("giver of all"), but in neither has he yet aged into the avuncular role he plays in Chaucer's *Troilus*, presiding over the rites of Troilus's loss of innocence from the feast to the ordering of the urn for his ashes.[19] In the *Filostrato*, Boccaccio's Pandar is full of platitudes and strategy, but he is still a young warrior, a contemporary who serves more as a courier between his "cousins" than a procurer. Pandar's sympathy with Troilo, before and after the event, is sincere, uncomplicated, and it lasts until the end of the eighth of Boccaccio's nine books; his last words are to declare that he has willingly sacrificed his honor for the sake of Troilo's love. His prayer to the gods to punish Criseida *si che piu 'n tal guisa non fallisca* ("so that she may not sin again in like fashion")[20] is seemingly devoid of irony. The Narrator is full of sympathy for both Pandar and Troilo.

Chaucer's Pandarus has become Criseyde's uncle and Troilus's closest companion; he is never described, but he dominates the action of the poem. He is Chaucer's most brilliant and subtle dramatic characterization, the source of all of the poem's wit, intelligence, and energy, and he makes its compromises with reality entirely with words. He virtually dictates, and then delivers, the letters, invents their occasions, tells the necessary lies, and makes the fictional crises "real."[21] Until the

18. *The Iliad of Homer*, trans. Richmond Lattimore (Chicago, 1951). All quotations are from Lattimore's translation.

19. *Troilus and Criseyde*, 5. 309–15.

20. *Il Filostrato di Boccaccio*, ed. with trans. by Nathaniel Griffin and Arthur B. Myrick (Philadelphia, 1929), 8. 24 (pp. 494–95). All quotations from Boccaccio are from this source, hereafter cited as Griffin and Myrick, *Filostrato*.

21. For example, in Book II, the need to consult Deiphebus, which brings Criseyde to

truce is declared in Book 4, he is, as Donaldson observes, Chaucer's master of illusion. His last words in the poem are, *I kan namore seye* (5. 1743).

Although the Narrator never describes him, Pandarus's physical presence is charismatic, close up, and his action is more vivid than any other movement in the poem—except, of course, the consummation scene where sensuous description of the lovers' bodies dissolves into similes that in effect sublimate their physical embrace. Pandarus, however, bustles in and out of doors, pokes Criseyde and chucks her chin, sings, and wants to dance. He fetches pillows and candles, thrusts Troilus, unconscious, into bed and rips off his shirt; he goes to house-parties and committee meetings, and walks the walls with Troilus. But in all of these scenes, the Narrator is looking, not at Pandar, but as if through him, toward what Pandar sees. As if he can be trusted as the witness of the events the Narrator can only imagine: Pandar's imaginative power to see, and to make what he sees seem to be, conjures the reality inside the poem, and it is through the Narrator's use of Pandar that the illusion of the action is conveyed to us by documentary reportage.

> Quod Pandarus: "thus fallen is this cas."
> . . . .
> "Ye woot, ye nece myn," quod he, "what is."
> $\qquad\qquad\qquad\qquad\qquad\qquad\qquad$ [3. 841;844]

> [PANDARUS.] "And, by my trouthe, I have right now of the
> $\qquad$ A good conceyte in my wit, as I gesse,
> $\qquad$ And what it is I wol now that thou se.
> $\qquad$ I thenke . . .
> $\qquad\qquad\qquad$ I wol thi thank deserve,
> $\qquad$ Have here my trowthe, and that thow shalt wel here";
> $\qquad$ And went his wey, thenking on this matere,
> $\qquad$ And how he best myghte hire biseche of grace,
> $\qquad$ And fynde a time therto, and a place.
> $\qquad\qquad\qquad\qquad\qquad$ [1. 995–98; 1060–64]

Both the Narrator's and Pandarus's roles are significantly increased in Chaucer's poem. Both are much older than the lovers and claim to be

---

Troilus's bedside; in Book III, the report of the "rival" (Oraste), which brings Troilus to Criseyde for her denial.

beyond *al swich hoot fare*: they are drawn into alignment close to parallel.[22] As the Narrator labors to transmit his knowledge of love, based on
the *olde bookes*, to the reader, Pandarus labors to teach Troilus and
Criseyde all the old words, the defenses that are no defense, the pros
and cons that are all true enough, so far as he can be trusted. The
Narrator serves Pandarus in his own cause, and both are alike, intermediaries.

> "Now, em," quod she, "what wolde ye devise?
> What is youre rede I sholde don of this?"
> "That is wel seyd," quod he, "certein, best is
> That ye hym love ayeyn for his lovynge;
> As love for love is skilful guerdonynge.
> . . . .
> Go love; for olde, ther wol no wight of the;
> Lat this proverbe a loore unto yow be:
> 'To late ywar, quod beaute, whan it paste';
> And elde daunteth daunger at the laste."
>
> [2. 388–92; 396–99]

> And with that thought [Troilus] gan ful sore syke,
> And seyde: "allas, what is me best to do?"
> To whom Pandare answerde: "if the like,
> The beste is that thow telle me al thi wo,
> And have my trouthe . . ."
>
> [1. 827–31]

Through Pandarus's ability to see and to make what he imagines
plausible, finally tangible, the Narrator overcomes his own limited
vision, ironically doubling his self-confessed impotence to alter the
events of the story.

> "Ye, haselwode!" thoughte this Pandare,
> And to hym self ful softeliche he seyde:
> "God woot, refreyden may this hote fare,
> Or Calkas sende Troilus Criseyde!"
>
> [5. 505–09]

22. In *Design in Chaucer's Troilus*, Meech observes that Chaucer's Pandarus "has more than
twice as many lines as Boccaccio's" (p. 9), and he comments on the expanded role of Chaucer's Narrator (p. 14), which he regards as an attempt to gain "closer rapport" with the audience, and as wide an audience as possible. Meech also quotes with approval the opinion of
John L. Lowes, that Chaucer's greatest achievement in *Troilus* is the "detachment" of his
presentation of love.

So, as Troilus sings, Pandarus thinks to himself. The tensions Chaucer manipulates, between illusion at the surface and bleak clarity, consciousness and unconscious recognition, are played out fully in the scene at the city wall on the evening of the tenth day (which in Shakspere is replaced by the nocturnal visit to the Greek camp, where Cressida does appear, "within"). As the light fades, Troilus beccmes calm, certain that he understands the meaning of the empty horizon: she doesn't wish to be seen. In a reversal that occurs in the ellipsis between stanzas, having "seen" why Criseyde does not wish to be seen, suddenly Troilus sees:

> " . . . Pandarus, now woltow trowen me?
> Have here my trouthe, I se hire! yond she is!
> Heve up thyn eyen, man! maistow nat se?"
> Pandare answerde: "nay, so mote I the!
> Al wrong, by god; what seistow, man? where arte?
> That I se yond nys but a fare-carte."
>
> [5. 1157–62]

The moment blurs, as Troilus accepts, with strange relief, and predicts that she will come by night. Answering in kind, keeping up the fiction, Pandarus replies

> "it may be wel ynough,"
> And held with hym of al that evere he seyde;
> But in his herte he thoughte, and softe lough,
> And to hym self ful sobreliche he seyde:
> "From haselwode, there joly Robyn pleyde,
> Shal come al that thow abidest heere:
> Ye, farewel al the snow of ferne yere!"
>
> [5. 1170–76]

Pandarus's sleight of hand with platitudes, taken at face value by the Narrator, implicitly affirms what he denies. Pandarus's angry denial of the power of Fortune in Book I, when he is rousing Troilus to confidence in his freedom to love, comes back in the mocking echoes of Book IV, at the anticlimax before Criseyde's departure. Pandarus again attempts to rouse Troilus from his despair by turning Fortune's wheel full circle once more. "You are doomed: we all are; cut your losses: time is running out; this town is full of ladies":

Quod Pandarus; "than blamestow Fortune
For thow art wroth, ye, now at erst I see;
Wostow nat wel that Fortune is commune
To everi manere wight in som degree?
And yit thow hast this comfort, lo, parde:
That, as hire joies moten overgone,
So more hire sorwes passen everychone.

For if hire whiel stynte any thyng to torne,
Than cessed she Fortune anon to be;
Now, sith hire whiel by no wey may sojourne,
What woostow if hire mutabilite,
Right as thy selven list, wol don by the,
Or that she be nat fer fro thyn helpynge?
Paraunter, thow hast cause for to synge."

[1. 841–54]

. . . .
                              "yis;
As wisly were it fals as it is trewe,
That I have herd, and woot al how it is.
O mercy, god, who wolde have trowed this?
Who wolde have wend that, in so litel a throwe
Fortune oure joie wolde han overthrowe?

For in this world ther is no creature,
As to my dome, that evere saw ruyne
Straunger than this, thorugh cas or aventure.
But who may al eschue, or al devyne?
Swich is this world; forthi I thus deffyne,
Ne trust no wight to fynden in Fortune
Ay propretee; hire yiftes ben commune.

But tel me this, whi thow art now so mad
To sorwen thus? whi listow in this wise,
Syn thi desir al holly hastow had,
So that by right it oughte ynough suffise?
But I, that nevere felte in my servyse
A frendly cheere, or lokyng of an eye,
Lat me thus wepe and wailen, til I dye.

And over al this, as thow wel woost thi selve,
This town is ful of ladyes al aboute;
And, to my doom, fairer than swiche twelve
As evere she was, shal I fynde in som route,
Ye, oon or two, withouten any doute.
Forthi be glad, myn owen deere brother;
If she be lost, we shal recovere an other."

[4. 380–406]

At a profounder level than the sophistry of his circular reasonings in
Book IV against Necessity, which Chaucer so clearly exposes for what
they are—the expedient contradictions of a man trapped by his own
pragmatism—in Book V, Pandarus's distrust and fear of dreams reject
the imagination itself, the very source of his own power to make things
seem. The Narrator relies on his *auctors*, but Pandarus prefers his own
intelligence.

"Thy swevenes ek and al swich fantasie
Drif out, and lat hem faren to meschaunce;
For they procede of thi malencolie,
That doth the fele in slepe al this penaunce.
A straw for alle swevenes signifiaunce!
God helpe me so, I counte hem nought a bene;
Ther woot no man aright what dremes mene.

For prestes of the temple tellen this:
That dremes ben the revelaciouns
Of goddes; and as wel they telle, ywis,
That they ben infernals illusiouns.
And leches seyn that of complexiouns
Proceden they, or fast, or glotonye.
Who woot in soth thus what thei signifie?

Ek oothre seyn that thorugh impressiouns,
As if a wight hathe faste a thyng in mynde,
That thereof comen swich avysiouns.
And oothre seyn, as they in bokes fynde,
That after tymes of the yer by kynde
Men dreme, and that theffect goth by the moone.
But leve no dreme, for it is nought to doone.

[5. 358–78]

This whole scene, with its insistent echoes of Pandarus's "Rise up!
Awake!" in Book I, and its ironic repetition of the *carpe diem* theme of
time's mutability, reveals more and more of Pandarus's inadequacy.
As the Narrator repeats, "as the booke seyth," Pandarus repeats himself:

> "For which with al myn herte I the biseche,
> Unto thi self that al this thow foryive;
> And ris now up, withouten more speche,
> And lat us caste how forth may best be dryve
> This tyme, and ek how fresshly we may lyve . . .
>
> [5. 386–90]

> Ris, lat us speke of lusty lif in Troie
> That we han led, and forth the tyme dryve;
> And ek of tyme comyng us rejoie,
> That bryngen shal oure blisse now so blyve.
>
> [5. 393–96]

The price of Pandarus's denial of *swevenes signifiaunce* is revealed in his
reduction to repetition: he is losing words, and soon will have no more
to say—as he has no more time, only the present moment. He is in fact,
redundant already: "*This town is ful of lordes al aboute | And trewes lasten
al this mene while*" (5. 400–01).

The audience knows, as the characters themselves know, the truce
will not last. Both the temporal necessity and the phantoms of possibility which Pandarus refused to admit may exist soon rise up in all
their power and expose his ignorance, the terrible darkness of the mind
that understands only itself. The power to make things of words, as if
language itself can create the human heart's desire, links Chaucer's
Pandarus to both poetry and idol making, and his ignorance is scepticism.

The common medieval source on idolatry is the Wisdom of Solomon
14:12 ff.:[23]

> For the idea of making idols was the beginning of fornication, and
> the invention of them was the corruption of life. For neither have
> they existed from the beginning, nor will they exist forever. For

23. *The Oxford Annotated Apocrypha*, RSV (New York, 1965), pp. 118–19. For a survey of the
medieval traditions, see J. D. Cooke, "Euhemerism: A Medieval Interpretation of Classical
Paganism," *Speculum* 2(1927): 396–410.

through the vanity of men they entered the world. . . . For the worship of idols not to be named is the beginning and cause and end of every evil.

The medieval exegetical tradition, Stoic and euhemerist, is still preserved in the modern biblical annotation of these verses: the evil in the invention of images—of the dead and of the living–which originated in images of the king, lies in the maker as well as the image itself. What is demonic is the human skill of the craftsman to make illusion beautiful, transcending nature,

> the likeness to take more beautiful form, and the multitude, attracted by the charm of his work, now regarded as an object of worship the one whom shortly before they had honored as a man. And this became an hidden trap for mankind.
>
> [19–21]

The commentators continue, "men, in bondage to misfortune or to power, bestow on objects of stone . . . the name that ought not to be shared" (14:21). By the power of art, man makes himself a god more beautiful than created nature and worships likenesses transcendent of himself; attempting to deny death and mutability, he ends in despair.

Pandarus however, is not an idol maker, and he does not believe in his own fiction making. He knows Criseyde. His antagonist is not Diomede, whom one can fight, but Calchas, the astrologer, who is unarmed. Calchas says almost nothing at all, and his vision is the poem's destiny. This, too, both the audience and the characters knew all along. As soothsayer, Calchas is the witness of human powerlessness, and like Cassandra's, his prophecy does not have to be believed to be true. Pandarus the magician, the plausible fraud, is ironically aware that his game is lost from the start, but, like Tantalus and Spenser's Despair, he compulsively performs his repertoire of legerdemain, and lets it go. At the moment of his triumph in Book III, he gives the game away to Troilus, but Troilus no longer understands the images of manipulation; what he now knows is beyond Pandarus, and his knowledge saves the poem. In response to Troilus's gratitude for his changed life, Pandarus replies,

> but—take it nat a-grief—
> For love of god be war of this myscheif:

> That there as thow now brought art in thy blisse,
> That thow thi self ne cause it nat to misse.

> For of fortunes sharp adversitee
> The worst kynde of infortune is this:
> A man to han ben in prosperitee,
> And it remembren whan it passed is.

[3. 1621–28]

As he abjures both memory and dreams, Pandarus confesses the only certainty he knows:

> For also seur as reed is every fir,
> As gret a craft is kepe wel as wynne.
>
> . . . .
>
> For worldly joie halt nat but by a wir.
> That preveth wel, it brest alday so ofte;
> Forthi, nede is to werken with it softe.

[3. 1633–38]

If the Chaucerian Pandarus's linguistic mirage making seems to suggest that the art of fiction itself is suspect, in the wider context of the poem, allegorical irony subsumes Pandarus's defeat in other paradoxes. For he is the Narrator's fictional creation, as the Narrator is Chaucer's, and in the transmission of the power of language through all the intermediary voices, the words for love are finally spoken, for what they are worth, by those who do mean what they say. Their ambiguity arises from the disbelief of Pandarus, who inspires them, and the doubt of his own credibility of the Narrator, who constantly intrudes his presence, breaking the fiction, with echoes of Pandarus's flexible proverbs and clichés. Pandarus's and the Narrator's language is prosaic and colloquial; their commonplaces offset the language of passion in Troilus's and Criseyde's soliloquies and lyrics.[24] In their early dialogue with Pandarus, the interplay indirectly arouses each to eloquence, setting the tone to follow, when he first persuades Troilus to reveal himself, and Criseyde to look in her mirror.

Like Alan de Lille's archetypal Genius, Chaucer's Pandarus is con-

---

24. See Payne, *Key of Remembrance*, pp. 171–216, for a full study of the stylistic effects of Chaucer's revisions.

stantly at work imagining *figurae*, and from the start he is presented as a rhetorician:[25]

> For everi wight that hath an hous to founde
> Ne renneth naught the werk for to bygynne
> With rakel hond; but he wol bide a stounde,
> And sende his hertes line out fro withinne
> Aldirfirst his purpos for to wynne.
> Al this Pandare in his herte thoughte,
> And caste his werk ful wisly er he wroughte.
>
> [1. 1065–71]

A Genius reduced to absurdity, Pandarus's inability to control his characters' destinies—like the Narrator's—and his scepticism of them and of himself, leave no further questions to be asked; he withdraws, with a curse against mortal frailty. That he has vanished from the scene in Henryson's *Testament* allows Henryson's Narrator to concentrate on the question Chaucer left open, the moral dilemma of Cresseid's guilt, in which Pandar is now superfluous. In both Shakspere's and Dryden's plays, Pandar's lost chance as a poet is ironically underlined and further debased by each in giving him songs to sing, in place of the lyrics given to Troilus in Boccaccio and Chaucer. Dryden recast Pandarus's exit, in the fourth act of Shakspere's play, into a grotesque and pathetic snatch of song, losing the last echo of Chaucer's Pandarus's power caught in the sound of rain.

> [PANDARUS (*sings*).] O Heart, as the saying is, O Heart,
>   heavy Heart, why sighs't thou without
>   breaking. . . . Because thou cans't not
>   ease my smart, by Friendship nor by
>   Speaking. There never was a truer Rhyme.
>   Let us cast away nothing, for we may live
>   to have Need of such a verse.
>
> [*Troilus and Cressida*, 4. 1]

Dryden's Pandarus goes home to die of "the Sullens, like an old Bird in a cage"; his helplessness is ridiculed by the vivid agility of Thersites,

---

25. Robinson, in his note on this passage, remarks that the stanza is taken "almost literally" from Geoffrey of Vinsauf's *Nova Poetria*, 43–45; Root, in his edition, cites Boethius, *Consolation* IV, prosa 6, 57–60. The simile is a commonplace.

who stays alive to speak the Epilogue, which "strews Rats bane," refusing to condemn or confess his failure.

For all their apparent historic and collateral continuities, then, this series of figures of Pandar is only superficially genetic. It is deceptive, if not entirely spurious, to call them analogues. What they have in common is their ancient association with a time of truce, their function as intermediaries, and their sacrifice of honor in a cause that, as expected, turns out to be futile. What the Pandar intended is always achieved, but the accomplishment ends in a greater disaster. In the medieval story, the exchange of Criseyde for Antenor brings home to Troy its final betrayer, for Antenor's theft of the Palladium from Athene's temple (where Troilus first saw Criseyde) offends the goddess, and her protection is removed from Troy.[26] Pandar has no role in these events, but it is clear that the peace he brings about between Troilus and Criseyde, in their sexual union, is as temporary as the truce which terminates it. Each replaying of his part reveals the deliberate and concealed revision of history, and although Pandarus's subtle humiliation in every version after Homer's seems to imply a kind of censure of artifice itself, the putting down of Pandarus in fact heightens the passionate *trouthe* of Troilus. The true poets make him, and break Pandar, to keep the fiction intact.

Analogical Criticism: Problems in Method

Michelangelo's painting of *Leda and the Swan*—which haunts the modern reader of Yeats—was made in 1529 for Alfonso d'Este during a temporary hiatus in his work on the Medici tombs. The gigantic figure of *Night* and the *Leda* are "two designs . . . variations on one theme, derived from a common model, an ancient image of 'Leda and the Swan' which frequently occurs on Roman sarcophagi."[27] Michelangelo made two versions of the myth of Leda, Helen's mother: the painting, at the moment of her rape by the huge swan of Zeus, and the marble figure, in the repose of despair, with Minerva's owl in the crook of her half-bent knee. The source or prototype is the image of sexual union in death, found in antique tomb sculpture, which Wind shows

26. In Homer, Odysseus and Diomede steal Pallas's image, and the will of Zeus is the binding necessity to be fulfilled; Chaucer gives the medieval version in 4. 204–10.

27. Wind, *Pagan Mysteries*, p. 129.

was inherited as a Renaissance commonplace. The symbolic elements of the formula can become swan, dove, or owl;[28] the moment in time is an epiphany, containing past, present, and future: the birth of Castor, Pollux, and Helen, in *Leda*; the death of all men in *Night*. Thus Wind's brilliant exegesis of the Renaissance mythology of "Amor as a God of Death" connects the two images to their common topos, the loves of the gods for mortals—the common theme of the myths of Bacchus and Ariadne, Mars and Rhea, Diana and Endymion—which Pico and the Florentine Platonists reinterpreted with the handbooks of medieval allegory such as Bersuire's *Ovide moralisé* (1340) and Boccaccio's *Genealogy of the Gods* (ca. 1360), based in turn on the old encyclopedias of Isidore of Seville, Fulgentius, Apuleius, and Cicero.

> To die was to be loved by a god, and partake through him of eternal bliss. As there are many kinds of death (according to Valeriano), this one is the most highly approved and commended both by the sages of antiquity and by the authority of the Bible: when those . . . yearning for God and desiring to be conformed with him (which cannot be achieved in the prison of the flesh) are carried away to heaven and freed from the body by a death which is the profoundest sleep, in which manner Paul desired to die when he said "I long to be dissolved and be with Christ." This kind of death was named the kiss by the symbolic theologians, . . . of which Solomon also appears to have spoken when he said in the Song of Songs, *Osculetur me osculo oris sui*. And this was foreshadowed in the figure of Endymion, whom Diana kissed as he had fallen into the profoundest sleep.[29]

Could the medieval Troilus's death and ascent to the eighth sphere and the Renaissance Criseyde's deathbed desire to walk with Diana, *quhair scho dwellis . . . in waist Woddis and Wellis* (*Testament*, 587–88), be reconciled with this kind of analogical exegesis? No doubt they could, if the prototype of medieval Pandarus is the biblical Jonadab, and he is "a priest of Satan," if Criseyde is cousin to "the Samaritan woman," Troilus is "Adam, as Everyman," and "night" is "spiritual ignorance,

---

28. These symbolic birds have a wide range of traditional associations: the swan is sacred to Apollo and Zeus; the dove is Venus's, Mary's, as well as the divine messenger to Noah in the Old Testament; the owl is Minerva–Athene's, Satan's, and at the Crucifixion, it may become Divine Light. All are associated with metempsychosis.

29. Wind, *Pagan Mysteries*, pp. 130–31.

or blindness, and adversity."[30] Reinterpreted, their Renaissance forms might be provided with a more glamorous and complicated ancestry, equally demonic, but more appropriately "humanist." The task of synthesizing all five of the major medieval and Renaissance Criseydes into one composite figure would, perhaps, discourage further attempts to mythologize her, as she has been so easily allegorized. But even in dealing with literary evidence alone, the language of criticism blurs, at the crucial point of discovery of a "source," and goes opaque with concessions, asserting a new analogy: "[Here] are parallels with Italian influences which suggest affinities."[31]

In aesthetics as in history, the risks of anachronism, overinterpretation, false simplicity, in "allegory" and analogy alike, are real and too often are not worth taking. Yet some survive; one image corroborates another, and the relation becomes a corollary of the evidence itself, and, after the fact, a commonplace. That the cycles of mosaics in the dome of the Baptistry in Florence bear a striking resemblance to the ascending circles of the saints in Dante's final vision in the *Paradiso*, as Ernest Wilkins and countless others have since seen, indeed confirms what is already a given in both cases; the perfection of the circle, and the circumscription of the many into one as the formal equivalent of the idea of the divine, in the temple and in the poem. The analogy does not obscure but illuminates, and the parallels are clear enough to be pressed in detailed comparison. Similarly, the pilgrimage depicted in the Lorenzetti frescoes in Siena (1345–49), entitled the "Allegory of Good Government and of Bad Government," extends beyond the walls of a contemporary image of the city. Its gate is the point of departure for the pilgrimage into a miraculously receding horizon of landscape, into which the long line of riders follows their winding road. The frescoes seem to me to image, and anticipate, the whole complex international spread of journey poems of the fourteenth century: the collections of *novella* and fabliaux, of Boccaccio and Sercambi, Chaucer's tales and Gower's anthologies, and the countless quests which depart from the city of man in search of the city of God—pilgrimages undertaken by individuals in bands, in *felawshipe* and *compaignye*, friars following St. Francis, knights following St. George. We cannot, however,

30. See D. W. Robertson, "Chaucerian Tragedy," *ELH* 19 (1952): 1–37; repr. Schoeck and Taylor, *Chaucer Criticism II*, pp. 92, 98–99, 104, 121 n. 15.

31. T. W. Baldwin, *Shakespeare's Five-Act Structure* (Urbana, Ill., 1963), p. 796, in a discussion of the *Commedia dell'arte*, *The Tempest*, and the *Comedy of Errors*.

pursue such analogies very much farther without confronting the deep chasms that divide the arts, separating the expression of a given common theme in one medium from its similar expression in a different vocabulary. The experience of the audience is altered, even when it is virtually certain that the artist has no wish to surprise, but assumes a given meaning is known in advance; reinterpretation is not originality but reinforcement, a new experience that confirms our expectations. The effects of changing media are difficult enough to describe even within one so-called "period style" in a static art. As J. A. K. Thomson observed,

> A discussion of the form or style of a Logos (a Traditional Story) in abstraction from its content is even more meaningless than talk about the qualities of a statue which should not consider whether it is made of marble, or bronze, or ivory.[32]

Similarly, late Gothic painting and relief, fresco and statue, in their illusions of light, depth, proportion, and aesthetic distance vis à vis the observer, resist simplification, even before the critic superimposes his subtle metaphors of motion and time, rhythm and duration, and their interplay, to explain by analogy his own experience. Giotto (to paraphrase Vasari) places the Virgin in an implied universal space into which both the spectator and the Christ look toward her averted gaze; that suspended linear space becomes a circular field, alive with movement and tensions, enveloping the marble Incarnation in the round. As in plastic and pictorial art, the analogies on one theme among narrative, lyric, and drama are proportionally more complex, vis à vis the reader and his poet, the audience and the playwright's company.

It is not easy, then, to compare by analogy the demands felt and met by the poet, writing for the reader in a private performance *(thow, redere, helpe me)*, for the public stage ("such dull and heavy-witted worldings as were never capable of the wit of a comedy"—the anonymous epistle in the second quarto of Shakspere's *Troilus*), and the altered consciousness of the later audience of Dryden. I shall not attempt to take the case to its modern extreme, the audience who read and hear the twentieth-century libretto of William Walton's opera, *Troilus and Cressida*, against its medieval and Renaissance literary backgrounds.

Two further questions of method should be briefly considered before we try to set the legends of Troilus in analogical relation: the relevance

32. *The Art of Logos* (London, 1935), p. 13.

of "myth" and symbolic archetypes. Three contingent frames of complex mythological reference in late medieval and early Renaissance literature and art offer opportunities for comparison, and symbolic interpretation, that seem easily to enlarge, but may not clarify understanding. In short, analogy, like allegory, may become an infinite regress in criticism. In works of art, however rich and strange the new synthetic symbols become, mythology is visible, concrete; but poetic myth is an abstraction, and it may be latent, unconscious, or "unintended." The analogies found for interpretation of difficult programs in Florentine painting, for example, are visual and in the public domain, as well as supported by texts. Literary historians begin and end with abstract conceptions, invisible images, from the same encyclopedias of symbolic archetypes: the Bible and the Apocrypha, Fulgentius, Isidore, Martianus Capella, *Ovide moralisé*. Beside the Christian supernatural of sacred allegory, late medieval and early Renaissance poetry is becoming more and more what it had always been, the vehicle for the "survival of the pagan gods" and the pagan mysteries, as well as the colloquial mythopocia of secular folk tale and romance.[33] "Sir Orfeo" and the Trojan ancestors of Arthur's heroes mingle with elves and fairies and other incubi in the limbo of popular poetry. As we have already noted, the ironies of the *Merchant's Tale*, and the *Wife of Bath's*, depend on such incongruities.

All three symbolic strains—Christian, classical, and northern legendary—come to the surface in the most sophisticated of the alliterative romances, *Sir Gawain and the Green Knight*, which opens at Christmas at Camelot:

> Siþen þe sege and þe assaut watȝ sesed at Troye,
> Þe borȝ brittened and brent to brondeȝ and askeȝ,
> Þe tulk þat þe trammes of tresoun þe wroȝt
> Watȝ tried for his tricherie, þe trewest on erthe:
> Hit watȝ Ennias þe athel and his highe kynde,
> Þat siþen depreced prouinces, and patrounes bicome
> Weleneȝe of al the wele in þe West Isles.
>
> [1–7]

In a famous critical impasse between irreconcilable mythological theories of this poem, the dazzling greenness of Sir Gawain's an-

33. See Jean Seznec, *The Survival of the Pagan Gods*, trans. Barbara Sessions (Princeton, 1953), pp. 11–36, for the Trojan legends and medieval and early Renaissance euhemerism.

tagonist was interpreted by the Jungian, Heinrich Zimmer (in 1948), as universally symbolic of Death.[34] The neo-Frazerian–Freudian, John Speirs (in 1949), read "greenness" as the potency of Life itself, the Nature God of Rebirth.[35] Zimmer's analogies are to "folk tale" and Tibetan art, Speirs's to "folk tale" and Celtic art. The greenness of the Green Knight is the only point of agreement between them; the example could be multiplied many times. Not all mythopoeic "analogical" interpretations can be so easily reduced to absurdity, but medieval and Renaissance poems are vulnerable to such abuse by virtue of three centuries of conflation and crossfertilizing of symbols, Northern pagan, Christian, and classical, which a hybrid poem such as *Sir Gawain and the Green Knight* so early epitomizes, in all its ambiguity. The later and more learned the poet, from Boccaccio to Chaucer to Spenser and his contemporaries, the more likely that multiple allusions and intentional ambiguities will be found. Boccaccio warns his reader, in the great textbook of early Renaissance mythological interpretation, the *Genealogy of the Gods*, to go slowly in reading ancient as well as modern poets,

> I repeat my advice to those who would appreciate Poetry, and unwind its difficult involutions. You must read, you must persevere, you must sit up nights, you must inquire, and exert the utmost power of your mind. If one way does not lead to the desired meaning, take another; if obstacles arise, then still another, until, if your strength holds out, you will find that clear which at first looked dark. For we are forbidden by divine command to give that which is holy to dogs, or to cast pearls before swine.[36]

Sidney's *Apologie* makes a similar case for the 1580's.

Given the abundance and fertility of the "sources" and their analogues, the temptation for criticism to reduce complex new forms to simpler, older archetypes is very strong. For example, the connection between the apparent "death" of Criseyde in Book IV of *Troilus and Criseyde* (ll. 1149 ff.), when Troilus lays out her body as if on a bier, melodramatically preparing to kill himself and join her in death, and the fully realized double suicide in the fifth act of *Romeo and Juliet*, has not been clearly seen as "imitation" for several reasons.[37] Behind

34. Heinrich Zimmer, *The King and the Corpse* (New York, 1948), pp. 27 ff.
35. John Speirs, "Sir Gawain and the Green Knight," *Scrutiny* 16 (1949): 274–300.
36. Osgood, *Genealogy*, 14.12, p. 62.
37. In his edition of "Romeus and Juliet" (*Shakespere Classics*, London, 1908) J. J. Munro

Romeo and Juliet, it is easy to find Arthur Brooke's poem, and beyond that, if we accept Brooke's preface, lies another play. In back of Brooke, there are (perhaps) Xenophon of Ephesus, Masuccio of Salerno, Luigi da Porto (or Cardinal Bembo), Bandello, and Boaistuau; somewhere in the near foreground are Painter's *Palace of Pleasure,* and Lope da Vega. But the archetype of all, as G. L. Kittredge long ago summed up the scholarship, is Ovid's "Pyramus and Thisbe," the tragic tale told in *Metamorphoses* IV, in defiance of Bacchus's festival.[38] Seeking the antecedents of Ovid's sophisticated late classical fables leads us further and further away from Shakspere's play and the meaning of the lovers' deaths. If the critical perspective is long enough, it becomes possible to see the hypostasized priest performing funeral rites, in Shakspere and in Ovid, as simply pagan and Christian variants of a single primal scene; at that distance, it is impossible to tell, and literary art no longer matters. In the converse, foreshortened perspective, the enigmatic relationships between *Romeo and Juliet* and *Troilus and Cressida* are close enough, and sufficiently oblique, to be also out of focus.

It may very well be true that, by the same processes of conscious and unconscious imitation, Aesculapius's sister, Circe, is the ancestral symbolic prototype for Morgan le Fay, Sir Gawain's Lady, as well as for Spenser's seductive Acrasia. I think there is, however, no more to be learned from tracing such suggestive similarities than from observing their irreducible differences. In critical analogies, "likeness" is best used to disclose the intractable, the unique, as translation reveals what is untranslatable, and imitation the imitator's art, but not the inimitable original. The uniqueness revealed in comparison of analogues is more valuable for criticism than the resemblance, which may equally be deliberate or chance; if we want to know, for example, how it comes about that Sir Guyon's victorious chastity resists Acrasia and ends in destructive violence, while Sir Gawain departs from the Green Castle humbled by the lady, with ceremony and witty repartee: how Chaucer's

---

comments on Brooke's "borrowing" from *Troilus.* In his note on the Troilus stanza, R. K. Root casts doubt on Young's suggestion of an analogy between the bedroom scenes in *Troilus* (2. 1394–3. 231; 3. 505–1309) and Boccaccio's *Filocolo,* "which has many similarities with Keats' *Eve of St. Agnes*" (p. xxix), because of the unlikenesses in the outcomes of the scenes. But Keats's reading is self-documented; the lovers' escape in the *Eve of St. Agnes* answers both *Romeo and Juliet* and *Troilus.*

38. In the Preface to Kittredge's edition of *Romeo and Juliet,* rev. Irving Ribner (New York, 1966), pp. x–xii. Cf. T. W. Baldwin, *Shakespeare's Five-Act Structure,* ch. 31 and ch. 32, passim, for parallels with Golding's Ovid and Brooke.

Criseyde awakens in time to snatch away Troilus's knife, but Juliet must find Romeo's and use it. Dryden's amazing Cressida, as we shall see, copies Juliet.

Finally, it is well known, and still worth repeating, that the antiquity of an apparent archetype is no guarantee of its validity or relevance to later analogues. Unless, of course, we admit to the condition of Jungian simplicity, in which symbolic archetypes "correspond to certain collective structural elements of the human psyche in general, . . . [and are] like the morphological elements of the human body, . . . inherited." Thus, in the words of Zimmer, the "central archetype present [in a work . . . can never be described, because] it does not refer to anything that is, or ever has been, conscious."[39] As the historical dimension in an analogy is stretched, the distinctiveness of each element shrinks, so that "resemblance" can be maintained. At the extreme point, as in the case of allegorical interpretation, where critical insight—our compulsion to see a pattern—goes beyond the evidence to pure conjecture, the integrity of separate images and symbols no longer holds; "likeness" itself becomes dim, obscure, and confused. Odinn, hanging from his tree for nine nights, and Christ on the Cross, at the critical distance entailed to see them analogically, lose more meaning than is gained by recognition of the structural pattern in their self-sacrifice. They become tautologies. The tree itself, in its cyclical death and revival, is the ultimate reduction of the complex human symbol to elementary, preverbal mystery. At this point, inarticulate nature itself, we are left with pattern that images pattern, and literature becomes evidence in another area of speculative knowledge, philosophy or anthropology; its distinctive asymmetries and styles are no longer definitive, and may be discarded. "I do not find / The Hanged Man . . . I see crowds of people, walking round in a ring." Before Pound edited *The Waste Land*, Eliot's clairvoyante Madame Sosostris had said, "I look in vain [for the Hanged Man]" and his Narrator had added, "('I, John, saw these things and heard them')". The key changes are the cutting of "in vain" and the line from *Revelations*; only the circular image, the allusion to Dante, was let stand in the revision. Every poet leaves some clues and signs for the perspective that will serve his poem best, and he takes pains to remove the superfluous. He may also leave false clues, like Chaucer's "Lollius," in order better to

---

39. Heinrich Zimmer, *The King and the Corpse*, quoted by C. W. Moorman in "Myth and Medieval Literature," *Myth and Literature*, ed. John B. Vickery (Lincoln, Neb., 1966) p. 171.

conceal the artfulness of his illusion, and to add suspense to the discovery of the archetypes, the familiar forms, we may expect to find.

The History of the *Troilus*

God he knoweth, not I, who plukt hir first-sprong rose,
Since Lollius and Chaucer both make doubt upon that glose.[40]

Having taken note of some of the problems which eclectic historical criticism cannot ignore, let us return to Chaucer's *Troilus*, its ancestry and descendants.

> The original story was written by one Lollius, a Lombard, in Latin verse, and translated by Chaucer into English; intended, I suppose, a satire on the inconstancy of women: I find nothing of it among the Ancients; not so much the name Cressida once mentioned. Shakespere, . . . in the apprenticeship of his writing, modelled it into that play . . . now called *Troilus and Cressida*, but so lamely is it left to us that it is not divided into acts. . . . For the play itself, the author seems to have begun with some fire . . . but the latter part of the tragedy is nothing but a confusion of drums and trumpets, excursions and alarms. The chief persons are left alive; Cressida is false, and is not punished.[41]

The *terminus ad quem* for our inquiry, Dryden's *Troilus and Cressida Or, Truth found too Late*, opens with a Preface which also contains an essay, "On the Grounds of Criticism in Tragedy," as well as a defense (quoted in part above) of his dealings with the story of Troilus.[42] Dryden comments on the defects of Shakspere's play, and by implication, Chaucer's *Troilus* as well, beginning with the barbarity of the language.[43] But it

---

40. George Gascoigne, *A Hundreth sundrie Flowers* (1573); text in J. W. Cunliff, ed., *The Complete Works of George Gascoigne* (Cambridge, Eng., 1907–10), 1:101.

41. The Preface to *Troilus and Cressida* (1679), in *The Works of John Dryden, Esq.* (London, 1685), vol. 5; repr. in W. P. Ker, ed., *Essays of John Dryden* (Oxford, 1900), 1: 202–29; hereafter cited as Ker, *Essays*. For quotations from Dryden's play, I have used the 1685 edition. Reuben Brower, in *Hero and Saint* (Oxford, 1971), ch. 6, praises Shakspere for precisely what Dryden deplores: the stage effects of so many flourishes and alarums, which interrupt as well as separate the scenes. Brower also reminds us of the sound of the voice who cries out from the crowd at Cressida's arrival at the Greek camp, with another fanfare, "The Trojan's trumpet!"

42. Sir Francis Kynaston's Latin translation of the first two books of Chaucer's *Troilus*, annotated, had been published in 1635; Kynaston's Preface distinguishes the *Testament* as not Chaucer's, but "by one Mr. Henderson," as did Francis Thynne, in his unpublished *Animadversions* against Speght in 1599. Dryden says nothing of these later "sources."

43. "It must be a allowed to the present age, that the tongue in general is so much refined

is the shapelessness and confusion of the play that disturb Dryden
most, as a dramatist, and he is concerned with the moral as well as
dramatic focus of the play:[44]

> As in perspective, so in Tragedy, there must be a point of sight in
> which all the lines terminate. . . . The last quality of the action
> is, that it ought to be probable as well as admirable and great.
> 'Tis not necessary that there should be historical truth in it, but
> always necessary that there should be a likeness of truth. . . . To
> invent . . . a probability, and to make it wonderful, is the most
> difficult undertaking in the Art of Poetry; for that which is not
> wonderful is not great; and that which is not probable will not
> delight.[45]

We may now consider some of the analogical relations that connect
Chaucer's *Troilus* with its traditional sources—Boccaccio's *Il Filostrato*
and the fictitious "Lollius"—and then the three major Renaissance
adaptations of its *matere*: Henryson's moral allegory, Shakspere's tragic
satire, and Dryden's tragedy.[46] What follows is not a short history of
the vast body of Trojan material, nor a critical analysis of its narrative
and dramatic forms and philosophical substance undergoing transformation in each new version of Troilus's story. Rather, we shall
attempt to use parallels selectively, in a negative sense, observing what is
most obvious: the curves away from the "sources," the avoidance of
imitation, divergences which permit each new version to claim autonomy. It was Chaucer's best imitator, Henryson himself, as MacQueen's
study of him as both humanist and poet shows, who first used the

---

since Shakespeare's time, that many of his words, and more of his phrases, are scarce intelligible. . . . 'Tis true, that in his latter plays he had worn off somewhat of the rust; but the
tragedy which I have undertaken to correct was in all probability one of his first endeavors on
the stage" (Ker, *Essays*, 1: 203). The commonplace "rust" was noted in Addison in ch. 1
above, and in Skelton, ch. 6.

44. Cf. Brower, *Hero and Saint*, p. 252: "We may ask those who find the Shakespeare of
Troilus 'lacking in constructive power' to produce an example from his plays that shows more
skillfull joining of relatively distinct lines of action, or better use of theatrical effect to focus
ear, eye, and mind on a change of relationships and character . . . it is doubtful whether
many of (his) contemporaries . . . could have built the play so surely toward a decisive
moment."

45. Ker, *Essays*, 1: 208.

46. By analogy, I mean likeness or resemblance between things not like in origin or kind;
analogues are comparable but by definition *not* identical.

rhetorical term "invention" in its modern sense to mean "a fiction, a fabrication, something devised," rather than "choice," "selection," "finding of a topic or an argument," or simply, as Caxton used it, "a work produced by the mind, a literary composition."[47] Henryson uses the new sense in the opening monologue of the *Testament*, precisely where we should expect it, where suspicion of the past is necessarily to be aroused:

> Quha wait gif all that Chaucer wrait was trew?
> Nor I wait nocht gif this narratioun
> Be authoreist or fenyeit of the new
> Be sum Poeit, throw his Inventioun.[48]

There are three major areas where traditional analogies among all five versions of Troilus's story break down, where the bridge is out, and the crucial opportunities for "invention" appear, in retrospect. Put very crudely, in the order in which they will be taken up, the divergences occur in structure, dramatis personae, and the cumulative effects of these on the theme itself. By structure, I mean nothing more subtle than the shape oɪ pattern imposed on the content, the events of the legend itself. By dramatis personae, I mean all of the speakers, presented directly by Shakspere and Dryden, indirectly by the Narrator, who is one of them, in Boccaccio, Chaucer, and Henryson. They determine the rhythms and the tempo the pattern takes, as well as its expressive range. Finally, the interpretation of the pattern of events portrayed in each successive version is cumulatively redefined. Its significance is affected, that is, by two causes; first by its altered presentation, and second by the increasing familiarity of the story. Criseyde's betrayal was already a literary allusion in Gower, long before Chaucer's poem was written, and the well-known Trojan "histories" of Lydgate and Caxton in the fifteenth century greatly amplified common knowledge.[49] The audience's knowledge is a given, implicit and always necessary,

47. See *OED*. s.v. "invention," I. 1d, 3b. and John MacQueen, *Robert Henryson, A Study of the Major Narrative Poems* (Oxford, 1967), p. 55.

48. *The Testament of Cresseid by Robert Henryson*, ed. Bruce Dickins (London, 1925), ll. 64–67. Dickins's text has been superseded by the edition of Denton Fox, for Nelson's Medieval and Renaissance Library (London, 1968). Hereafter, I shall cite both editions as Dickins, *Testament*, and Fox, *Testament*.

49. Mieszkowski, *The Reputation of Criseyde*, cites seven references to the story in Gower, in all his major poems from *Mirour de l'Homme* (1375) to *Cinkante Balades* (?1400), balade xx.

from Chaucer to Dryden; but the appeal for pity to the fourteenth-
century audience—*ye loveres*—to supply their own sympathetic awareness of Chaucer's *Troilus* disappears by the seventeenth century.

> Who koude telle aright or ful discryve
> His wo, his pleynte, his langour, and his pyne?
> Naught alle the men that han or ben on lyve!
> Thow, redere, maist thiself ful wel devyne,
> That swich a wo my wit kan nat defyne.
>
> [5. 267–71]

As Shakspere's Rosalind, who has heard it once too often, remarks,
everyone knows

> Troilus had his brains dashed out with
> a Grecian club; yet he did what he could to die
> before, and he is one of the patterns of love. . . .
>
> [*As You Like It*, 4. 1. 97–99]

The meaning of Troilus's "pattern of love" is supplied by the larger
context, through which the audience interprets it. The fifth act of the
Merchant of Venice opens on the moonlit scene between Lorenzo and
Jessica, who exchange an increasingly ominous series of analogies (in
stichomythia), to "such a night" for lovers: "as Thisby, . . . as Dido,
. . . as Medea, . . . so Jessica,"[50] But the chain of associations in the
dialogue is set in motion by Lorenzo's opening speech:

> The moon shines bright: in such a night as this
> When the sweet wind did gently kiss the trees
> And they did make no noise, in such a night
> Troilus methinks mounted the Troyan walls
> And sigh'd his soul toward the Grecian tents,
> Where Cressid lay that night.
>
> [*Merchant of Venice*, 5. 1. 1–6]

The scene Lorenzo is imagining does not occur, of course, in Shakspere's own *Troilus*, nor in Henryson; Chaucer found it in Boccaccio's
Filostrato (an echo of his own *Filocolo*). Yet such a situation, visualized
once, becomes a pattern for countless imitations: the Elizabethan

---

50. R. K. Root, *Classical Mythology in Shakespeare*, Yale Studies in English 19 (New York,
1913), notes allusions to Troilus in *Merry Wives*, *Henry V*, *Twelfth Night*, *Much Ado*, *All's Well*,
and *Rape of Lucrece*.

ballads and Tudor poetic epistles modelled on Book V of Chaucer's *Troilus* and the *Testament,* as well as the "lost" plays. All that Shakspere needs for the ironies of Lorenzo's lyric to take effect is the common knowledge of "Troilus," not in Middle English, but in colloquial speech. As Nerissa says, later in the same scene, "When the moon shone, we did not see the candle" (5. 1. 96).

The Medieval Versions: Boccaccio and Chaucer

The metamorphosis of the Troilus story, from a fragmentary anecdote in a mid-twelfth-century verse chronicle to Boccaccio's romantic *novella,* to Chaucer's Boethian tragedy, is the medieval phase of its evolution. The source studies of Griffin and Myrick, Kittredge, Root, Meech, Pratt, and their successors have gathered the evidence for interpretation, and it is possible to recapitulate the medieval phase in a very brief outline.[51] After its appearance in Benôit de Ste. Maure's *Roman de Troie* (1155), the story of Troilus was successively translated (and conflated) into Latin prose, French prose, Italian verse, and finally Middle English rime royal. Before Chaucer, then, serial changes in language were accompanied by structural variations in overall length, addition, expansion, deletion of episodes, shifts of stress and change in characters, and by stylistic heightening and rhetorical emphases of various kinds. These formal aspects of the evolution of the story are more or less quantifiable and have been measured.[52] Nevertheless, the statistical results of comparison of the early versions, against one another and against Chaucer's, are only slightly less open to dispute than speculative interpretation of their functions and effects. Legitimate questions have arisen over the cataloguing of rhetorical devices, for example; whether Pandarus's habitual proverbs should be counted as exemplifying *digressio, sententia,* or *exclamatio,* to say nothing of whether they are benign, if confusing platitudes, or in effect banal debasements of the figures he employs.

There is of course no such thing as an objective criticism, even when it seems to be supported by textual facts and allusions which have been

51. See Mieszkowski's bibliographical summary, and the surveys in the bibliographies of Griffith (1908–53), Crawford (1954–63), and Baugh (to 1968).

52. Robert Payne, *The Key of Remembrance* (New Haven, 1963), casts doubt on the statistics of Meech, Ludeke, and Traugott Naunin, pp. 187, 192 n. 37. See his study of Chaucer's revisions, pp. 171–216, and also Meech, *Design,* pp. 432–34, nn. 5–19. I am much indebted to Payne's clear analyses of the dream–vision structure.

counted. In order for analysis to begin, in order to count things, they must first be named; therein lies metonymy. When weights are assigned, inferences are drawn, but statistical solutions are very few. Those who confess their subjectivity are also, no matter how sincere, equally likely to be contradicted by the same reversible ironies. Thus, Karl Young saw Chaucer's revisions in *Troilus* as an attempt to "transport the reader . . . [back] from contemporary reality to a distant and romantic Troy [by means of strategic addition of ancient, 'archaizing' Trojan details]."[53] In virtually complete disagreement, C. S. Lewis reached the opposite conclusion; he saw Chaucer as a "medievalizer," bringing the story up into a late Gothic romance perspective for his "courtly" audience [by means of contemporary psychology and anachronistic "English" details].[54] Meech supplies evidence for both views.[55]

Like the greenness of the Green Knight, these contradictions at the surface of Chaucer's *Troilus and Criseyde* are subsumed by the greater paradoxes at the center and at the ending of the poem: the irreconcilable conflict inherent in its structure, which Chaucer created and deliberately let stand. At the surface, *Troilus* is both "archaized" and "medievalized," by the copious anachronisms coexistent in its atmosphere: Ovid and Statius, Boethius and Dante; "Bishop" Amphiorax; "courtly love" etiquette; medieval Fortuna, but Greek Tisiphone; Troilus's virginal innocence.

The question of Chaucer's Troy is in fact moot, because the premises of the questioners are clearer and more stable than the poem's, which begin to disintegrate as soon as they are abstracted from it. One thing is certain: the modern critic is more sure of his ground than Chaucer's Narrator, in informing us that, according to medieval interpreters,

> Troy is the human body, the introduction of the Trojan horse, Lechery. Troilus is then in a sense a personification of Troy, as understood by medieval interpreters. The destruction of a man is

53. Karl Young, "Chaucer's Troilus and Criseyde as Romance," *PMLA* 53 (1938): 38–63. Young enlarges upon the comments of J. S. P. Tatlock in "The Epilog to Chaucer's *Troilus, Modern Philology* 18 (1921): 627–59, on Chaucer's "archaizing."

54. C. S. Lewis, "What Chaucer Really Did to *Il Filostrato,*" *Essays and Studies* 17 (1932): 56–75. Lewis seems to have relished using his defense of "courtly love" as a weapon to attack modern moralists and writers he disapproved of, in particular D. H. Lawrence: "the teeming marshlands . . . whose depths the wisest knows not, and on whose bank the hart gives up his life rather than plunge in." This is the concluding sentence of his essay on *Troilus.*

55. In his *Design,* passim.

the destruction of a city, when we consider that every man builds either Babylon or Jerusalem within himself, and Babylon is destined to fall.[56]

The question of his vision of Troy is one that the Narrator would not have been able or willing to answer; it is in the poem, as it is read:

> Wherfore I nyl have neither thank ne blame
> Of al this werk, but prey yow mekely,
> Disblameth me, if any word be lame;
> For as myn auctor seyde, so sey I.
>
> . . . .
>
> For every wight which that to Rome went,
> Halt nat o path, nor alwey o manere;
> Ek in som lond were al the game shent,
> If that men ferde in love as men don here,
> As thus, in opyn doyng, or in chere,
> In visityng, in forme, or seyde hire sawes;
> Forthi men seyn, ech contree hath his lawes.
>
> [2. 15–19; 36–42]

The serene relativism of Chaucer's Narrator is the reflex of his evasive, self-abnegating attitude toward his *matere*:

> Ek though I speeke of love unfelyngly,
> No wonder is, for it no thyng of newe is;
> A blynd man kan nat juggen wel in hewis.
>
> [2. 19–21]

While it is true that modern interpreters—Payne, Robertson, Donaldson, Lewis, and Young—have brought back to light one stratum after another of the image of Chaucer's Troy, it still rebuilds itself in the imagination of the reader, in his subconscious response to the Narrator's invitation to participate in the aesthetic illusion of the lovers' experience, and if need be, to perfect it:

> But how although I kan nat tellen al,
> As kan myn auctor of his excellence,
> Yit have I seyd, and god toforn, and shal,
> In every thing the gret of his sentence;

56. D. W. Robertson, "Chaucerian Tragedy," in Schoeck and Taylor, *Chaucer Criticism, II,* p. 120, n. 6.

And if that I at loves reverence,
Have any thing in eched for the beste,
Doth therwithal right as youre selven leste.

For myne wordes, heere and every part,
I speke hem alle under correccioun
Of yow that felyng han in loves art,
And putte hem hool in youre discressioun,
Tencresce or maken diminucioun
Of my langage, and that I yow biseche.

[3. 1401–13]

As he leaves the emotions and motives of his characters to be understood, so the Narrator's notations of setting in time and place where
actions occur are at once elusively familiar and indescribably vague.
Perhaps three years in the war elapse, condensed into some half-dozen
significant days and nights. The seeming concreteness of the "History of
Troilus and Creseyde," as the poem is entitled in the earliest editions,
yields evidence to reading after reading, few of which can be called
false, and many true. Like Schliemann's multi-levelled Troy, the indeterminate evidence is the result of long occupation of the site, and in
Chaucer's poem, of overlapping layers of allusion which suggest one
kind of specificity, in the perspective of one plane, that later emerges in
retrospect as an element in a larger design, on a deeper plane. The
effect is of perspective within perspective, like the dream within a
dream, and the play within the play, as Shakspere used it. A clear
example of this is Chaucer's complex ironic exploitation of the "Siege of
Thebes," which lies like a microdot in Book II, where it is named four
times; when it is finally developed in Book V, the "Siege of Thebes"
retroactively shifts the plane of the action into new lines, convergent
and receding, from fictional Troy—the "historical present"—into the
dream world of the past, where Cassandra looks and reads its future.
The structural effects of such allegorical ironies, in Chaucer's revisions
of Boccaccio, can be compared to the double vision Harold Osborn
describes as "artistic illusion" in a painting:

When the pictorial image emerges, and we see the field with cows,
we still see simultaneously the textured and pigmented surface of
the canvas. . . . This dual seeing, and the seen relation, between
the painting as a pigmented surface and the pictured image,

enhance the aesthetic interest. This reciprocal relation of the real surface and deep illusion is apparently inexhaustible.[57]

Unlike its prototype, the *Filostrato*, and unlike any of the subsequent reinterpretations of the theme, Chaucer's *Troilus is* an artistic illusion, a double image, because its moral and aesthetic meanings do not converge, in Dryden's phrase, at a "point of sight in which all the lines [must] terminate." The afterimage of the affirmation of human love persists and is irreconcilable with the perspective of divine love which contains it. In all the other redactions of the story, the moral and aesthetic perspectives finally coincide on the fixed point of the meaning of Criseyde. The question every version of *Troilus* raises is, not, why was she false with Diomede, but what was her love with Troilus? In every version but Chaucer's, there is an answer.

In Boccaccio's *Il Filostrato*, Criseida is the *bellissima donna* to whom the *Proemio* is addressed; she is the poet's Muse, and is invited to identify herself with the heroine of Troilo's romance:

> How often you find Troilo weeping and grieving at the departure of Criseida, so often may you clearly understand and recognise my very cries, sighs, and distresses; and as often as you find good looks, good manners, and other thing praiseworthy in a lady written of Criseida, you may understand them to be said of you.[58]

Boccaccio returns to the pseudoautobiographical outer frame of his poem in the epilogue, his ninth book, which commends the *dolci versi*, *canzon . . . pietosa* to the Lady and ends with an appeal for a favorable response. The fiction is thus set up and consistently maintained as an extended epistle, a courtly love letter which mirrors the poet's relation to a lady.[59] The poetic conventions of the *dolce stil nuovo* and the *chansons de geste* are combined in the narrative, and the Narrator interrupts it only twice, as if by accident, to comment on its fictionality.[60] The pattern of the *Filostrato* is very clear, and its imbalance is consistent with the Narrator's chief interest, the presentation of the sudden rise and

---

57. Harold Osborn, "Artistic Illusion," *British Journal of Aesthetics* 9 (1969): 121; Osborne quotes in this passage from George Kubler, *The Shape of Time* (New Haven, 1962,) p. 24.

58. Griffin and Myrick, *Filostrato, Proemio*, p. 129.

59. Griffin and Myrick identify her as one Maria d'Aquino and propose a grand affair between the lady and the poet in Naples during the years when his romances were written; there is little other evidence that the relationship was not simply Boccaccio's version of Petrarch's love for Laura and Dante's for Beatrice.

60. See above, ch. 4, n. 8.

long fall of Troilo, the passive victim of the Lady's deadly beauty. The
nine books comprise three sequences of episodes. The first three (Troilo's infatuation, wooing, and winning of Criseida) quickly rise to the
turn, from which the last six books gradually descend as Boccaccio
amplifies his theme—the fear, suffering, and disillusion of the lover.
Books four through six contain the parliamentary decision to exchange
Criseida, the lovers' grief, and the handing over of the heroine to Diomede. The last three books describe Troilo's waiting, his disillusioning
dream and its proof, and his death at the hands of Achilles:

> And one day, after a long stalemate, when he had already killed
> more than a thousand, Achilles slew him miserably.
>
> [8. 27]

Boccaccio's Criseida, in whom the destructive passions inherent in the
theme of the Trojan war are reduced to "perfidious Love," is "fickle
and desirous of many lovers" because all women are; she is as beautiful
and inconstant as a leaf in the wind, "Volubil sempre come foglia al
vento" (8. 30). She appears to Troilo "as was her usual wont" carrying
a flaming torch (3. 27; 4. 114), and in his pathetic defense of her virtues
against Cassandra's contempt, Troilo epitomizes her power in the
metaphoric context of the rigid elegant game in which she plays the
queen:

> I do not believe there are any knights in this city, be there as many
> courteous ones as you will, whom she would not mate in the middle
> of the chessboard in courtesy.
>
> [3. 97]

Boccaccio's urbane ironies polish the surface, and do not penetrate the
conventions acted out by his Lover, Lady, Rival, and Go-between. The
pattern of the action and the characters develop clearly and unambig-
uously out of romance cliché: the reductio ad absurdum of *la donna è
mobile*—the beautiful fiction—reflects itself without contradiction, and
without excuse.

Chaucer's reduction of the *Filostrato* from nine books to five gave his
poem symmetry and exposed a paradox which he deliberately let stand.
His subsequent brilliant revisions of his own work increased its in-
consistency. In so doing, Chaucer opened the way toward Henryson's
solution to his paradox, and therein, its subsequent development on the
stage, in Renaissance and neoclassic tragedy.

Concerning tragedy, Horace warns the Piso's of certain rules:

Let your play, if it is to continue to have appeal and be produced, have five acts, no more nor less. And do not have a god—a *deus ex machina*—intervene unless there is a knot worthy of having such a deliverer to untie it. Nor should there be a fourth actor trying to speak.[61]

Within the narrative proper of *Troilus and Criseyde*, Calchas and the "Siege of Thebes" are as close as Chaucer comes to using a *deus ex machina*, and he indeed left a knot "worthy of a god to untie," but it is the "fourth actor, trying to speak" who transforms the narrative of *Il Filostrato* into "Chaucerian tragedy." Chaucer's revisions, both of Boccaccio and of his own poem, systematically reproportion the pattern of the action toward greater symmetry. New, longer Proems replace Boccaccio's letter to his Lady and brief Hymn to Venus in Books I and III, and Proems are added to Books II and IV; the first stanza of Book V is sufficient to finish off the design. The latent possibilities for balance and parallel, implicit in Pandarus's alternating visits to the lovers, are developed at all levels of structure and imagery. For example, the houseparty at Sarpedon's in *Filostrato* becomes, in Chaucer, the last of a sequence of dinners, the first in Book II, at the house of Deiphebus (the first tryst), followed by the climactic celebration at Pandarus's in Book III, and finally, the time-killing visit to Sarpedon's in the aftermath of Book V. The midpoint of the romance is constantly in focus as the action approaches Book III, and then recedes away from its moment of stasis. As Meech and Payne have shown, most of Chaucer's revisions and additions work toward heightening the third book, so that the prolonged delays in Books I and II leading up to it balance the two books of long descent; 900 lines are needed, for example, for the nine days of Troilus's wait. The contrast between Boccaccio's pattern, three books of rise against six of falling action, and Chaucer's seemingly symmetrical design, looks clear, and it is only from the perspective of the ending that we see we have been misled. As in artistic illusion, when we catch sight of the static frame, we see that the highest point of the poem must be Troilus's ascent to the stars, which Chaucer added to the death Boccaccio dramatically underplayed. In retrospect, it appears that the larger, circular pattern—from Troilus's laughter in Book I to his laughter in Book V, at the woe of *this wrecched world*, and *al oure werk that folweth so | The blinde lust . . . that may nat laste*—contradicts and denies the balanced arch that rises to Book III.

61. Horace, *Ars Poetica*, 189–92.

Chaucer's two tasks of revision, the one moral, the other aesthetic, produce an antinomian result. The symmetries effected on either side of Book III (the dream of the eagle; the dream of the white boar; Pandarus's interviews; the letters exchanged; the ruby ring, Troilus's signet; Criseyde's empty "shrine") are artificial patterns to enhance the central episode, the consummation framed by the two Boethian hymns to Love, the Narrator's and Troilus's, in Book III. Yet, in the final perspective of the Narrator, that which elevates Troilus's death to the eighth sphere where the *erratik stars herkning armonye | With sounes ful of hevennish melodye* replace the moon, he sees Troilus look down, and back in time, to where he was slain. From that perspective, human love, *trouthe*, and betrayal are all reduced to insignificance, to the level of Pandarus's futility. Chaucer's architectural patterning of the narrative which leads to Troilus's end projects one shape, prospectively—the shape of tragedy, latent in *Filostrato*. But in retrospect, all of the artificial balancing and lyric elaboration which built the arch seem to disintegrate and the proportions fade. In the perspective of the ending, the natural world becomes remote and indistinct, as the circular imagery of the last stanza circumscribes all human art, and human love, in the paradox of love that is the Christian meaning of death:

> And loveth hym which that right for love
> Upon a cros, oure soules for to beye,
> First starf, and roos, and sit in hevene above;
> For he nyl falsen no wight, dar I seye,
> That wol his herte al holly on hym leye.
> And syn he best to love is, and most meke,
> What nedeth feyned loves for to seke?
>
> [5. 1842–48]

Answering Boccaccio's last stanza, the prayer to Apollo to give grace to his poem for his Lady's pleasure, *Troilus* ends in rebuke:

> Lo here, of payens corsed olde rites!
> Lo here, what alle hire goddes may availle!
> Lo here, thise wrecched worldes appetites!
> Lo here, the fyn and guerdoun for travaille
> Of Jove, Appollo, of Mars, of swich rascaille!
> Lo here, the forme of olde clerkes speche
> In poetrie, if ye hire bokes seche!
>
> [5. 1849–55]

> Thow oon, and two, and thre, eterne on lyve,
> That regnest ay in thre, and two, and oon,
> Uncircumscript, and al maist circumscrive,
> Us from visible and invisible foon
> Defende.

[5. 1863–67]

As I have suggested, the "Siege of Thebes" is a paradigm of Chaucer's discovery and development of what was latent in *Il Filostrato*, at one of the points of tangency between the two. Boccaccio's Troilo, during the waiting period after Criseida's departure, dreams of a white boar, which he sees trample Criseida under its feet and tear out her heart with its snout (7. 23). Troilo knows at once what his dream means, and he explains it to Pandarus (7. 26–9): Criseida has betrayed him, taken for a new lover Diomede, whose ancestors slew the boar of Calydon, and his dream of love and constancy is over. He rushes to grab a knife, and only with difficulty can Pandarus keep him from suicide (7. 36). Troilo's dream is *ex post facto*, for Boccaccio has already introduced Diomede and given his proud ancestral line to Tydeus and the Calydonian kingdom, his "credentials" in wooing Criseida (7. 23–25). This Chaucer suppressed as he turned the dream of the boar into a complex web of symbolic imagery which interlinks three books. One strand of it is metamorphic animal imagery, the other the myth–history which the white boar signifies.

In *Troilus and Criseyde*, the dream of the white boar which Cassandra interprets for Troilus in Book V is the culmination of a series of associated omens, each anticipating the next, each ambiguous at first, and ironic in retrospect. Troilus's dream in Book V links back to Criseyde's dream of the eagle, who tears out her heart in Book II, which dream in turn came to her after the nightingale's song under her window. The nightingale's song, in its turn, is part of a sequence which connects it to Antigone's song in the garden, and further, to the singing of Procne the swallow, under Pandarus's window, awakening him on the day of his first approach to Criseyde. The sequence extends to the beautiful simile in Book III, at the moment of Criseyde's surrender.

> And as the newe abaysed nyghtyngale,
> That stynteth first whan she bygynneth to singe,
> Whan that she hereth any herde tale,
> Or in the hegges any wight sterynge,

> And after, siker, doth hire vois out rynge;
> Right so Criseyde, whan hire drede stente,
> Opned hire herte, and tolde al hire entente.
>
> [3. 1233–39]

As the narrative continuously reflects back on itself, we see the evolution of the animal imagery (boar, eagle, nightingale, swallow) linking symbols of rape and death with sexual union.

The white boar, as emblem of Diomede in Troilus's dream (5. 1457–1519), is interpreted for him by Cassandra by means of a ninety-line summary of the "Siege of Thebes." She goes back to the beginning of the enmity between gods and men, *as olde bookes tellen us*, in order to make clear the history of the son of Tideus, who outraged Diana, and whom she punished. In this monologue, the authority formulae (*as us the bookes telle . . . or elles olde bookes lie*) recur six times, adding to the already heavy weight of the convention in the fifth book. The Narrator interrupts Book V thirteen times to refer to his *olde stories, as men do in bookes finde*, in the course of his increasing detachment and withdrawal from responsibility, and he refers to *myn auctor* five times, for verification. In another reversal of the episode in *Filostrato*, where Troilo believed at once his own reading of his dream, Troilus furiously rejects what Cassandra says; in effect,

> Wepe if thow wolt, or lef; for, out of doute,
> This Diomede is inne, and thow art oute.
>
> [5. 1518–19]

> "Thow seyst nat soth," quod he, "thow sorceresse,
> With al thy false goost of prophecy!
> Thow wenest ben a gret devyneresse.
>
> [5. 1520–22]

This is the second time in the poem that the "Siege of Thebes" has been rejected as irrelevant, untrue—in short, a fiction—so that the irony of its meaning is denied by those inside the frame, and intensified for those without. The first time is, as I have previously noted, at the outset of the vivid, concretely realized scene in Book II on the day of Pandarus's first visit. When Pandarus arrives, he finds Criseyde reading with her ladies in the little paved parlor where they *herden a maiden reden hem the geste | Of the sege of Thebes whil hem leste*. Pandarus lightly asks what is being read—is it of love?

With that thei gonnen laughe, and tho she seyde:
"This romaunce is of Thebes that we rede;
And we han herd how that king Layus deyde,
Thorugh Edippus his sone, and al that dede;
And here we stynten at thise lettres rede,
How the bisshop, as the book kan telle,
Amphiorax, fil thorugh the ground to helle."

Quod Pandarus; "al this knowe I my selve,
And al thassege of Thebes, and the care;
For herof ben ther maked bookes twelve.

[2. 99–108]

In the fourth reference to it in this scene, the *geste . . . romaunce . . . book* becomes a convenient bit of stage property, as Pandarus pushes it aside in order to begin his game, the invitation to the dance:

Do wey youre wympel, and shewe youre face bare;
Do wey youre book, rys up and lat us daunce,
And lat us don to May som observaunce.

[2. 110–12]

The love affair—the celebration of those rites of May—when the book is put away, lasts until the "Siege of Thebes" is picked up again and Cassandra repeats the very rubricated lines where Criseyde stopped listening *(How) Amphiorax fil thurgh the ground to helle* and how *Tydeus was slain* (2. 105; 5. 1500–01). So Chaucer uses the "Siege of Thebes" within the siege of Troy, as an allegorical irony, as a frame to enclose the action of Criseyde's romance with Troilus, and as a key to its dissonant symbolic harmonies. The affair is seemingly suspended during the time elapsed between the reading of the book and the interpretation of the dream. As the cyclical irony of the old war—the past—plays against the new, at one level of convergence inside the poem, from another angle outside the frame, as in artistic illusion, the double images of "history" and fiction, *"romaunce"* and dream, seem to be reflected and turned toward each other, making the "real" time and space imaged between them, the crown of the arch of Book III, a hallucination, contained in a *déjà vu*.

Like the other repeated elements in the larger design of the poem, the "Siege of Thebes" is used to create an artificial symmetry, and thus it calls attention to the poet's art, his mastery of the theme. At the same time, its artistic repetition is subversive, if the ambiguity of history itself is read as a dubious attempt to impose a pattern on events. The "Siege of Thebes" is a book, an old romance to be cast aside when "the real world" intrudes, and the messenger of the real world is, in his *fantasye*, creating a way to escape it. He has no use for history, or for dreams. Yet, in the light of the ending, and only then, the "Siege of Thebes," Troilus's dream, and Cassandra's prophecy become in fact the real world in which the Trojans and the Greeks have roles to play in linear time, which is not free, artistic, and symmetrical, but bound, inescapable, and irreversible, unwinding from the past. The temporal dimension of the poem is thus symbolically fixed, and then universal- ized, from the moment in Book II when *Amphiorax fil thurgh the grounde to helle* to the escape of Troilus's *lighte gost*

> Up to the holughnesse of the eighte spere,
> . . . .
> And ther he saugh, with ful avysement,
> The erratik sterres, herkenyng armonye
> With sownes ful of hevenyssh melodie.
>
> [5. 1809–13]

The Narrator's art achieves an image of human love which lasts only so long as it is unfolding, in the process of becoming; when it comes to the mortal limit of mutability, its decay, the poem turns back upon itself, and condemns its own illusion.

In Boccaccio's romance, the Narrator does not attempt to explain Criseida's treachery, nor reconcile Troilo's death with anything other than the war, in which he is an inevitable casualty, one body among a thousand more. Chaucer's Narrator, from the very beginning of the first Proem, undertakes the role of moralist as well as historian, and it is the redefinition of his role that redefines Chaucer's poem. He interprets, rather than narrates, as the Narrator of *Filostrato* does, and through his perception of the characters, the double focus of Chaucer's irony— foreknowledge, contradiction, human impotence and blindness—magni- fies Troilus, Criseyde, and Pandarus from romance clichés to universals. He is the "fourth actor trying to speak," who calls attention to the fictionality of these *pagans' cursed rites* in the very process of making them more concretely real.

The symbolic imagery Chaucer found latent in Boccaccio, Ovid, and Dante gives his characters the surrealistic landscape in which the

natural world has supernatural shadows. The illusion of Criseyde's
aungelik beautee transcends Criseida's sexual magnetism, as Troilus's
innocence and Diomede's brutality transcend Boccaccio's gallants. The
Narrator's constant shifts of focus and change of lens—consulting his
auctor, the "Lollius" of his ingenious invention—make it increasingly
difficult to maintain a single view of any of his characters, as we oscil-
late between awareness of "the frame and painted canvas," the moral
allegory of fallen sensuality made explicit at the outset, and the "deep
illusion" of the beauty of desire. The Narrator's oblique turn at the end
to make his disavowal precludes pathos, for Troilus has risen beyond
what men can see. Yet the "deep illusion," the satisfaction of human
desire, remains to the end the afterimage of the poem, the arch achieved
within the circumscription of Christian comedy.

The Renaissance Versions: Henryson's *Testament of Cresseid*

To invent a probability, and to make it wonderful, is the most
difficult undertaking in the Art of Poetry.

> Dryden, preface to *Troilus and Cressida*

The second phase of the evolution of the Troilus legend from the
Middle Ages to the Renaissance begins with Robert Henryson's *Testament of Cresseid* (?1490).[62] In the hundred-odd years between the
presumed dates of composition of Chaucer's poem (?1385) and Henryson's supplementary *tragedie*, there accrue in print several further
inflations of the history of Troy, in which the famous lovers figure—
Lydgate's huge *Troy Book* (1420), Caxton's prose *Recuyell of the Histories
of Troye* (1475), and ephemeral imitations known to us chiefly in
allusions.[63] Henryson's Narrator assumes that his reader knows well the
previous history of the lovers in the book *writtin be worthie Chaucer
glorious*. It is worth noting that he writes for a reading public, not for

62. In addition to the notes of Fox and Dickins in their editions and MacQueen's full
length study (see above, nn. 47–48), useful criticism of Henryson may be found in R.D.S.
Jack, *Italian Influence on Scottish Literature* (Edinburgh, 1972); A. C. Spearing, *Criticism and
Medieval Poetry* (London, 1964), pp. 118–44; and E. M. W. Tillyard, *Five Poems, 1478–1870*
(London, 1948), pp. 5–29. The only complete edition of Henryson is still H. Harvey Wood,
ed., *The Poems and Fables of Robert Henryson* (Edinburgh, 1933).

63. Allusions to Troilus in Lydgate's *Troy Book* occur in 3. 4077 ff., 4197 ff. See *Lydgate's
Troy Book*, ed. Henry Bergen, *EETS*, extra series 97 (London, 1906): 278–79, 410, 515–17,
873. Caxton and Mansion also printed the French text of Le Fevre, the source of Caxton's
Recuyell, in 1476.

the ideal audience depicted on Duke Humphrey's manuscript, the Corpus Christi *Troilus and Criseyde* frontispiece, where "Chaucer" gives a reading for the Ricardian court. Henryson is a poet of the new, post-Caxton generation, and while his elegant alliteration reads aloud extremely well, he writes for readers. The attrition of the medieval narrative formulae, worn out by Lydgate, is apparent in their relative rarity in Henryson. The naming of Chaucer as his *auctor* three times in the opening stanzas (11. 41, 58, 64) in fact serves to question the authority of the ending of *Troilus*; the reference is at once pious and deliberately dubious, as I have suggested:

> To brek my sleip ane uther quair I tuik
> In quhilk I fand the fatall destenie
> Of fair Cresseid, that endit wretchitlie.
>
> Quha wait gif all that Chauceir wrait was trew,
> Nor I wait nocht gif this narratioun
> Be authoresit or fenyit of the new
> Be sum Poeit, throw his Inventioun
> Maid to report the Lamentatioun
> And wofull end of this lustie Cresseid
> And quhat distres scho thoillit, and quhat deid.

[61–70]

Who knows, if what he, or any poet, writes is true? As Peter Burke has suggested, commenting on the phenomena of scepticism and the rise of new conceptions of what it is to write history in the early Renaissance, the discovery and comparison of documents are the beginning of the unmasking of authority. "An author ceased to be treated as an authority when he could easily be compared with many others." The authenticity of Dares' and Dictys' "eyewitness" accounts of the Trojan war had been questioned as early as 1401 by Petrarch's disciple Coluccio Salutati.[64]

Henryson's Narrator is laconic, not given to asides, and the poet never resorts to the authority formula after he has established his conventional framework in the first dozen stanzas: *myn auctor seyth* is already an archaism, and it is because he is deliberately imitating Chaucer that Henryson uses it. The opening of the *Testament* is the traditional entrance into the two-dimensional world of medieval dream vision, but

---

64. Peter Burke, *The Renaissance Sense of the Past* (London, 1969), pp. 150, 55.

what is lacking is the self-conscious medieval *humilitas* of the dreamer in Gower and Chaucer. In the *Book of the Duchess*, the *Parliament of Fowls*, and the *Legends of Good Women*,[65] the insomniac poet, too old for love, comforts himself with poetry. Chaucer does not pose as a dreamer in *Troilus and Criseyde*; to its Narrator, credibility is a serious matter. For Henryson, the distinction between fable and fact is a matter of interpretation, and his theory of allegory is plainly put in the *Prolog* to his *Morall Fabills of Esope the Phrygian*, and in his epilogue to *Orpheus and Eurydice*.[66]

> Thocht feinyit fabils of ald poetre
> Be not al grunded upon truth, yit than
> Thair polite termes of sweit Rhetore
> Richt plesand ar Unto the eir of man;
> And als the caus that thay forst began
> Was to repreif the haill misleving
> Off man be figure of ane uther thing.
>
> [Prolog to the *Fabills*, 1–7]

Henryson moralizes the *olde bokes* topos of the *Parliament of Fowls*, 11. 22–25[67] to justify *subtell* secular poetry:

> In lyke maner as throw the bustious eird,
> Swa it be labourit with grit diligence
> Springis the flouris and the corn abreird,
> Hailsum and gude to mannis sustenence,
> So dois spring ane Morall sweit sentence,
> Oute of the subtell dyte of poetry:
> To gude purpois quha culd it weill apply.
>
> The nuttes schell, thocht it be hard and teuch,
> Haldis the kirnill, and is delectabill.
>
> [Prolog, 8–16]

The *Testament's morall sentence* is an allegorical interpretation of the

---

65. In all editions after 1532, the *Legends* follow the *Testament*.

66. See Wood's edition of the *Fabills*, 11. 1–18, 1099–1100, 1380–90, 1890–91, and *Orpheus*, 11. 415–633.

67.
> For out of olde feldes, as men seyth,
> Cometh al this newe corn from yer to yere,
> And out of olde bokes, in good feyth,
> Cometh al this newe science that men lere.

consequences of the *Troilus*'s *payens corsed olde rites* / . . . and *what alle hire goddes may availle* (5. 1849–50), which Chaucer had denied with ironic contempt. Henryson's plot is, to my knowledge, entirely his own invention. The paradox that the best of all the fifteenth-century imitations of Chaucer was for two centuries accepted as Chaucer's last judgment on Criseyde is one of the most famous in literary history. Although the *Testament* had been printed in Scotland in the first decade of the sixteenth century,[68] by some as yet untraced connection, a copy of it came to William Thynne in time for him to insert a relatively bad text, evidently at the last minute, into the first edition of his 1532 collected *Works* of Chaucer. There is a copy of Thynne's 1532 text in the Beinecke Library of Yale University which contains a "cancelled leaf" at fol. ccxix; on it, the last stanzas of *Troilus*, Book V, are followed by the colophon *Here endith the fyfth and laste book of Troylus / and here foloweth the Legends of Good Women*, with a woodcut filling out the lower half of the page. The verso is blank. After the "cancelled leaf," the next folio, ccxix again, contains the last stanzas of *Troilus* and a new colophon, introducing the *Testament of Cresseid*. Thus Denton Fox's hypothesis[69] is confirmed, as to how the *pyteful and dolorous testament of fayre Creseyde* was sandwiched in on four extra leaves (Qq³, Qq⁴, Qq⁵, Qq⁶) between *Troilus* and the *Legends*, which come next in all the sixteenth-century reprintings of Thynne's 1532 text. Thynne revised his table of contents so that the reader has no suspicion that the *Testament* was not Chaucer's, but rather a poem written in Scotland nearly a century after his death. In Stowe's 1561 and Speght's editions of 1598 and 1602, the *Testament* appears in the table of contents, but is printed in its usual position after the fifth Book of *Troilus*, as its traditional afterpiece. The conspicuous Middle Scots dialect features that would have betrayed the poem's Northern origin have been smoothed away by substitution of London forms in rhyme words, and within the lines. Thus the *Testament*, ironically, reached a much wider public, and influence, than its poet could have hoped for when he meditated critically on Chaucer's poem and composed his moral imitation.

It should be obvious that Henrysons's allusions to Chaucer in the opening stanzas of the *Testament* are in fact the converse of the Chaucerian Narrator's habitual deference to his *olde books*. Henryson pro-

68. Fox, *Testament*, pp. 2–3; Dickins, *Testament*, pp. 43–44.
69. Fox, *Testament*, p. 10.

poses not to translate, but to continue, the story of *the fatall destinie | Of fair Cresseid, that endit wretchetlie* (9):

> Ane doolie sessoun to ane cairfull dyte
> Suld correspond, and be equivalent,
> Richt sa it wes quhen I began to wryte
> This tragedie.
>
> [*Testament*, 1–4]

He begins the story from a point in the middle of *Troilus*'s Book V, when, *sum men sayis*, Cresseid had become filthy *with fleschlie lust*, Diomede has gotten rid of her, and Troilus is still alive. The point of departure for Henryson's version is thus a denial of Chaucer's ending, both of its Christian *moralitas* and its angry rejection of the pagan gods— *Jove, Appollo, Mars and swich rescaille* (5. 1853). For his poem, Henryson needs the gods, "worthy to untie the knot" of Cresseid's ambiguity, and he assumes without a qualm that his allegorical planet–gods will be properly interpreted as divine, not demonic. For the dramatic crisis of his action, the pathetic nonrecognition scene at the roadside between the oblivious Troilus and the deformed, leprous Cresseid, he needs Troilus alive and unchanged, with her image still perfect in his mind.

After 1532, Henryson's grotesque Cresseid becomes the stereotype complement to Chaucer's *flour of ladies*, his *hevennish parfit creature* (1.104) of the first three books, as both Criseyde's are read together, in apparent continuity, in all editions of Chaucer until Urry's of 1721. Criseyde and Cresseid are like the before-and-after emblems of innumerable *memento mori* images in medieval diptychs and Renaissance woodcuts, such as the ubiquitous "Three Living and Three Dead," which depicts three beautiful richly dressed ladies facing three rotting skeletons, their counterpart "real" images, in parallel. Henryson is a Christian humanist poet; the *Testament* manifests a glittering pride in its own artistry and in its brilliantly appropriate humiliation of Cresseid's worldly weakness. Everything that she possessed and valued, described in rich detail—her beauty, the comforts of life, her *mirth* and *jolitee*— can be used against her, and the judgment executed by Saturn and Cynthia makes her die twice, with the leper's living death between. It is a far more rigorous and severe conception of what she was, and what Troilus loved, than any of the earlier versions, and it, more than *Troilus*, established *false Cresseid* as the literary type of feminine traitor, until the incomparably greater image of Milton's Eve.

One of Henryson's great virtues as a poet, his brevity, is also in part responsible for his unique status as the most Chaucerian of all Chaucerians. Better than any other fifteenth-century poet, he learned to imitate not only Chaucer's *Troilus* stanza and the high style (e.g., that of *Anelida and Arcite* and the *Knight's Tale*) but also learned his control over the *matere*. We shall take further note of Henryson's significance in chapter 8, in the context of the apocryphal poems in sixteenth-century editions which Renaissance readers accepted as "Chaucer." However, a question arises here as well, in that it might be concluded, if Henryson so successfully modelled his style on Chaucer's, then his poem is its closest analogue, since it was for so long indistinguishable from its source.[70] Granting the intentional resemblances in style, it is still nevertheless clear that the *Testament* presents not merely a sequel but a distinct departure, and in effect an alternative ending, for Chaucer's poem, a conclusion which substitutes the punishment of Cresseid's sin for the Chaucerian reward of Troilus's virtue. The moral allegory in the *Testament*, unequivocal in the plant–gods' trial and conviction of her, is as clear as it is richly mythological, for in this poem, matters *suld correspond, and be equivalent.* Henryson's poem leaves no doubts as to the issues it raises, and settles; his Narrator claims to have found the true answer to the paradox of Cresseid, and having found it, he records her epitaph and succinctly concludes, Q.E.D.:

> Beir in your mynd this schort conclusioun
> Of fair Cresseid, as I have said befoir,
> Sen scho is deid, I speik of hir no moir.

> [614–16]

What is, in Donaldson's phrase, mist-enshrouded in *Troilus and Criseyde*, becomes as clear as the night sky that the Narrator looks up to in the *Testament*:

> The Northin wind has puryfit the Air
> And sched the mistie cloudis fra the sky,
> The froist freisit, the blastis bitterly
> Fra Pole Artick come quhisling loud and schill.

> [17–20]

---

70. The Chaucerian *brevitas* of Henryson's style is discussed by Spearing, *Criticism*, ch. 6 passim.

　　The formal structure of the *Testament* is based on the old book-dream formula which descends from Chrétien de Troyes and the *Roman de la Rose* to become the fifteenth-century structural stereotype.[71] Henryson's neatly balanced pattern of 86 stanzas (616 lines) can be analyzed, as MacQueen has shown, into eight separate parts, four containing the narratative of the new action devised for Cresseid in the Greek camp, alternating with four nonnarrative parts. The latter are distinct units: the Narrator's introduction (11. 1–70), Cresseid's vision of the gods (141–343), her Complaint (in seven 9-line stanzas, 11. 407–69), and her last lament (547–74). These monologues and lyrics occur at the pivotal points in the narrative, which is thus an alternative series of inset scenes of action and reflection, rising to the confrontation in the sixth of the eight parts. Each narrative episode builds toward the next, and the interspersed vision, complaint, and lament are each at once the effect of the preceding scene and the ground of the next to come, in a balanced sequence of action and interpretation, in four and four. This very tight weave works out the consequences of Cresseid's curse of her father's gods and her own, Venus and Cupid (11. 72–140), which brings about her final accusation of herself. The dream of the gods' trial and sentence of her ends with Cresseid's discovery of its real meaning, and her immediate entrance into the leper house (344–406), where she "dies" to the world and makes her Complaint. The ensuing scene (470–546) of her begging with cup and clapper brings on Troilus, his pity and largess to the unknown leper, and Cresseid's swoon when she hears, after the fact, who he was. After the lament to fortune and acceptance of her guilt, the final scene describes her last letter to Troilus, her second, "real," death and burial (11. 575–616). Her last words are, *his trew lufe, and with that word scho swelt* (1. 591).

　　Henryson's skill in creating such a compact and densely woven pattern is equalled by no other fifteenth-century poet. His plot is succinct, the lyric interludes precisely timed, and the whole design of alternating parts organized with economy that strengthens the impact of its crises: the verdict of the gods, the confrontation with Troilus, and Cresseid's self-condemnation. In keeping with the compression of the poem, Henryson's dramatis personae are condensations of basically simple formulae rather than complex characterizations. The Narrator is a wry parody of Chaucer's comic dreamer of the *Legends* and the

71. See Payne, *Key of Remembrance*, ch. 4.

Parliament, not the humble historian of *Troilus.* Henryson's Narrator both accuses and excuses Cresseid's *filthy fleschlie lust, brukkilnes,* and feminine beauty, and with heavy irony he condemns *cruell Saturne, fraward and angrie* for the inhuman malice of his punishment of her, *quhilk was so sweit, gentill, and amorous.* Henryson's Narrator is self-satirized at the outset by his own excuse for reading *Troilus* and imagining his Cresseid. Like Chaucer's melancholy, impotent old Reeve, he is too old for Venus's works, but warms himself by the fire with a drink and a tale of *fleschlie lust sa maculait,* while the unnatural arctic wind blasts the Lenten night with *schouris of Haill . . . fra the North.* Thus, his judgment of Cresseid is tainted, but since Henryson makes virtually no use of him in asides to the reader, the self-characterizations of Calchas and Cresseid are relatively free-standing and autonomous. Cresseid is Chaucer's *flour* (5. 792 [Diomed]; 1317 [Troilus]; 1841 [Narrator]) in seven telling instances,[72] but her beauty is already fading when the action begins. She grows increasingly shrill, and finally monstrous as Henryson reduces her self-pity to blasphemy (against Cupid, then Fortune), and her venereal crime becomes macabre disease (as leprosy was understood to be akin to syphilis in the sixteenth century). Henryson's Cresseid is not ambiguous, but irredeemably guilty, in simple absolute terms. Like the double-faced Venus of her dream, whose symbolic gown, half green, half black, represents inconstancy and death, Cresseid is a vile antinomy:[73]

> [VENUS.] Under smyling scho was dissimulait,
> Provocative, with blenkis Amorous,
> And suddanely changit and alterait,
> Angrie as ony Serpent vennemous
> Richt pungitive, with wordis odious.
> Thus variant scho was, quha list tak keip,
> With ane Eye lauch, and with the uther weip.
>
> [*Testament,* 225–31]

The planetary gods are Henryson's most fully and vividly described dramatis personae, and their attributes are probably traceable to Boccaccio's *Genealogy.*[74] With Mercury, god of medicine and poetry,

---

72. *Testament,* ll. 78, 128, 137–9, 279, 435, 461, 608.

73. See Fox, *Testament,* note to l. 221, for several interpretations of Venus's symbolic colors.

74. MacQueen, *Robert Henryson,* pp. 47–49, discusses Lydgate's *Assembly of Gods* and other parallels, but argues strongly for the Italian source. See also R. D. S. Jack, *Italian Influence,* ch. 1 passim.

speaker for the prosecution, their "parliament" is a brilliant tableau; its rigid morality and pompous decor recreate as a serious trial the "court of love" Chaucer so lightly mocks in the Prologue to the *Legends of Good Women*, where Cupid condemns him for creating Criseyde. Henryson's Cupid is the Platonized Renaissance Cupid, *Cupide the King, ringand ane silver bell*, and Cresseid's curse against him is a blasphemy against the laws "of love, of nature, and of God."[75] This episode prefigures the Spenserian pageantry of the *Mutability Cantos*, and of course supplements the elaborate images of Saturn, Mars, Venus, and Diana of the *Knight's Tale*, which Renaissance readers could assume were by the same hand, rather than among the sources of Henryson's imitative adaptations.

Henryson's Calchas has none of the malign soft-spoken power of Chaucer's Calchas, and he is no longer Apollo's priest, but is now Venus's. He accepts his fallen child with egregious piety: *Quod Calchas, douchter, weip thow not thairfoir | Peraventure all cummis for the best* (11. 103–04). He takes her off to the spital-house, as the law dictates, *wring-and his handis, oftymes he said allace | That he had livit to se that wofull hour* (11. 394–95).

The total absence of Pandarus (and of Diomede, except by report), alters the terms in which Cresseid's guilt must be understood. As he, by implication, will be responsible for his own shame, so she bears the full punishment for hers. Henryson judges his characters as individual symbolic types, distinct and unique, not as the interdependent congeries of qualities in flux which Chaucer presents, in complex reciprocities. The laws of God, operating through the laws of kind, in Henryson's Platonized cosmos, are visible in the patterns and powers of the planets. Against divine and natural law, Cresseid is a heretic, and she is judged with the certainty that must be summoned for a witch trial: her mesmerizing beauty and sexual desire must be put down and Troilus, the *trew knicht*, saved. Troilus, for *knichtlie pietie and memoriall* of the love he suffered for, lives to write its epitaph (11. 607–09). The marble and gold of the tombstone *sum seid* he made for her will cover over the pollution of her mutability, but there is no escape for him from knowledge of her fall. For the last time, Troilus faints, as he did at Criseyde's bedside in Chaucer and in the Trojan parliament in *Filostrato*; neither Shakspere nor Dryden let him swoon or weep.

For greit sorrow his hart tobrist and boun,

75. Fox, *Testament*, p. 37.

> Siching full sadlie, said: I can no moir,
> Scho was untrew, and wo is me thairfoir.
>
> [*Testament*, 600–03]

Henryson's Troilus is still bound to the earth, where his passion lies dead. He is the only character in the poem who escapes Henryson's scorn. It is true, as Fox and MacQueen have argued, that Cresseid's recognition of her guilt—*her greit unstabilness | Brukkil as glas*—assures a Christian audience of her contrition. But in spite of this and the bitter moral judgment she recognizes after Troilus "sees" her, her great moment in the poem comes before, while she is still in ignorance, blaming Fortune for all the woe in the world and seeing herself as the victim of beauty and desire, as all women may so be:

> O Ladyis fair of Troy and Grece, attend
> My miserie, quihilk nane may comprehend:
> My frivoll Fortoun, my Infelicitie:
> My greit mischeif, quhilk na man can amend.
> Be war in tyme, approchis neir the end,
> And in your mynd ane mirrour mak of me:
> As I am now, peradventure that ye
> For all your micht may cum to that same end,
> Or ellis war, gif ony war may be.
>
> [*Testament*, 452–60]

This passage, "The Complaint of Cresseid," was often printed separately in Renaissance anthologies, among the Ovidian "Letters of Dido" and others, like "The Lament of the Duchess of Gloucester" (1441), whose refrain runs, *All women may be ware by me.*[76] Cresseid the betrayer is a more powerful moralist than Aeneas's victim, or even Eleanor Cobham, could be.

Henryson did not achieve, because he did not attempt, Chaucerian allegorical irony, "that which affirms and denies at the same time." His conception of the *moralitas* of his poem precludes uncertainty, and his ironies are all at the expense of the weak. His allegory of Saturn and Cynthia's curse and punishment—incurable physical and psychic disease—exempts nothing mutable from "the wrath of time's destruc-

---

76. See R. H. Robbins, *Historical Poems of the XIV and XV Centuries* (New York, 1959), pp. 176 ff. and notes. The second duchess of Gloucester, Eleanor Cobham, was tried and convicted for sorcery in 1441 and sentenced to life imprisonment.

tive power."[77] That he has divine authority speaks for itself, but whereas Chaucer left an image of this world that *passeth sone as flowres faire* (5. 1841), Henryson leaves a dignified stone, signifying death, *his ressoun, in goldin letteris,* in answer to Cresseid's cry,

> Quhair is thy gardins, with their greisses gay? . . .
> Nocht is your fairnes but ane faiding Flour,
> Nocht is your famous Laud and hie honour,
>
> . . . .
>
> Lo fair Ladyis, Cresseid, of Troyis Toun,
> Sumtyme countit the flour of Womanheid,
> Under this stane lait Lipper lyeis deid.
>
> [*Testament,* 425; 461–2; 607–09]

Shakspere's *Troilus and Cressida*

Henryson's *Testament,* the first and greatest of the reinterpretations of Chaucer's *Troilus,* isolates Cresseid and dramatizes her alone. For the spectacle necessary in the theatre, Shakspere multiplied the dramatis personae of the legend, speeded up the action to the last confused days before and after the truce, and ended with a return to unfinished battle. The familiar plot of Cressida's unfaithfulness is subsumed in the deeper futility of the war, and the great men who are attempting to end it, knowing it is no longer worth fighting. In the play's profusion of scene shifts, Troilus and Cressida are alone only once; they have only one night together and, the morning after the consummation, she is handed over to Diomede. Her famous entrance (4. 5) with a kiss for each of the enemy generals is sardonic comedy, and it emphasizes the mockery of *amour courtois,* its secrecy and ennobling virtue, among the "merry Greeks" and lecherous Trojans. Paris calls Helen "Nell," and Troilus praises her as "she whose youth and freshness / Wrinkles Apollo's, and makes stale the morning" (2. 2. 78–9). Cressida's sex is open and teasing and Troilus fears the act will disappoint the ecstasy of its anticipation. Shakspere's Troilus and Cressida are satirized, within as well as outside the fiction, by the ironic awareness of their affair among all the other characters, both their inferiors and superiors, enemies and friends: Thersites and Pandarus, Ulysses, Paris, Aeneas watch them with as much contempt as pity.

77. The phrase is MacQueen's, *Robert Henryson,* p. 75.

The difficulties both audiences and readers must face in Shakspere's
Troilus arise in considerable measure from the crowding of the stage
with famous heroes, far too many for any one to carry the play. The
world of the play opens as widely into the Greek camp as it does into
Priam's court, and there are two dozen speaking parts, as well as bands
of retainers and soldiers. The action is prolonged by epic inflation of
the issue at stake in the war: the honor of the heroes, which gives
meaning to their death. The delays for the Greek council in act 1 and
the Trojan parliament in act 2 raise problems of far more profound
philosophical difficulty than the tragedy of Troilus alone. The theme
of mutability passes from Cressida, its sexual symbol, to the turbulence
we see going out of control in the murder of Hector, alone and unarmed, and the inability of intelligence, sane or mad, Ulysses' or Cassandra's, to reason with and control appetite. The issue has become the
flux of time itself, "great-sized monster of ingratitude," which devours
all. Saturn–Chronos is more terrible in mortal shape, reduced to the
"fashionable host" who welcomes each, ever smiles, and makes the
whole world kin.

> [ULYSSES.] Time hath, my lord, a wallet at his back,
>   Wherein he puts alms for oblivion,
>   A great-sized monster of ingratitudes.
>   Those scraps are good deeds past, which are devoured
>   As fast as they are made, forgot as soon
>   As done.
>
> . . . .
>   Let not virtue seek
>   Remuneration for the thing it was. For beauty, wit
>   High birth, vigor of bone, desert in service,
>   Love, friendship, charity, are subjects all
>   To envious and calumniating time.
>   [3. 3. 145–50; 169–73]

Shakspere and his audience, in some indeterminate sense, knew two
irreconcilable versions of the Trojan legends: the "medieval" tradition
of Chaucer and Caxton's *Recuyell*, and the newly translated *Seaven
Books of the Iliades* (1598) of Chapman.[78] The first derives from Virgil
and Latin sources, and is partisan to the Trojans; the second glorifies

---

78. The seven books are *Iliad* 1–2, 7–10, 12, and 18 (The Shield of Achilles).

the attacking Greeks, and exposes the factional quarrel among them over Achilles' sullen anger. In the words of Reuben Brower,

> We need not attempt to determine what no one has yet determined, the exact debt of Shakespeare to ancient, medieval and Renaissance versions of the Troy story and the tale of Troilus and Cressida. . . . More certain than his reading of any particular work is his familiarity with the traditions of chivalry and courtly love (and with contemporary mockery of them), and with the Renaissance remaking of the ancient heroic tradition.[79]

Shakspere does not attempt to reconcile the discrepant histories in his mélange of sources; rather, he intensifies the stalemate itself as the matrix of corruption which debases the honor of the warriors on both sides, and all their women: decadent Trojans, barbarian Greeks, trapped on the stage in a war of words that finally erupts into carnage. Since Dryden, critics have struggled to determine the play's proper genre, whether tragedy or satire, faced with its overwhelming ironies.[80] Brower's excellent essay concludes,

> The end of *Troilus and Cressida* is no demonstration of poetic or any kind of justice: all effort, all values, are equally subject to "envious and calumniating time."[81]

In the concurring opinion of Philip Edwards, "it refuses all consolation and resolution":

> Since life is fundamentally arbitrary and meaningless, all art which . . . seeks to show pattern and meaning is false. . . . *Troilus and Cressida* is anti-art, because its very structure is a kind of defiance of the certainty, consequence, and unity which the more usual kind of play will provide. Shakespeare dispenses with suggestions of order and meaning, which a unified plot

79. Reuben Brower, *Hero and Saint*, p. 272.
80. For example, Irving Ribner, in *Patterns in Shakespearian Tragedy* (London, 1960), p. 11, excludes *Troilus* from his book "for although there is strong bibliographical evidence that Shakespeare and his contemporaries regarded it as a tragedy, this evidence is far from conclusive. If it was designed as a tragedy, it is . . . so different from the others as to require separate treatment." See also O. J. Campbell, *Shakespeare's Satire*; and Alice Walker, ed., *Troilus and Cressida* (Cambridge, 1957); both argue in favor of satire.
81. Brower, *Hero and Saint*, p. 266.

with a single hero must impose on any material. His reasons for
doing so are in the matter of the play.[82]

In the "matter of the play," the theme of love is drowned out by the
epic hyperbole of the generals' rhetoric, but all are struggling to deny
the same premise: the futility of the attempt to make an act conclusive.
Shakspere's expansion of the tale of Troilus, putting it back into the
context of the siege, is a change of scale and perspective which would
seem to give the audience distance and detachment; but instead of making the issue clear, the dramatization of Troilus's betrayal and Hector's
death brings the ambiguity of heroism and passion so close that they
can no longer be distinguished from slaughter and lechery. The imagination can still conceive an ideal, but none of these Greeks and
Trojans stands a chance of achieving honor, or love.

> [TROILUS.] This is the mostruosity in love, lady,
>   that the will is infinite and the execution
>   confined; that the desire is boundless, and
>   the act a slave to limit.
>   [3. 3. 74–77]

In his last scene, Troilus brings word to the Trojans that Hector has
been murdered, and "dragged through the shameful field," in a speech
that is crosscut with ironies:

> [TROILUS.] Go in to Troy, and say there Hector's dead.
>   There is a word will Priam turn to stone,
>   Make wells and Niobe's of the maids and wives. . . .
>   But march away,
>   Hector is dead; there is no more to say.
>   [5. 10. 17–18, 22]

> [TROILUS.] What knowe I of the quene Niobe?
>   Lat be thine olde ensamples, I thee praye . . .

> [PANDARUS.] Right fain I wolde amende it, wiste I how.
>   And fro this worlde, almighty God I praye
>   Delivere hir soone; I can namore saye.
>   [*Troilus and Criseyde*, 1. 759–60; 5. 1741–43]

Such echoes as these are of course inevitable and unprovable; Niobe is

82. Philip Edwards, *Shakespeare and the Confines of Art* (London, 1968), p. 97.

a classic synonym for grief, and the defection of Criseyde and the death of Hector are unspeakable, in the same terms—they are the defeat of the imagination's ideals. Yet the irony of Pandarus's famous last words for Criseyde's betrayal, spoken now by Troilus of the death of Hector, has the impact of hallucination.

What gives Shakspere's *Troilus and Cressida* its unique power as a fiction, distinct from all the preceding versions of the legend, is that the transfer to the stage magnifies and makes explicit and concrete all the ironic implications of Troilus's tragedy: the war, Cressida's weakness and lust, Pandarus's chicanery, and the difficult struggle to reason out the meaning of events, the Boethian dialectic of Troilus's soliloquy on necessity and human freedom in Chaucer's fourth book. But in Shakspere there is no Narrator to shield and filter the action as it unfolds in retrospect: the play proceeds, episodically and out of control, as the actors pontificate, and make love, all too visibly and near. The limits of the spectator's patience are tested, as Dryden saw, by the distortions in the play's structure. Twenty-four scenes crowd one another, as time runs out; the seven scenes of the nuclear love story give the action narrative continuity, from Troilus's desire in act 1, scene 1, to Cressida's yielding to Diomede in 5. 2, but the superimposed dialectics of the generals, and the battle in progress at the end, make up two-thirds of the whole. The effect is to disintegrate the tragedy, and to make the history of the war a meaningless sequence of episodes whose *moralitas* is a commonplace: "men cannot do what they choose, nor be what they choose."[83]

In place of the Narrator, the manipulators, Thersites and Pandarus, comment on the war theme and the love theme; each is being used in turn by their more eloquent employers in the basic action set in motion in act 1, the goading of Ajax and the persuasion of Cressida. Without the intervening fiction of a dream world, as in the *Testament*, or a sympathetic Narrator, as in *Filostrato* and Chaucer's *Troilus*, the seduction of the lady and the meaning of the hero's military prowess can no longer be distanced by an illusion of detachment; they are only one dimension away from the audience, made more, not less than real. The ambiguity that clouds the tale is not from the effusions of pity of the Narrator, but in the nature of the events and the characters themselves. The victorious warrior and the embodiment of sexual pleasure—Achilles and Cressida, and all their similars—play out their roles to the

83. Ibid., p. 106.

foregone conclusion, but in the play, doubt is not an option. The *olde books* are gone, and we are forced to trust our eyes. There is no evasion of the fact, "This is, and is not Cressida!" (5. 2. 142). Hector is slain. "He's dead, and at the murderer's horse's tail / In beastly sort, dragged through the shameful field" (5. 10. 4–5).

Shakspere's Prologue is perhaps the last remnant of the medieval narrative interpreter of Troilus's tragedy left in the Renaissance evolution of the legend. It has been suggested that the device of the Prologue is part of the classical machinery that Shakspere is awkwardly manipulating in the play.[84] Given the rarity of formal prologues in Shakspere, and their scattering, to go beyond the separate case is hazardous.[85] In *Troilus*, the effect the Prologue achieves is not only to hypothesize the epic landscape, to overcome the bare stage, but also to reiterate ironically the old formulaic denial of authority, and undercut it. First the Prologue ("armed") fixes the illusion of historicity, of real men and women; he is not a *deus ex machina*:

> In Troy there lies the scene. From isles of Greece
> The princes orgulous, their high blood chafed,
> Have to the port of Athens sent their ships. . . .
> The ravished Helen, Menelaus' queen,
> With wanton Paris sleeps; and that the quarrel.
>
> [1. 1–3, 9–10]

The Prologue ends with a sardonic *occupatio*, offering no guarantee, no apology, and making no plea for tolerance. Himself "vizarded," he leaves the interpretation of "what may be digested in a play" arbitrary and indeterminate:

> Hither am I come,
> A Prologue armed, but not in confidence
> Of author's pen or actor's voice, but suited
> In like conditions of our argument. . . .
> Beginning in the middle, starting thence away
> To what may be digested in a play.
> Like or find fault; do as your pleasures are:
> Now good or bad, 'tis but the chance of war.
>
> [1. 22–25, 28–31]

84. See J. A. K. Thomson, *Shakespeare and The Classics* (London, 1952), pp. 141–45.
85. The plays with Prologues are *Taming of the Shrew, Romeo and Juliet, 2 Henry IV, Henry V, Troilus, Pericles;* Time appears in *Winter's Tale*, 4.1, to provide the transition.

In Shakspere's *Troilus*, the "Siege of Thebes" has become the Siege of Troy, in an image of war of timeless contemporaneity. If there is anything in the play to set against its pessimism, it is the self-awareness of the characters, who know their state, and defy time's mutability. They attempt to imagine a pattern which the experience offered by the play refutes. Shakspere leaves the paradox of the mortal love men die for unresolved, vastly enlarged from the meaningless death of Troilus; and, in leaving him alive, going back into battle at the end, with Cressida still at large in the Greek camp, Shakspere set free the tragic irony of the myth from its medieval Christian sublimation.

Dryden's Revision of Shakspere: *Troilus and Cressida Or, Truth Found Too Late*

Dryden, as he explains in his Preface, honors the original play because it was Shakspere's, and he

> undertook to remove the heap of rubbish under which many excellent thoughts lay wholly buried. Accordingly, I new-modelled the plot, threw out many unnecessary persons, improved those characters which were begun and left unfinished, as Hector, Troilus, Pandarus, and Thersites, and added that of Andromache.

Dryden goes on to describe in detail how he made

> with no small trouble, an order and connexion of all the scenes (so), that there is a coherence of them with one another, and a dependence on the main design; no leaping from Troy to the Grecian tents, and thence back again, in the same act, but a due proportion of time allowed for every motion.

The reduction of Shakspere's chaos to Dryden's conception of dramatic order and design involved not only invention of new scenes, and re-proportioning of actions and dramatis personae, but reduction of the antinomian themes of Shakspere's double plot to a "single, great and probable action, which by moving us to fear and pity, is conducive to the purging of those passions in our minds."[86] Dryden undertook to reconcile the paradoxes of Shakspere's play, and to allay, indeed to "rectify" them. In his essay, Dryden applies both Aristotle and his French contemporary Bossu to the problem of transformation of reality

86. Ker, *Essays,* 1: 204, 207.

in tragic drama, which must enclose the "terrible"—the existence of evil, and of unmerited suffering—in a greater and more wonderful whole that affirms order and frees us from the fear of unorganized experience. Tragic fear is that in which "the only certain thing is eventual extinction. The fear is two-fold: the fear of confusion, and the fear of time."[87]

For his play, Dryden reconstructed Shakspere's plot in accordance with the "three Unities, Time, Place and Action" in order to facilitate expression of the moral, the focus of the play:

> 'tis the moral that directs the whole . . . to one center, and that action or fable is the example, built upon the moral, which confirms the truth of it to our experience.

At great cost, Dryden achieved the resolution of both the theme of war and the tragic love affair, in the synchronized battle scene of the last act (5. 2). Cressida proves her innocence, and dies on Troilus's sword, blessing both her destiny and her lover:

> Since I question not your hard Decree
> That doom'd my days unfortunate, and few,
> Add all to him, you take away from me;
> And I die happy, that he thinks me true.

Ulysses arrives after the final slaughter, in which Troilus kills Diomede and is in turn killed by Achilles, to deliver the "precept of morality which [the play] would insinuate into the people":

> Now peaceful Order has resum'd the Reins,
> Old Time looks young, and Nature seems renew'd:
> Then since from home-bred Factions Ruin springs,
> Let Subjects learn Obedience to their Kings.

In order to achieve this final synthetic result, the astounding vindication of Cressida's honor and the justification of the victorious Greeks, Dryden transformed the twenty-four scenes of Shakspere's play to eleven, and rewrote the fifth act entirely; scenes of his own are "mingled" with those remodelled from Shakspere's, and the language, "which was obsolete," has been "refined."[88] He divided the result into five acts, with the action rising to an anticlimactic confrontation

87. Edwards, *Shakespeare*, p. 3
88. Ker, *Essays*, 1:213, 204.

between Troilus and Diomede, where Aeneas intervenes to save the truce (4. 2), and then to the catastrophe (act 5) which fulfills the lovers' anticipation of their union in death:

[CRESSIDA.] What have we gained by this one minute more?

[TROILUS.] Only to wish another, and another,
　　　　A longer struggling with the Pangs of Death.

　　　　　　　　　　　　　　　　　　　　　　　[4.1]

Dryden's moral theme is stated in his subtitle, "Or, Truth Found Too Late." Troilus is unable to perceive what Cressida's interview with Diomede really means: her vain attempt to save her father and herself and get safe-conduct back to Troy. Troilus is guilty of misreading the evidence, which is ambiguous, but Cressida herself is not guilty and not a paradox. She is as virtuous as she seems, in her yielding innocence in act 3, scene 2, when she piteously asks Pandarus, without irony, "And will you promise that the holy Priest / Shall make us one forever?" She willingly kills herself to prove that love can be, and is, true. She is, in effect, no longer Cressida, but a martyr to her own beauty and *trouthe*, and victim of Troilus's incredulity. Chaucer's Troilus loved his betrayer to the end:

　　　　　　　　and I ne kan nor may,
　　　For al this world, withinne myn herte fynde
　　　To unloven yow a quarter of a day!
　　　In corsed tyme I born was, weilaway!
　　　That yow, that doon me al this wo endure,
　　　Yit love I best of any creature.

　　　　　　　　　　　　　　　　[5. 1697–1701]

So too, Henryson extended the integrity of Troilus's love, without sentimentality, to give him the resolution of burying her. Shakspere's bitter Troilus, seeing Cressida with Diomede *in playe*, splits what he sees in two, keeping the ideal image ("Cressida is mine, tied with the bonds of heaven") and rejecting her mortal counterpart, "Diomed's Cressida," in "the madness of discourse . . . within his soul." But Dryden's Troilus can bear no more, when Pandarus taunts him with the common gossip (4. 2):

[TROILUS.] 　　　　　　　　She's Falshood, all,
　　　False by both kinds; for with her Mother's Milk·

> She sucked the Infusion of her Father's soul.
> She only wants an Opportunity—
> Her Soul's a Whore already.

Dryden's tragedy is a failure, doomed from the start by his reinterpretation of the meaning of Troilus's tragedy. He revised not only
Shakspere's play, but the fundamental elements in the conflict at its
heart: that Troilus loved a beautiful illusion and was true to the death
to a symbol of mortal mutability. To revise the symbolism, making
Cressida true, and Troilus's *trouthe* unstable, violates the integrity of the
legend in order to moralize its paradox. Dryden attempted to affirm
dramatic order and coherence by means of a new myth: to reconcile in
a single action the fall of Troy and Hector's death, and at the same time
save the phenomena of innocent love, even at the price of suicide. But,
as Thomson observes of ancient tragedy,

> In a traditional tale, such as the myths, which
> form the subject [of tragic drama], the characters
> have traditional qualities; alter these qualities,
> and the myth no longer makes sense.[89]

The audience of *Troilus* knows too well that Cressida will not be true;
there have been too many witnesses, and the myth, in Dryden's play,
no longer makes sense. By subjecting it to rational principles of design,
he made the myth conform to morality external to it, and in so doing
damaged it beyond repair. Criseyde's betrayal is inexplicable, and it is
a given. The fall of Troy, and the triumph of the strong, is more amena-
ble to rationalizing, for both Hector and Achilles know the meaning of
honor, and in Homer, Priam's recovery of Hector's body binds Greek
and Trojan together in their common grief. Dryden's futile attempt to
justify, to make a balance and a synthesis out of the conflicting forces let
loose in Shakspere's unruly play, bears a curious antithetical relationship to Henryson, who first pursued Cresseid to her death and made her
see herself in her own mirror. She then became the mirror of all mortal
beauty, in her lament to Fortune:

> Exempill mak of me in your Memour,
> Quhilk of sic thingis wofull witnes beiris.
> All Welth in Eird, away as Wind it weiris,
> Be war thairfore, approchis neir the hour.
>
> [*Testament*, 465–68]

---

89. Thomson, *Shakespeare and the Classics*, p. 225.

Dryden's heroine bears woeful witness, but not to justice: to tragic injustice, and her death leaves pity unrelieved. Dryden was unwise, for once, to tamper with the truth of the old story: that Cressida was false, and Troilus loved her to the end.

As part of his scholarly defense of his reworking of Shakspere with interspersed elements he borrowed from Euripedes, Dryden quotes a passage of Longinus's *On the Sublime* concerning Plato's imitations of Homer:

> We ought not to regard a good imitation as theft, but as a beautiful idea of him who undertakes to imitate, by framing himself on the invention and the work of another man; for he enters the lists like a new wrestler, to dispute the prize with the former champion . . . when we combat for victory with a hero [we] are not without glory even in our overthrow.[90]

The history of the legend of *Troilus and Criseyde* in the Renaissance is the metamorphosis of "a beautiful idea" which became increasingly more difficult to keep alive as it became more clearly visualized, passing from the myth-history of Chaucer's *auctors*—*In Omer, or in Dares or in Dite, | Who so that can may reden hem as they write* (1. 146–47)—to more and more self-conscious works of art. As Francis Beaumont wrote to Speght in 1597 in his prefatory letter congratulating the editor for bringing England's greatest poet back to the light, *Troilus and Criseyde* is still "the most excellent of all imitations of Homer, Virgil, and Horace," because, more than any other quality,

> one gifte hee hath aboue other Authors, and that is, by the excellencies of his descriptions to possesse his Readers with a stronger imagination of seeing that done before their eyes, which they reade, than any other that ever writ in any tongue.

In conclusion, let us consider one last analogy. Chaucer's *Troilus and Criseyde* may be seen to stand, in relation to all of its Renaissance imitations, as in the first and greatest of them, Criseyde remains an indelible image:

> The Idole of ane thing in cace may be
> Sa deep Imprented in the fantasy
> That it deludes the wittis outwardly
> And so appeares in form and lyke estait
> Within the mynd, as it was figurait.
>
> [*Testament*, 505–11]

90. Ker, *Essays*, 1. 206.

VIII

The Renaissance Chaucer: From Manuscript to Print

Chaucers woorkes bee all printed in one volume, and therfore knowen to all men.

John Fox, 1570

In one open parliamente . . . when talke was had of Bookes to be forbiden, Chaucer had there for euer byn condempned, had yt not byn that his woorkes had byn counted but fables.

Francis Thynne, 1599

Conflation: The Earliest Editions

In an "Observation on Method," Edgar Wind defended his approach to the study of art history through "exceptions" rather than the "typical," even though it is true that "the symbolical creations of geniuses are harder to nail down to a definite subject than the allegorical conventions of minor artists." Wind concludes,

> it seems to be a lesson of history that the commonplace may be understood as a reduction of the exceptional, but the exceptional cannot be understood by amplifying the commonplace. . . . That this relation is irreversible should be an axiom in any study of art.[1]

As in art, the difficulty for the literary historian of the later Middle Ages and the early Renaissance is the anonymity of many poems, both exceptional and commonplace, in manuscript and in print. The corollary of this is attribution of both kinds of poetry, the sublime and the indifferent, to famous poets, whether there is evidence for authorship or not. Great poets do write bad poems, and the converse may sometimes happen, but the usual tendency is to give the benefit of the doubt to the admirable. In the case of Chaucer, his early editors admired, accepted,

---

1. Wind, *Pagan Mysteries*, p. 191.

and attributed to him a very large number of works in verse and prose which were subsequently understood to be representative of his style and thought for four hundred years. In Wind's sense, then, the evolution of Henryson's *Testament* as a part of Chaucer's *Troilus* is both commonplace and exceptional; commonplace in that the *Testament* is only one of forty-odd non-Chaucerian pieces assimilated into the canon of Chaucer's works in the sixteenth century; exceptional, in its catalytic power and excellence. It is necessary to take account of both kinds, however; so we turn now to mediocrity, the reductive "commonplace" which amplifies in the context of the exceptional, in the manuscripts and early editions of Chaucer's *Works*. In effect, the modern reader, accustomed to fully edited texts purged of non-Chaucerian accretions, reads a different poet from the "Chaucer" of English literary history before the nineteenth century. Some serious questions, perhaps unanswerable ones, remain as to the authenticity of a few poems, but the evidence of Renaissance conflation is clear enough, and certainly important enough, to justify a summary review of the apocrypha in the black letter editions of the sixteenth-century "Chaucer," and a brief glance at the problems of linguistic evolution. The facts are at once familiar, complex, and depressing. We can best begin with the general problem of the Renaissance editor.

In the earliest printed texts of Chaucer's poems, the editions of Caxton, Wynkyn de Worde, Julian Notary, and Richard Pynson, from ca. 1478 to the first quarter of the sixteenth century, separate works are published as separate entities. Caxton, however, printed two non-Chaucerian lyrics with the genuine minor poems in his *Parliament of Fowles*, entitled *The Temple of Bras* (1477), and after Pynson's three-part publication of ten of "Chaucer's" poems (five apocryphal) in 1526, conflation of the spurious with the genuine grew on a significant scale. Three-quarters of a century after Chaucer's death, Caxton described his difficulty in obtaining a true copy of the original poems in the famous Prohemye to his second edition of the *Canterbury Tales* (1484). He tells of his dismay at learning of the flaws in his first edition of the *Tales* of a few years before, and he rightly blames his bad text on a bad manuscript.[2] The textual problems presented by the *Tales* alone, to their earliest editors and to all their successors, are perhaps as fascinating as they are tedious, given the number of variables in the fragments Chaucer left.

2. W. J. B. Crotch, ed., *The Prologues and Epilogues of William Caxton, EETS*, o.s. 176 (1928, repr. 1956): 90–91. Pynson printed Caxton's *Tales* (2nd ed.) in 1491–92.

The "intended" arrangement of the surviving *Tales*, after the General Prologue, is still intelligently debated, as is the extent of Chaucer's "influence" in the incomplete and quite pedestrian *Romaunt of the Rose*, still published as an open question in some modern texts. But since Caxton published the *Boke of Fame* in 1483 with a twelve-line conclusion and apologetic epilogue,

> I fynde nomore of this werke to fore sayd / For as fer as I can vnderstonde / This noble man Geffrey Chaucer fynysshyd at the sayd conclusion of the metyng of lesyng and sothsawe / where as yet they ben chekked and may not departe, . . .

one by one the minor poems have been disentangled and authenticated, and several other hands discovered, earlier and later than Caxton's. Taking for granted the innumerable textual problems that remain to be solved for individual poems, it is now no longer so difficult to see how the modern canon developed by a peculiarly literary and non-Darwinian evolution. The great period of growth is the sixteenth century, when increasing numbers of ghost poems and imitations began to be associated with Chaucer's *Works*. Reviewing the chaos of the evidence of contaminated texts seems to me to raise critical questions perhaps as insoluble as the proper order of the *Tales*, but no less relevant to interpretation. Much still remains to be seen: not only, who were the anonymous "other" poets, and why were the apocrypha attributed to Chaucer (although these are interesting questions) but further, how do the accretions of Chauceriana cumulatively affect later readings of the originals, and their subsequent imitation by his successors? If there are answers to such questions, they will be found only by individual readings of individual poets and not by a general census. But a survey of the Renaissance texts is needed, if only to set the parameters within which the important texts can be read. This chapter purports to do no more than review the period of Renaissance confusion, in the most general sense, which C. S. Lewis characterized in a paradox:

> From the varied excellence of the fourteenth century to the work of the early sixteenth century it is a history of decay . . . [yet], it might be called a transition from barbarism to civilization.[3]

It is well known that the gradual process of conflation of poems began before 1500, and it lasted until the later eighteenth century: Urry added

3. C. S. Lewis, *English Literature in the Sixteenth Century* (Oxford, 1954), p. 120.

two new *Canterbury Tales* in 1721, and it was not until Tyrwhitt in the 1770's that the purification of the canon began.

In addition to the steady multiplication of textual variants in every poem—the inevitable debasement of the text which picks up from scribal errors and goes on in printers' errors, line by line—the proportion of spurious to genuine poems in every edition of Chaucer's *Works* rises throughout the sixteenth century. It reaches its highest level in the last of the great Renaissance folios, Speght's two editions of 1598 and 1602, at once the worst and the most interesting of all the black letter texts. Speght's 1602 folio was not reprinted until 1687, and in that year there also appeared a remarkable publication derived from Chaucer's preeminent and self-proclaimed Elizabethan heir, *Spencer Redivivus* [*sic*], containing the first book of the *Faerie Queene*, its "Essential Design preserv'd, but his obsolete Language and manner of Verse totally laid aside, Deliver'd in Heroick Numbers."[4] Except for the last clause, that subtitle brings into focus the problem of reading Chaucer and his contemporaries in the Renaissance. The author concludes his preface with precisely the questions still to be pursued in the present study, for which the review of the editions and the language needs to be undertaken.

> Not but I grant that it is a Work of highest difficulty, and no less to be admir'd, if perfect, than some wondrous Architecture hardly to be equall'd in point of Design, Magnitude, and Beauty.
>
> But not impossible to be effected since there needs not be urged a surer Refutation of all Opposers, than the marvellous esteem of this Author, notwithstanding the obsoliteness of his English and Verse, who liv'd within a hundred years of our times. But how to excuse the choice of the Language he writ in, that he could not but know, was of too antiquate a Date, if not generally exploded by all Writers in the time he liv'd; or why he should not conceive himself oblig'd to impart the Tongue of that season as currant as he found it, I cannot apprehend.
>
> Unless he was resolv'd, as is reported of him, to imitate his ancient Predecessor Chaucer, or affected it out of design to restore our Saxon English.

It is a paradox, like the Restoration "modernization" of Shakspere, that Spenser, translated, "improv'd," and made intelligible, was published in the same year as the reprinting of Speght's *Chaucer* of

4. *Spencer Redivivus.* . . . *by a Person of Quality* (London, 1687).

eighty-five years before, and thirteen years before Dryden's modern translations in the *Fables* of 1700. The Elizabethan language of the *Faerie Queene* (like Shakspere's in *Troilus*, to Dryden) had become, by 1687, as remote as its medieval ancestor's in Speght's folio.[5]

> howsoever admirable, [the *Faerie Queene*] is so far from being familiarly perceptible in the language he deliver'd it in, that his Stile seems no less unintelligible at this Day, than the obsoletest of our English or Saxon dialect.

The Chaucer Apocrypha: Linguistic and Stylistic Imitation

In order, then, to approach the speculative question of Spenser's imitations of Chaucer, it is necessary to return first to the problematic facts of the growth of the "Chaucer" the Renaissance inherited, with all the apocrypha intact. It is not a task that can be approached with the ebullience of the author of *Spencer Redivivus*, who was confident that he had discharged his obligation both to his poet and to his audience. In an overview such as this, many questions will be begged; the mass of the evidence itself—some 21,000 lines of additions to the medieval canon—precludes discussion of the individual pieces of Chauceriana here in any detail. The impact of conflation is cumulative, and the linguistic complexities technically difficult. Among the Chauceriana alone, there is an immense surplus of evidence, of great interest to specialists; the question remains, however, which is most relevant to Chaucer and Spenser, as "Spenser's Chaucer"? If it is against the background of the commonplace that the exceptional emerges, then perhaps enumeration of the commonplace can be foregone; some of those who have read these poems may be willing to forgive their absence. In the general discussion that follows, then, no pretense is made of a full and adequate coverage of the literary evidence, much of which I consider worthless; the anonymous imitations are of interest chiefly by association. This is, however, a minority dissent, against the testimony of the Chaucerian imitations of Dryden, Keats, and Wordsworth, who were charmed by

5. A second curious parallel occurs in the 17th century history of Chaucer and Spenser, the two independent attempts made to preserve their poems from further linguistic decay by translation into Latin. Sir Francis Kynaston's partial publication of his version of *Troilus and Criseyde* appeared in 1635, and Theodore Bathurst's *Shepherd's Calendar* in 1653, *Calendarium pastorale sive Aeglogae duodecim totidem anni mensibus accomodatae Anglice olim scriptae ab Edmundo Spensero. Nunc autem eleganti Latino carmine donatae a Theodoro Bathurst with glossarie.*

The Flower and the Leaf, and Lewis's generous estimate of the *Court of Love,* for example, which he admits is a pastiche, but finds an amazing performance.[6] In my opinion, that so turgid and mindless an allegory should be taken for Chaucerian love poetry is somewhat more to be deplored than applauded. P. M. Kean's reassessment of Chaucerian influence on his fifteenth-century successors provides a much clearer view, but her approval of the "easy, conversational style" of the *Court of Love,* the *Assembly of Ladies,* and the *Flower and the Leaf* is nearly as misleading as Lewis's peremptory abuse of the "stupid" Chaucerians who gilded their language with Latinisms.[7] Kean corrects narrow modern readings of the early panegyrics on Chaucer's style, reexamining what was meant by the terms "illumyne" and *ornare;* she rightly stresses the Horatian concepts of the unity of style and content in Caxton's praise of the brevity, clarity, and richness of Chaucer's rhetoric. Nevertheless, I think the questions remain as cloudy and compelling as before: did Spenser believe that the *Letter of Cupid,* the *Lamentations of Mary Magdalen,* and the *Mossie Quince* were Chaucer's poems, and, if so, what difference does it make?

Wind's "Observation on Method" would appear to be as appropriate for poetry as for painting: "the exceptional cannot be understood by amplifying the commonplace." Just as fifteenth-century manuscript miscellanies juxtaposed Gower, Chaucer, and Lydgate, often without titles or colophons, or with equivocal scribal marginalia, so the expanding black-letter editions continually interpolated the commonplace into the immediate context in which the exceptional was read. The inevitable, immediate effect is blur. As time passed, uncertainty grew as to what "Chaucer's" poems were; the greater poems acquired an increasingly heavy hidden burden of anonymous and trivial verse, neither original—as Henryson's is—nor truly imitative—as Spenser's is to be—but derivative, dull, and redundant. The history of the black-letter folios is easily summarized in their ample tables of contents and ornate title pages, which announce, in succession, discoveries of "diverse works never before imprinted," brought to light for the first time, again and again. New manuscripts are found and compared, and new Chauceriana accepted into the canon; each subsequent edition revises the aggregate whole and reduces the proportion of genuine poems. The lengthening lists and tables clearly reveal, then, two kinds of change or

6. Lewis, *English Literature,* p. 240.
7. P. M. Kean, *Chaucer and the Making of English Poetry* (London, 1972), 2: 210 ff.

literary evolution. They are qualitative and quantitative metamorphoses of Chaucer's *Works*, as the gap between the fourteenth-century poet and the sixteenth-century editions of his poems grows longer and the secondary links more tenuous and insecure. First, there is the direct evidence of abundant inflation and debasement occurring in each edition; from this, indirectly, we may infer the gradual change in the conception of Chaucer and medieval poetry which the folios in succession conveyed to contemporaries.

In the course of the century, it was apparent, as it was proudly announced, that the shape and the content of the canon of Chaucer, *oure auncient laureate poete*, were changing and growing with newly printed poems. Simultaneously, the increasing tempo of linguistic change made Chaucer's poetic language less and less intelligible. The consciousness of "medieval" obscurity and linguistic obsolescence becomes increasingly evident; it eventually becomes something of a fashionable affectation, worth public comment, as in Thomas Wilson's *Arte of Rhetorique* of 1553:

> The fine Courtier wil talke nothyng but Chaucer. The misticall wise menne, and Poeticall Clerkes will speake nothyng but quaint prouerbes, and blynd allegories, delityng muche in their awne darkenesse, especially, when none can tell what thei dooe saie.[8]

It is worth noting that three decades later, in his definitions of the ornaments of poetry, Puttenham named the rhetorical figure *Allegoria* after a symbolic figure in the *Romaunt of the Rose*: "*Allegoria*, or *False Semblant* (dissimulacion), the chief ringleader and captain of all the other figures."[9] Far more significantly, both the glosses "E.K." provided for the archaisms in Spenser's *Shepherd's Calendar* of 1579, and the Latin *Vocabula Chauceriana* of "P. Greenwood's" *Gramatica Anglicana* (1594), (which borrows words from "E.K.") set out to define and explain obsolete colloquialisms and native words, rustic "Chaucerisms," not "poetic diction." The elegant polysyllabic Romance–Latinate language of Chaucer's *Complaint of Mars and Venus* needs a learned reader; the simpler levels of his ordinary speech had already become lost, even to the learned. Aureate poetic diction is relatively stable and self-defining, as Francis Beaumont tries to explain in his

---

8. Thomas Wilson, *The Arte of Rhetorique*, ed. G. H. Mair (London, 1909), 3:162; quoted in Spurgeon, *Five Hundred Years*, 1: 91–92.

9. Puttenham, *The Arte of Englishe Poesie*, p. 197.

Letter of 1597 (with examples from Latin), but ordinary speech wears quickly away by attrition:

> [even though] many of his wordes, as it were with ouerlong lying, are grown too hard and vnpleasant [to be] gratious. . . . But yet so pure were Chaucers wordes in his owne daies, as Lidgate that learned man calleth him The Loadstarre of the English language.[10]

Insofar as Chaucer used the language of his own day for poetry, he could only be awkwardly imitated by those born later, and the tone and meanings of his language blurred in a single generation. Insofar as he used elevated, Latinate, and continental poetic diction, his meaning and tone remained "polished" and clear, and he could be copied with relative ease. The same holds true for speech rhythms: what is based on colloquial usage is ephemeral, while polysyllabic poetic language has its own accentual flexibility, in Shakspere as in Chaucer.

Cumulatively, then, the effect of successive enlargements of the canon of Chaucer's poems and of irreversible evolution in the spoken language, of which men were aware, is that literary imitations became increasingly indistinguishable from their older originals. Of this, how many men were aware? From the earliest printed texts onward, less than a century after Chaucer's death, the spurious began to become part of the definition of the genuine. Thus, as more and more non-Chaucerian poems come into the canon, the criteria for what is "Chaucerian" fade and widen again. After 1532, when the *Testament* and even later sixteenth-century poems and prose are printed and accepted as Chaucer's *Works*, the distinctive qualities of his fourteenth-century language and style, imitated because they are prized and famous, became increasingly "rusted" and indistinct. The concept of "Chaucerian" poetry is redefined in the Renaissance by its imitations, from the best to the worst. Who could doubt, or challenge, a majestic volume,

10. Sir Francis Beaumont, Letter to Speght (1597), in Speght's *The Workes of our Antient and Learned | English Poet, Geffrey Chaucer* (London, 1598). I have consulted the following editions in the collection of the Beinecke Library at Yale University: Caxton, 1483, 1484; Pynson, 1526; Thynne, 1532, 1542, ca.?1550; Stowe, 1561; Speght, 1598, 1602. D. S. Brewer has edited Thynne's text in a new facsimile, *Geoffrey Chaucer, The Works of 1532, with supplementary material from the editions of 1542, 1561, 1598, & 1602* (London, 1969); this valuable edition was not available to me when this chapter was written. A full bibliographical description of the black letter folios is in Charles Muscatine's *The Book of Geoffrey Chaucer* (San Francisco, 1963); more details will be found in Eleanor Hammond's *Chaucer, A Bibliographical Manual* (New York, 1908), which is out of date but still reliable.

published with the patronage of Henry VIII, compiled by a member of his household, which superseded all previous editions? Readers as acute as William Thynne's friend John Skelton were rare; speaking in defense of Chaucer in *Phyllyp Sparow* (ca. 1505), Skelton noted the problems of language and clarity already apparent, long before the major editions were in print:

> His Englysh well alowed
> (So as it is enprowed),
> For as it is enployed,
> There is no Englysh voyd,
> At those dayes moch commended;
> And now men wold have amended
> His Englyssh whereat they barke
> And mar all they warke;
> Chaucer, that famus clerke,
> His termes were not darke,
> But plesaunt, easy, and playne;
> Ne worde he wrote in vayne;
>   Also Johnn Lydgate
> Wryteth after an hyer rate;
> It is dyffuse to fynde
> The sentence of his mynde.[11]

But Skelton could distinguish Lydgate from Chaucer as few later readers could. As for Lydgate himself, his typical modest apology is a cliché as true as it is sincere; again and again, he demurs,

> We may assay forto countrefete
> His gay style, but it wyl not be;
> The welle is drie, with the lycoure swete
> Both of Clye and of Caliope.

These lines, ironically, from the thirty-fifth stanza of Lydgate's *The Flower of Courtesy*, were printed as "Chaucer's" by Skelton's friend Thynne, in his huge 1532 edition of the *Works*, reprinted twice thereafter (1542, ca. 1550), and not properly attributed to Lydgate until Stowe's edition of 1561, which in its turn brought a new flood of Lydgatean pseudo-Chaucerian verse into the already contaminated canon.

    After 1400, then, while the ordinary speech of the fourteenth century

---

11. John Skelton, *Phyllyp Sparow*, ll. 792–807; text in Kinsman, *ed. cit.*, pp. 50–51.

went quickly out of date, the superficial elements of the literary "high style" became more fashionable. The conventions picked up and copied by Lydgate and his lesser contemporaries had already begun to harden into polished "poetic diction," anonymous and formulaic, before 1450. Chaucer himself had mocked it playfully in *Rosamunde* and the triple rondel called *Merciles Beaute*:

> Madame, ye ben of al beaute shryne
> As fer as cercled is the mapemounde,
> For as the cristal glorious ye shyne,
> And lyke ruby ben your chekes rounde.
> Therwith ye ben so mery and so jocounde
> That at a revel whan that I see you daunce,
> It is an oynement unto my wounde,
> Thogh ye to me ne do no daliaunce.[12]
>
> . . . .
>
> Your yen two wol slee me sodenly;
> I may the beautee of hem not sustene,
> So woundeth hit thourghout my herte kene.[13]

The lover, trapped like a fish in a dish (*a pik walwed in galauntine*) in *Rosamunde*, too fat to fear Love's prison in the rondel (*I nevere thenke to been in his prison lene | Sin I am free, I counte him nat a bene*), escapes the chiming *amourous plesaunce: daliaunce* by means of brilliant burlesque, both of the style and the gestures of the *matere* of his French models. These two witty lyrics were never printed with Chaucer's *Works*, however, and remained in single manuscripts until the twentieth century. The *Complaints* that in print exemplified Chaucerian high and serious art—*to Pity, to His Lady, of Mars*—are somberly formal, untainted by irony, and not leavened by wit:

> The ordre of compleynt requireth skylfully
> That yf a wight shal pleyne pitously,
> Ther mot be cause wherfore that men pleyne;
> Or men may deme he pleyneth folily
> And causeles, alas! that am not I!
> Wherfor the ground and cause of al my peyne,
> So as my troubled wit may hit atteyne,

12. *Rosamunde*, ll. 1–8.
13. *Merciles Beaute*, ll. 1–3.

> I wol reherse; not for to have redresse,
> But to declare my ground of hevynesse.[14]

In the mocking complaint of the Wife of Bath, the half-line formula of self-pity comes back with a ricochet—*He spak to hem that wolde live parfitly | And, lordinges, by youre leve, that am not I!* (D 117–18). Far more amenable than Alison to echo by another poet are the personified abstractions of the *Complaint unto Pity*:

> Hit stondeth thus: youre contraire, Crueltee,
> Allyed is ayenst your regalye,
> Under colour of womanly Beaute,—
> For men shulde not, lo, knowe hir tirannye,—
> With Bounte, Gentilesse, and Curtesye,
> And hath depryved yow now of your place
> That hyghte "Beaute apertenant to Grace."
>
> Eke what availeth Maner and Gentilesse
> Withoute yow, benygne creature?
> Shal Cruelte be your governeresse?
> Allas! what herte may hyt longe endure?
> Wherfore, but ye the rather take cure
> To breke that perilouse alliaunce,
> Ye sleen hem that ben in your obesiaunce.[15]

It was this Chaucerian poetic language, not an "easy, conversational style," which was kept artificially alive by poets for another century, in the conventional preservative of the *reyne [of] gold dewe dropis of rethorik so fyne*, both in the original, and the alloy of the imitators. The admired "high style" of the fifteenth-century "Chaucer" is typified by the seven-line stanza, elevated aureate diction, and arbitrary versification based on syllabic final -*e*, apparent to the eye, but no longer audible to the ear. The baffling randomness in the use of final -*e* and -*en* is already apparent in scribal confusion and arbitrary spellings in the corrupt fifteenth-century manuscripts, which therefore can be seen as both effect and cause: they reflect confusion, and in turn produce more. After 1500, when the editions of Caxton and his successors added the weight of printed authority to crippled rhythms, the artificiality of "Chaucerian" poetic technique was perpetuated as deliberately awk-

---

14. *Complaint of Mars*, ll. 155–63.
15. *Complaint unto Pity*, ll. 64–70, 78–84.

ward metrical archaism. It is evident in the apocrypha: *The Cuckoo and the Nightingale* abounds in headless lines, syllabic final *-e*, and avoidance of elision; in *La Belle Dame Sauns Merci*, final *-e* is rarely used at all; the *Court of Love* is distinguished by total confusion of final *-en*, enjambment of stanzas, and eye-rhymes which lead Skeat to exclude it, "not only from the fourteenth, but even from the fifteenth century."[16] As Norman Eliason sensibly comments, "the repetition of meter requires for regularity no more than the ability to tap with one's foot," and the fifteenth-century ballads are as rhythmically regular as those of any other era.[17] However, poets who attempted to manipulate more than a four-beat line were in increasing difficulty. Skelton's pithy brevity was one, radical solution, when he eschewed the stanza and ran the risk of doggerel:

> For though my ryme be ragged
> Tattered and jagged
> Rudely rayne-beaten
> Rusty and mothe-eaten
> Yf ye take well therwith
> It hath in it some pyth.
>
>   [*Colin Clout*, ll. 53–58]

The other way out, the alexandrines, fourteeners and sixteenth-century poulters' rhyme, can be seen in the verse Lewis calls "Drab," anthologized in the reprintings of Tottel's *Miscellanies* from 1557 to the 1580's.[18] But poets like Hawes, whose *Pastime of Pleasure* ran to four editions (1509, 1517, 1554, 1555), floundering in the wake of Lydgate, made the rime royal stanza a visual unit in which words move according to measures no longer intelligible:

> Connynge ys lyght and also pleasaunt
> A gentyll burden without greuousnes
> Vnto hym that is ryght well applyaunt
> For to bere it with all his besenes
> He shall attaste the well of fruytfulnesse

16. W. W. Skeat, *Supplement to the Works of Chaucer* (Oxford, 1897), 7: lxxx.

17. Norman E. Eliason, "Chaucer's Fifteenth Century Successors," in *Medieval and Renaissance Studies*, ed. O. B. Hardison (Chapel Hill, 1971), pp. 103–21.

18. "Fourteeners" (couplets of eight and six) and "poulters' measure" (six and seven) are pausing meters, which superimpose pattern on the sense of the line; the caesura is required by metrical force, not meaning. See John Thompson, *The Founding of English Meter* (New York, 1961).

Whiche Vyrgyll claryfyed and also Tullyus
With latyn pure swete and delycyous

From whens my mayster Lydgate deryfyde
The depured rethoryke in englysshe language
To make oure tongue so clerely puryfyed
That the vyle termes shoulde nothynge arage
As lyke a pye to chattre in a cage
But for to speke with Rethoryke formally
In the good ordre withouten vylany

And who his bokes lyste to here or se
In them he shall fynde elocucyon.

[*Pastime of Pleasure*, 1165–71]

Hawes begs his readers to see, to look through the *dymme and derke* curtain of ignorance, to find the poet's *elocucyon*, and yet even his stanzas on utterance itself (ca. xii, ll. 1184–1239) force prose stress against the stanza frame, resulting in verse without cadence or flow:

And thus the gentyll rethorycyan
Through the labour of his ryall clergy
The famous nurture orygynally began
Oppressynge our rudenes and our foly
And for to gouerne vs ryght prudently
The good maner encreseth dygnyte
And the rudeness also inyquyte

[*Pastime of Pleasure*, 1219–25]

Thus Hawes alludes to the myth of Orpheus.

First in manuscript, then in print, the extraordinary ease and colloquial freedom of Chaucer's patterns of stress, elision, and caesura, in both the rime royal stanza and the couplet, were the earliest casualties lost in the transmission of his style to his successors. First the sounds, then the meanings of ordinary speech undergo metamorphosis and become more difficult to understand, and to imitate. But in poetic language they remained half-alive and half-dead, quaintly anachronistic, pseudo-Chaucerian.

The Growth of the Renaissance Canon

The task of analysis of the unwieldy mass of the evidence suggests first of all the need to simplify, as much as possible, and to seek order wherever it may be found. Fortunately, we can survey and summarize what was preserved as authentically "Chaucerian" in the three major publications of the sixteenth century of his *Works*: the folios of Thynne of 1532 (revised in 1542 and in the "booksellers" edition of ca. 1550), Stowe of 1561, and Speght, of 1598 (revised in 1602, reprinted in 1687). The Renaissance "Chaucer" takes shape in these editions, which successively reveal the three interlinked phenomena of linguistic obsolescence, pseudo–Chaucerian enrichment, and the growth of the canon of "true" poems discovered and printed for the first time. It will be quickly apparent that the pseudo–Chaucerian additions far outnumber the authentic new texts, and much of what was published has no identity at all and is likely to remain anonymous. It is equally obvious that we cannot broaden the perspective to survey the wider range implicit in the apocrypha, the extraordinary Chaucerian influence on English and Scottish poets of the fifteenth and early sixteenth centuries, ranging in quality from the strength of Dunbar to the weakest of Lydgate's imitators. Wyatt, Surrey, and Sackville too have rightly been called "Chaucerian"; and insofar as the *Fall of Princes* transmitted Lydgate's postmedieval vision, access to the Ricardian poets, his forebears, Chaucer and Gower, becomes a labyrinth of direct and indirect allusion. The "other" Chaucerians, beyond the scope of this study, must be taken as a historic given, within which we seek to narrow the problem of "Chaucer's" spurious poems in the transmission of what was believed to be genuine by the buyers and readers of "*Chaucer's Works.*" Finally, the question of the judgment of the early editors, who may or may not have been aware of the provenance of their texts, will also have to remain open. It would seem that, as in the case of William Thynne, the zest of an antiquarian like Stowe and the scholarly ambitions of Speght and Francis Thynne were engaged in heightening Chaucer's poetic reputation and influence, certainly not damaging it, however mixed and diluted their productions were. By whatever means, they meant to do their poet honor, as well as make a profit, if only in reflected glory.

It is the competition among poems, however, that is significant for criticism. That the last major edition of Gower, the *Works* of Berthelette of 1533, was reprinted only once, twenty years later, would seem to suggest that Chaucer alone survived in the later Renaissance as a living influence and a medieval model. So it seemed to Puttenham, in

1589, as we shall see. But the shadow of Lydgate and his immense production, both recognized and hidden in Chaucer's *Works*, was even longer than Chaucer's and Gower's in the sixteenth century. There is much more of Lydgate among the apocrypha than of any other poet— seventeen poems, according to Bonner's estimate[19]—and it is the grim and massive *Fall of Princes*, rather than Malory's *Morte Darthur* or Chaucer's *Boece* that reflects the authoritarian moral and political image of the fifteenth century to its immediate heirs. Estimates of "influence" based on numbers of editions of an author are not much more reliable than those based on surviving manuscripts. Two of Sir Robert Cotton's collection contain *Beowulf* (Cotton Vitellius A xv) and *Pearl, Patience, Purity and Sir Gawain* (Cotton Nero A x), the unique remnants of two strong poetic traditions, Anglo-Saxon verse epic, Middle English alliterative romance. On the other hand, as R. W. Chambers has shown, Richard Rolle, the Yorkshire mystic who died in 1349, was "in English or in Latin . . . during the latter half of the fourteenth century and the whole of the fifteenth probably the most widely read in England of all English writers."[20] Chambers's examination of probated wills found a dozen owners of Rolle manuscripts for every one or two of the *Canterbury Tales*; even though devotional books tend "to get read to pieces," between four and five hundred of Rolle's works survived in manuscript, against less than a hundred of the *Tales*. Similarly, there were twenty editions of Richard Whitford's translation of the *Imitatio Christi* of Thomas à Kempis between 1530 and 1585, and, according to Curtius, between 1499 and 1599, eight editions of Martianus Capella's *de nuptiis Philologiae et Mercurii*, a book of five hundred pages of erudite Latin allegorical verse and prose.[21] In the same period, there were six of Chaucer's *Works*, and two of Gower's.

Our purpose is not to measure popularity, however, nor to review the growing body of anecdotal criticism and allusions to Chaucer collected in Spurgeon's anthology, but rather to try to observe the changing shape of the body of poems understood to be his, against which his successors

19. Francis W. Bonner, "The Genesis of the Chaucer Apocrypha," *SP* 48 (1951); 461–81. Bonner's "A History of the Chaucer Apocrypha" (Ph. D. diss., University of North Carolina, 1949), catalogues the contents of the early editions.

20. R. W. Chambers, "On the Continuity of English Prose from Alfred to More and his School," an extract from the Introduction to *Harpsfield's Life of Sir Thomas More*, ed. E. V. Hitchcock and R. W. Chambers *EETS*, o.s. 191A (1932, repr. 1966): ci; see also H. S. Bennett, *English Books and Readers, 1475–1550* (London, 1956); and N. F. Blake, *Caxton and His World* (London, 1969).

21. Curtius, *European Literature*, p. 38, n. 5.

measured their own achievement and attempted their imitations in the
later sixteenth century. As the editorial prefaces grow measurably
longer, more pompous and richly decorated with Chaucer's "laurels,"
he becomes ever more reverently remote. The epithets from the dedicatory letter to Henry VIII written by Sir Brian Tuke for Thynne in
1532 are passed on, from Ascham to Francis Meres: "England's
Homer"—antique, obscure, magnificent, the precursor who made
Spenser's language possible. Speght explains, in 1598, noting the
breadth of Chaucer's reading,

> Chaucer had alwaies an earnest desire to enrich and beautifie
> our English tongue, which in those daies was verie rude and
> barren: and this he did following the example of *Dantes* and
> *Petrarch*, who had done the same for the Italian tongue; *Alanus*
> for the French; and *Iohannes Mena* for the Spanish: neither was
> Chaucer inferior to any of them in the performance hereof. And
> England in this respect is much beholden to him.
>
> [Preface, 1598]

To bring his poet up to the highest contemporary critical esteem,
Speght then turned to "two of the purest and best writers of our daies:
the one for Prose, the other for Verse, M. Ascham and M. Spenser";

> Master Ascham . . . calleth him *English Homer* [and says] that he
> valueth his authoritie of as high estimation as euer he did either
> *Sophocles* or *Euripedes* in Greeke. [Of English versifying] he vseth
> these wordes: *Chaucer* and *Petrarke*, those two worthy wittes, deserve
> iust praise. . . . [Finally], hee putteth him nothing behind either
> *Thucidides* or *Homer* for his liuely descriptions of site of places, and
> nature of persons both in outward shape of bodie, and inward
> disposition of mine. . . .

> Master Spenser . . . calleth him *Titirus*, the god of Shepheards,
> comparing him to the worthiness of the Romane *Titirus Virgil*.
> In his *Faerie Queene* in his discourse of friendship, as thinking him-
> selfe most worthy to be Chaucers friend, for his like naturall dis-
> position that Chaucer had, hee sheweth that none that liued with
> him, nor none that came after him, durst presume to reuiue
> Chaucers lost labours . . . but only himselfe: which he had not
> done, had ne not felt [as he saith] the infusion of Chaucers owne
> sweete spirite, suruiuing within him.

Speght concludes with a truncated quotation from the *Faerie Queene*—the famous image of the "clear stream"—suggesting that the praise of modern Spenser, the true disciple, will magnify ancient Chaucer:

> Dan Chaucer, Well of English vndefiled,
> On Fames eternal beadrole worthy to be filed,
>
> . . . .
> I follow here with footing of thy feet,
> And with thy meaning so I may the rather meet.
>
> [4. 11. 32, 35]

Spenser, of course did not follow the footing of Chaucer's feet; he sought Chaucer's authority for making his own new way and acknowledged that he knew his predecessor's, in the *Shepherd's Calendar* and the *Faerie Queene*, "Mother Hubberd" and Colin Clout. Moreover, the *eternal beadrole* is not in Chaucer's House of Fame, for there, time and justice are askew: Spenser means his own power to confer poetic immortality, *That with thy meaning I may the rather meet*. Speght did not quote, for obvious reasons, the intervening stanza from his source, wherein Spenser meditates on devouring Time:

> But wicked Time that all good thoughts doth waste,
> And workes of noblest wits to nought out weare,
> That famous moniment hath quite defaste,
> And robd the world of threasure endlesse deare,
> The which mote haue enriched all vs heare.
> O cursed Eld the cankerworme of writs,
> How may these rimes, so rude as doth appeare,
> Hope to endure, sith workes of heauenly wits
> Are quite deuoured, and brought to nought by little bits?
>
> [4. 2. 34]

The Sixteenth-century Editions

Chaucer left three enigmatic inventories of what his works once were: the deprecatory lists of the *Man of Lawes Prologue* and the *Prologue to the Legends of Good Women*, both given by fictional characters, and the problematic epilogue found in some of the manuscripts of the last fragment of the *Canterbury Tales*. It is called "The Prayer" in Caxton's second edition of the *Tales* in 1484, and has been entitled the *Retraction* since 1721, when Urry restored it to its original place after the *Parson's Tale*. Chaucer begs the reader to forgive him his faults:

> for the mercy of God, that ye preye for me that Crist have mercy on me and foryeve me my giltes; / and namely of my translacions and enditynges of worldly vanitees, the which I revoke in my retracciouns.
>
> [I., 1084–85]

The authorities for adding poems to the canon of Chaucer's works then are three: two are embedded in the poetry itself, and hence transmitted; the third, strangely, was not. Chaucer's *Retraction* was omitted by Thynne in 1532, and it does not appear in any subsequent edition until the eighteenth century; its curious list of "lost" poems, books, and balades, which Chaucer claims to have forgotten, was however always known from Caxton's text and the manuscripts in which it occurs, and it gave invisible support to the sketch of a canon in the two Prologues. In the *Retraction*, Chaucer "revokes" not only *Troilus*, the *Book of Fame*, the *Book of the Duchesse*, the *Parlement of Briddes*, and the *tales of Caunterbury, thilke that sownen into synne* but also

> the book of the Leoun, and many another book . . . and many a song and many a lecherous lay that Crist for his grete mercy foryeve me the synne.

It is this open category of other *bookes* and *songs* which offered early scribes and editors the invitation to attribute to Chaucer what seemed likely to have been his. Thus, for example, the professional scribe John Shirley attempted in 1450 to account for all he knew, in his versified lists and marginalia, to preserve

> þe moral and famous Chaucyer which first enlumyned þis lande with retoryen and eloquent langage of our rude englisshe modere tonge.[22]

Although Caxton had printed a poem of Chaucer's friend Scogan, a stanza ("With empty hands man may no hawkes lure") and some proverbial couplets as authentic minor poems of Chaucer before 1500, the first significantly contaminated publication of Chaucer's *Works*

---

22. From the ending of his *Boethius de Consolacione Philosophiae*, Add. MS. 16,165, f. 94; quoted in Spurgeon, *Five Hundred Years*, 1: 49.

is the three-part edition published by Richard Pynson in 1526. Pynson printed *the boke of Troylus / and Creseyde / newly prin / ted by a trewe / copye /* as part one; *the boke of Fame / made by Geffray Chaucer / with dyuers other of / his workes /* as part two, and *the boke of Caunter/ bury tales / dilygently and / truly corrected / and / newly printed* as part three. The three parts were evidently intended to be all-inclusive, and later owners bound them together as one book. It is part two that contains the spurious poems: Pynson's *Troilus* is not yet supplemented with the *Testament*, and he used Caxton's second edition of the *Canterbury Tales*, with the *Retraction*, for part three. In part two, along with *the boke of Fame* (which has Caxton's ending and epilogue),[23] Pynson printed the *Assemble of Foules, la bele Dame Sauns / mercy . . . translate out of French in to Englysshe by Geffray / Chaucer*, . . . and the short poem now called *Truth*, headed *Ecce bonum consilium . . . contra fortunam*. The *Morall Prouerbes of Christyne* is listed in the table of contents, but the colophon of *La Belle Dame* calls them *Certayne morall proverbes of the foresayd Geffray Chaucers doyng* (101 couplets); then follow three more non-Chaucerian pieces, the *Lamentations of Mary Magdalen*, the *letter of Dydo to Eneas*, and *a lytell exortacioun howe folke shulde behaue them selfe in all companyes*, which is Lydgate's poem, "Utter thy Language. . . ." Pynson had found the moral proverbs of Christine da Pisan in Caxton, there attributed to Earl Rivers as their translator.

The pattern of inflation thus set in 1526 is maintained throughout the sixteenth century. Each editor bases his canon on the publication of his predecessor, and in addition, consults all such manuscripts as he can obtain, in order to surpass the previous editions in both diversity and completeness by compiling a fuller collection. The chief exception to the rule of inclusion is Thynne's first edition of 1532, which omits Pynson's *letter of Dydo* and the *Morall proverbs*. But the rule is, of course, to publish more, not less, and Thynne set another kind of precedent in omitting the *Retraction* and attempting to restore all that its covering fiction implied, including what Chaucer rejected. Thynne printed not only the *Romaunt of the Rose*, but *othere books . . . and omelies, and moralitee, and devocioun*, and the *Testament of Cresseid* as well:

> I thought it in maner appertenant unto my dewtie and that of very honesty and love to my country I ought no less to do than to put my helpyng hand to the restauracion and bryngynge agayn to

23. See Crotch, *Caxton*, p. 69.

lyght of the said workes after trewe copies and exemplaries afore-
said.

[*Preface*, 1532]

The Chauceriana are not, typically, new *Canterbury Tales* (although
there are notable additions, as we shall see), but more and more additions to the open category of minor poems: *translaciouns*, *balades*, and
the *lecherous lays* abjured in Chaucer's *Retraction*. While the links between
the *Canterbury Tales*, and consequently, their order, are editorially
revised and amended, the *Tales* themselves suffer much less contamination than the miscellaneous collection of *dyuers other of his workes*.
The *Tales* were famous, but who knows what were the *worldly vanitees*
and forgotten poems of Chaucer's youth? It is thus that the proportions
begin to change, and the context in which "Chaucer" was understood
grew vague and dim. Of the forty-eight pieces which are found in the
Renaissance editions, now regarded as non-Chaucerian or known to
be by other poets, only two purport to belong to the *Canterbury Tales*
(the *Plowman's Tale*, added by Thynne in 1542, and *Jack Upland*,
added by Speght in 1602, the "revised" editions of both editors). All
the rest are moral, allegorical, or amorous verse, and most are in the
high style of the fifteenth century.[24]

The majority of the apocrypha are of doubtful authorship or by
unknown poets, but attribution is virtually certain in the case of at
least eight other authors: Thomas Usk, Gower, Hoccleve, Scogan,
Lydgate, Clanvowe, Henryson, and Sir Richard Ros. As we have
observed, the addition of a single short poem to the canon, Henryson's
Testament, significantly changed the reading of Chaucer's *Troilus*; the
impact of twenty more pieces in the same edition, Thynne's of 1532, is
of another order of magnitude altogether. The *Works* of 1532 enlarged
its predecessor by approximately fifteen thousand lines; all of the
extant *Romaunt of the Rose*, the three books of Usk's prose *Testament of
Love*, the *Book of the Duchess* (entitled "Chaucer's Dreme"), and *dyuers
more*.

Thynne's edition of 1532 established the Renaissance "Chaucer";

24. For texts, see e.g., Eleanor Hammond's anthology, *English Verse between Chaucer and
Surrey* (Durham, N. C., 1927). Aage Brusendorff, *The Chaucer Tradition* (London, 1925); and
Skeat, *Supplement*, vol. 7, provide short philological comments on selected poems. The sum-
mary essay of Derek Pearsall, "The English Chaucerians," in *Chaucer and Chaucerians*, ed. D. S.
Brewer (London, 1966), pp. 201–39; and Denton Fox's "The Scottish Chaucerians," ibid.,
pp. 164–200, provide together an excellent survey.

his text is modified only by the additions (and further errors) of his successors. The traditional order of the poems, after 1532, follows his sequence up to the point of conflation. After the front matter, preface, tables, and four short non-Chaucerian moral warnings, the *Canterbury Tales* come first; then, for the first time in 1532, the *Romaunt of the Rose*; *Troilus and Criseyde*, followed by the *Testament*, in 1532 and thereafter; then, the *Legends of Good Women*, "A Goodly ballad," and *Boece*. Thereafter, all the preceding are printed in Thynne's order; the following poems, however, are open to fluctuation, and among the shorter poems, opportunities occur for interpolating shorter and longer poems. Thousands of lines accrue, "after folio 340," as Lounsbury put it: pseudo-Chaucerian dream visions, complaints, and ballads. Thynne's largest and most conspicuous contribution to the new canon was the Middle English *Romaunt of the Rose*. It was probably so prominently placed, immediately after the *Tales*, because of the current strong interest in moral allegorizing in the new French editions of the *Roman*: Clement Marot's prose redactions of 1529, 1531, and 1537, and Molinet's *Romant de la rose moralisé cler et net* (composed ca. 1482), published in 1500, 1503, and 1521.[25] The fresh impetus thus given to English imitations of the *Roman* came from both Paris and London, and it kept the allegory of Faux Semblant, Nature, Genius, and the etiquette of the Rose alive for another century.

By far the greater part of the Chauceriana printed by Thynne in the latter part of his volume is second-rate stanzaic verse on the subjects of women, love, and misfortune. The [Lydgatean] *Complaint of the Black Knight*, [his] *Flower of Courtesy*, [Hoccleve's] *Letter of Cupid*, the *Lamentations of Mary Magdalen* suggest the range.[26] In addition to the *Romaunt*, there are nineteen non-Chaucerian pieces added to the canon. The facsimile of Thynne's edition, published in 1905 with a long introduction by W. W. Skeat, gives a clearer impression of the "Chaucer" read in the Renaissance than Skeat's other, more heterogeneous volume of *Chaucerian and Other Pieces*, compiled, edited, and revised from manuscripts as well as the black letter texts.[27] Of the thirty spurious pieces in Skeat's miscellany, ten are by Lydgate.

25. Rosamond Tuve, *Allegorical Imagery* (Princeton, 1966), pp. 233, 237, discusses Marot and Molinet.

26. The latter was finally shifted to the section "Poems Attributed to Chaucer" in Skeat's revised edition of Bell's *Chaucer* in 1875.

27. See above, n. 16; Skeat also discusses the apocrypha in vol. 1 of his *Complete Works of Geoffrey Chaucer, Romaunt of the Rose and Minor Poems*, 2d ed. (Oxford, 1899), pp. 20–91.

The second edition of Thynne, published in 1542, contains the first major addition to the *Canterbury Tales*, the anticlerical satire entitled the *Plowman's Tale*, 1380 lines in eight-line stanzas, placed immediately after the *Parson's Tale*.[28] In the so-called "booksellers'" edition of ca. 1550, the *Plowman's Tale* was moved back to precede the *Parson's*, where it remained until the eighteenth century. Apparently even before Francis Thynne reopened the question of his father's troubles with threatened censorship in his *Animadversions* of 1599, there was some uncertainty about the Protestantism of the Plowman and his *Tale*. It was always printed, but in 1598 Speght took note of the question in his defense of reprinting it; he describes it as

> a complaint against the pride and couetousness of the cleargie: made no doubt by Chaucer with the rest of the Tales. For I have seen it in writen hand in Iohn Stowes library in a booke of such antiquity, as seemeth to have been written near to Chaucer's time.

Several points are noteworthy in this passage: Speght's hesitant tone, the evident difficulty of dating manuscripts from such distant antiquity ("near Chaucer's time"), and finally, the mention of Speght's predecessor, the London tailor and bibliophile John Stowe. Stowe's efforts as an antiquary and collector of old documents ended in governmental suspicion, harassment, search, seizure, and ultimately his reduction to poverty. Dedicated to his poets, Lydgate and Chaucer, Stowe got his discoveries into print, but his contributions to the Chaucer canon have been reviled as "a heap of rubbish," "soiled and mangled" trash, by orthodox Chaucerians since the work of authentication began, by Tyrwhitt at the end of the eighteenth century, carried on by the later Victorians. Of the nineteen additions Stowe made to the canon, all but three have been rejected; the last public notice of him recorded in the seventeenth century was the license granted him by James I to beg and put alms basins in London churches.[29]

"Spenser's Chaucer": The Stowe Folio of 1561

The *workes of Geffray Chaucer* of 1561 contains Stowe's *diuers addicions*

---

28. See Hammond, *Bibliographical Manual*, p. 119; the *Plowman* is now attributed to Hoccleve.
29. See *Animadversions . . . by Francis Thynne*, ed. G. H. Kingsley, rev. F. J. Furnivall, *EETS* 9 (1865): p. 130.

neuer in print before, which so outraged Tyrwhitt and Skeat; it contains also, as the title page announces, *the siege and | destruccion of | the worthy citee of Thebes, compiled | by Ihon Lidgate| Monk of Berie.* Thus the *Siege of Thebes* takes its place at the end of Chaucer's *Works* for the rest of the century, a convenient "source" for readers of *Troilus and Criseyde.* The poem is an early "imitation," in Lydgate's heavy-handed approximation of the couplets of the *Canterbury Tales.* It opens, as we have seen, with a grossly obscene Harry Bailly in dialogue with "Lydgate," and then proceeds to recount the story of Thebes in 4716 lines, in the characteristically retarded Lydgatean style. Here is a familiar passage, the dramatic moment where Criseyde's reading ended and Cassandra's prophecy began:

> And richely I-armyd in his char
> Amphiorax cam with his meyne,
> Ful renomyd of antiquite
> And wel expert becouse he was old
> And whil that Grekys as I haue ȝou told,
> wer bysiest her wardys to ordeyne,
> Myd of the feld bifyl a cas sodeyne,
> Ful vnhappy lothsom and odyble
> For liche a thing þat wer invisible
> This olde bisshop with char and hors certeyn
> Disaperyd and no mor was seyne
> Only of fate which no man can repelle
> Þe erth opnede and he fille doun to helle
> with all his folk þat vpon hym abood
> And sodeynly the ground on which he stood
> Closyd ageyn and togydre shette
> Þat neuer after Grekis with hym mette.
> And thus the devel for his old outrages
> lich his decert paied hym his wages.
>
> [*Siege of Thebes,* 4023–4040]

When Spenser's Sansjoy falls, and Duessa and Night recover his body to carry it down to Aesculapius in the underworld in the first book of the *Faerie Queene,* the setting will have long been foreseen by the reader of Lydgate and Chaucer in the 1560's:

> For he ful lowe is discendid doun
> Into the dirk and blake Regyoun

> wher that Pluto is crownyd and ystalled
> with his quene proserpina I-called
> with whom this bisshop haþ made his mansioun
> Perpetually as for his guerdoun.
> lo here the mede of ydolatrie,
> Of Rytys old and of fals mawmetrye
> lo what auayllen Incantaciouns
> Of exorsismes and coniurisouns.

[*Siege of Thebes*, 4041–50]

The list of the eighteen other of Stowe's additions to the 1561 reprint of Thynne's *Works* consists mainly of minor poems of Lydgate or their near likenesses.[30] They are collected as an appendix, with a separate heading,

> Here foloweth certaine woorkes of Geffray Chaucer which hath not here tofore been printed, and are gathered and added to this booke by Iohn Stowe.

Among the spurious are two genuine poems of Chaucer, *Gentilesse*, and, ironically, the wry warning entitled *Chaucers Wordes unto Adam, his Owne Scriveyn*.

> Adam scriveyn, if ever it thee bifalle
> Boece or Troylus for to wryten newe,
> Under thy long lokkes thou most have the scalle,
> But after my makyng thou wryte more trewe;
> So ofte a-daye I mot thy werk renewe,
> It to correcte and eek to rubbe and scrape;
> And al is thorugh thy negligence and rape.

The other poems are, as their titles suggest, chiefly trivia: *How Mercurie with Pallas, Venus, and Minerva appeared to Paris of Troie, he slepyng by a fountain*; *The Ten Commandments of Love*; *The Nine Ladies Worthy*; the *Craft of Lovers*; the *Court of Love*. However insignificant these poems are individually, it is obvious enough that they alter the profile of Chaucer as a love poet; he is becoming more and more the poet of the Squire's and the Franklin's romantic sentiments, and their genteel loquacity. This volume, then, is the crucial text for studies of Spenser's Chaucer. Gabriel Harvey's interspersed marginalia on the *Tales* and the *Siege of*

---

30. The list is given in Hammond, *Bibliographical Manual*, pp. 119–20.

Thebes, in a book given him by Spenser, imply the composite edition of
Stowe, but it is even more interesting that Harvey implies knowledge of
Chaucerian poems not available in print, yet already associated with
the aggregate "Chaucer" of the 1560's. In 1585, Harvey commends
the *Flower and the Leaf*, which was not published in Chaucer's *Works*
until 1598, and his comment epitomizes the composite poet created by
editorial conflation:

> The Description of the Spring, in the beginning of the prologues of
> Chawcers Canterburie tales. In the beginning of the Complaint of
> the Black Knight. In the beginning of the flo[wre] and the leafe.
> In the beginning of Lidgats Storie of Thebes. In the romant of
> the Rose: 122.6. In the beginning of the testament of Creseide,
> a winterlie springe.[31]

The only genuine poem of Chaucer's own in Harvey's note is the
General Prologue, but with the exception of Lydgate's *Siege*, the rest were
already attributed, or about to be, to Chaucer in his *Works*: all but the
Flower and the Leaf are in the Stowe folio of 1561.

The 1598 Folio of Speght

We may now turn to the last and largest of the black letter folios,
Thomas Speght's *Works* of 1598, which contains all of the spurious
poems of its predecessors, Thynne's and Stowe's editions, and, as his
title page announces, *Two Bookes of his neuer before Printed*. Speght's
contributions to the canon are the *Flower and the Leaf* (noted by Harvey
more than a dozen years before), and *Chaucers dreme, neuer before this
time published in print*. The headnote preceding this poem continues,

> That which here tofore hath gone under the name of his dreame, is
> the book of the Duchesse: or the death of Blanch Duchesse of
> Lancaster.

The new poem Speght calls *Chaucers Dream* is now called *The Isle of
Ladies*, and has recently been claimed for Sir Richard Ros, the fifteenth-
century translator of *La Belle Dame Sauns Merci* (printed as "Chaucer's"
since Pynson added it in 1526). Speght gives generous acknowledg-

31. MS notes in Gabriel Harvey's hand, ca. 1585; quoted in Spurgeon, *Five Hundred Years*,
1: 127: cf. G. C. Moore Smith, *Gabriel Harvey's Marginalia* (Stratford on Avon, 1913), p. 159–
61.

ment of his indebtedness to the labors of Stowe in his "annexations" published in the 1561 "Chaucer": he reprints "all [poems] collected and adioned to his former workes" as well as a "catalogue of translations and Poeticall deuises, in English mitre or verse, done by Iohn Lidgate Monke of Bury, wherof some are extant in Print, the residue in the custody of him [Stowe] that first caused this *Siege of Thebes* to be added to these works of G. Chaucer."

Speght's elaborate front matter and editorial apparatus include a great deal more than any of his predecessors' volumes, and he reprints Thynne's letter to Henry VIII as well as his own dedicatory epistle to Sir Robert Cecil, followed by an address to the reader, and Sir Francis Beaumont's congratulatory letter to Speght, recalling their days in Cambridge twenty years before, when they first learned to love Chaucer's poems. Speght's prefatory pages are decorated with woodcut borders, epigraphs from Chaucer and Ovid, and a full-page copperplate engraving of the poet, surrounded by the leaves and branches of a family tree drawn up by the Somerset Herald. On the title page, the scope of Speght's work as an editor is set forth; it consists of six parts, the seventh being the two Books *neuer before Printed*:

1. His Portraiture and Progenie shewed
2. His Life collected
3. Arguments to every Booke gathered
4. Old and obscure words explaned
5. Authors by him cited, declared
6. Difficulties opened

In short, then, Speght presents our *Antient and Learned | English Poet* with more grandeur, apparatus, and annotation than he had ever before received. With all the fanfare, both the antiquity and the difficulty of Chaucer's poems are made strongly apparent. A great deal still remains to be learned from detailed investigation of what Speght and Beaumont thought worthy of discussion, and from more careful study of the glossaries and annotation, as well as of the relation of this text to Stowe's. An overview, such as this chapter attempts to provide, can only suggest a return to the texts of the folios themselves, so long despised and ignored, for the wealth of their evidence of "error" Elizabethans took for truth.

Speght's pride is in the *auncient* English greatness of his poet: *he himselfe an Englishman borne—*

For els how could he have come to that perfection in our language
as to be called The first illuminer of the English tongue?

The scope of Speght's *Life* can be summarized in its subheadings: "his
country; parentage; education [both Oxford and Cambridge, and the
Inns of Court]; his marriage [and noble connections]; his children;
revenues; service; rewards; friends; books [where Speght notes, "*The
Letter of Cupid* is none of Chaucers doing, but was compiled by Thomas
Occleue"]; his death, epitaph, and funerary verses," concluding with
the recent praise of Sidney from the *Apologie*, for *Troilus and Criseyde*:

> Of whom truly I know not, whether to merveile more either that
> he in that mistie time could see so clearly, or that we in this cleare
> age walke so stumblingly after him.

Again, it is the distance between the modern reader and the ancient
poet that is reemphasized as a wonder to be honored.

Since Speght's editions of 1598 and 1602 are the last major revisions
of Chaucer's works before the eighteenth century, it is worthwhile to
pause briefly over his presentation of the poems. In his 1598 address
"to the Reader," Speght apologizes for having left incomplete much of
the editorial collation and commentary he had hoped to provide. He
knows there are errors, but it is too late to correct them. In his second
edition of 1602, he claims to have repaired many deficiencies, with the
aid of Francis Thynne, son of the William Thynne whose book provided
the ground for all the sixteenth-century editions of Chaucer. Francis
Thynne's bitter and pedantic *Animadversions*, written in 1599, had
reached Speght, and although he made some use of the criticism of his
text, he did not heed it all. The *Testament*, which Francis Thynne
rejected, remains in the 1602 text, but corrections of egregious errors in
the glossary and notes were made. The second glossary is almost twice
as large as the first of 1598, and both, with the supplementary commentaries on the texts, form an interesting comparison for the work of
"E.K." on Spenser's *Calendar* twenty-odd years before. As for the
major revisions of his book in 1602, Speght's Preface announces:

1. In the life of Chaucer many things inserted
2. The whole works by the old copies reformed
3. Sentences and Prouerbes noted
4. The Signification of the old and obscure Words

    proued: also caracters shewing from what Tongue
    or Dialect they be derived.

5. The Latin and French, not Englished by Chaucer,
    translated.

6. The Treatise called Jacke Upland, against Friers;
    and Chaucers A. B. C. called La Priere de nostre
    Dame, at this Impression added.

Speght's final addition to the canon, *Jack Upland*, is perhaps the least
defensible and the most puzzling of all the Chauceriana. The *Tale* itself
is a polemic, 435 lines of vituperative sixteenth-century prose, whose
tone is set in its opening lines:[32]

> To veri God & to alle trewe in Crist, I, Iacke Vplond make my
> moone, þat Anticrist and hise disciplis bi coloure of holynes
> wasten and disceiuen Cristis chirche bi many fals signes.

There is a strange secondary history of the *Tale of Jack Upland*, to which
we shall presently return. It is complex, but, I think, even more than the
linguistic evolution apparent in Speght's glossaries, it is relevant to the
whole sixteenth-century sequence of conflation, manipulation, and
suppression of supposed Chaucerian works, which took place in a context of remembered rebellion, usurpation, and religious strife. The
disrupted continuity between the past and present is stated in the
expressive language of the *Acte for thadvauncement of true Religion and for
thabolishment of the contrarie . . .* of 1542:

> Provided allso that all bokes in Englishe printed before the year of
> our Lorde a thousand fyve hundred and fourtie intytled the Kinges
> Hieghnes proclamaciouns, injunctions, translacion of the Pater
> noster, the Ave Maria and the Crede, the psalters, prymers,
> prayers, statutes and lawes of the Realme, Cronycles, Canterbury
> tales, Chaucers bokes, gowers bokes, and stories of mennes lieves,
> shall not be comprehended in the prohibicion of this acte, oonlesse
> the Kinges saide Majestie shall hereafter make speciall procla-
> macion for the condempnacion and reproving of the same or any
> of them.

---

32. In *Jack Upland, Friar Daw's Reply and Upland's Rejoinder*, ed. P.L. Heyworth (Oxford,
1968), p. 54. Heyworth's edition and commentary make sense out of the confusion of these
texts for the first time in their history.

As Furnivall commented, when he rediscovered this clause in the statute, unlike the abominations specified,

> pestiferous and noysome . . . craftye false and untrue translacion of Tyndall . . . [and] the printed bookes . . . balades, playes, rymes, songes, and other fantasies . . . subtilly and craftilye instructing his Hieghnes people, and speciallye the youthe of this his Realme, untrulie and otherwyse thann the scripture ought, or sould be, thaught, declared, or expounded.

Chaucer and Gower survived.[33]

At the dissolution of the monasteries, special searches were made to recover such manuscripts as could be found containing works of those two poets, to whom royal favor had been shown, from the days of Richard II to the era of Henry VIII, down to that of his daughter Elizabeth. The tale of *Jack Upland* resumes in 1897, when Skeat found an earlier print of it than Speght's in the 1602 *Chaucer*, in the library of Caius College, Cambridge; he conjectured its date to be ca. 1536. This treatise is attributed to "the famous Geoffrey Chaucer," and its headnote reads, "These ben the lewed questions of Friers rytes and observaunces the whyche they chargen more then goddes lawe, and therfore men shulden not gyve hem what so they beggen, tyll they hadden answered these questions." *Jack Upland*, its reply and counter-reply (the "Friar Daw–Jack Upland debate") belong to the contentious tradition of *Piers Plowman* and its descendants, the *Plowman's Crede*, the *Layman's Complaint*, and the like. Yet, in 1602 it became part of the "Chaucer" of the *Plowman's Tale*, in the canon since 1542. Both the prose abuse of *Jack Upland* and the allegorical argument between the Pellican and the Griffon, which abruptly ends the *Plowman's Tale*, distort the covering fiction of Chaucer's pilgrims and crudely expand Chaucerian irony into the dangerously recent past. In Speght's last folio, the lower registers of archaic colloquial style are exploited, as well as the artificial *courtoisie* affected by the author of *The Flower and the Leaf*.

Finally, one more subtle revision should be noted in Speght's 1602 text, a change more significant than the rearrangement of his notes and

33. Furnivall's note in Thynne's *Animadversions*, p. xiv. The question of the *Courte of Love* is reexamined in E.K. Chambers's essay on Wyatt, in his *Sir Thomas Wyatt* (New York, 1965), pp. 98–145, and Appendix A, pp. 207–27. See the edition of Russell A. Fraser, *The Court of Venus* (Durham, N.C., 1955).

the expanded lists of "hard words." The reference to Spenser's relation to Chaucer in Sir Francis Beaumont's epistle has been silently revised, since Spenser's death in 1599. In the 1598 text, the letter reads

> his much frequenting of Chaucers antient speeches causeth many to allow farre better of him, then otherwise they would.

In the 1602 version, Beaumont's comment has become less condescending to Spenser:

> his much frequenting of Chaucers auncient words, with his excellent imitation of diverse places in him, is not the least helpe that hath made him reach so hie.

The shift in relation between ancient and modern is, in the second case, clearly much closer to balance, for the excellence, the reputation, and the name of Spenser have risen: the *antient speech* of Chaucer's poetry remains what it was, a dead language, if anything more obscure because of the heavier weight of annotation which the editor thought he must provide.

The Reformers' Chaucer

Even such a cursory summary as the foregoing makes it plain that the approach first taken by Thynne in 1532, and then followed and extended by all his successors, was an effort to do homage to the past. The ideal of each edition is inclusiveness, the gathering in of as much as can be saved. In this context, let us pause to reconsider the significance of *Jack Upland* and the *Plowman*, admitted into the canon sixty years apart. It is difficult to determine the truth in Francis Thynne's muddled story of his father's thwarted attempt to print a *Pilgrim's Tale* in 1532. There is extant however, a fragment of a printed *Pilgrim's Tale*, dated by Bradshaw to be ca. ?1536–40, which was found among the Douce papers in the Bodleian. This text also contains part of another work called *The Courte of Venus*. Neither, of course, is Chaucer's. The two titles are together entwined in the labyrinth of censorship, moral and political, that was growing stronger as more and more books were published in the first half of the sixteenth century. The Pilgrim, the Plowman, and the *Courte of Venus* cling, like broken spider webs, to the history of Thynne's *Animadversions* of 1599. Thynne addressed his attack indirectly to Speght, to defend his father's edition, which Speght's new

Works superseded; he questioned Speght's competence, authority, and his facts. Among his anecdotes in support of his father's *Chaucer* is the strange story of Henry VIII's advice to William Thynne not to risk the ire of the bishops of Wolsey's faction by publishing the *Pilgrim's Tale* in Chaucer's *Works*, for fear that its anticlerical attack would bring about suppression, or worse. The elder Thynne already had made enemies, and was known to be a friend of the satirist Skelton,

> and had furthered Skelton to publishe his *Collen Cloute* against the Cardinall, the moste part of whiche Boke was compiled in my father's house at Erithe in Kent.[34]

So far as is known, William Thynne did not publish a *Pilgrim's Tale*, but someone did; the fragment that remains is on the verso of a leaf of *The Courte of Venus*, and this poem, in turn, seems to correspond to a "lost" poem of "Chaucer's" listed in Bale's inventory of unprinted manuscripts he said he had seen. Bale's list of 1557 records, *In Maio cum virescerent*; the extant *Courte of Venus* begins, *In the moneth of May when the new tender grene* . . . . There is no evidence, other than this confused note, to connect Geoffrey Chaucer with either the lyrics of the *Court of Venus* or a *Pilgrim's Tale*; but these two ghost-Chaucerian chimaeras are linked in Bale's incipits, in the Douce fragments, and finally in the larger context of another powerful struggle to repress poetry:

> Likewise the Lacedemonians bothe banyshed Archilochus the Poet, and also burnt his bookes, althoughe neuer so learned and eloquent, because they woulde not haue the mindes of their youthe and other Citizens corrupted and defiled by the reding of them. These men shall rise vp against vs English men at the day of iudgement, whyche banishe not, nor burn not, but rather Print, publishe, set forth and sell baudy balades and filthy bookes, vnto the corruption of the reders, as the *court of Venus*, and suche like wanton bookes. Is the commaundement of God geuen by S. Paule thus obserued of vs Englishe men? Let no filthy communication procede out of your mouth, but that which is good to edefie withall, as oft as nede is.[35]

While the extant fragment of the *Pilgrim's Tale* quotes from the Wife of Bath and from the Chaucerian *Romaunt of the Rose* (with page and line

34. Thynne, *Animadversions*, p. 10.
35. Quoted from Becon, *Works*, 1: f. Dclxii (A.D. 1564) in Thynne, *Animadversions*, p. xlvi.

references to a printed text!) it never got into the canon, nor did the *Courte of Venus*, denounced in 1564. Chaucer's *Complaint of Venus* and the apocryphal *Plowman's Tale* were safely preserved, exempt from the Statute of 1542, in the growing collected *Works*, and they carried with them the mass of pseudo-Chaucerian balades, virelais, Lydgatean complaints and allegories in the *Works* which comprise the anomalous *threasure* of medieval Chaucerian poetry—saved from the zealots and from the disintegration of the language itself.

The Elizabethan Legacy

By the end of the sixteenth century, then, if the *Romaunt of the Rose* is counted as not authentic, the proportion of spurious and dubious Chauceriana rises to roughly forty percent of the whole. So, in the Renaissance editions of his works, the precedent Chaucer seems to set, as the first "true poet" in English, is doubly ironic; his *Works* are celebrated for poems of his own which he specifically abjured and renounced, and the publication of them is enhanced with many others' poems, in kinds he disowned, in language he would have ridiculed—as worthy as *Sir Thopas's* to counterfeit his own.

In order to simplify still further this review of the conflation and debasement of the texts of the Renaissance "Chaucer," the facts can be very crudely quantified, by reductio ad absurdum. The medieval canon of "Chaucer's Works"—those explicitly acknowledged by him in the *Prologues*, the *Retraction*, and in the consensus of the early manuscripts—comprised approximately 34,000 lines of finished and unfinished poems. The Renaissance "Chaucer" which finally emerged in the summary edition of Speght in 1602 had grown to about 55,000 lines, an increase of roughly 21,000 lines accomplished by the successive efforts of William Thynne in 1532 and 1542, Stowe in 1561, and Speght in 1598 and 1602. With his publication of the *Romaunt of the Rose* and his other discoveries, Thynne began the process of recovery and expansion by adding to the work of his predecessors some 15,000 lines by 1542; Stowe added another 2,400 (of which approximately 150 are accepted as genuine by modern editors). Speght completed the process with his addition of 3,000 lines more, to which he promised to add the lost *Pilgrim's Tale*, if it could be found. In the 1687 reprint of Speght, a note added among the corrigenda apologizes for the omission of the *Pilgrim*, the text of which had been reported "seen" but could no longer be located.

At this level of generality, there is very little to be learned from the evidence. At the other extreme, in the cacophony of the individual additions, it is equally difficult to be precise as to the relationships that obtain between, for example, *The Cuckoo and the Nightingale* and the *Parliament of Fowls,* as separate entities and as related parts in the larger whole of Chaucer's love poetry. Since their separation and disentanglement, it has become possible to describe the genuine poems in the canon, and the rejected ones have become irrelevant to interpretation. But for the Renaissance "Chaucer," these questionable poems still remain open for criticism and have yet to be fully explored in context. They lie in the murky area of uncertainty, where quantitative change becomes qualitative, where the effect of "amplification of the commonplace" occurs and alters the perspective in which the extraordinary—the greater originals—are understood. It is impossible, of course, to divest ourselves of modern scepticism and to read the derivative pastiche poems begotten by the Middle English *Roman de la Rose* and Chaucer's *Complaints* with the unsuspecting confidence that they were Chaucer's, as did Spenser, Dryden, Keats, and Wordsworth. The eighteenth-century editors continued to print the interminable *Court of Love* (1442 lines in rime royal stanzas), as well as the *Tales of Gamelyn,* and of *Beryn,* the *Cuckoo,* and the *Flower and the Leaf.* It would seem to me, however, that no selection, no matter how judicious, of "typical" pseudo-Chaucerian pieces from the mass inflation of the canon in the sixteenth century could be adequately representative, in range of content, quality, and style, of the thickening and blurring effects brought about by their aggregate inclusion. To say the pseudo-Chaucerian poems are redundant and their effect reductive is true, but it is not true enough.

As I have suggested, the task of criticism is complicated by the various kinds of linguistic confusion in the texts. The authentic Chaucerian diction, archaic and perplexing to scribes and early printers, became more confused in the simultaneous presence of fifteenth- and early sixteenth-century pseudoarchaisms in the imitations, and by such linguistic anomalies as the smoothed London version of Henryson's Scots in the *Testament.* The prime example of the mutation of the language is, of course, Spenser's *Shepherd's Calendar;* to a lesser extent it is also apparent in *Daphnaida, Colin Clout,* and *Mother Hubberd's Tale.* We shall reexamine "E.K.'s" glosses and the Chaucerian Spenser in the following chapter, for of all the readers of the Renaissance Chaucer, perhaps none was as subtle as he, and none more certain of his own identity as a poet and willing to invest his inheritance.

In conclusion, then, the Renaissance reediting of Chaucer involved two kinds of conflation: the evolution of the language and the amplification of the text. Both are quantitative in kind and qualitative in effect, and their fusion produced the unique, ambivalent status of Chaucer the poet in the sixteenth century. He was at once a remote and primitive ancestor, and a model; his antique poetic diction and his "learning" were a national treasure, preserved from that age of "darkness and error" primarily because he satirized its ignorance and civilized its language. In 1589, Puttenham looked back to the origins of modern English poetry in the fourteenth century:

> before [the time of Edward III and Richard II], by reason of the late Normane conquest, which had brought into this Realme much alteration both of our langage and lawes, and ther withall a certain martiall barbarousnes, whereby the study of all good learning was so much decayd, as long time after no man or very few entended to write in any laudable science: so as beyond that time there is little or nothing worth commendation to be founde written in this arte. And those of the first age were *Chaucer* and *Gower*, both of them as I suppose Knightes.

After a short history of the fifteenth- and sixteenth-century writers, Puttenham returned to evaluate the "makers" in more detail.

> But of them all particularly this is myne opinion, that Chaucer, with Gower, Lidgate and Harding for their antiquitie ought to haue the first place, and Chaucer as the most renowned of them all, for the much learning appeareth to be in him aboue any of the rest. And though many of his bookes be but bare translations out of the Latin and French, yet they are wel handled, as his bookes of Troilus and Cresseid, and the Romant of the Rose, whereof he translated but one half, the deuice was Iohn de Mehunes, a French Poet, the Canterbury tales were Chaucers owne inuention as I suppose, and where he sheweth more the naturall of his pleasant wit, then in any other of his workes, his similitudes comparisons and all other descriptions are such as can not be amended.

Puttenham's praise of *Troilus's* "meetre Heroicall . . . graue and stately" singles out its versification: "keeping the staffe of seuen, and the verse of ten." He notes also the Horatian decorum of the "pleasaunt pilgrimage, in which every mans part is playd with much decency." More surprising are his contrasting opinions of Gower and Lydgate:

Gower's moralities are "many times very grossely bestowed, neither doth the substance of his workes sufficiently aunswere the subtiltie of his titles." Of Lydgate, "no deuiser of that which he wrate, but one that wrate in good verse."[36]

To the sixteenth-century reader, Chaucer was presented as a precursor of their own Renaissance, valuable for moral wisdom, excusably obscene in wit, and preeminently a love poet of the vanished Courts of Love and chivalry which Tudor and Elizabethan court pageantry revived in masquerades. Inigo Jones consulted Speght's *Chaucer* for the scenic production of Ben Jonson's *Masque of Queenes Celebrated from the House of Fame* in 1609; the *Knight's Tale* was dramatized twice, in Richard Edwards's *Palamon and Arcite*, acted before Elizabeth in 1566, and in *The Two Noble Kinsmen* of Shakspere and Fletcher of 1613.

The most acutely sensitive of the sixteenth-century readers of the surviving Chaucer's *Works* read them, as did Shakspere, for their immediate use to himself as a poet. Spenser's *Chaucer* (Stowe's "edition") is a heterogeneous and corrupt text in which the spurious outweighs and complicates interpretation of the genuine. The task of reading through the "rust of time" was not yet eased by Speght's editorial addenda of 1598, which in fact follow the precedent set by Spenser's own scholarly *Calendar*, his homage to Chaucer of 1579. In that poem, he defined his relation to his ancestor, and his own commitment to poetry, not in the spirit of rebellion against the past, but as its favored heir:

> The God of shepheards Tityrus is dead,
> Who taught me homely, as I can, to make.
> He, whilst he lived, was the soueraigne head
> Of shepheards all, that bene with loue ytake:
> Well couth he wayle his Woes, and lightly slake
> The flames, which loue within his heart had bredd
> And tell vs mery tales, to keep vs wake,
> The while our sheepe about vs safely fedde.

Spenser's Envoy follows "E.K.'s" gloss of the December Embleme, "The meaning wherof is that all thinges perish and come to theyr last end, but workes of learned wits and monuments of Poetry abide for euer. . . ." Perhaps nowhere else in the *Calendar* does Spenser reveal so clearly the sense of exhilaration and dread of the young poet pro-

36. Puttenham, *Arte of English Poesie*, pp. 74, 75, 76.

claiming his independence, and his full consciousness of time's decay: his new poem goes forth to stand the test of mutability, in the presence of its progenitors.

> Loe I haue made a Calender for euery yeare,
> That steele in strength, and time in durance shall outweare:
> And if I marked well the starres reuolution,
>   It shall continewe till the worlds dissolution.
> To teach the ruder shepheard how to feede his sheepe,
> And from the falsers fraud his folded flocke to keepe.
>   Goe lyttle Calender, thou hast a free passeporte,
> Goe but a lowly gate emongste the meaner sorte.
>   Dare not to match thy pype with Tityrus hys style,
>   Nor with the Pilgrim that the Ploughman playde a whyle:
> But followe them farre off, and their high steppes adore,
> The better please, the worse despise, I aske nomore.[37]

37. *The Shepherd's Calendar by Edmund Spenser*, ed. W.L. Renwick (London, 1930), *June*, ll. 81–89; *December, Envoy* ll. 235–46.

IX

Chaucer and Spenser

> Others commend Chaucer and Lydgate for their witt, pleasaunt
> veine, varietie of poetical discourse, and all humanitie: I specially
> note their Astronomie, philosophie, and other parts of profound
> or cunning art. Wherein few of their time were more exactly
> learned. It is not sufficient for poets to be superficial humanists:
> but they must be exquisite artists, and curious universal schollers.
>
> Gabriel Harvey (ca. 1585)

The Shepherd's Calendar

Gabriel Harvey, the "most excellent and learned friend" to whom
"E.K." addressed his preface and commended the *Shepherd's Calendar*,
"for the good lykyng . . . of his labour and the patronage of the new
Poet," while he is praising Chaucer, seems rather to be describing
Edmund Spenser, who was already famous by 1585 as perhaps "the most
exactly learned . . . exquisite . . . and curiously universall" scholar
of the astonishing generation of new poets of the last quarter of the
sixteenth century in England. The publication of the *Shepherd's Calendar*
in 1579 marked the beginning of the new age, and it was, as everyone
knows, as definitive a turning point for poetry as "E.K." claimed it to
be, comparable in retrospect to the publication of the *Lyrical Ballads* in
1798. Renwick, its modern editor, describes the *Calendar* as

> the first English example of High Renaissance art: a clearly per-
> ceptible self-conscious personality, working within a well-under-
> stood convention.[1]

In this chapter, I shall attempt to explicate the terms of Renwick's
definition as they relate to Spenser's homage to Chaucer.

---

1. *The Shepherd's Calendar by Edmund Spenser*, ed. W.L. Renwick (London, 1930), p. 163;
all quotations from the *Shepherd's Calendar* are from Renwick's edition, cited hereafter as Renwick, *Calendar*. Quotations from Spenser's "Complaints" are from Renwick's edition, *Complaints by Edmund Spenser* (London, 1928), hereafter cited as Renwick, *Complaints*.

The *Calendar* is preeminently "artificial" art, a highly wrought composite of pastorals, emblems, and two-dimensional interpretation. "E.K." presents suggested "readings" of Spenser's intention and his language that are, in effect, inseparable from the reader's experience of the poems. The commentary, published with the poet's authority, stands between the text and the reader to focus the allegory and to clarify intentional obscurity so that the fictional audience can be controlled. Unlike Chaucerian allegorical ironies, Spenser's use of *ironia* is unambiguous and explicit, and "E.K." makes its polarities clear. In the *Faerie Queene*, the commenting role of "E.K." is assimilated into the fictional role of the Narrator, analogous to Chaucer's Dreamer or Chaucer the Pilgrim. The consequent effect on interpretation is kaleidoscopic, for the narrator's "I" is free to speak with authority, to feign ignorance, and to create enigma.[2] In this chapter, I shall not attempt to describe such effects of multiple perspective in the narration of the *Faerie Queene* but shall focus mainly on the first appearance of "a clearly perceptible self-conscious personality," as Spenser presented himself, in the "new Poete" of the *Shepherd's Calendar*.

Superficially like the *Canterbury Tales*, Spenser's *Calendar* presents a series of voices in conversation and debate, in twelve interlaced eclogues, with the figure of Colin Clout the poet (identified by "E.K." as Spenser's alter ego) playing the leading part. But obviously the analogy will not hold: the *Canterbury Tales* has a linear structure, unfolding unpredictably in fixed time and space, and the fictional pretext Chaucer sets forth is spontaneous interaction, among widely varied characters, recorded with quasi-naturalistic faithfulness to a historical occasion. Spenser's *Calendar* and his shepherds have the timeless conventionality of universals: winter and summer, youth and age, in micro- and macro-rhythms of symbolized time. The twelve parts of Spenser's circular structure (as "E.K." tells us, proportional to the months, seasons, and the stages of the life cycle of the poet) have variously been seen as six pairs of two, four groups of three, and three groups of four elements, variously balanced and contrasting in theme, tone, and dominant style, ranging from the harsh and crude "Chaucerian" mode of *February* to

---

2. The Narrator of the *Faerie Queene* is discussed at length in the study of Robert M. Durling, *The Figure of the Poet in Renaissance Epic* (Cambridge, Mass., 1965), pp. 211–37. See Paul J. Alpers, *The Poetry of the Faerie Queene* (Princeton, 1967); and Lewis J. Miller, Jr. "The Ironic Modes in Books I and II of the *Faerie Queene*," *Papers on Language and Literature* 7 (1971): 133–49.

the fluid smoothness of *April* to the grand melancholy of *November*.[3] In
"E.K.'s" words, "his dewe observing of Decorum everywhere, in
personages, in seasons, in matter, in speache," is self-evident in the
"goteheards' Tales," variously "moral, plaintive, and recreative." An
inner frame is provided by the two poems in the first-person singular,
the prologue "To His Book," and the epilogue, Spenser's farewell after
December. Both of these derive from the same convention, and make a
double use of their common source, Chaucer's famous farewell to his
book at the ending of *Troilus*. Spenser ends where he began, appropriately, at the point of departure and withdrawal in Chaucer's greatest
poem. Throughout the *Calendar*, the asserted relationship—Spenser's
bond to Chaucer—is apparent, implicit in Spenser's allusions, and
explicit in "E.K.'s" commentary, separate introductions and glosses
on each eclogue, and in his explanations of the mottoes and woodcut
emblems which decorate the text. Nothing quite so elaborately "made"
and presented had ever been published before by an English poet:
interlaced pastorals with a supporting apparatus worthy of a newly
found Renaissance antique. Spenser's eclogues are the traditional
debut, the introduction of the new poet in classic Virgilian style; the
voices of his shepherds are expressed self-consciously, in the fine-tuning
of first performance, and their awkwardness is intentional. The eclogues
are interesting, but they are uneven. "E.K." praises their novelty of
breadth, freshness of form, and the artificiality of their language, from
which, however, spontaneity, natural ease, and freedom are excluded by
definition. Whether one calls it rigidity or tension, the *Calendar* is tightly sprung on its frame; every syllable in every song is calculated for its
effects in the immediate context and its radiating relationship to the
larger circular setting. The manipulations of balance among the voices
are perhaps comparable to madrigal, but Spenser's variations on the
set topics of desire, death, poetry, and politics are not dramatic for
characterization, but tonal and rhythmic, varying with the pattern of
heavy and light, bright and dark, themes. As "E.K." again and again
points out, the proprieties are based on Horatian decorum: what words
such "rusticks" could be expected to use, for example, in praising their

---

3. The allegory of the *Shepherd's Calendar* is treated at length by Paul E. McLane in *Spenser's Shepherd's Calendar* (Notre Dame, Ind., 1961); and in passing by Hallett Smith in his
essay on pastoral in *Elizabethan Poetry* (Cambridge, Mass., 1952), pp. 31–59. See also Sam
Meyer, *An Interpretation of Edmund Spenser's Colin Clout* (Notre Dame, Ind., 1969); A.C. Hamilton, "The Argument of Spenser's *Shepherd's Calendar*," JELH 23 (1956): 171–82.

"Elyza," the Queen. Spenser uses an unparalleled variety of metrical schemes and experimental stanzas, not all of which are equally successful. The subject matter, like the styles of the voices, is proportioned rhythmically to the season, the month, the speaker, and the limited devices of pastoral convention. The *Calendar* opens up, then, the range of themes traditional to eclogue, love, moral allegory, and political satire, again not unlike the *Canterbury Tales*. However, the performance of Colin Clout, and hence, the role of the poet, are at the center of the *Calendar* as a whole. The *Calendar*'s cycle is the life of Colin Clout, and it is separated only by the transparent "I" of the Prologue and Epilogue from Spenser himself, as "E.K." explains: "As for Colin, vndur whose person the Authore selfe is shadowed,"

> Colin Clout is a name not greatly vsed, and yet haue I sene a Poesie of M. Skelton's vnder that title. But indeede the word Colin is French . . . and used of Marot. Vnder which this Poete secretly shadoweth himself, as sometimes did Virgil vnder the name of Tityrus . . . for the great vnlikelyhoode of the language.[4]

Spenser's Colin Clout, in other words, is the first Spenserian poet, who himself became almost at once a model and prototype of the "new Poete" for contemporary imitation. But for all the heavy emphasis on introducing the "new Poete" in a first performance unique in several notable ways, both "E.K." and Spenser give equal weight and attention to the continuity of the new poetry in older English traditions, specifically and insistently, the "Chaucerian." Mutation has occurred, and the new poetry is to be henceforth "Spenserian," but it is introduced and defined in the context of the old poetry. The *Calendar* is not, obviously, imitation, but a kind of dedication to Chaucer, who wrote moral, political, and love allegory, and artificial natural description, but no "pastoral." The eclogue is a Renaissance form, which Spenser self-consciously medievalized.

Beginning with his first words, "E.K.'s" commentary asserts the association; misquoting Pandar's encouragement to Troilus to speak ("Vnknowe, vnkiste, and lost that is vnsought"), "E.K." presents Spenser as he wished to be found, and made famous:

> Vncouthe, vnkiste, sayde the olde famous Poete, Chaucer: whom for his excellencie and wonderful skil in making, his scholler

4. Renwick, *Calendar*, p. 19.

Lidgate, a worthy scholler of so excellent a maister, calleth the
Loadestarre of our Language.[5]

The new poet, to be made famous by his worthy scholar in turn, is in
"E.K.'s" eyes the new "Loadestarre," made more brilliant by the
light of his distant predecessor; in effect, the more "ancient" the old
poetry now seems, the more remarkable the achievement of the new.
"E.K.'s" task is to commend both, simultaneously. Throughout his
commentary and annotation, "E.K." calls attention to Spenser's
wonderful "skill in making" and his incomparably varied language.
Since 1579, as "E.K." foresaw, such disagreement as there has been in
the almost unanimous acclaim for the *Calendar* has been concerned with
Spenser's deliberate re-creation of English poetic diction, the words and
forms which "E.K." stresses, defends, and admires. The newest aspect
of the *Calendar*, to contemporaries, was its conspicuously old, remote,
apparently "Chaucerian" language. "E.K." commends

> his wittinesse in deuising, his pithinesse in vttering, his complaints
> of loue so louely, his discourses of pleasure so pleasuntly, his pasto-
> ral rudeness, his moral wiseness . . . in matter, in speache, and
> generally in all seemely simplicytee of handeling his matter and
> framing his words; the which of many things in him be straunge,
> I know well seeme the straungest, the words themselues being so
> auncient, the knitting of them so short and intricate, and the whole
> Period & compasse of speache so delightsome for the roundness
> and so graue for the straungeness.

"E.K." continues for another eighty lines, discussing the state of decay
into which the language of English poetry had fallen and the ill-founded
remedies attempted by Spenser's recent predecessors, those whom
Polyhymnia denounces in the *Teares of the Muses*,

> Heapes of huge words uphoorded hideously,
> With horrid sound though having little sence,
> They thinke to be chiefe praise of Poetry;
> And thereby wanting due intelligence,
> Have mard the face of goodly Poesie,
> And made a monster of their fantasie.

[ll. 553–58][6]

5. Ibid., pp. 3–4.
6. Renwick, *Complaints*, p. 46.

In the *Calendar*, the "present state of poetry" is the subject of the
October eclogue, where Spenser treats it in both ethical and historical
terms. Cuddy says,

> But after vertue gan for age to stoupe,
> And mighty manhode brought a bedde of ease:
> The vaunting Poets found nought worth a pease,
> And put in preace emong the learned troupe.
> Tho gan the streames of flowing wittes to cease,
> And sonnebright honour pend in shamefull coupe.
>
> And if that any buddes of Poesie
> Yet of the old stocke gan to shoote agayne:
> Or it mens follies mote be forst to fayne,
> And rolle with rest in rymes of rybaudrye:
> Or as it sprong, it wither must agyne:
> Tom Piper makes vs better melodie.
>
> [*October*, 67–78]

While Cuddy compares the greatness of the past with the present state
of the "withered sproutes" on the "olde stocke," "E.K." would "scorne
and spue out the rakehellye route of our ragged rymers," not only for
their ignorance but for their pride in neologism (Latinizing "aureation")
and their penchant for loan words from other languages (the anglici-
zation of French and Italian), in short, for their acceleration of the
processes by which English had steadily enriched its stock for the past
thousand years. Spenser, in practice, simply reversed the terms of the
humanist-purist dispute on the poverty of the language by turning
attention to its inherited wealth. It is unnecessary to patch it up by
borrowing foreign words, if one looks into the available supply, as
Spenser looked and found what could be used in the recent editions of
Langland's *Piers Plowman* (1555) and Chaucer's *Works* (1542, 1550,
1561).

"E.K.'s" expectation of controversy was soon confirmed by Sidney's
disapproval of Spenser's "archaism," expressed in the *Apologie*, and Ben
Jonson's famous comments to Drummond in 1619. Both Sidney and
Jonson disliked, and rebuked, the impropriety of Spenser's affectation
of rustic antiquity and the strange dialect words he bound so "tightly
and intricately" into his language that they create its distinctive tone.
The following stanzas, also from the October eclogue, exemplify the

mixture of levels of diction to which Sidney objected. The words "E.K."
glossed are italicized:

> *Cuddie*, for shame hold vp thy heauye head,
> And let vs cast with what delight to chace,
> And weary thys long lingring Phoebus race.
> *Whilome* thou wont the shepheards laddes to leade,
> In rymes, in ridles, and in bydding base:
> Now they in thee, and thou in sleepe art dead.
>
> Cvddye.
> Piers, I haue pyped erst so long with payne,
> That all mine *Oten reedes* bene rent and wore:
> And my poore Muse hath spent her spared store,
> Yet little good hath got, and much lesse gayne.
> Such pleasaunce makes the Grasshopper so poore,
> And *ligge so layd*, when Winter doth her straine:
>
> The *dapper* ditties, that I wont deuise,
> To feede youthes fancie, and the flocking *fry*,
> Delighten much: what I the bett for thy?
> They han the pleasure, I a sclender prise.
> I beate the bush, the byrds to them doe flye:
> What good therof to Cuddie can arise?
>
> [*October*, 1–18]

While this is Spenser's relatively homogeneous "middle style" in the
Calendar, far from his most "Chaucerian," the admixture of rural and
"artificial" modes is conspicuous, and the effect is neither ancient nor
modern, literary nor colloquial enough to fulfill "E.K.'s" claims for it
("so delightsome for the roundness, . . . so graue for the straungeness
. . ."). I suspect that Sidney and Jonson would have preferred that
Spenser emulate the narrower, and hence seemingly purer range of the
Renaissance "Chaucer" as exemplified in such as the following, the
opening stanzas of the *Court of Love*, published in the 1561 *Works*; they
are a relatively free imitation of the formulaic opening of the *Parliament of Fowls*, in the high style of the fifteenth century:

> With temerous herte, and trembling hand of drede,
> Of cunning naked, bare of eloquence,
> Unto the floor of poort in womanhede

I write as he that none intelligence
Of metres hath, ne floures of sentence
Saufe that me lest my writing to convey
In that I can to please her heigh nobley.

The blosmes fresh, of Tulius gardein soote
Present then not, my matter for to borne
Poemes of Virgile taken here no roote
Ne crafte of Galfride may not here soiuourne
Why nam I cunning o wel maie I morne
For lack of science that I can nat write
Unto the princes of my lyf aright.

In contrast to the more elegant "Chaucerian" imitator, Chaucer
himself had simplified the same rhetorical figure, the "impossibility"
variant of the modesty topos, with wry seriocomic *ironia*:

The life so shorte, the craft so long to lerne
Thassai so hard, so sharp the conqueryng
The dredful ioy, alwaie that flt so yerne
All this meane I by loue, that my felyng
Astonieth, with his wonderfull werkyng
So sore iwis that when I on hym thinke
Naught wete I well, whether I flete or sink.

For out of the olde feldes, as men saith
Cometh all this newe corne, fro yere to yere
And out of old bookes, in good faieth
Cometh all this newe science that men lere.[7]

In the *Calendar*, Spenser's poetic diction both rises higher and falls
far lower than the range exemplified in the *Courte of Love* and *Parliament* stanzas, and it is, as "E.K." says, "strange" in heterogeneous
mixtures, as in *October*—Phoebus and the grasshopper, Orpheus's pipe
and the bird in the bush. Spenser's metrical stress patterns also intensify
the effects of alliteration, "hard words" and affected simplicity, in low,
middle, and elevated poetic speech. Again, "E.K's" glosses are italicized
to indicate his perception of "difficulty" for the Elizabethan reader:

They looken bigge as Bulls that bene bate

7. The Chaucerian texts here quoted are from the 1561 (Stowe) folio in the Beinecke
Library of Yale University.

And bearen the *cragge* so stiffe and so *state*
As cock on dunghill, crowing cranck

Diggon I praye thee speake not so dirke
Such *myster* saying me seemth to *mirke*
[*September* 44–46, 102–03]

In not *thilke* same a *goteheard* prowde
that sittes on yonder *bancke*
Whose *strayng heard* them selfe doth shroude
emong the bushes rancke?
[*July* 1–4]

Ye *daynte* Nymphes, that in this blessed Brooke
doe bathe your brest
Forsake your watery bowres, and hither looke
at my request
[*April* 37–40]

O *trustless* state of earthly things, and slipper hope
Of mortal men, that swincke and sweate for nought,
And shooting wide, doe misse the marked scope:
Now haue I learnd (a lesson derely bought)
That nys on earth assurance to be sought.
[*November* 153–57]

In the past fifty years' work on Spenser's language, especially in the *Calendar*, a consensus seems gradually to have emerged among modern philologists, who have gathered evidence in defense of Spenser in order to demonstrate that, despite "E.K.'s" pedantic pride in the oddity of some few words, in fact Spenser did not, alone and single-handedly, enlarge the boundaries of Elizabethan poetic language by his stress on rustic, archaic, dialectal, and obsolete colloquial speech. Vere Rubel, B. R. McElderry, and A. C. Partridge have published lists to show how much of Spenser's "straunge" vocabulary was already in use, or still in print, tentatively concluding that he did not depart "very far" from the norms of Elizabethan English.[8] Nevertheless, in spite of modern

8. See Vere Rubel, *Poetic Diction in the English Renaissance* (New York, 1941); Bruce R. McElderry, "Archaism and Innovation in Spenser's Poetic Diction," *PMLA* 47 (1932): 147–70; A.C. Hamilton, *The Language of Renaissance Poetry* (London, 1971); Patricia Ingham, "Spenser's Use of Dialect," *English Language Notes* 8 (1971): 164–68; Emma F. Pope, "Renais-

opinion, both to contemporaries and to the seventeenth-century reader (as *Spencer Redivivus* witnesses in 1687), it indeed seemed that Spenser had cast an aura of strangeness on his language, and in presenting himself as Chaucer's "heir," he had taken full advantage of the "graveness" of the association. In effect, the assertion, and "E.K.'s" gloss, add another invisible outer frame to the *Calendar*, its halo of artificial "Chaucerian" "delightsomeness." Spenser revitalized poetic language by making his innovations seem more ancient and strange than they probably were, in fact.

The "New Poete": The Chaucerian *Maker* and Spenserian Inspiration

The *Calendar*, with its elaborate apparatus and emblems, was a remarkable publication, the first vernacular example of its kind in England. While "E.K." takes note of Spenser's continental models (the eclogues of Marot and Mantuan) and pompously describes their classical ancestors in Virgil, Ovid, Theocritus, and Bion, Spenser's debut was not so striking as an essay in Renaissance pastoral (already extant in Barclay and Googe) as it was the creation of the "new English Poete." Throughout both text and commentary, Spenser and "E.K." raise again and again the questions of the state of poetry and the nature of the true poet. I think more can be learned, from Spenser and "E.K.," concerning "Spenser's Chaucer" and the "Chaucerian," by examining their definitions of poetry and imitation, and the new description of the "perfect patterne of a Poete" who is variously "Tityrus," Colin Clout, Cuddye, and Spenser himself, than by reviewing the familiar ground of the *Calendar*'s allegory and diction. Spenser's debut was a turning point, which self-consciously looked both forward and back, toward the Chaucerian past and the Elizabethan present, and attempted to incorporate both in the new poetry of "the new Poete." "E.K.'s" Argument to the *October* eclogue provides our starting point; it leads straight to the issue of the history of *makyng*:

---

sance Criticism and the Diction of the *Faery Queene*," *PMLA* 41 (1926); F.M. Padelford, "Aspects of Spenser's Vocabulary," *PQ* 20 (1941): 279–83; Hallett Smith, "The Use of Conventions in Spenser's Minor Poems," in Wm. Nelson, ed., *English Institute Essays* (New York, 1961), pp. 122–45; C.L. Wrenn, "On Re-reading Spenser's *Shepherd's Calendar*," *Essays and Studies* 29 (1943): 30–49; Martha Craig, "The Secret Wit of Spenser's Language," in Paul Alpers, ed., *Elizabethan Poetry: Modern Essays in Criticism* (Oxford, 1967).

> In Cuddie is set out the perfecte paterne of a Poete, which finding
> no maintenaunce of his state and studies, complayneth of the
> contempte of Poetrie, and the causes thereof: Specially hauing bene
> in all ages, and euen amongst the most barbarous always of
> singular accoumpt & honor, & being indede so worthy and com-
> mendable an arte: or rather no arte, but a diuine gift and heauenly
> instinct not to bee gotten by laboure and learning, but adorned
> with both: and poured into the witte by a certain *enthousiasmos*,
> and celestiall inspiration, as the Author hereof els where at large
> discourseth, in his booke called the English Poete.[9]

Whether or not Spenser intended Cuddye to exemplify the true poet,
Cuddye himself defers to Colin Clout, and in both figures the conception of the poet's role and art is clearly Spenserian: "no arte, but a
divine gift, poured into the witte by . . . celestiall inspiration."

Now let us also take into account the Spenserian senses of the medieval verb, *make*, which "E.K." found it necessary to gloss in the *April*
eclogue:

> [THENOT.] And hath he skill to *make* so excellent
>   Yet hath so little skill to bridle love?
>
> [April, 19–20]

> [GLOSS.] to make) to rime and versify. For in this word
>   *makyng*, our olde Englishe Poetes were wont to com-
>   prehend all the skil of Poetrye, according to the Greeke
>   woorde *poeien*, to make, whence commeth the name of
>   Poetes.

In effect, "E.K." is adding his erudite Greek etymology to the common
Middle English sense of "makyng" as applied to poetry in, for example,
Chaucer's description in the *General Prologue* of the courtly art of the
Squire, "He koude songes make and wel endite" (A, 95), or the Man of
Law's dismissal of "Chaucer" in his *Prologue*, "I speke in prose, and lat
him rymes make" (B, 96), or, in Chaucer's *Words to Adam the Scrivener*,

> Under thy long lokkes thou must have the scalle
> But after my makyng thou wryte more trewe
> So ofte a day I mot thy werk renewe.

By the end of the sixteenth century, from the earliest readings of the

---

9. Renwick, *Calendar*, p. 128.

Shepherd's Calendar of "E.K." to the treatises of Sidney and Puttenham in the following decade, it becomes evident that the medieval conception of the poet as a "maker," like the medieval allegorical figure of Genius, had undergone metamorphosis, which developed the radical meaning of *enthousiasmos*—invisible powers—and reclothed the image in Renaissance dress. It became apparent, that is, within five years of its first publication, that Spenser and his Colin Clout in the *Shepherd's Calendar* were the first modern English "makers" to fit Sidney's Elizabethan image of the true poet, and the meaning of imitation, as he defined them in the *Apologie*, written shortly after 1580. It is, of course, the same learned etymology which "E.K." explains and glosses as the "Chaucerian" meaning—"as the olde English Poetes use" the word *make* (*poeien*)—from which Sidney derived the divine authority for poetry and defended the freedom of the poet's imagination as "maker" of a golden world, more pure and true than the grosser world of nature. The new definition of "What a Poet and Poesie is" was restated, within the decade, in Puttenham's *Arte of English Poesie* of 1589 (six years before Sidney's already famous *Apologie* was printed). The first chapter of Puttenham's book begins with the meaning of the old word, *maker*:

> A Poet is as much to say as a *maker*. And our English name well conformes with the Greeke worde: for of *poeien* to make, they call a maker *Poeta*. Such as (by way of resemblance and reuerently) we may say of imagination, make all the world of nought, nor also by any paterne or mould as the Platonicks with their Idees do phantastically suppose. Even so the very Poet makes and contriues out of his owne braine, both the verse and matter of his poeme, and not by any foreine copie or example, as doth the translator, who therfore may well be sayd a versifier, but not a Poet.

We will later in this chapter return to Plato, whom Puttenham here brushes aside; he is engaged in the delicate problem of accommodating the dedication of his book to the Queen, whom Spenser's Polyhymnia calls

> Most peereles Prince, most peereles Poëtresse,
> The true Pandora of all heavenly graces,
> Divine Elisa, sacred Emperesse.
>
> [*TM* 577–79]

Puttenham turns from the creative to the imitative power of the poet, and the nature of his "sources":

because he can expresse the true and liuely of euery thing is set
before him, and which he taketh in hand to describe: and so in
that respect is both a maker and a counterfaitor: and Poesie an
art not only of making, but also of imitation. . . . It is of Poets
thus to be conceived, that if they be able to deuise, and make all
these things of themselues, they be (by maner of speech) as creating gods. If they do it by instinct diuine or naturall, then surely
much fauoured from aboue. If by their experience, then no doubt
very wise men. If by any president or paterne layd before them,
then truly the most excellent imitators and counterfaitors of all
others.[10]

Contrary to the overwhelming evidence of the pejorative meanings of
counterfeit, from its earliest history in the fourteenth century, to mean
"to make an imitation with intent to deceive," "to forge, adulterate,
disguise, falsify," "to feign, pretend, simulate," Sidney and Puttenham
tried to turn the negative meaning of *counterfeit* into an excellence of
art. As was seen in chapter 2, the Elizabethan defenders of the arts of
imitation and "makyng" affirm, with high and serious confidence, the
power of poetry to confer true fame, never lie, and speak truth, which is
wholly different from the scepticism of Chaucer's *Book of Fame* and the
ironies of Alan's *Plaint of Kind*. As Boccaccio defended the myths of the
ancients and pagan poetry, Sidney declares that *makyng* and imitation
are not a deeper debasement of nature, but that by *poeien* and *mimesis*,
artists and poets perfect the model: they bring it to a higher state.

From the perspective of Elizabethan criticism, we can now turn to
the evidence: the conceptions of *makyng* in the outer frame of the
Shepherd's Calendar and in its inner frame, the modesty topoi of the
Prologue and Epilogue, where Spenser first alludes to Chaucer and
takes, as his points of both departure and return, one of the most famous
of Chaucerian self-deprecations, the humility of the Narrator as the
maker of *Troilus and Criseyde*:

> Go, litel book, go, litel myn tragedye,
> Ther god thi makere yit, or that he dye
> So sende myght to make in some comedye!
> But, litel book, no makyng thow nenvie,

---

10. *The Arte of English Poesie*, pp. 19, 20–21. Puttenham's description of pastoral is worth
comparing with that of "E.K."; see ibid., pp. 52–53.

> But subgit be to alle poesie;
> And kis the steppes, where as thow seest space
> Virgile, Ovide, Omer, Lucan, and Stace.
>
> [V, 1786–92]

Now it has long been argued that Chaucer intends, here and everywhere else in his work, a special, highly symbolic sense for *poesie* and the title "poet," which he reserves for others and does not attribute to himself. According to this view, Chaucer thought of himself as a "mere *maker*," humble, profane, vernacular. It is necessary to keep this twentieth-century interpretation in mind, as Spenser's Elizabethan version is set against its apparent source.

While "E.K.'s" gloss of the verb *make* comes in the *April* eclogue, the first Spenserian use of *maker* as an archaism in the *Calendar* comes, paradoxically, as a silent echo of Chaucer, by means of metaphor, in the opening lines of the Prologue, *To His Book*. As he does in the epilogue after *December*, Spenser makes a direct appeal to the reader's memory, by allusion to the famous lines of the farewell to *Troilus*:

> Goe little booke: thy selfe present,
> As child whose parent is unkent:
> To him that is the president
> Of noblesse and of chevalree,
> And if that Envie barke at thee,
> As sure it will, for succoure flee
>   Under the shadow of his wing,
> And asked, who thee forth did bring,
> A shepheards swaine saye did thee sing,
> All as his straying flocke he fedde:
> And when his honor has thee redde,
> Crave pardon for my hardyhedde.
>   But if that any aske thy name,
> Say thou wert base begot with blame;
> For thy therof thou takest shame.
> And when thou art past jeopardee,
> Come tell me, what was sayd of mee:
> And I will send more after thee.
>
> [*To His Book*]

The text of Chaucer's *Troilus* which Spenser is most likely to have known, and expected his reader to know, was the version printed in 1561, in which the stanza reads as follows:

> Go litel boke, go my litell tregedie
> There god thy maker yet er that I die
> So sende me might to make some comedie
> But litell boke, make thou none enuie
> But subiect ben vnto al poesie
> And kisse the steppes, wher as thou seest pace
> Of Vergil, Ouide, Homer, Lucan, and Stace.

The confusion apparent in the Stowe text makes the second line of Chaucer's stanza highly ambiguous: who is the maker of the *litell tregedie*? Chaucer's elliptical indirect address to himself ("thy maker, er that he die") has undergone a revision to avoid parallelism ("god thy maker, er that I die"), and *me* has been added to the third line (with Chaucer's "make in som comedye" contracted to "make some"). Yet Spenser understood the sense well enough to transform it, omitting the Chaucerian ambiguity of *make* and *maker* by substitution.

Spenser varies the Chaucerian diminutive *litel boke* (Boccaccio's *piccolo mio libro*, in Chaucer's source) by turning the *Calendar* into his child, "whose parent is unkent." Spenser's verbs play on the old metaphorical meanings of *make* and *maker* implicit in the symbol of Genius, the intermediary in the imagination's begetting of new forms. Spenser's *Calendar* can claim that "a shepheard swain . . . thee forth did bring"; "thou wert base begot with blame." As "E.K." notes, Spenser also uses the medieval meanings for *make*, "to rime and versify," nonmetaphorically, seven times elsewhere in the Calendar, and he uses it in this sense in *Colin Clout's Come Home Again*, but not, so far as I have been able to discover, in the *Faerie Queene*, nor elsewhere in his works.[11] As for *maker*, the "noble name of a poet" in Dunbar and Malory, in Spenser the case is not the same: except for the *Shepherd's Calendar*, Spenser's *maker* is almost invariably a "heavenly Maker," with or without the epithet (20 times), or he uses it in the positive sense of "artificer" (of, e.g. Canacee's chariot). Twice, however, it is a metonymy for Archimago, and once for the witch who terrorizes Florimell. It is clear that, in the *Faerie Queene*, Spenser's preference is for the name *poet* (35 times), and he variously refers to his art as *poesie* (7 times), *poetry* (3 times), *rime* (43 times), or *verse* (65 times). The evidence is that after the *Calen-*

11. See Charles G. Osgood, *A Concordance to the Poems of Edmund Spenser* (London, 1963).

dar, the "olde Poetes use" of *make* and *maker*, so vague in scope and unclear in status, has been supplanted by the increasingly honorific *poet*. "E.K.'s" gloss of *make* ("to rime and versify, in our olde Poets") may have been merely pendantry, but it would seem that the brief revival of *maker* in Spenser, Sidney, and Puttenham did not restore the poetic sense. Nor did they reverse the connotations of *counterfeit*; the next recorded use of it to mean "imitate, with no sense of deceit," is in Charles Darwin's *Origin of Species* in 1859, and, as will be noted presently, Spenser himself uses the negative senses for Duessa. *Maker*, as the clearly archaic name for a poet, is not recorded again until Joseph Warton's *Essay on Pope* in 1756. As I have earlier mentioned, Shakspere plays on its punning ambivalence in the self-parody of his art in *A Midsummer Night's Dream*, in the playwright of Pyramus's tragedy, Peter Quince the carpenter. After Dunbar's splendid *Lament for the Makars*, and Sidney's rhetorical

> I know not, whether by lucke or wisedome,
> wee Englishmen haue mette with the Greekes in
> calling him a maker: which name, how high and
> incomparable a title it is, . . . [12]

the medieval name for a poet seems to fade into obsolete ambiguity. Throughout the *Apologie*, Sidney relies on the modern term to distinguish the poet from others who claim to know, philosophers and historians.

We can now turn to the subtle and difficult argument over Chaucer's *maker*, in which it is claimed that he intended and preserved in all his work a significant distinction among these terms. This is most apparent, it is said, in the ending of *Troilus*, his greatest poem, where he, a mere *maker*, commends his book to "submit to his ancient masters, the poets." J. S. P. Tatlock first stated the case, in his reading of "The Epilog to Troilus," and his opinion forms the basis of many later interpretations.

> [Chaucer makes] a clear distinction between the two sets of words, "poete," "poetical," "poesye" on the one hand, and on the other "makere," "makyng," "make." As applied to poetry, both sets of words seem about coeval in English, both hardly antecedent to the fourteenth century.[13]

12. Smith, *Sidney*, p. 155.
13. J.S.P. Tatlock, "The Epilog of Chaucer's *Troilus*," *MP* 18 (1921): 625–59.

On this assumption, Tatlock then interpreted the farewell stanza ("Go, litel boke") of *Troilus*: Chaucer does not regard the words *maker* and *poet* as synonymous or interchangeable. He is, in effect, telling his *litel book* to envy none, but be *subiect to alle poesie*: "envy not your peers, and submit yourself to your betters." Thus, *makyng* is inferior art, while *poesie* and the name *poet* are restricted to the great; Chaucer lists the past masters—Virgil, Ovid, Homer, Lucan, and Statius—naming elsewhere both Dante and Petrarch as "poetes" (but never Boccaccio), all in reverent homage. Tatlock's reading looks very plausible indeed; it would be impossible to deny that Chaucer intends veneration, and an "aura of the sacred" for the names of poets, and self-deprecation of his own modest *craft* as a *maker*. So, it would seem, Spenser venerates his *olde maker*, Chaucer. The argument concludes with a broad distinction between Chaucerian reverence for "classical poetry" and for Dante— "the esoteric sacredness of loftier symbolic literature"—citing Chaucer's *Retraction* and the low regard for his own worldly poems of passion and comedy which Chaucer the *maker* acknowledged. The unstated assumption is that Chaucer the poet is Chaucer the Narrator, and that the modesty convention is to be taken straight and read as homage. But surely there is a question, as Donaldson raised it, as to how humble Chaucer's "epilogue" stanza may be, and whether the humility professed by the Narrator is perfectly sincere and uncomplicated as he sends *Troilus* off in the footsteps of five of the greatest poets of antiquity.[14] In comparing Spenser's version, in the *Faerie Queene*,

> I follow here with footing of thy feet
> And with thy meaning so I may thee rather meet.
>
> [IV, ii, 35]

I think the modesty formula is well understood and used precisely: to enforce in the mind of the reader the new poet's sense of his own achievement, strong enough to bear comparison with the master's work. In each case, the poetic "I" has the advantage of both center stage and the present tense and is gaining, not losing, by the acknowledgment.

Now, there appears to be a similarity between the dichotomy between *poesie* and *makyng* proposed for Chaucer, and that separating

---

14. Donaldson's essay on "The Ending of Chaucer's *Troilus*," in Arthur Brown and Peter Foote, eds., *Early English and Norse Studies Presented to Hugh Smith* (London, 1963), is reprinted in his *Speaking of Chaucer* (New York, 1970), ch. 6.

"Nature" and "Art," which lies at the heart of C. S. Lewis's interpretation of Spenser's allegory in the *Faerie Queene*.[15] Lewis's famous explication of the antithesis shows the seductive, sterile artifice of Acrasia's Bower as the negative image of the natural, fertile love created in the Gardens of Adonis, with the boar in chains below. When the parallels are extended in exegesis, it becomes relevant to bring in the Platonic distinction between Socrates' "fiction," his Aesop's fables, and the sacred Hymn to Apollo, and gradually there seems to appear a great cultural bifurcation, in medieval and Renaissance thought, in which the root meanings of *poet* and *maker*, *craft* and *art*, proliferate from poetry via allegory into metaphysics. It is the very vagueness and generality of the terms involved which permits such abstraction, makes such hypotheses plausible, and finally trivializes them. Let us reevaluate the terms, in Chaucer and Spenser.

To recapitulate, and return to the texts, we began in the first instance with a hypothesis: that Chaucer expressed profound respect for Virgil and Ovid, Dante and Petrarch, as poets, and revered their art, is incontrovertible. That he regarded his own secular art with contempt is unlikely, but the oblique conclusion, that he then saved it, or attempted to transform profane poetry to sacred, *Cristes lore*, by means of secretly encoded allegory, has not been proved and probably cannot be proved. *Allegoria* and *ironia* in poetry agree with, and evoke, a multiplicity of readings, any one of which can be disproved only by strong "refuting facts": contradictory and paradoxical interpretations compete in terms of probabilities.[16] Thus, Chaucer's farewell to his *litel tragedie* and his juxtapositions of *makyng* and *poesie*, ancient and modern, can be read either as expressions of exquisite humility or as "something close to arrogance." Similar questions can be asked of Spenser's modest acknowledgements of his masters, but in the virtual absence of *ironia*.

15. In *The Allegory of Love* (London, 1936), ch. 7.

16. Cf. Quintilian, *Institutes,* 8.6.44, 54: "Allegoria . . . quam inversionem interpretantur, aut aliud verbis aut aliud sense ostendit aut etiam interim contrarium. . . . In eo vero genere, quo contraria ostendatur, ironia est, illusionem vocant. Quare aut pronuntiatione intellegitur, aut personam aut rei natura; nam, si qua earum verbis dissentit, apparet diversam esse orationi voluntatem" [On the other hand, . . . that class of allegory in which the meaning is contrary to that suggested by the meaning of the words, . . . involves an element of irony, or, as the rhetoricians call it, *illusio*; this is made evident to the understanding either by the delivery, the character of the speaker, or the nature of the subject. For if any one of these is out of keeping with the words, it at once becomes clear that the intention of the speaker is other than what he actually says.] See the discussion of *allegoria*, above, ch. 6 passim.

The issue of the poet's fame is the crux, implicit in "E.K.'s" paraphrase of Pandarus on "humility": "vncouth, vnkiste (and lost that is unsought)."

In the *Troilus* stanza, Chaucer does distinguish between *maker* and poet, and he uses the latter term in homage to Dante and Petrarch elsewhere; but it does not therefore follow either that he regarded his own art as inferior or that he concealed its deeper "sacred truth." The modesty topoi are among the subtlest of all the conventions which descend in the evolution from early medieval to Renaissance poetry; when they are used ironically, as Chaucer so frequently uses them, they and their subsequent imitation must be interpreted with the greatest caution. The transformation of the name *maker* by Sidney and Puttenham belongs to the new age, but it is not retroactive. Chaucer's ironic detachment from his fiction was obscured, and frequently unobserved by the Elizabethans, who read his poetic "I" as evidence of the naive, primitive state of the art of poetry before the new learning, the new printing, and the new poetry, their own. Spenser and "E.K.'s" conflation of the old and new meanings of *maker* reveals the Elizabethan revision of the past. "To rime and versify" became, finally, in Sidney, "no art, . . . but a divine gift, and heavenly instinct, adorned with labor and learning."

We can pursue the diverging parallels somewhat further, in Spenser's reading and imitation of the ending of *Troilus*. Immediately following the so-called "farewell," there is a second, equally famous Chaucerian stanza (marked by a marginal pointing hand in Speght's folio of 1602), which seems to me to contradict the theory of self-deprecation. I think it is not, certainly, an "invitation to correction, . . . in self-conscious humility," but rather an ironic prayer to the future scribes and readers of the poem, that they value it and protect it—every word is vulnerable. As it stands in the 1561 (Stowe) text, the stanza reads

> And for there is so great diuersite
> In English and in writing of our tonge
> So praie I to god that none miswrite the
> Ne the misse metre for defaute of tonge
> And redde wher so thou be, or els songe,
> That thou be vnderstonde, God I beseche
> But yet to purpose of my rather speche.

[V, 1793–99]

The poignancy of the literal meaning of the stanza is not to be denied, but it is undermined by the ending of the struggle, through five long books, as the Narrator tries to explain what he admits is inexplicable and to extricate himself from involvement in, and the ultimate moral responsibility for, the experience his poem creates as the reader discovers its meaning. I think the stanza is a brilliant variation of the "impossibility" topos, in effect, which deflects the inevitable misinterpretation the Narrator foresees away from himself to the ink on the page, and its scribes.

Spenser's answer to this stanza is not in the *Shepherd's Calendar*, but in the patently Chaucerian context of the fourth book of the *Faerie Queene*, where the theme of the *Squire's Tale* is taken up and its "lost labours revived" (IV, ii, 34). Here, Spenser addresses the theme of mutability in an aside to the reader, which pities the decay of "famous moniments" and glances at the future of his own work, in a tone quite different from the positive conviction he expressed at the end of the *Calendar*. In Book IV, there is apparent anxiety, confronted and overcome by the Narrator:

> But wicked Time, that all good thoughts doth waste,
> And workes of noblest wits to nought out weare,
> That famous moniment hath quite defaste,
> And robd the world of threasure endlesse deare,
> The which mote have enriched all us heare.
> O cursed Eld, the cankerworme of writes!
> How may these rimes, so rude as doth appeare,
> Hope to endure, sith workes of heavenly wits
> Are quite devourd, and brought to nought by little bits?
>
> [IV, ii, 33]

In his compassion for the "antique story" of Chaucer's "heavenly wit," Spenser also stresses his own demonstration of restorative art. The true meaning of Cambello and Canacee can continue,

> Though now their acts be nowhere to be found,
> As that renowmed poet them compyled,
> With warlike numbers and heroicke sound,

for it is now to be carried to its conclusion, through the survival and preservation of Chaucer's "sweete spirit" in Spenser's fiction: the page decays, but the work of the imagination is indestructible. Spenser had already raised and answered the question of "sources" and the historicity of fiction in the Proem to his second book, and his defense—like Socrates' belief in his vision of the other world in the passage of the *Phaedo* discussed in chapter 1—protects the myth from scepticism.

> Right well I wote, most mighty Soveraine,
> That all this famous antique history
> Of some th'aboundance of an ydle braine
> Will judged be, and painted forgery,
> Rather then matter of just memory;
> Sith none that breatheth living aire does know,
> Where is that happy land of Faery,
> Which I so much doe vaunt, yet no where show,
> But vouch antiquities, which no body can know.
> . . . .
> Yet all these were when no man did them know,
> Yet have from wisest ages hidden beene;
> And later times thinges more unknowne shall show.
> Why then should witlesse man so much misweene,
> That nothing is, but that which he hath seene?
> What if the moones fayre shining spheare,
> What if in every other starre unseene,
> Of other worldes he happily should heare?
> He wonder would much more; yet such to some appeare.
>
> [II, pr. 1, 3]

In the *Shepherd's Calendar*, however, where he is closest to the text of Chaucer's *Troilus* stanzas (the *go, litel book* and prayer for careful copying), Spenser ignored the themes of decay and misinterpretation and stressed instead the power of his imagination, at the beginning and end of his poem:

> And when thou art past jeopardee,
> Come tell me what was said of mee,
> And I will send more after thee.
>
> [To His Book, 16–18]

> That steele in strength and time in durance shall outweare.
>
> [*Epilogue*, 2]

Thus, while he ends in modesty, intending only

> To teache the ruder shepheard how to feede his sheepe,
> And from the falsers fraude his folded flock to keepe,

and claiming only to waik in Chaucerian footsteps, to follow "farre off, and their high steppes adore," Spenser's two imitations of Chaucer's farewell to *Troilus*, in the prologue and epilogue of the *Calendar*, even more strongly and unequivocally proclaim his faith in his own art. I think Spenser found, in the professed humility of the Chaucerian Narrator's self-abnegation of unworthiness in the company of self-chosen forebears, the model for his own self-conscious acceptance of his legacy, "the infusion sweete" of power "which doth in me survive." Far more significantly, Spenser also transformed the Chaucerian Narrator's defensive anticipation of textual decay and fading meaning from fear into defiance of time and denial of mutability:

> Loe I haue made a Calendar for euery yeare,
> That steele in strength, and time in durance shall outweare:
> And if I marked well the starres reuolution,
> It shall continewe till the worlds dissolution.
>
> [*Epilogue*, 1–4]

Spenser's final lines, like Chaucer's, descend also from Ovid's *Vade, liber verbique meis, loca grata saluta*, and they preserve the traditional sense of modest withdrawal, invoke the shadow of Virgil in Tityrus, and obscurely suggest both Langland and Chaucer as greater literary ancestors, while they simultaneously assert his own identity as the new Poet, who has the last word:

> Goe but a lowly gate emongst the meaner sorte.
> Dare not to match thy pype with Tityrus hys style,
> Nor with the Pilgrim that the Ploughman playde a whyle:
> But followe them farre off, and their high steppes adore,
> The better please, the worse despise, I aske nomore.
>
> [*Epilogue*, 8–12]

We can now reconsider the implications of the distinction Tatlock first generalized, between *makyng* and *poesie* in Chaucer, and in the "Go, litel boke" stanza particularly, and consider whether it is possible to be sure that the former conception implies lower, and the latter, higher art, as we can, certainly, with Spenser's moral distinctions between unnatural artifice and the perfected nature of Venus, in her Garden and her Temple. The evidence in Chaucer's poetry would seem to me to blur, rather than support that distinction. Chaucer uses the poetic senses of the verb *make* and the noun *maker* relatively rarely, and in neutral contexts; there are less than a dozen cases in the hundreds of citations of *make* in all its forms in Tatlock and Kennedy's *Concordance*.[17] Chaucer uses various forms of "poet" as an honorific adjective, but again infrequently (19 times). Rather, it would seem that both "poet" and "maker" are subsumed in the larger conception of *craft*, the *art* that *countrefeteth kynde*, of which Chaucer is a practitioner and an ardent reader, but not a theoretician. The poet in Chaucer is presented as an ambiguous witness of what he sees *ymarked in min hed* (as the Dreamer prays to Apollo in the *Book of Fame*), or what he can find in his reading (in his *olde bokes*), or of what other men say—the tales of pilgrims. Unlike Spenser, Chaucer evaded ("myn auctor seyth"), rather than stressed allusions to his role in the artifice of *makyng* fictional worlds. In the *Shepherd's Calendar*, where he needed both a modest withdrawal from the fiction and a historical allusion to his "Tityrus," Spenser chose the one telling instance—even in the twisted version in which he knew the stanza—where Chaucer's Narrator does take responsibility, and then lets go, as the *maker* of Troilus's tragedy.

Spenser's new interpretation of the verb *poeien* means more than simply the "olde poetes" general sense, "to rime and versify," comparable to other kinds of craft. Spenser, "E.K.," and Sidney attempted to give *makyng* a new, high Renaissance sense of divine creativity, and the new Poet seeks a fame who soars far beyond the Temple of Chaucer's ambiguous Fame. The metamorphosis implied for the *maker* is entailed for his Fame as well, as is clearly illustrated in Spenser's elegy for Sidney in the *Ruines of Time*:

> For deeds doe die, how ever noblie donne,
> And thoughts of men do as themselves decay,
> But wise words taught in numbers for to runne,
> Recorded by the Muses, live for ay;
> Ne may with storming showers be washt away,
> Ne bitter breathing windes with harmful blast,
> Nor age, nor envie shall them ever wast.
>
> . . . .
> But fame with golden wings aloft doth flie,

17. J.S.P. Tatlock and Arthur Kennedy, *A Concordance to the Complete Works of Geoffrey Chaucer* (Washington, D.C., 1927).

> Above the reach of ruinous decay,
> And with brave plumes doth beate the azure skie,
> Admir'd of base-borne men from farre away:
> Then who so will with vertuous deeds assay
> To mount to heaven, on Pegasus must ride,
> And with sweete Poets verse be glorifide.
>
> [*Ruines of Time*, 400–07, 421–28][18]

Spenser here affirms the power of his poetry to confer immortality, to create a world, and to outlast time, without equivocation or self-doubt. I think the midpoint in the evolution of this figure, from Chaucer's arbitrary and capricious goddess Fame with her attendant trumpeters to the beautiful flying figure of Spenser's Fame, can be discerned in a poem of Lydgate's, which Spenser might have seen; there are manuscripts still extant in Trinity College, Cambridge, and in Lincoln. The puzzling figure of Spenser's "Genius of Verulam" in the first part of the *Ruines of Time* may be traceable to such a source; Lydgate's image is also in Hawes's Lady Fame, on Pegasus, glanced at briefly in chapter 7.

> The golden trompet of the house of Fame
> With full swyfte wynges of pegsee
> Hath [blown] full farre the knyghtly mannes name
> Borne in Verolame, a famous olde citee.[19]

The infusion of divine creativity into the old meanings of *maker* for poet is apparent in Spenser's pride and confidence in his own art, expressed for the first time in the *Calendar*. His sense of mastery is climaxed in the dramatic gesture of making Colin Clout forsake his pipe at the close of the cycle, completing the revolution from *January* to *December*, for it is not that Colin doubts his art, or his capacity to master his audience, or his inspiration:

> Fro thence I durst in derring doe compare
> With shepheardes swayne, whatever fedde in field:
> And if that Hobbinol right iudgement bare
> To Pan his owne selfe pype I need not yield.
> For if the flocking Nymphes did follow Pan,
> The wiser Muses after Colin ranne.
>
> [*December*, 43–48]

18. Renwick, *Complaints*, p. 17.
19. "The glorious lyfe and passion of seint Albon . . . and saint Amaphabel," quoted in Spurgeon, *Five Hundred Years*, 1: 44.

The fictional pretext for Colin's withdrawal is the loss of his love, Rosalind, who

> does teach him climbe so hie,
> And lyftes him vp out of the loathesome myre:
> Such immortal mirrhor, as he doth admire,
> Would rayse ones mind aboue the starry skie.
>
> [*October*, 91–94]

"E.K." cites Petrarch, in his gloss on the image of the immortal mirror, but the divine love and poetical fury of Cuddye and Colin Clout are Plato's in the *Phaedrus* and *Symposium*.[20] It is the rejection of Colin's love which makes him long for death, not the loss of his art, which to the end is as powerful as ever: "Was neuer pype of reede did better sounde" (*December*, 142).

In the *Calendar*, Spenser and "E.K." elevate *makyng* to the level of *poesie*: both are divinely inspired by *enthousiasmos*, in the true poet's art. On the other hand, a distinction is made, and maintained, between the ancient maker and the modern poet: *February*, *July*, and *September*, the three Chaucerian eclogues (animal fables, and the tale of "The Oak and the Briar"), are moral allegories in the heavily rustic and archaic style, while the most elevated and modern parts of the *Calendar* are Colin's performances as "Poet." The ancient Chaucerian maker is imitated in a harsh, antiquated style to offset the brilliant lyrics of the modern poet, the lay to Eliza in *April*, and the lament for Dido in *November*. Spenser, both maker and poet, is master of both ancient and modern styles; he is the creator of the *Calendar* as a whole. In the distance between ancient and modern, Spenser also reveals another dimensional shift in which the conceptions of authority, and of the individual, are altered. The old occupatio, heavy with echoes of Lydgatean and Chaucerian disavowal, becomes a kind of claim of independence for Colin Clout:

> I neuer lyst presume to Parnasse hyll,
> But pypyng lowe in shade of lowly groue,
> I play to please my selfe, all be it ill.
>
> [*June*, 70–72]

20. Diotima, to Socrates: "There is poetry, which as you know is complex and manifold. All creation or passage from non-being into being is poetry or making; and the processes of all art are creative; and the masters of arts are all poets or makers." *Symposium*, 205B,C; text in Demos, *Plato*, p. 260.

Sidney's assertion in the *Apologie* of the poet's true autonomy—"he nothing affirms, and therefore never lieth"—is, in fact, a denial of lying, and it entailed the redefinition of *counterfeit* as well. In Spenser the burden of suspicion of art is shifted to the past, to the cave of the witch, the hut of the hermit, and to those who "boast they han the deuill at commaund" (*September*, 94). The deeply ambiguous and demonic meanings of art as subversion of "man's mynd, and man's will" (in Ascham's words), as *counterfeit* "with intent to deceive" (as in the false Florimell), as the making of idols and unclean *sprites*, were not abolished by the changing of the meanings of words. There had been accusations against Petrarch of paganism, and charges of necromancy against Boccaccio, to which the new Poet was evidently still liable. Both in theory and in poetry, new defenses had to be found, or alternatives offered, to preserve the "pure" power of the poetic imagination from contamination by the "other," the voices and eyes of the mind which belong to the history of magic. In Spenser, the dark powers are transferred to the domain of the past and to the figure of the hypocrite priest. Like the Pardoner, old Archimago with his muttering spells and his magic book is the evil intermediary between the underworld and the fictional "real" world, in Faerie Land. The *maker* who deals in words as *craft*, who counterfeits *kynd* and can invade the imagination, is symbolized as the superstition of the old Church, not in disguise, but in full regalia. As we would expect, this first appears in the *Shepherd's Calendar* in the Chaucerian moral allegory, explicitly in the "goteheard's tales," which "E.K." explains in a redundant gloss, "By Gotes in scrypture be represented the wicked and reprobate, whose pastour also must needes be such." Thomalin describes them,

> They bene yclad in purple and pall,
> > so hath theyr god them blist,
> They reigne and rulen ouer all,
> > and lord it, as they list:
> Ygyrt with belts of glitterand gold,

> [*July*, 174–77]

and they have been seen, "late on Pilgrimage / To Rome . . ." (1. 182). Fully developed into the allegorical context of the first book of the *Faerie Queene*, the subtler power of the artificer is subsumed in the priestly Archimago, the enemy from whom the new Christian must free himself, alone. The individual, without corrupt intermediaries and face to face with God, trusts his vision of the new Jerusalem and his inner voice. The Protestant poet who makes his faith explicit, as Spenser does, has nothing to fear if he believes in his inspiration, *enthousiasmos*, and eschews ambiguity in himself. In the *Faerie Queene*, Spenser shifts the dangerous meanings of hallucination and seductive power to the demonic magician, away from the poet, who retains the "divine breath" and visionary truth through his celestial Muses, those "whores" whom Boethius banished, Boccaccio called back and reclaimed, and Sidney sanctified:

> both Roman and Greek gaue diuine names unto [Poetry], the one of prophesying, the other of making; . . . considering that where as other Arts retaine themselues within their subiect, and receiue, as it were, their beeing from it, the Poet onely bringeth his own. . . . Sith neither his description nor his ende contayneth any euill, the thing described cannot be euill; Sith his effects be so good as to teach goodnes and to delight the learners. . . . But all, one and other, hauing this scope—to knowe, and by knowledge to lift vp the mind from the dungeon of the body to the enioying of his owne diuine essence.[21]

Spenser's Homage to Chaucer

Spenser exemplifies the power of the poet in the *Calendar* in Colin, Cuddye, the shepherds, and, just outside the fiction, he took his stance at the beginning and the end as humble successor to his master:

> The God of shepheards Tityrus is dead,
> Who taught me homely, as I can, to make.
> He, whilst he liued, was the soueraigne head
> Of shepheards all, that bene with loue ytake:
> Well couth he wayle hys Woes, and lightly slake
> The flames, which loue within his heart had bredd,
> And tell vs mery tales, to keep vs wake,
> The while our sheepe about vs safely fedde.
> Nowe dead he is, and lyeth wrapt in lead,
> (O why should death on hym such outrage showe?)
> And all hys passing skil with him is fledde,

21. Smith, *Sidney*, pp. 180, 161.

The fame whereof doth dayly greater growe.
But if on me some little drops would flowe,
Of that the spring was in his learned hedde,
I soone would learne these woods, to wayle my woe,
And teache the trees, their trickling teares to shedde.

[*June*, 81–96]

Immerito (immediately identified by "E.K.") addresses his poem with
a new confidence, unthinkable in Chaucer, that his own work will
last. The first indication of his "High Renaissance art . . . the clearly
perceptible self-conscious personality, working within a well-understood
convention" is Spenser's transformation of Chaucer's farewell to
Troilus into his own entrance line, "Goe little book: thy selfe present,"
and he ends with a self-reflexive farewell of his own: "The better please,
the worse despise, I aske nomore."

It was a brilliant debut, and it made all previous attempts to make
a new kind of English poetry obsolete. Ten years later, in the published
version of the first three books of the *Faerie Queene*, it is apparent that
Spenser has fully mastered and assimilated the traits of his style and
habits of conflation which first appear in the *Calendar*, where it is still
possible to trace and more or less disentangle "sources," "influences,"
and the linguistic trademarks developed and transmuted in the greater
allegory, the sonnets, and the *Hymns*. But even in the *Calendar*, to pick
up one "Chaucerian" half line—"Goe, little book"—lifts a whole web,
and reveals complex, half-visible transformation. The adjective "Chaucerian" in "Spenser's 'Chaucer' " is, of course, intentional; for any
Elizabethan reading of his *Works* must mean the whole range of the
sixteenth-century "Chaucerian" poetry, which lies latent and virtually
ignored in interpretations of Spenser's allusions and uses of medieval
convention. The 1561 *Chaucer* was the biggest and most recent edition
available to Spenser, and it was considerably more corrupt than the
1532, 1542, and 1550 folios. It is the Stowe text which provides the
reservoir of the "olde Poetes makyng" both in Spenser's memory and
in his intentional adaptations. At any crux, the question must arise,
whether Spenser recognized the "Chaucerian" apocrypha; only tenta-
tive answers are possible, but the transformation of Sir Thopas's dream
of his elfin queen into Arthur's dream of Gloriana would suggest that
no "source" can be ruled out as improbable, and that the "imitations"
of Chaucer were as likely to be valuable to Spenser as the genuine

poems. As I noted in chapter 8, it is likely that Spenser accepted the composite *Canterbury Tales* of the mid-century folios, on the evidence of direct quotations from the spurious *Plowman's Tale* in three of the eclogues of the *Shepherd's Calendar* (*February*, 149, *April*, 99, *July*, 169–204). Whether or not Spenser doubted the common ascription to Chaucer, he used the source in the *Calendar* as if it were Chaucer's *Tale*, chiefly in order to heighten the effects of his conscious evocation of "Tityrus's" style: to make moral satire more rough and rustic in *February* and *July*, and to set off the smoothness of the song from the "rude" singer in Colin's lay to Eliza:

> (Shee is my goddesse plaine
> And I her shepherds swayne)
> *Albee forswonck and forswatt I am.*

[*April*, 97–99]

Although the line is a quotation from the *Plowman*, "E.K." identifies this as the style of Tityrus, "whom our Colin Clout . . . calleth the God of Shepherds, comparing him to the Roman Tityrus Virgil,"

> whose prayses for pleasaunt tales cannot dye, so long as the memorie of his name shal liue, & the name of Poetrie shal endure.[22]

If Spenser himself saw through the spurious and apocryphal poems in the sixteenth-century *Chaucer*, he left only enigmatic evidence and used both false and true, as if all were equally useful to his purpose.

The first line of the lament of Polyhymnia, the last of the *Teares of the Muses*, illustrates another, more problematic kind of allusion, perhaps unintentionally "Chaucerian."

> A dolefull case desires a doleful song,
> Without vaine art or curious complements,
> And squallid Fortune into basenes flong,
> Doth scorne the pride of wonted ornaments.
> Then fittest are these ragged rimes for mee,
> To tell my sorrowes that exceeding bee.

[*TM*, 541–46][23]

The first lines of Henryson's *Testament of Criseyde*, it will be remembered, (printed as Chaucer's from 1532 throughout the sixteenth century) read, "A doly season tyl a careful dyte / Shulde corespond and be

22. Renwick, *Calendar*, pp. 3, 33.
23. Renwick, *Complaints*, p. 46.

equivolent." These lines, in turn, deliberately imitate the opening of the second stanza of the proem to the first book of *Troilus*:

> (For wel sit it, the sothe for to seyne)
> A woful wight to han a drery feere
> And to a sorwful tale, a sory chere.

The theme is a commonplace, and the apparent echo could have come from either *Troilus*, the *Testament*, or neither. The idea is ultimately Horatian: *si vis me flere, dolendem est primum ipse tibi* (if you wish me to weep, you must first feel grief youself).[24] Like the "farewell" stanzas and the modesty topoi in the *Calendar* and the *Faerie Queene*, the striking of an archetypal pose for the complaint of Polyhymnia exemplifies the indeterminate Renaissance inheritance of medieval conventions from many sources at once. Such formulas are the enabling devices through which tacit cues to interpretation, controlled by the author, are conveyed to the reader.

A convention is in essence a nameless allusion; it is an empty frame, preshaped by its history, and dependent for effect on recognition of its symbolic form. Its meaning shrinks insofar as its history is forgotten, and grows, proportionally, with repetition, echo, and cross-reference. In his study of Spenser's epithalamia, Thomas Greene gives a clear description:

> One might define a convention as a set of allusions. A convention exists when the full literary meaning of a word or line requires a knowledge of many past works in order to be wholly understood. . . . It follows that the first example one encounters in a convention cannot be read as the poet expected his work to be read.[25]

In Spenser, it is the metamorphoses of postclassical and medieval conventions, which already have evolved long histories, that become apparent and undergo further change. Conventions based on Chaucer and his imitators, and Spenser's imitations of them, exert a multiplier or halo effect on his meaning and on our interpretation, which is often stronger and more complex than the seemingly more clear-cut kind of allusion which names names, yet conceals more than is revealed. Such was the case, for example, in Spenser's allusion to "old Dan Geffrey",

---

24. Horace, *Ars Poetica*, ll. 102–03. Cf. Quintilian, *Inst.*, VI, ii, 26–35: "Fire alone can kindle, and moisture alone can wet, nor can one thing impart any colour to another save that which it possesses itself. . . . We should be moved ourselves before we attempt to move others."

25. "Spenser and the Epithalmic Convention," *Comp. Lit.* 9 (1957): 215–28.

who did not describe Nature's gown and face, but transferred the task to Alan in the *Plaint of Kind*. As was seen in chapter 2, both the allusion to Chaucer, and the convention of Nature's dress, turn out to be more enigmatic than the simple naming of a source and form would suggest. Spenser used Chaucer and Alan, in effect, as Chaucer used Virgil and "Lollius": that is, to veil his own art. The concealment of himself does not reduce but rather extends his freedom of invention. The poet gains the advantage of the convention and its historical meanings, and the fresh increment of his own.

In Spenser, however, allusion and imitation are not ironic evasion of originality, self-doubt, or intentional ambiguity, as has been argued in the case of Chaucer's "Lollius," his Dreamer, and his Pilgrim. Spenser's solemn Narrators, and the absence of irony and comedy in his imitations of Ariosto and Chaucer, reflect his high conception of the poet and his "celestiall vision." Spenser's freedom and authority as a *maker* are, as Sidney describes the true poet, his assertion of autonomy over the whole domain of nature and art. Like Faerie Land itself, the field of imitation in Renaissance *mimesis* is open to the creation of new meaning, by all the arts of language, in the name of homage to the past, in order to make

> formes such as neuer were in Nature, . . so as [the Poet] goeth hand in hand with Nature, not inclosed within the narrow warrant of her guifts, but freely ranging onely within the Zodiack of his owne wit.[26]

Hence, in Faerie Land, the conventions of pastoral, romance, and epic are fused in the Narrator's presentation of himself, in the traditional modesty formula, through which he asserts his authority over the fiction:

> Lo! I the man, whose Muse whylome did maske,
> As time her taught, in lowly shepherds weeds,
> Am now enforst, a farre unfitter taske,
> For trumpets sterne to chaunge mine oaten reeds,
> And sing of knights and ladies gentle deeds;
> Whose praises having slept in silence long,
> Me, all too meane, the sacred Muse areeds
> To blazon broade emongst her learned throng:
> Fierce wars and faithfull loves shall moralize my song.
>
> [*FQ* 1, Pr. i]

26. Smith, *Sidney*, p. 156.

In the "lowly shepherds weeds" of the *Calendar*, Spenser revealed much of what he learned from medieval poetry beyond the "strange olde words"; he found examples of the uses of humility and professed subservience, which he could adapt for the advantage of their prestige and his own self-definition. But I think he also reveals more in what he omitted and revised: the irony and ambivalence characteristic of medieval Chaucer's attitude toward his art, its credibility, and its submission to time. The Spenserian conception of the new Poet begins his career fully confident: Colin Clout ends in despair over the loss of his lady, but with undiminished pride in his art. Colin's performance as the most eloquent of Spenser's shepherds is the antithesis of Chaucer's bumbling Geffrey, the Pilgrim, the Dreamer, and the anxious Narrator of *Troilus and Criseyde*.

What is more significant in the *Calendar*, I think, is that here, Spenser strongly denies for the first time the paradox of mutability, and anticipates the answer his Nature gives in her trial, in the last fragment of the *Faerie Queene*. As "E.K." glosses the *Calendar's* symmetrically circular conclusion, Spenser intends it to express the exact contrary of Chaucer's lament to the scribes. The emblem of *December* means "that all things perish and come to their last end, but workes of learned wits and monuments of Poetry abide for euer."[27] The ultimate source of both Chaucer's farewell stanzas to *Troilus* and Spenser's imitation of them in the *Calendar*, the common analogue which provides for both negative and positive interpretations, is the end of the Book of Revelations, 22:18–19, where John affirms the truth of his vision, and commands that it remain as he has written it. The history of the medieval convention of the epilogue begins in these words:

> For I testify unto every man that heareth the words of the prophecy of this book, If any man shall add unto these things, God shall add unto the plagues that are written in this book. And if any man shall take away from the words of the book of this prophecy, God shall take away his part of the book of life, and out of the holy city, and from the things that are written in this book.

Where Spenser stands in secure and clear agreement, at precisely this point, the profane love poem of Chaucer's *Troilus* stands in its most ambiguous relation to the power of the poet to see, and to make visible, that which enchants him. Just so, his secular goddess Fame and her Muses are profoundly satirized by the sceptical Dreamer's allusion to

27. Renwick, *Calendar*, pp. 159–60.

the *bestes foure* "That Goddes tronne gunne honoure / As John writ in th' Apocalips" (*HF*, 1383–85). Neither in the *Faerie Queene*, nor anywhere else in his poetry, does Spenser's Poet face such a dilemma as the ending of his poem forced on the poet of *Troilus*. Spenser does not need to affect the disguise of the humble Dreamer to take the consequences of his own ambiguity. When Spenser's Narrator imagines Mutability's trial, he sees Nature dressed in the robe of Christ at the Transfiguration before John, Peter, and James, and he deliberately suppresses the powerful convention of his medieval sources: the torn gown symbolic of Adam's fall. In remaking her "celestiall image," irony and ambiguity are irrelevant to his purpose, for Spenser controls the *allegoria*, to the furthest extent that such control can be exerted. Through the Narrator's interpretation, before and after the fact, and the self-identification of the symbolic figures in the allegory, Spenser attempted to contain ambiguity within the fiction. Doubt and uncertainty are presented and acted out, but the Narrator and the reader share superior knowledge and moral certainty from a single point of view, in which the allegory can be seen in perfect focus. The author's command depends on his control of the meaning of words. Thus, at the end of canto 8 of the first book of the *Faerie Queene*, when Una exposes the witch Duessa, she expounds the meaning of the allegory, and uses the old medieval meaning of *counterfeit* for its full force :[28]

> Such is the face of Falsehood, such the sight
> Of fowle Duessa, and her borrowed light
> Is laid away, and counterfesaunce knowne.
>
> [I, viii, 49]

The Narrator's irony in this episode, for example in his *occupatio*, as he describes the withered ugliness of Duessa's naked deformity, is simple, heavy scorn, without ambivalence.

At the literal level, Duessa's defeat (in addition to all its other implications in the mind of the Red Cross Knight) signified to the Elizabethan reader the exposed and banished whore of Rome, the medieval Church, whose perversion of biblical truth Spenser believed to have been restored at last to its ancient originality, freed from the intermediate corruption of idolotrous ritual, superstitious dogma, and false priests.

---

28. Spenser uses forms of *counterfeisance* and *counterfeit* 13 times, with negative implications in all but three cases, in all his poems; Chaucer uses forms of *counterfeit* 21 times, all but two negative. See the Concordances cited above, nn. 11 and 17.

That the triumph of Una was still precarious and incomplete is also suggested, by the survival of Archimago, who is still at large at the end of Book I: "Who then would thinke, that by his subtile trains / He could escape fowle death or deadly paines?" (I, xii, 36). When he is caught sight of later by others, he has become more debased by grotesque comedy and has lost the aura of his first appearance. It is, of course, the literal level of the allegory where the richest evocation of Spenser's sense of the meaning of the immediate past is to be found, where the landscape of Lucifera's castle, Archimago's hut, and the monastic House of Holiness convey the vividness of a world still visible. It is always a risk to try to weigh the presence of the real world in a poem, and in the chiarascuro of Spenser's Faerie Land, the unseen and the latent history of the imagery are even more powerful and mysterious than what is described as seen. Nevertheless, the literal level of the allegory of Book I presents broad historical underthemes, which develop and enlarge the moral allegory of the Chaucerian eclogues of the *Shepherd's Calendar* and suggest Elizabethan assumptions which Spenser shared and took for granted with his reader. Spenser's personifications articulate and make visible a contemporary interpretation of history in which what is unsaid—as in the allegorical landscape, what is invisible—is as important as what is asserted.

Spenser's personified "Chaucer"—the Tityrus of the *Calendar*, and old "Dan Geffrey"—combines and relates several of the contradictory elements in the evidence that remains of Elizabethan reactions to medieval Chaucer, of those who interpreted him as editors, critics, or practicing poets and inheritors of his art. In the foreshortened perspective of receding recent time, and the deepening awareness of remote classical antiquity, the Middle Ages were paradoxically both despised by Elizabethans as the primitive darkness of superstition and ignorance from which they had emerged, and yet honored, as the origin of uniquely English institutions, the common law, the English language, and the monarchy itself. The second, epic sense of the English past is expressed in the literal level of Spenser's allegory. In his Renaissance "Chaucer," the image Spenser created by allusion, both parts of the paradox are compounded, reverence and condescension. The medieval Chaucer survived chiefly as archaic fiction, mutilated by time and separated from the new world by an irreparable alienation, the hiatus that ended all pilgrimages.

The decisive break in the continuity of Elizabethan history, to men

then looking back, was the reign of Henry VIII and the subsequent
restoration of English glory which culminated in their Queen. In a
reign of increasingly spectacular events, and of continuous and seemingly irreversible gains in royal power, Henry made himself a monarch
more absolute than any medieval English king had ever been. His
power became so great that the assertion of his authority in one of the
most profoundly shocking events in the religious history of England
occurred in a virtual vacuum of silence, without celebration and without protest. In the relatively brief and increasingly chaotic reigns of his
children, Edward and Mary, the event was not publicly alluded to,
either as a triumph or a sacrilege, nor was it mentioned by any writer in
the reign of Elizabeth, when history and poetry and finally drama
found reason to turn again and again to Tudor chronicles and biography for images and themes. The act, so far as I have found, was never
mentioned in English literature after it had accomplished its purpose;
nevertheless, it was of immense symbolic significance, relevant to the
present context, the interpretation of Chaucer in the Renaissance. In
1538, after proceeding against the smaller abbeys, Henry finally ordered
the destruction of the shrine of Thomas à Becket in Canterbury cathedral and the confiscation of its treasure of relics, gold, and various
jewels. The sanctuary was destroyed, the pilgrim routes shut down, and
Henry finally acquired the cathedral's greatest ornament, the so-called
Regale de France, brought in honor of St. Thomas by Louis VII in
1179. This, the most precious and famous of the treasures of Becket's
tomb, was made into a thumb ring for the king, the visible symbol of
his power over the superstition he had overthrown. After Mary Tudor,
who inherited it and wore it on a gold collar, the jewel disappeared and
has never been traced. When the shrines of St. Thomas were completely
destroyed, not a word of public protest could be published; such reac-
tion as there was, was silenced, and the new archbishop, Thomas
Cranmer, presided without incident at Canterbury. In 1542, four years
later, Cranmer wrote the preface to the new *Calendar* of the liturgy for
the Christian year, to be published in the new *Book of Common Prayer* for
the king's reformed church. The *Calendar* still opens with the following
words:

> There was never anything by the wit of man so well devised, or so
> sure established, which in continuance of time hath not been cor-
> rupted.

Mutability and Assimilation

Cranmer's theme is the theme of Mutability—Spenser's theme—and the poet's answer is as orthodox as the Archbishop's; it is epitomized in Nature's Boethian reply to Mutabilitie's challenge:

> I well consider all that ye have sayd
> And find that all things steadfastnes doe hate
> And changed be: yet being rightly wayd,
> They are not changed from their first estate,
> But by their change their being doe dilate,
> And turning to themselves at length again,
> Doe worke their owne perfection so by fate
> Then over them Change doth not rule and raigne,
> But they rayne over change, and do their states maintaine.
>
> [*FQ* VII, vii, 58]

It is tempting, but I think ultimately fruitless, to seek in Nature's speech incontrovertible evidence of Spenser's interpretation of the *Knight's Tale*, and the analogous speech of Theseus on the Prime Mover and the fair chain of love. Both are congruent and unique imitations which remake a common source in antiquity: Spenser had both sources, *Boece* and the Knight, simultaneously in his *Chaucer*. C. L. Wrenn, writing on the *Shepherd's Calendar*, asked, and left unanswered the question implicit in these speculations:

> Is [Spenser's] Tityrus Virgil, or Chaucer, or both? Spenser's sources of inspiration are vague and widely diffused, rather than individual or clearly definable. The influence of Virgil goes deeper than that of Chaucer.[29]

In other words, Spenser's "Tityrus" is not Virgil *or* Chaucer, but both. His Christian Platonism is Chaucerian, and Boethian, as well as "influenced" by Ficino; but his Mutabilitie is his own.

The evidence of Spenser's literary indebtedness accumulated by his editors, from "E.K." of the *Calendar* onward for nearly four hundred years, confirms the naive reader's immediate apprehension: Spenser's simplicity belies immense learning ("not . . . a superficial humanist, but . . . a curious universall scholler"). For the modern, as for the

29. "On Re-reading Spenser's *Shepherd's Calendar*,' p. 36.

Elizabethan reader, Faerie Land is at once utterly remote, and yet
perfectly familiar, like Chaucer's Troy. The task of discovering how
much of both the medieval erudition and the "familiarity" in Spenser
are Chaucerian, however, is far more difficult than tracing the literary
history of *Troilus and Criseyde* from Chaucer's antecedents to his imitators in the Renaissance and after. In Spenser, there is no clear parallel
case of a single work of imitation, of one unfragmented "Chaucerian"
source left whole, although *Mother Hubberd's Tale* belongs to the genre
Chaucer legitimized for poetry, and *Daphnaida* is an adaptation of both
Chaucer's and Lydgate's Black Knight's laments, cast not in the form
of a dream, but as the twilight experience of Spenser's poetic "I." In
addition to the diffusion of the "Chaucerian" in varying ratios in all of
Spenser's poems, study of "indebtedness" is complicated by the fact
that both conscious and unconscious echoes and imitations of "Chaucer" are derived from bad texts, themselves contaminated by imitations.
But more than these, the problems hardest to define, and most difficult
to elucidate once they are recognized, are the effects of the profound
change, apparent in Spenser and his contemporaries, in the conception
of the individual poet's role in his poem, and of the value of poetry as a
means of knowing and creating truth. These effects are inseparable, and
it is very difficult to discuss them in isolation, and in terms of only a
limited number of texts. Properly to explore them would require
exegesis of all of the *Faerie Queene*, as well as the *Fowre Hymnes*. The
rehabilitation of the imagination, in Spenser and Sidney, is an aspect
of the revival of the study of philosophy in the Renaissance, when,
after about 1550, the impact of the Platonic dialogues and their Italian Neoplatonic commentaries became increasingly important in
English thought, coincident with the revolution in the state religion.
Although Neoplatonism in Spenser is a vexed issue, which extends far
beyond the subject of this book, neither can it be ignored, for it is one
of the crucial early signs of the change of the role of the poet in the
poem, between Chaucer's narrators and Spenser's, in the *Shepherd's
Calendar*. It contains, as I have tried to show, the Elizabethan renewal
and elevation of the idea of the *maker*, as Chaucer used it, to the visionary, as Plato describes the divine madness of poets in the *Phaedrus*:

> There is a third form of possession or madness, of which the Muses
> are the source. This seizes a tender, virgin soul and stimulates it to
> rapt passionate expression, especially in lyric poetry, glorifying

the countless mighty deeds of ancient times for the instruction of posterity. But if any man come to the gates of poetry without the madness of the Muses, persuaded that skill alone will make him a good poet, then shall he and his works of sanity with him be brought to naught by the poetry of madness, and behold, their place is nowhere to be found.[30]

This is the image of the poet inspired by divine *enthousiasmos* which Spenser first described in the *Shepherd's Calendar* and "E.K." repeated in his gloss and commentary on Spenser's meaning; it is "for the glorification . . . of ancient times, [and] the instruction of posterity" that the new poet turns to the past, and feels the "sweete spirit" within him.

I shall not attempt to define the impact of the empty space behind the altar at Canterbury, the destination of Chaucer's pilgrims, on the Elizabethan readers of his poems. "Chaucer" was safely read as a satirist of the vices of his decadent age. The quest for divine love and certainty of medieval pilgrimage and dream vision, as everyone knows, turned inward, to the fiction that could be made more than merely "real," in the imagination of the Poet, for the triumph of the new religion over the old is a vindication of the inner voice, the divine breath of the *Phaedrus*, the *Apology*, and Spenser's Muse. The Elizabethan defense of poetry became a full victory, finally, in Milton's divine voice and inner vision. To contain these expanding themes in one focus, in all of Spenser's work, has not at all been my intention; I have tried rather to reduce them to the clearer, earlier images of the "true poet" visible in the *Shepherd's Calendar*. It is Spenser's first major poem, and the one in which he makes the most of his homage to medieval Chaucer. The result was a reinterpretation of the "model"—Chaucer the *maker*—comparable to the Renaissance transformation of *Troilus*. A fuller study of the *Calendar* would reveal more of Spenser's use of Chaucerian conventions, of fragmentary quotations, and the borrowed meanings of old words, at the point of metamorphosis. Although I have discussed only a few aspects of the *Calendar*—the modesty formula, the interpretation of the verb *make*, and the concept of mutability—they are as important as its "archaism" and its allegory, and perhaps definitive of Spenser's remaking of what he found, and valued, in "Chaucer": the composite symbol of transition from medieval to Renaissance, which the *Calendar* seemed, to Elizabethans, to have achieved.

30. Plato's *Phaedrus*, 245A; ed. and trans. R. Hackforth (Cambridge, Eng., 1952), p. 57.

Index

Starred page numbers locate quotations.

301